哈佛燕京圖書館文獻叢刊第十五種
Harvard-Yenching Library Reprint Series, No. 15

美國哈佛大學
哈佛燕京圖書館藏
鋼和泰未刊往來書信集

The Unpublished Correspondence of Alexander von Staël-Holstein in the Harvard-Yenching Library, Harvard University

鄒新明　編

中

GUANGXI NORMAL UNIVERSITY PRESS
广西师范大学出版社
·桂林·
北京大学出版社
PEKING UNIVERSITY PRESS
·北京·

目　録

序號	書信人	信件擬目	頁碼
049	I. V. Gillis	01 I. V. Gillis to Alexander von Staël-Holstein, Jun. 15, 1928	1
		02 I. V. Gillis to Alexander von Staël-Holstein, Jun. 18, 1928	2
		03 I. V. Gillis to Alexander von Staël-Holstein, Sept. 6, 1929	3
		04 I. V. Gillis to Alexander von Staël-Holstein, Feb. 11, 1930	4
		05 I. V. Gillis to Alexander von Staël-Holstein, Sept. 16, 1930	5
		06 Alexander von Staël-Holstein to I. V. Gillis, 1930？ 此信無日期。信末説：“I enclose a cheque for the amount of your bill dated March 31st 1930.” 據此大致可以推斷，此信寫於 1930 年，在 3 月 31 日之後。	7
		07 I. V. Gillis to Alexander von Staël-Holstein, Nov. 7, 1931	8
		08 Alexander von Staël-Holstein to I. V. Gillis 此信日期不詳。信中説：“I am very glad to hear that Mr. De Vere Barley likes my article ‘On Some Divine Metamorphoses’.” 此文發表於 *The China Journal of Sciences and Arts* 1926 年第 4 卷第 2 期，故可大致推斷，此信寫於 1926 年，或之後。	9
		附 01 I. V. Gillis to George H. Chase, Jan. 30, 1930	10
050	Helmuth von Glasenapp	01 Helmuth von Glasenapp to Alexander von Staël-Holstein, Feb. 1, 1933	11

序號	書信人	信件擬目	頁碼
051	Goette	01 Alexander von Staël-Holstein to Goette, May? , 1930 此信無日期，與此信寫於同一頁的另一封信的日期爲 1930 年 5 月 5 日，故推斷此信大致寫於 1930 年 5 月。	14
		附 01 Alexander von Staël-Holstein to Someone, May 5, 1930 此信收信人僅寫爲“Baron”，具體不詳。此信與鋼和泰 1930 年 5 月致 Mr. Goette 一信寫於同一頁，該信位於頁面下部，暫繫於此。	14
052	V. Goloubew	01 V. Goloubew to Alexander von Staël-Holstein, Sept. 24, 1929	15
053	Roger S. Greene	01 Alexander von Staël-Holstein to Mrs. Roger S. Greene, Mar.?, 1929–1930 此信從内容看爲鋼和泰寫給顧臨，從筆迹看，應爲他人抄録或代筆。信中説 Mr. Gordon Bowle 是自己一年前在哈佛任教時的學生。鋼和泰 1928—1929 學年在哈佛任教，則此信大致寫於 1929—1930 年。	17
		02 Alexander von Staël-Holstein to Mrs. Roger S. Greene, Mar.?, 1930 此信收信人爲顧臨夫人，暫繫於此。此信無日期。信中提到 4 月 12 日周六，查萬年曆，結合顧臨與鋼和泰在北京交往的時間範圍，應爲 1930 年。又信中提到“next month (April)”，故可確定此信寫於 1930 年 3 月。此信下半頁有鋼和泰寫給 Mr. Plomp 書信。	18
		03 Roger S. Greene to Alexander von Staël-Holstein, Jan. 13, 1932	19
		04 Roger S. Greene to Alexander von Staël-Holstein, Apr. 24, 1933	20
		05 Alexander von Staël-Holstein to Roger S. Greene, Oct. 28, 1934	21
		06 Alexander von Staël-Holstein to Roger S. Greene, Nov. 28, 1934	22
		07 Alexander von Staël-Holstein to Roger S. Greene, Apr. 16, 1935	23

序號	書信人	信件擬目	頁碼
		08 Alexander von Staël-Holstein to Roger S. Greene, Jun. 22, 1935	24
		09 Alexander von Staël-Holstein to Roger S. Greene 此信無日期，信中開頭說：“In letter dated November 18th 1931 I wrote ……”，可以確定此信寫於 1931 年 11 月 18 日之後，具體日期不詳。	25
		10 Alexander von Staël-Holstein to Roger S. Greene 此信日期不詳。	26
		11 Alexander von Staël-Holstein to Roger S. Greene 此信日期不詳。信中說：“I am very glad to know that the Trustees of the Harvard-Yenching Institute have ordered my report to be placed on file.” 故此信應寫於哈佛燕京學社任命鋼和泰擔任中印研究所所長之後，大致在 1930 年之後。此信背面有鋼和泰致 Mrs. Hussey 書信一封。	27
		12 Alexander von Staël-Holstein to Roger S. Greene 此信日期不詳。	28
		附 01 Someone to Roger S. Greene, Nov. 2, 1929 此信爲他人寫給顧臨，暫繫於此。有鋼和泰抄件和打印複印件各一。	29
		附 02 Alexander von Staël-Holstein to Baronne, Mar.?, 1930 此信寫於 1930 年 3 月鋼和泰致顧臨夫人一信的背面，收信人僅署 “Bronne”，具體不詳，暫繫於此。此信無日期，其背面書信及同頁另一封信的日期均爲 1930 年 3 月，故大致推定此信日期爲 1930 年 3 月。	32
		附 03 Alexander von Staël-Holstein to Doctor 此信無日期。寫於鋼和泰致顧臨的開頭爲 “Dear Mr. Greene, A great weight has been lifted off my mind.” 一信的背面。收信人僅寫爲 “Doctor”，具體人物不詳。暫繫於鋼和泰致顧臨一信之後。	33

序號	書信人	信件擬目	頁碼
		附 04 Alexander von Staël-Holstein to Monsieur 此信寫於鋼和泰約 1929—1930 年給顧臨一信的背面左部，收信人僅署爲 “Monsieur”，暫繫於此。	34
		附 05 Alexander von Staël-Holstein to Professor 此信寫於鋼和泰約 1929—1930 年給顧臨一信的背面右部，收信人僅署爲 “Professor”，暫繫於此。	34
054	J. Hackin	01 J. Hackin to Alexander von Staël-Holstein, Sept. 16, 1936	35
055	Hilda L. Hague	01 Hilda L. Hague to Alexander von Staël-Holstein, Oct. 15, 1931	37
		02 Hilda L. Hague to Alexander von Staël-Holstein, Apr. 2, 1932	38
		03 Alexander von Staël-Holstein to Hilda L. Hague, Apr. 3, 1932 此信寫於鋼和泰 1932 年 4 月 3 日致傅斯年一信背面。此信收信人僅署 “Miss Hague”，從書信内容看，收信人應爲哈佛燕京學社駐北平辦事處秘書 Hilda L. Hague。	39
		04 Hilda L. Hague to Alexander von Staël-Holstein, May 6, 1932	40
		05 Alexander von Staël-Holstein to Hilda L. Hague, Jun. 26, 1932	41
		06 Hilda L. Hague to Alexander von Staël-Holstein, Aug. 30, 1932	42
		07 Hilda L. Hague to Alexander von Staël-Holstein, Sept. 12, 1932	43
		08 Alexander von Staël-Holstein to Hilda L. Hague, Sept. 18, 1932	44
		09 Hilda L. Hague to Alexander von Staël-Holstein, Apr. 9, 1935	45
		10 Hilda L. Hague to Alexander von Staël-Holstein, Apr. 11, 1935	46

序號	書信人	信件擬目	頁碼
		11 Alexander von Staël-Holstein to Hilda L. Hague, Apr. 14, 1935	47
		12 Hilda L. Hague to Alexander von Staël-Holstein, Apr. 18, 1935	49
		13 Alexander von Staël-Holstein to Hilda L. Hague, Apr. 27, 1935	51
		14 Hilda L. Hague to Alexander von Staël-Holstein, May 3, 1935	52
		15 Hilda L. Hague to Alexander von Staël-Holstein, May 4, 1935	53
		16 Hilda L. Hague to Alexander von Staël-Holstein, May 29, 1935	54
		17 Alexander von Staël-Holstein to Hilda L. Hague, Jul. 2, 1935	55
		18 Alexander von Staël-Holstein to Hilda L. Hague, Feb. 14, 1936	56
		19 Hilda L. Hague to Alexander von Staël-Holstein, Monday 此信無具體日期，僅署“Monday”。	57
		20 Hilda L. Hague to Alexander von Staël-Holstein, Tuesday 此信無具體日期，僅署“Tuesday”。	59
		附 01 Hilda L. Hague to Mr. P'an, Jun. 29, 1935	61
		附 02 Alexander von Staël-Holstein to Doctor, Summer?, 1932 此信寫於鋼和泰 1932 年 6 月 26 日致 Miss Hague 一信背面下半頁，年代大致應與背面書信接近，暫定爲 1932 年夏季前後。	62
056	Clarence H. Hamilton	01 Clarence H. Hamilton to Alexander von Staël-Holstein, Apr. 26, 1929	63
057	Sven Hedin	01 Sven Hedin to Alexander von Staël-Holstein, Feb. 23, 1927	64

序號	書信人	信件擬目	頁碼
		02 Sven Hedin to Alexander von Staël-Holstein, Apr. 5, 1930	65
		03 Sven Hedin to Alexander von Staël-Holstein, May 4, 1930	66
		04 Sven Hedin to Alexander von Staël-Holstein, May 24, 1930	67
		05 Sven Hedin to Alexander von Staël-Holstein, May 28, 1930 此信内容位於頁面上部。	68
		06 Alexander von Staël-Holstein to Sven Hedin, Jun.?, 1930 此信寫於斯文·赫定 1930 年 5 月 28 日致鋼和泰一信底部，無日期，或爲鋼和泰的復信，時間暫定爲 1930 年 6 月前後。	68
		07 Sven Hedin to Alexander von Staël-Holstein, Jun. 16, 1930	69
		08 Sven Hedin to Alexander von Staël-Holstein 此信日期不詳。	70
		09 Sven Hedin to Alexander von Staël-Holstein 此信日期不詳。	71
058	Howard Coonley Hollis	01 Howard Coonley Hollis to Alexander von Staël-Holstein, Nov. 12, 1929 此信附有 Hollis 寫的一篇關於鋼和泰的剪報，寫於 1929 年 8 月 12 日，刊登的報紙名稱、日期不詳。	72
		02 Howard Coonley Hollis to Alexander von Staël-Holstein, Feb. 15, 1930	80
		附 01 Howard Coonley Hollis to The Rector of the University of Dorpat, Feb. 15, 1930 此信爲給鋼和泰的抄件。	81
059	Horstmann	01 Alexander von Staël-Holstein to Horstmann 此信德文，日期不詳，原置於“Porter, Lucius C. 回發”信封内，寫於鋼和泰致博晨光夫人一信下半頁。	82

序號	書信人	信件擬目	頁碼
060	Prof. Hsü	01 Alexander von Staël-Holstein to Prof. Hsü, Mar. 24, 1932 此信收信人僅署爲“Prof. Hsü”，具體不詳。	83
061	Hu Shih	01 Hu Shih to Alexander von Staël-Holstein, Mar. 29, 1919	84
		02 Hu Shih to Alexander von Staël-Holstein, Sept. 30, 1919	85
		03 Hu Shih to Alexander von Staël-Holstein, Sept. 20, 1923	86
		04 Alexander von Staël-Holstein to Hu Shih, Sept. 20, 1923	89
		05 Alexander von Staël-Holstein to Hu Shih, Jul.–Aug., Dec. 20, 1923 此信爲鋼和泰致胡適書信草稿，無日期，據中國社科院近代史所檔案館“胡適檔案”所藏此信補充日期。	91
		06 Alexander von Staël-Holstein to Hu Shih, Jun. 7, 1924	93
		07 Alexander von Staël-Holstein to Hu Shih, Jun. ?, 1925 此信無日期。信末説作者暑期將去上海，到商務印書館查看《大寶積經迦葉品梵藏漢六種合刊》序言。據哈佛燕京圖書館藏“鋼和泰檔案”，鋼和泰 1925 年 8 月 31 日給商務印書館書信的第三頁提到，他將爲《大寶積經迦葉品梵藏漢六種合刊》書稿的題名頁、中文導言及序言等的修改一事，到上海去一趟。兩信所説似應爲一事，故此信應寫於 1925 年。從信中内容看，鋼和泰當天要去大連度暑假，故大致推定此信日期爲 1925 年 6 月。	95
		08 Alexander von Staël-Holstein to Hu Shih, 1925 此信無日期。信中提到鋼和泰請于道泉幫助抄寫藏文《大寶積經》注，查哈佛燕京圖書館藏“鋼和泰檔案”，有一封于道泉給鋼和泰的信，信中提到抄寫注釋的事情。該信無日期，但從内容看，應寫於于道泉 1925 年 10 月 6 日給鋼和泰的另一封信之前不久。據此，可以大致推斷，此信寫於 1925 年。	97
		09 Alexander von Staël-Holstein to Hu Shih, Jun. 17, 1926	99

序號	書信人	信件擬目	頁碼
		10 Hu Shih to Alexander von Staël-Holstein, Jun. 15, 1927	101
		11 Alexander von Staël-Holstein to Hu Shih, Jun.–Jul.?, 1927 此信無日期，信中提及胡適從日本給鋼和泰發明信片，從上海給鋼和泰寫信，“在西方一年”，應該指胡適 1926 年赴英國參加英庚款咨詢委員會會議，然後去美國，1927 年經日本回國，到上海。應爲對胡適 1927 年 6 月 15 日書信的回復。信中又説，很高興知道商務印書館希望我今年夏天去查看藏文圖書。因此，可以大致推斷此信寫於 1927 年六七月間。	104
		12 Alexander von Staël-Holstein to Hu Shih, Jul.–Aug.?, 1927 此信無日期。信中説據日本新聞 7 月 23 日報道，上海當局在奉命抓捕鮑羅廷。此事應發生在 1927 年。此外，信中提到 7 月 14 日星期四，查萬年曆，1927 年 7 月 14 日確爲周四。則此信寫於 1927 年當無疑問。信中開頭説 6 月 28 日到警察廳申請到上海的護照，信中説 7 月 28 日給胡適發過電報，又説 8 月 2 日將動身去青島，則此信大致寫於 1927 年 7 月 29 日至 8 月 1 日這幾天。此信爲草稿，有幾段内容重複。	106
		13 Alexander von Staël-Holstein to Hu Shih, Aug. 17, 1929 此信爲鋼和泰致胡適書信草稿，無日期，據中國社科院近代史所檔案館“胡適檔案”所藏此信補充日期。	112
		14 Hu Shih to Alexander von Staël-Holstein, Dec. 21, 1929	114
		15 Alexander Von Staël-Holstein to Hu Shih, Jul. 5, 1927–1930 此信日期不詳，從内容看，大致應在胡適居住上海之時。即 1927—1930 年。信中提到“iconographical material”，鋼和泰大約寫於 1927 年七月底八月初給胡適的信中也提到“iconographical material”。	115
		16 Alexander von Staël-Holstein to Hu Shih, May 8, 1932 此信第二頁内容似與第一頁不銜接，暫繫於此。	116

序號	書信人	信件擬目	頁碼
		17 Alexander von Staël-Holstein to Hu Shih, Jul.?, 1935 此信無日期，信中提到爲 Mr. Roger S. Greene（顧臨）餞行，顧臨 1935 年回美國，則此信應寫於 1935 年。另信中提到的時間爲 7 月 11 日星期四，查萬年曆，1935 年 7 月 11 日確爲周四。考慮到宴會的時間爲 7 月 11 日，大致推定此信寫於 1935 年 7 月初。此兩頁信爲草稿，内容部分重複，第二頁更爲完整。	118
		18 Alexander von Staël-Holstein to Hu Shih, Jan. 31, 1936	120
		19 Alexander von Staël-Holstein to Hu Shih, Apr. 8, 1936	121
		20 Alexander von Staël-Holstein to Hu Shih, Jul. 5, 1936	123
		21 Alexander von Staël-Holstein to Hu Shih, Jul.?, 1936 此信無日期，信前提到 1933 年、1935 年去日本旅行不需要簽證的事實，以説明作者當下也該不需要簽證。則此信大致寫於 1936 年或以後。鋼和泰 1937 年 3 月 16 日去世，此信中提到要馬上去旅行，似不應在 1937 年。此外，信中提到胡適即將去美國，當指胡適 1936 年去美國參加太平洋國際學會會議，胡適是 1936 年 7 月 14 日從上海啓程的。鋼和泰信中説胡適出發的日子臨近，則可大致推定此信寫於 1936 年 7 月。此外，鋼和泰 1936 年 7 月 5 日寫給胡適的信中，請胡適幫忙辦理去日本的許可證，此信説此事已經辦妥，則此信應寫於上一封信之後，胡適出國之前。即 1936 年 7 月 5 日至 14 日間的某一天。	127
		22 Alexander von Staël-Holstein to Hu Shih 此信日期不詳。	128
		23 Alexander von Staël-Holstein to Hu Shih 此信日期不詳。	129
062	Huang Chung Chiang	01 Huang Chung Chiang to Alexander von Staël-Holstein, Apr. 23, 1928	130
063	Arthur William Hummel	01 Arthur William Hummel to Alexander von Staël-Holstein, Oct. 23, 1928	131

序號	書信人	信件擬目	頁碼
		02 Alexander von Staël-Holstein to Arthur William Hummel, Winter?, 1928 此信無日期，恒慕義 1928 年 10 月 23 日給鋼和泰的信開頭説：“The Library of Congress has just sent you from its Chinese Collection the volume of Dulva from the Tibetan sacred books……”，鋼和泰此信中説：“That is why the Harvard Library has asked you to be so kind as to send us now the volume Dulva I of the Derge Kanjur.” 可知此信爲鋼和泰對恒慕義 1928 年 10 月 23 日一信的回復，大致時間應在 1928 年冬季。	132
064	William Hung	01 William Hung to Alexander von Staël-Holstein, Oct. 13, 1931	133
		02 Alexander von Staël-Holstein to William Hung, Nov. 7, 1931 此信無日期。洪業 1931 年 10 月 13 日給鋼和泰的信中説：“I am thinking of a little social gathering possibly to be scheduled in the course of the next few months in which those who are engaged in the various branches of work of the Harvard-Yenching Institute might have an opportunity to get acquainted with one another.” 此信開頭説：“Please do excuse me for answering your letter dated October as late as this. I quite agree with you in thinking that a meeting of all the Harvard-Yenching scholars etc. should meet this winter, and I suggest that the meeting might take the form of a tea party at my house which is certainly large enough for fifty people.” 此信應爲對洪業 1931 年 10 月 13 日信的回信。此後，洪業在 1931 年 11 月 25 日給鋼和泰的信中説：“It is very kind of you to suggest in your letter of November 7 that you may invite all the persons connected with the Harvard-Yenching Institute to a tea party at your house……”，綜上，此信當寫於 1931 年 11 月 7 日。	134
		03 William Hung to Alexander von Staël-Holstein, Nov. 25, 1931	135
		04 William Hung to Alexander von Staël-Holstein, Dec. 1, 1931	137
		05 Alexander von Staël-Holstein to William Hung, Dec.?, 1931 此信無日期，開頭説：“My dear Professor Hung, I shall be delighted to attend the Yenching tea Party on Saturday December 5th……”，洪業 1931 年 11 月 25 日書信中説：“The list of names we have at present amounts to 65, and President Stuart has suggested now the date of Saturday afternoon, December 5.” 由以上可以推斷，此信爲對洪業 1931 年 11 月 25 日一信的回復，大致寫於	138

序號	書信人	信件擬目	頁碼
		1931 年 11 月 25 日至 12 月 5 日之間。大致定爲 1931 年 12 月初前後。	
		06 William Hung to Alexander von Staël-Holstein, Jan. 11, 1932	139
		07 William Hung to Alexander von Staël-Holstein, Feb. 25, 1932	140
		08 William Hung to Alexander von Staël-Holstein, Jun. 23, 1932	142
		09 William Hung to Alexander von Staël-Holstein, Jun. 25, 1932	144
		10 Alexander von Staël-Holstein to William Hung, Mar. 10, 1935	145
		11 William Hung to Alexander von Staël-Holstein, Mar. 28, 1935	146
		12 Alexander von Staël-Holstein to William Hung, Mar. 28, 1935	147
		13 William Hung to Alexander von Staël-Holstein, Apr. 6, 1935	148
		14 Alexander von Staël-Holstein to William Hung, May 12, 1935	149
		附 01 Alexander von Staël-Holstein to Doctor, Dec.?, 1931 此信寫於鋼和泰 1931 年 12 月初前後寫給洪業書信的下半頁，時間應該比較接近，故暫定爲 1931 年 12 月。收信人僅爲 "Doctor"，暫繫於此。	150
065	Mrs. Hussey	01 Alexander von Staël-Holstein to Mrs. Hussey 此信寫於鋼和泰致顧臨開頭爲 "Dear Mr. Greene, Many thanks for your kind note!" 一信的背面。原置於 "Greene 回發" 信封中。	151
066	J. H. Ingram	01 J. H. Ingram to Alexander von Staël-Holstein, Nov. 26, 1932	152
067	K. Ito	01 K. Ito to Alexander von Staël-Holstein, Nov. 16, 1916	153

序號	書信人	信件擬目	頁碼
		02 K. Ito to Alexander von Staël-Holstein, Mar. 14, 1917 明信片，上署日期爲 3 月 14 日，郵戳爲 6.3.15。年代似應爲大正六年，即 1917 年。此外，另一封信的年代爲 1916 年，比較接近。明信片上的日文名字爲伊東教順。	154
		03 K. Ito to Alexander von Staël-Holstein, Jul. 29 此信僅署月日，無年代。	156
		04 K. Ito to Alexander von Staël-Holstein, Oct. 16 此信僅署月日，無年代。	158
068	A. L. Lvanov	01 A. L. Lvanov to Alexander von Staël-Holstein, Aug. 27, 1921	159
		02 A. L. Lvanov to Alexander von Staël-Holstein, Dec. 1, 1922	161
		03 A. L. Lvanov to Alexander von Staël-Holstein, Feb. 3, 1923	163
		04 A. L. Lvanov to Alexander von Staël-Holstein, Sept. 21, 1923	166
		05 A. L. Lvanov to Alexander von Staël-Holstein, Jul. 13, 1924	168
069	Prof. Jackson	01 Alexander von Staël-Holstein to Prof. Jackson 此信日期不詳。	170
070	Nelson Trusler Johnson	01 Nelson Trusler Johnson to Alexander von Staël-Holstein, Mar. 17, 1933	171
071	Kam ?	01 Kam ? to Alexander von Staël-Holstein 此信寫信人姓不能辨識，大致爲日本人，無年代。	173
072	Mr. Keller	01 Alexander von Staël-Holstein to Mr. Keller, Oct. 22, 1935	175
		02 Alexander von Staël-Holstein to Mr. Keller, Feb. 27, 1936	184

序號	書信人	信件擬目	頁碼
		03 Alexander von Staël-Holstein to Mr. Keller, Jul. 15, 1936 此信月日寫爲 "Mitte Juli" 即 7 月中，大致爲 1936 年 7 月 15 日。	185
073	F. S. Kershaw	01 F. S. Kershaw to Alexander von Staël-Holstein, Apr. 9, 1929	187
		02 Alexander von Staël-Holstein to F. S. Kershaw, Apr. 10, 1929	188
074	Kungpah T. King	01 Kungpah T. King to Alexander von Staël-Holstein, Jun. 22, 1923 此信無年代，僅署 6 月 22 日周五，查萬年曆，結合寫信者其他書信年代，大致爲 1923 年，且是年 6 月 22 日爲周五。故推定此信寫於 1923 年 6 月 22 日。	189
		02 Kungpah T. King to Alexander von Staël-Holstein, Jun. 6, 1924	191
		03 Kungpah T. King to Alexander von Staël-Holstein, Jul. 5, 1924	192
		04 Kungpah T. King to Alexander von Staël-Holstein, May 1, 1925	193
075	Sohtsu G. King	01 Sohtsu G. King to Alexander von Staël-Holstein, Jun. 4, 1925	197
		02 Sohtsu G. King to Alexander von Staël-Holstein, Aug. 6, 1925	198
		03 Alexander von Staël-Holstein to Sohtsu G. King, Summer ?, 1925 此信無日期，信末說："Many thanks for sending me Mr. Yin-Kuan's（印光）books." Sohtsu G. King 1925 年 6 月 4 日寫給鋼和泰的信中說："Herewith a book of 4 volumes of the collected writings of the Buddhist Priest 'Yin Kwon' 印光 ." 故此信應爲鋼和泰對 Sohtsu G. King 1925 年 6 月 4 日一信的回復，時間大致在 1925 年夏。	200
076	Kazuo Kitamura	01 Kazuo Kitamura to Alexander von Staël-Holstein, May 10, 1929	201

序號	書信人	信件擬目	頁碼
077	Nobuji Kitamura	01 Nobuji Kitamura to Alexander von Staël-Holstein, May 11, 1929	205
078	Sten Konow	01 Sten Konow to Alexander von Staël-Holstein, Nov. 4, 1926	207
		02 Sten Konow to Alexander von Staël-Holstein, Aug. 15, 1927	209
		03 Alexander von Staël-Holstein to Sten Konow, Aug.?, 1927	211
		04 Alexander von Staël-Holstein to Sten Konow, Aug. -Sept.?, 1927 此信無日期。信末説：“The document in the language No. 2, a photograph of which I send you under separate cover, is said to come from Tun Huang ……”，此前談到 “I have found much a good deal of new iconographical material lately”，Konow1927 年 9 月 14 日寫給鋼和泰的書信開頭説：“Many thanks for your kind letter and for the photographs of iconographical material……”，可以大致確定 Konow 1927 年 9 月 14 日一信是對此信的回復，故此信大致寫於 1927 年八九月間。	212
		05 Sten Konow to Alexander von Staël-Holstein, Sept. 14, 1927	216
		06 Alexander von Staël-Holstein to Sten Konow, Winter, 1927 此信無日期，信中提及一位挪威政府部長 Mr. Michelet 表示願意資助鋼和泰創辦的中印研究所，希望 Konow 幫忙，Konow 1928 年 5 月 24 日給鋼和泰的信開頭説：“I have delayed answering your letter about the Sino Indian Research Institute, because I wanted to await Mr. Michelet’s arrival.” 故 Konow 1928 年 5 月 24 日給鋼和泰的信應爲對此信的回復。此信末又説：“I hope you got my New year’s cards.” 綜上，可以大致推斷，此信寫於 1927 年冬季前後。	218
		07 Sten Konow to Alexander von Staël-Holstein, May 24, 1928	221
		08 Alexander von Staël-Holstein to Sten Konow, Aug. 14, 1934	223
		09 Sten Konow to Alexander von Staël-Holstein, Feb. 8, 1935	225

序號	書信人	信件擬目	頁碼
		10 Alexander von Staël-Holstein to Sten Konow 此信無日期。	227
		附 01 Alexander von Staël-Holstein to Professor, 1927 此信收信人爲 "Professor", 具體不詳, 寫於鋼和泰 1927 年 8 月致 Konow 一信的背面, 暫繫於此, 時間大致定爲 1927 年。	229
		附 02 Sten Konow to Kollega & Freund, Oct. 1, 1933 此信原置於 "Konow, Sten 來" 信封内, 收件人爲 "Kollega & Freund", 生平不詳, 暫繫於此。	230
079	Dr. Kotvicz	01 Alexander von Staël-Holstein to Dr. Kotvicz, Dec. 24, 1929	232
080	Robert Keen Lamb	01 Robert Keen Lamb to Alexander von Staël-Holstein, 1928–1929 此信無日期, 從内容看, 當寫於鋼和泰在哈佛講學期間, 故暫定爲 1928—1929 年。	234
081	Charles R. Lanman	01 Charles R. Lanman to Alexander von Staël-Holstein, Jul. 21, 1934	235
082	K. S. Latourette	01 K. S. Latourette to Alexander von Staël-Holstein, Oct. 11, 1928	237
083	Owen Lattimore	01 Alexander von Staël-Holstein to Owen Lattimore, Apr. 2, 1935	238
		02 Owen Lattimore to Alexander von Staël-Holstein, May 21, 1936	239
		03 Alexander von Staël-Holstein to Owen Lattimore 此信日期不詳。	241
		附 01 Alexander von Staël-Holstein to Mrs. Lattimore, Nov. 11, 1935	242
		附 02 Alexander von Staël-Holstein to Mrs. Lattimore 此信日期不詳。	243

序號	書信人	信件擬目	頁碼
084	Dr. Laufer	01 Alexander von Staël-Holstein to Dr. Laufer, Apr. 4, 1929	244
085	Madame Lauru	01 Alexander von Staël-Holstein to Madame Lauru, Sept. 10, 1934	245
		02 Alexander von Staël-Holstein to Madame Lauru, Dec. 5, 1934	246
		03 Alexander von Staël-Holstein to Madame Lauru, Dec. 9, 1934	248
		04 Alexander von Staël-Holstein to Madame Lauru, Feb. 25, 1936	249
		05 Alexander von Staël-Holstein to Madame Lauru 此信日期不詳。	250
		06 Alexander von Staël-Holstein to Madame Lauru 此信日期不詳。	251
		07 Alexander von Staël-Holstein to Madame Lauru 此信日期不詳。	252
		08 Alexander von Staël-Holstein to Madame Lauru 此信日期不詳。	253
		附 01 Alexander von Staël-Holstein to Someone, Dec.?, 1932 此信寫於鋼和泰致 Madame Lauru 一封信的背面上半部，收信人不詳，僅寫爲“Mr.”，暫繫於此。此信無日期，與此信同一頁的鋼和泰致博晨光的信寫於 1932 年 12 月。此信也提到聖誕和新年，故大致也寫於 1932 年 12 月。	254
086	F. Lessing	01 F. Lessing to Alexander von Staël-Holstein, Dec. 16, 1921	255
		02 F. Lessing to Alexander von Staël-Holstein, Sept. 22, 1922	257
		03 F. Lessing to Alexander von Staël-Holstein, Sept. 28, 1922	259

序號	書信人	信件擬目	頁碼
		04 F. Lessing to Alexander von Staël-Holstein, Jul. 23, 1924	261
		05 F. Lessing to Alexander von Staël-Holstein, Apr.?, 1927 此信無日期，郵戳爲 1927 年 4 月 11 日，故可推斷此信寫於 1927 年 4 月。	262
		06 F. Lessing to Alexander von Staël-Holstein, Jun. 6, 1931	264
		07 F. Lessing to Alexander von Staël-Holstein, Jun. 15, 1932	265
		08 F. Lessing to Alexander von Staël-Holstein, Aug. 13, 1932	266
		09 F. Lessing to Alexander von Staël-Holstein, Oct. 8, 1932	267
		附 01 Someone to F. Lessing, Oct. 17, 1922 此信寫信人無法辨識，暫繫於此。	274
087	Ernst Leumann	01 Ernst Leumann to Alexander von Staël-Holstein, Apr. 14, 1928	275
		02 Ernst Leumann to Alexander von Staël-Holstein, Mar. 4, 1929	284
088	Sylvain Lévi	01 Sylvain Lévi to Alexander von Staël-Holstein, Jul. 16, 1921	288
		02 Alexander von Staël-Holstein to Sylvain Lévi, Nov. 6, 1924	291
		03 Alexander von Staël-Holstein to Sylvain Lévi, Jul. 8, 1928 此信原置於 “Letters (not identified) 回發” 中，與 “Lévi, Sylvain 回發”中 1924 年 11 月 6 日鋼和泰致 Lévi 一信稱呼相同，原排列位置接近，故暫定爲收信人爲 Lévi。此信包括打印件和手寫件各一份。	293
		04 Alexander von Staël-Holstein to Sylvain Lévi 此信無日期。	298

序號	書信人	信件擬目	頁碼
		05 Alexander von Staël-Holstein to Sylvain Lévi 此信無日期，信中提到 1932 年發表的論文，故此信應寫於 1932 年或之後。	300
089	Lin Li Kuang	01 Lin Li Kuang to Alexander von Staël-Holstein, Jul. 4, 1933	302
		02 Lin Li Kuang to Alexander von Staël-Holstein, Aug. 19, 1933	303
		03 Lin Li Kuang to Alexander von Staël-Holstein, Aug. 21, 1933	304
090	H. C. Hua-jin Lin	01 H. C. Hua-jin Lin to Alexander von Staël-Holstein, Jan. 4, 1928	305
091	Francis C. Liu	01 Francis C. Liu to Alexander von Staël-Holstein, Dec. 2, 1931	309
		02 Francis C. Liu to Alexander von Staël-Holstein, Dec. 15, 1931	310
		03 Francis C. Liu to Alexander von Staël-Holstein, Jan. 26, 1932	311
092	H. Lüders	01 H. Lüders to Alexander von Staël-Holstein, Mar. 18, 1934 此信後附有 Lüders 的論文十頁。	312
		02 H. Lüders to Alexander von Staël-Holstein, Jun. 28, 1936	324
093	Herbert M.	01 Herbert M. to Alexander von Staël-Holstein, Sept. 22, 1926 此信寫信人姓不能辨識。	325
094	Ma Heng	01 Alexander von Staël-Holstein to Ma Heng, Aug. 28, 1933 此信收信人僅寫爲“Professor Ma”，與 1934 年 12 月 27 日寫給“Director Ma”的信同在“Ma 回發”信封中，收信人應爲同一人。1934 年 12 月 27 日寫給 Director Ma 的信中説：“I am indeed proud to be a corresponding member of the Palace Museumand, I thank you very much for the new Pin Shu, which I received, not long ago.” 馬衡 1934 年 4 月任故宮博物院院長，故此 “Director	326

序號	書信人	信件擬目	頁碼
		Ma”應爲馬衡。同樣，“Ma 回發”信封中的 Proessor Ma 也應爲馬衡。	
		02 Alexander von Staël-Holstein to Ma Heng, Dec. 27, 1934	327
		03 Alexander von Staël-Holstein to Ma Heng, 1934?	328
		此信無日期，信開頭說：“I venture to send you a copy of my latest paper（On a Peking edition etc.）……”，所提到的論文即 *On a Peking Edition of the Tibetan Kanjur which seems to be unknown in the west*, 發表於 *Harvard Sino-Indian Series* 3, 1934。則此信大約在 1934 年。	
095	MacMurray	01 Alexander von Staël-Holstein to MacMurray, Mar. 18, 1934	329
		此信收信人僅寫“MacMurray”，全名不詳。背面有鉛筆書寫兩頁。	
		附 01 Alexander von Staël-Holstein to Someone, 1934?	333
		此信寫於鋼和泰致 MacMurray 一信背面，無開頭結尾，收信人不詳，暫繫於此。	
096	H. F. MacNair	01 H. F. MacNair to Alexander von Staël-Holstein, Feb. 18, 1924	335
		02 Alexander von Staël-Holstein to H. F. MacNair, Feb.– Jun.?, 1924	336
		此信無日期，信開頭說：“Many thanks for your kind letter. I feel indeed honored by your suggestion that I should lecture at St. John's University in July 1924……”，MacNair 1924 年 2 月 18 日致鋼和泰的信中說：“the Christian colleges and universities of East China are uniting for purposes of advanced instruction during the month of July. …… I should like very much to have you offer courses for advanced students in the Philosophy and Religion of the East.” 故可確定，鋼和泰此信應爲對 MacNair 1924 年 2 月 18 日一信的回復。信中又說：“I shall have to devote the summer months to writing up the notes……”，則此信應寫於 1924 年暑期之前，大致推定爲 1924 年 2—6 月。	
097	Mrs. Mamen	01 Alexander von Staël-Holstein to Mrs. Mamen, Jan. ?, 1931	337
		此信無日期，寫於鋼和泰 1931 年 1 月 22 日致博晨光一信	

序號	書信人	信件擬目	頁碼
		的背面,時間應接近,大致定爲 1931 年 1 月。此信原置於"Porter, Lucius 回發" 信封内。	
098	Georges Margouliès	01 G. Margouliès to Alexander von Staël-Holstein, Apr. 3, 1931	338
099	Prince Mdivani	01 Alexander von Staël-Holstein to Prince Mdivani 此信日期不詳。	339
		附 01 Alexander von Staël-Holstein to Someone, Feb. 20, 1934 此信爲俄文，收信人不能辨識，原置於 "Mdivani, Prince 回發" 信封内，暫繫於此。	341
		附 02 Alexander von Staël-Holstein to Someone, Feb. 22, 1934 此信法文，寫於上俄文信背面，收信人寫爲 "Monsieur"，原置於 "Mdvani, Prince 回發" 信封内，暫繫於此。	342
100	Father Mostaert	01 Alexander von Staël-Holstein to Father Mostaert, May 24, 1933	343
101	Herbert Mueller	01 Herbert Mueller to Alexander von Staël-Holstein, Jan. 12, 1928	344
		02 Herbert Mueller to Alexander von Staël-Holstein, Jan. 17, 1932	345
		03 Herbert Mueller to Alexander von Staël-Holstein, Nov. 26, 1933	346
		04 Herbert Mueller to Alexander von Staël-Holstein, Saturday 此信日期僅署爲 "Samstag"，即 Saturday。	348
		05 Herbert Mueller to Alexander von Staël-Holstein, 17 此信日期僅署爲 "17"，年月不詳。	349
102	G. K. Nariman	01 G. K. Nariman to Alexander von Staël-Holstein, Jan. 2, 1925	350

序號	書信人	信件擬目	頁碼
103	Mr. Nixon	01 Alexander von Staël-Holstein to Mr. Nixon, Summer ?, 1932 此信寫於鋼和泰 1932 年 6 月 26 日致 Miss Hague 一信背面上半頁，年代大致應與背面書信接近，暫定爲 1932 年夏季前後。	352
104	Y. Obala	01 Y. Obala to Alexander von Staël-Holstein, Mar. 14, 1922 此信原置於 "Embassies (and Legations) (Letters from-) 來" 信封内，僅署 3 月 14 日，信中提到 3 月 19 日周日，查萬年曆，與鋼和泰在北京的時間相合的爲 1922 年和 1933 年。信中還提到喜仁龍將參加寫信人的家庭聚會，喜仁龍 1921、1930、1934、1935 年多次來華，綜合考慮，此信可能寫於 1922 年 3 月 14 日。	353
105	B. I. Pankratoff	01 B. I. Pankratoff to Alexander von Staël-Holstein, Mar. 31, 1927	354
		02 B. I. Pankratoff to Alexander von Staël-Holstein, Mar. 10, 1929	366
106	Willys R. Peck	01 Willys R. Peck to Alexander von Staël-Holstein, Sept. 27, 1923	368
		02 Alexander von Staël-Holstein to Willys R. Peck, Oct., 1923 此信無日期。信中解釋遲交某譯文的原因，并説明大致可能完成的時間。Peck 1923 年 9 月 27 日寫給鋼和泰的開頭問："May I inquire how the translation is getting on?" 則此信應爲對 Peck 1923 年 9 月 27 日一信的回復。此信中提到寫信日期幾天之後爲農曆初九。查萬年曆，Peck 寫信時的 9 月 27 日爲農曆八月十七，因此此信提到的農曆初九，大致應爲九月初九，西曆爲 10 月 18 日，此信寫於前幾天，可以確定爲 1923 年 10 月。	369
		03 Willys R. Peck to Alexander von Staël-Holstein, Oct. 18, 1923	371
		04 Willys R. Peck to Alexander von Staël-Holstein, Jan. 4, 1924	373
		05 Willys R. Peck to Alexander von Staël-Holstein, Dec. 12, 1924	374

序號	書信人	信件擬目	頁碼
		06 Alexander von Staël-Holstein to Willys R. Peck, Dec.?, 1924 此信無日期。信開頭說："I beg to express my sincerest gratitude to you, to Mrs. Rockhill, and to Dr. Harris for the permission to publish the Tibetan documents in a philological journal, and also for the photographic reproductions ……"，據 Peck1924 年 12 月 12 日寫給鋼和泰的信："Dr. Harris also forwarded to me, to be presented to you, the photographic copies for which you asked……"，則此信當爲對上信的回復，時間大約在 1924 年 12 月底前後。	376
		07 Alexander von Staël-Holstein to Willys R. Peck 此信日期不詳，附有鋼和泰所寫 B. I. Pankratoff 簡歷。	378
		08 Alexander von Staël-Holstein to Willys R. Peck 此信日期不詳。	381
107	Paul Pelliot	01 Alexander von Staël-Holstein to Paul Pelliot, Winter, 1922 此信無日期，信中說："Mon edition du Kaçyapaparivarta n'est pas encore prêt. Il n'y a que 105 pages d'impriniees."大意是說《大寶積經迦葉品梵藏漢六種合刊》没有完成，衹印了 105 頁。王雲五 1922 年 10 月 4 日給鋼和泰的信中說："we beg, herewith, to forward to you 6 copies of 2nd proof from page 79 to 105……"。王雲五 1922 年 12 月 20 日寫給鋼和泰的信中又說："we send you herewith 5 copies of the last proof of the Pao Chih Ching(寶積經) from page 106 to 121"，則此信當寫於 1922 年 10 月 4 日至 12 月 20 日之間，大致定爲 1922 年冬季。	382
		02 Alexander von Staël-Holstein to Paul Pelliot, Apr.?, 1922 此信無日期，信中說："Le manuscrit est prêt depuis six mois mais jusqu'cici 17 pages seulement ont été imprimées." 大意是說：手稿已經完成六個月了，但到目前爲止，衹印了 17 頁。1922 年 4 月 20 日王雲五給鋼和泰的信中說："The pages 1–17 with your signature returned to us by express mail was received on February 20th." 王雲五 1922 年 5 月 6 日給鋼和泰的信中說已經修改了鋼和泰對 35—59 頁的校對。故此信大致寫於 1922 年 4 月。	385
		03 Alexander von Staël-Holstein to Paul Pelliot, Oct.?, 1923 此信無日期，信中說："Voilà díja plus de deux ans que le manuscrit est terminé, et la Commercial Press' n'a imprimé que 143 pages'." 大意是說：手稿完成兩年多了，商務印書館才印了	386

序號	書信人	信件擬目	頁碼
		143 頁。鋼和泰約寫於 1922 年 4 月的信中提到手稿完成 6 個月了，則此信大致寫於 1922 年之後一年半多，大致在 1923 年 10 月之後。	
		04 Alexander von Staël-Holstein to Paul Pelliot, Jul.?, 1926 此信無日期。第一頁中說："Mon 'Sino-Indian Research Institute'a reçu certaines sommes de l'Université de Yenching pour l'année 1. 7. 26–30.6.27, qui vient de commercer……"，大意是說：鋼和泰主持的中印研究所從燕京大學得到一筆 1926 年 7 月 1 日至 1927 年 6 月 30 日的資助，剛開始執行。故此信大致寫於 1926 年 7 月。	389
		05 Paul Pelliot to Alexander von Staël-Holstein, Apr. 26, 1931	392
		06 Alexander von Staël-Holstein to Paul Pelliot, Jul.?, 1933 此信時間僅署爲 "Jeudi" 即 Thursday，具體時間不詳。	396
		07 Paul Pelliot to Alexander von Staël-Holstein, Thursday 此信時間僅署爲 "Jeudi" 即 Thursday，具體時間不詳。	403
108	W. B. Pettus	01 W. B. Pettus to Alexander von Staël-Holstein, May 22, 1925	404
		02 Alexander von Staël-Holstein to W. B. Pettus, Sept. 22, 1934	405
		03 Alexander von Staël-Holstein to W. B. Pettus 此信日期不詳。	406
109	Mr. Plomp	01 Alexander von Staël-Holstein to Mr. Plomp, Mar. ?, 1930 此信無日期，寫於鋼和泰 1930 年 3 月致顧臨夫人一信下半頁，日期應該接近，故暫定爲 1930 年 3 月。	407
110	Lucius C. Porter	01 Alexander von Staël-Holstein to Lucius C. Porter, Feb.?, 1926 此信日期不詳。信中提到在上海出版著作的校樣，似應指《大寶積經迦葉品梵藏漢六種合刊》，并且說："I hope you will find time to read that part of the preface pages V, VI and XIII, in	408

序號	書信人	信件擬目	頁碼
		which the two further volumes which I am preparing are mentioned."博晨光在 1926 年 3 月 1 日給鋼和泰的信中説:"Herewith your package of proof, Mr. Hummel & I have been glad to read the preface and to see what you are planning." 故可確定博晨光 1926 年 3 月 1 日給鋼和泰一信應爲對此信的回復。鋼和泰寄給博晨光校樣的目的，不是爲了請其幫助校對，而是爲了讓其瞭解自己進一步編寫兩卷相關圖書的計劃，此似與争取燕大資助有關。博晨光的回復大致不會需要太多時日，故推定此信寫於 1926 年 2 月。另此信背面除了結尾外，尚有鋼和泰起草的德文書信一封，收信人僅寫爲 "Professor"，暫繫於此。	
		02 Lucius C. Porter to Alexander von Staël-Holstein, Mar. 1, 1926 此信日期僅署 "Monday"，另有鋼和泰手寫德文日期 "Frühjahr 26"即 Spring 26，故爲 1926 年春季。信中提及資助 Mr. Yü (應爲于道泉) 的事，并説希望 Mr. Pettus 也會同意。博晨光 1926 年 3 月 6 日的信中，又説自己把此事跟 Mr. Pettus 談了，故此信應寫於 3 月 6 日之前，一般春天從 3 月開始，此信又寫明爲周一，查萬年曆，當爲 3 月 1 日。	410
		03 Lucius C. Porter to Alexander von Staël-Holstein, Mar. 6, 1926	411
		04 Lucius C. Porter to Alexander von Staël-Holstein, Jun. 10, 1926	412
		05 Alexander von Staël-Holstein to Lucius C. Porter, Jun. 15, 1926	413
		06 Lucius C. Porter to Alexander von Staël-Holstein, Jun. 18, 1926	423
		07 Lucius C. Porter to Alexander von Staël-Holstein, Jun.–Jul.?, 1926 此信無日期，有鋼和泰鉛筆注明德文日期: Juni. Juli 26，即 June. July 26。	424
		08 Lucius C. Porter to Alexander von Staël-Holstein, Summer, 1926 此信原無日期，據鋼和泰鉛筆注明補。	426
		09 Lucius C. Porter to Alexander von Staël-Holstein, Sept. 24, 1926 此信原署日期爲 "Friday morning"，另有鋼和泰鉛筆注明德文日期 "Ende Sept. 1926" 即 End Sept. 1926（意为 1926 年 9	427

序號	書信人	信件擬目	頁碼
		月底），查萬年曆，1926 年 9 月最後一個周五爲 24 日。故此信大致寫於 1926 年 9 月 24 日。	
		10 Lucius C. Porter to Alexander von Staël-Holstein, Sept. 30, 1926	428
		11 Lucius C. Porter to Alexander von Staël-Holstein, Oct. 27, 1926	429
		12 Lucius C. Porter to Alexander von Staël-Holstein, Oct. 29, 1926	430
		13 Lucius C. Porter to Alexander von Staël-Holstein, Oct. 29, 1926 此信原無日期，據鋼和泰鉛筆注明日期補。	431
		14 Lucius C. Porter to Alexander von Staël-Holstein, Nov. 18, 1926 此信原無年代，信中提到周五將要安排的事情，應寫於周五之前，此信前後的書信均爲 1926 年，查萬年曆，1926 年 11 月 18 日爲周六，故暫定此信爲 1926 年。	432
		15 Lucius C. Porter to Alexander von Staël-Holstein, Nov.?, 1926 此信僅在信末署 “Thursday noon”，另有鋼和泰鉛筆德文注明 “Auf. Nov. 26” 即 “On Nov. 26”，故此信寫於 1926 年 11 月。查萬年曆，1926 年 11 月最後一個周四是 24 日，此信最晚寫於 1926 年 11 月 24 日。	433
		16 Alexander von Staël-Holstein to Lucius C. Porter, Nov, 1926 此信無日期，開頭說：“I have great pleasure in accepting your kind invitation to tea on Monday December 6th, ……”，博晨光 1926 年 11 月給鋼和泰的信中說：“Our school is giving a tea on Monday（Dec. 6th）.” 故此信應爲對博晨光 1926 年 11 月一信的回復，時間大致也在 11 月。	434
		17 Lucius C. Porter to Alexander von Staël-Holstein, Nov. 26, 1926	435
		18 Lucius C. Porter to Alexander von Staël-Holstein, Jan.?, 1927 此信原無日期，首頁有鋼和泰鉛筆德文注明 “Januar 1927”，即 “January 1927”。	437

序號	書信人	信件擬目	頁碼
		19 Lucius C. Porter to Alexander von Staël-Holstein, Feb. 25, 1927	439
		20 Lucius C. Porter to Alexander von Staël-Holstein, Apr. 11, 1927	440
		21 Alexander von Staël-Holstein to Lucius C. Porter, 1927 ? 此信無日期。信中提到博晨光將向 Lévi 等人徵詢關於中印研究所的意見。在中印研究所 1929 年歸入燕京學社之前，鋼和泰曾尋求燕京大學的資助，1927 年 7 月司徒雷登曾向伯希和等人寫信，請他們對鋼和泰的研究做出評價，故此信大致寫於 1927 年前後。	441
		22 Lucius C. Porter to Alexander von Staël-Holstein, Apr. 13, 1928	445
		23 Alexander von Staël-Holstein to Lucius C. Porter, Apr. ?, 1928 此信無日期。信中說："My plans have been entirely upsetby a letter just received from Sir Charles Eliot in which he tells me that he has given up his planned visit to Peking and that he is leaving for England directly." 查 Eliot 1928 年 4 月 8 日給鋼和泰的信中說："On the 26th of this month I leave for England & shall not be able to manage a visit to Peking. " 則此信當寫在 1928 年 4 月 8 日之後不久。另查博晨光 1928 年 4 月 13 日給鋼和泰的信，第二段說："As to the funds, our treasure has been authorized to pay to you the amounts due up to Oct. 1st 1928." 此當是鋼和泰在此信中說的"have solved the financial question"。故此信當是對博晨光 1928 年 4 月 13 日一信的回信，博晨光此時在燕京大學，鋼和泰尚未去哈佛，仍在北平，故此信極有可能寫在 1928 年 4 月。	446
		24 Alexander von Staël-Holstein to Lucius C. Porter, Apr. 7, 1929	447
		25 Lucius C. Porter to Alexander von Staël-Holstein, Oct. 14, 1929	448
		26 Lucius C. Porter to Alexander von Staël-Holstein, Nov. 11, 1929 此信原無日期，第一頁末說："The only time for this trip is on Saturday, Sunday & Monday of this Week, namely Nov. 16. 17. 18." 查萬年曆，此信當爲 1929 年，具體時間爲 11 月 11 日周一早上。	449

序號	書信人	信件擬目	頁碼
		27 Lucius C. Porter to Alexander von Staël-Holstein, Jan. 9, 1930	451
		28 Alexander von Staël-Holstein to Lucius C. Porter, Jan.?, 1930 此信無日期。信中說："My statement of account is not quite ready yet, but will be sent to you as soon as possible. The representation cheque has been received here with many thanks." 博晨光 1930 年 1 月 9 日給鋼和泰的信說："The check for Mr. Panratoff goes direct, and the quarterly payment for 'representation' goes to yourself." 則此信應爲對 1930 年 1 月 9 日一信的回信。故此信應寫於 1930 年 1 月。	452
		29 Alexander von Staël-Holstein to Lucius C. Porter, Jan. 28, 1930 此信第二頁寫於第一頁背面，具體日期不詳，暫繫於此。	453
		30 Alexander von Staël-Holstein to Lucius C. Porter, Apr. 27, 1930	455
		31 Lucius C. Porter to Alexander von Staël-Holstein, Jun. 6, 1930	456
		32 Alexander von Staël-Holstein to Lucius C. Porter, Jun. 11, 1930	458
		33 Lucius C. Porter to Alexander von Staël-Holstein, Oct. 22, 1930	459
		34 Alexander von Staël-Holstein to Lucius C. Porter, Oct. 28, 1930 此信原存入 "Chase, George H. 回發 3" 信封中。	461
		35 Alexander von Staël-Holstein to Lucius C. Porter, Oct. 30, 1930	463
		36 Lucius C. Porter to Alexander von Staël-Holstein, Jan. 19, 1931	464
		37 Alexander von Staël-Holstein to Lucius C. Porter, Jan. 22, 1931	465
		38 Lucius C. Porter to Alexander von Staël-Holstein, Jan. 26, 1931	466

序號	書信人	信件擬目	頁碼
		39 Lucius C. Porter to Alexander von Staël-Holstein, Jan. 30, 1931	467
		40 Alexander von Staël-Holstein to Lucius C. Porter, Feb.?, 1931 此信無日期。第一頁說：“I could not discuss it with Mr. Tschen Yin Koh last Saturday, because he did not appear at our meeting. His wife had fallen ill and he had to take her to the P. U. M. C.” 陳寅恪 1931 年 1 月 30 日的信中說：“I have to accompany my wife to go to P. M. U. C. this morning unexpectedly.”查萬年曆，1931 年 1 月 30 日確爲周六，故此信大致寫於 1931 年 2 月初。	468
		41 Lucius C. Porter to Alexander von Staël-Holstein, Apr. 15, 1931	470
		42 Lucius C. Porter to Alexander von Staël-Holstein, Jun. 25, 1931	471
		43 Lucius C. Porter to Alexander von Staël-Holstein, Jan. 7, 1932	473
		44 Lucius C. Porter to Alexander von Staël-Holstein, Dec. 19, 1932	474
		45 Lucius C. Porter to Alexander von Staël-Holstein, Dec. 30, 1932	475
		46 Alexander von Staël-Holstein to Lucius C. Porter, Dec.?, 1932 此信原入 “Laurn, Mme 回發” 信封中，寫於鋼和泰致 Madame Laurn 一封信的背面。此信無日期，信中提到 12 月 29 日周四，查萬年曆，應爲 1932 年，故此信當寫於 1932 年 12 月。	476
		47 Lucius C. Porter to Alexander von Staël-Holstein, May 2, 1933	477
		48 Alexander von Staël-Holstein to Lucius C. Porter, Jun. 5, 1933	478
		49 Lucius C. Porter to Alexander von Staël-Holstein, Jun. 8, 1933	479
		50 Alexander von Staël-Holstein to Lucius C. Porter, Jun.?, 1933 此信無日期，信中說：“Dean Chase writes that Professor	480

序號	書信人	信件擬目	頁碼
		Eliséeff hopes to be here towards the end of this month." 博晨光 1933 年 5 月 9 日給鋼和泰的信中説："He (Eliséeff) is therefore, planning to sail May 26th on the PRESIDENT HARRISON from San Francisco, which will bring him to Shanghai on June 19th and to Peking some time later." 據此，此信當寫於 1933 年 6 月。另，此信説："I am very much obliged to you for having dealt so promptly with my expense account." 博晨光 1933 年 6 月 8 日給鋼和泰的信開頭説："I have asked our treasurer to send you at once the amount you request ……"，故此信應爲對博晨光 6 月 8 日一信的回復，時間當在 1933 年 6 月 8 日之後幾天。	
		51 Lucius C. Porter to Alexander von Staël-Holstein, Jun. 13, 1933	481
		52 Lucius C. Porter to Alexander von Staël-Holstein, Jul. 19, 1933	482
		53 Lucius C. Porter to Alexander von Staël-Holstein, Dec. 28, 1933	484
		54 Lucius C. Porter to Alexander von Staël-Holstein, Dec.?, 1933 此信原無日期，開頭説："Thank you so much for your remembrance of Wolcotto'Stamp collection." 鋼和泰 1933 年 12 月 24 日給博晨光的信中説："I have lately received a number of letters etc. bearing stamps which might interest your youngest son. May I ask you to present the enclosed envelopes to him?" 故可確定，此信爲對鋼和泰 1933 年 12 月 25 日一信的回復，此信又有"a Merry Christmas to you" 等語，應大致寫於 12 月 24 日或 25 日。	486
		55 Alexander von Staël-Holstein to Lucius C. Porter, 1933 此信無日期，信中説："I have written an article for the Yenching Journal ……"，博晨光 1932 年 12 月 19 日寫給鋼和泰的信中説："I have had a talk with Professor Ku the editor of our YenchingJournal and he bids me tell you that he will be very happy to have an article from you for some future number of the journal." 則此信可能寫於 1933 年。另，此信背面有俄文信一封，寫信人不能辨識，暫繫於此。	487
		56 Lucius C. Porter to Alexander von Staël-Holstein, Feb. 3, 1934	489
		57 Lucius C. Porter to Alexander von Staël-Holstein, Feb. 15, 1934	490

序號	書信人	信件擬目	頁碼
		58 Alexander von Staël-Holstein to Lucius C. Porter, Feb. 15, 1934 此信日期寫於倒數第四行。	491
		59 Lucius C. Porter to Alexander von Staël-Holstein, Jun. 17, 1934	492
		60 Lucius C. Porter to Alexander von Staël-Holstein, Oct. 15, 1934	494
		61 Alexander von Staël-Holstein to Lucius C. Porter, Oct. 23, 1934	495
		62 Lucius C. Porter to Alexander von Staël-Holstein, Nov. 5, 1934	497
		63 Alexander von Staël-Holstein to Lucius C. Porter, Nov. 9, 1934 此信第二頁寫於第一頁背面，從内容看，似乎相關，暫繫於此。	498
		64 Lucius C. Porter to Alexander von Staël-Holstein, Dec. 14, 1934	500
		65 Alexander von Staël-Holstein to Lucius C. Porter, Dec. 24, 1934	501
		66 Lucius C. Porter to Alexander von Staël-Holstein, Jan. 25, 1935	502
		67 Lucius C. Porter to Alexander von Staël-Holstein, Feb. 7, 1935	503
		68 Alexander von Staël-Holstein to Lucius C. Porter, Feb. 7, 1935	504
		69 Lucius C. Porter to Alexander von Staël-Holstein, Mar. 23, 1935 此信第三頁爲前兩頁的打印件。	505
		70 Alexander von Staël-Holstein to Lucius C. Porter, Apr.?, 1935 此信無日期，博晨光 1935 年 3 月 23 日給鋼和泰的信 (信上地址爲：West China Union University, Chengtu) 開頭説："I am	508

序號	書信人	信件擬目	頁碼
		well established here and am greatly enjoying my work and the opportunity to get acquainted with this region. It is full of natural and historical interest, including many fine Buddhist temples which I am visiting. I hope to visit Mt. Omei before my return in May." 鋼和泰在此信中說："I am very glad to hear that you enjoy your stay at Chengtu and that you will return to Peking in May." 據此，此信當爲對 Porter 1935 年 3 月 23 日一信的回信，時間大約在 1935 年 4 月前後。	
		71 Lucius C. Porter to Alexander von Staël-Holstein, Sept. 11, 1935	509
		72 Alexander von Staël-Holstein to Lucius C. Porter, Oct. 1, 1935	510
		73 Alexander von Staël-Holstein to Lucius C. Porter, Oct.?, 1935 此信無日期，開頭說："Many thanks for having arranged the matter with the authorities of the Yenching Journal so satisfactorily. I am very glad to hear that they have accepted my offer, and that an article of mine will appear in their periodical." 博晨光 1934 年 10 月 15 日給鋼和泰的信中說："The editorial staff has only just decided to make your article the first article in No. 17 of our journal which will appear in June 1935." 故此信應爲對博晨光 1935 年 10 月 15 日一信的回信，時間大致在 1935 年 10 月底前後。	511
		74 Lucius C. Porter to Alexander von Staël-Holstein, Apr. 16, 1936	512
		75 Lucius C. Porter to Alexander von Staël-Holstein, Oct. 20, 1936	513
		76 Alexander von Staël-Holstein to Lucius C. Porter, Sept., 1935–Jun., 1936 此信無日期，信中提到"下學年"爲 1936、1937，故此信大致寫於 1935—1936 學年，即 1935 年 9 月至 1936 年 6 月。	515
		77 Alexander von Staël-Holstein to Lucius C. Porter, 1934–1936 此信無日期，開頭說："In case I get a good price from Langdon Warner I might sell him my collection." 鋼和泰在 30 年代曾想賣掉自己的收藏。Langdon Warner 1934 年 1 月 12 日給鋼和泰的信中說："As you may will imagine, there is no chance of selling such a collection in these dark days of depression." 此信或在此之後，大約 1934—1936 年。	516

序號	書信人	信件擬目	頁碼
		78 Alexander von Staël-Holstein to Lucius C. Porter 此信日期不詳。	517
		79 Alexander von Staël-Holstein to Lucius C. Porter 此信日期不詳。	518
		附 01 Alexander von Staël-Holstein to Mrs. Lucius C. Porter 此信日期不詳，爲鋼和泰致博晨光夫人，暫繫於此。	522
		附 02 Alexander von Staël-Holstein to Mrs. Lucius C. Porter, Dec. 24, 1933	523
		附 03 Alexander von Staël-Holstein to Someone 此信德文，日期不詳，寫於鋼和泰致博晨光夫人一信背面，收信人僅寫爲 “Herrn” 即 “Lord”，暫繫於此。	524
		附 04 Lucius C. Porter to Madame Lauru, Oct. 27, 1926 此信末署明日期爲 “Wednesday, October twenty seventh”，另在首頁有鋼和泰鉛筆注明 “Oct.–Nov. 26”，查萬年曆，1926 年 10 月 27 日確爲周三，故可推定此信寫於 1926 年 10 月 27 日。此信爲博晨光致 Madame Lauru，暫繫於此。	525
		附 05 John Leighton Stuart to Paul Pelliot, Jul. 15, 1927 此信原無寫信人署名，從内容看應爲燕大校長司徒雷登所寫。且信末提到 1924 年在美國與伯希和見面，司徒雷登 1924 年上半年在美國。原置於 “Porter, Lucius C. 來” 信封内，暫繫於此。	527
		附 06 John Leighton Stuart to F. Lessing, Jul. 15, 1927 此信原無寫信人署名，從内容看應爲燕大校長司徒雷登所寫。書信内容與司徒雷登同日致伯希和信多相同。原置於“Porter, Lucius C. 來” 信封内，暫繫於此。	529

序號	書信人	信件擬目	頁碼
		附 07 Alexander von Staël-Holstein to Madame, 1928 此信無日期，具體收信人不詳，寫於鋼和泰 1928 年 4 月致博晨光一信的背面上部，時間應比較接近，故大致推定爲 1928 年。	531
		附 08 Alexander von Staël-Holstein to Baronne, 1928 此信無日期，具體收信人不詳，寫於鋼和泰 1928 年 4 月致博晨光一信的背面中部，時間應比較接近，故大致推定爲 1928 年。	531
		附 09 Alexander von Staël-Holstein to Comte, 1928 此信無日期，具體收信人不詳，寫於鋼和泰 1928 年 4 月致博晨光一信的背面下部，時間應比較接近，故大致推定爲 1928 年。	531
111	Alan Priest	01 Alan Priest to Alexander von Staël-Holstein, Dec. 7, 1928 此信日期僅署爲 "Dec. 7"，所用信封爲紐約大都會博物館遠東藝術部，此信開頭説："I will forward the photographs as soon as the slides are ready." 紐約大都會博物館教育工作部的 Huger Elliot 1928 年 11 月 2 日給鋼和泰的信中説："Thank you for replying so promptly to my letter and for consenting to give the talk suggested by Mr. Priest." 故 Priest 此信中説的幻燈片應該是與此演講有關。Huger Elliot1928 年 12 月 18 日給鋼和泰的信説："I find that I have done something which I should not have done in allowing you to take with you the lantern slides made in the Museum for use by your delightful talk last Friday." 鋼和泰應該是 12 月 14 日（周五）做的演講。綜上，此信當寫於 1928 年 12 月 7 日。	532
		02 Alan Priest to Alexander von Staël-Holstein, Dec. 8, 1931 此信日期僅署爲 "Tuesday, December 8"，查萬年曆，1931 年、1936 年的 12 月 8 日均爲周二。鋼和泰 1934 年 12 月 5 日給 Madam Lauru 的信中説："This summer Alan Priest asked me to find a Chinese scholar who could assit him in interpreting a certain inscription. I recommended Professor Teng, and Priest, who worked with Teng for a number of months told me, when he left for America, that Teng had proved a great success." 説明 Priest 1934 年夏天後幾個月就回美國了。此信的内容看，當時 Priest 還在中國，故此信當寫於 1931 年 12 月 8 日。	533

序號	書信人	信件擬目	頁碼
		03 Alan Priest to Alexander von Staël-Holstein, Sept.–Oct., 1932 此信無日期，信中説：“When I have this I will do you another statement and I want to do it before the visit to the palace.” 鋼和泰 1932 年 10 月寫給 Priest 的信中説：“your non-photographic visit to the palace can take place very soon on a day to be fixed by yourself……”，此信應寫於鋼和泰 1932 年 10 月一信之前，故大致推定爲 1932 年 9—10 月。	536
		04 Alexander von Staël-Holstein to Alan Priest, Oct.?, 1932? 此信無日期，信中提到 Thursday October 13th，查萬年曆，與鋼和泰 Priest 在北平書信往來符合的時間内，1932 年 10 月 13 日爲周四，從書信内容看，此信應寫於 10 月 13 日之前不久，故大致推定爲 1932 年 10 月。	537
		05 Alan Priest to Alexander von Staël-Holstein, Oct.?, 1932 此信無日期，信中説：“I have opened up a new avenue of possible help and beg you to take a hand. It is a bother I know but I want Mrs. Cal and her two guests to see the Llama temple in the palace,……”，鋼和泰 1932 年 10 月寫給 Priest 的信中説：“your non-photographic visit to the palace can take place very soon on a day to be fixed by yourself……”，此信似應爲 Priest 對鋼和泰 1932 年 10 月一信的回復，他得知可以去故宫參觀後，又提出帶三個人同去。故此信大致寫於 1932 年 10 月。	538
		06 Alexander von Staël-Holstein to Alan Priest, 1932? 此信無日期，信中提到慈寧宫花園，Priest 1931 年 12 月 8 日給鋼和泰的信中也提到慈寧宫花園，大致時間不會相差太多。此外，信開頭説“Mr. Bishop has gone to Ta-t'ung-fu”，畢安祺 1932—1934 年在中國，故大致推定此信寫於 1932 年。	539
		07 Alexander von Staël-Holstein to Alan Priest, Sept.?, 1934 此信位於頁面上部，無日期，信中提到 Wednesday (Sept. 19th)，查萬年曆，1934 年 9 月 19 日爲周三，此信當寫於此前不久，故應推定爲 1934 年 9 月。	540
		08 Alexander von Staël-Holstein to Alan Priest, Oct. 10, 1934	541

序號	書信人	信件擬目	頁碼
		09 Alexander von Staël-Holstein to Alan Priest, Oct.–Dec., 1934 此信無日期，開頭説："Dear Mr. Priest, I am awfully sorry that I must not see you off." 鋼和泰 1934 年 12 月 5 日給 Madam Lauru 的信中説："This summer Alan Priest asked me to find a Chinese scholar who could assit him in interpreting a certain inscription. I recommended Professor Teng, and Priest, who worked with Teng for a number of months told me, when he left for America, that Teng had proved a great success." 説明 Priest 1934 年夏天後幾个月就回美國了。此外，鋼和泰 1934 年 10 月 10 日給 Priest 的信中説："I enclose his address. We gave it to your coolie last night when he came here with a letter addressed to Pankratoff but he has evidently not delivered the letter yet." 説明 Priest1934 年 10 月 10 日還在北京。故此信大致寫於 1934 年 10 月到 12 月間。	542
		10 Alan Priest to Alexander von Staël-Holstein, Tuesday 此信日期不詳。	543
		附 01 Alexander von Staël-Holstein to Bolschafts-rath, Sept.?, 1934 此信無日期，與鋼和泰 1934 年 9 月給 Priest 的信寫於同一頁，内容部分相同，均爲 9 月 19 日聚會之事，故也應寫於 1934 年 9 月。另，此信收信人辨識不完全準確，暫繫於此。	544
112	Przyluski	01 Alexander von Staël-Holstein to Przyluski, Jul.?, 1933	545
113	Reid	01 Alexander von Staël-Holstein to Reid, Sept. 27, 1922 此信寫於鋼和泰 1922 年 12 月致戴何都一信第二頁背面上部，無日期。與此信同在一頁的第三封信寫於 1922 年 9 月 27 日，此信時間應比較接近。信中提到寫信的第二天爲周四，查萬年曆，1922 年 9 月 28 日爲周四，則此信大致寫於 1922 年 9 月 27 日。	547
		02 Alexander von Staël-Holstein to Reid, Nov.?, 1922 此頁寫於鋼和泰 1922 年 12 月致戴何都一信第一頁背面，無日期。信中説："I look forward very much to seeing you on December 1st ……"，故此信大致寫於 1922 年 11 月。	548

序號	書信人	信件擬目	頁碼
		03 Alexander von Staël-Holstein to Someone, Sept. 27, 1922 此信寫於鋼和泰 1922 年 12 月致戴何都一信第二頁背面中部，無日期。此頁前後其它兩封信的日期均爲 1922 年 9 月 27 日，故推定此信爲同日。此信收信人寫爲 “Doctor”，具體不詳，暫置於此。	549
114	John D. Rockefeller	01 John D. Rockefeller to Yeh Pei Chi, Jan. 23, 1930 此信爲抄送件，原置於“Rockefeller (Foundation) 來”信封内，暫置於此。	550
115	Rolf	01 Alexander von Staël-Holstein to Rolf, Oct. ?, 1929 此信無日期，寫於鋼和泰 1929 年 10 月致 James H. Woods 的背面，時間應大致接近，故暫定爲 1929 年 10 月。	551
116	F. Rosenberg	01 F. Rosenberg to Alexander von Staël-Holstein, Aug. 18, 1916	552
		02 F. Rosenberg to Alexander von Staël-Holstein, Sept. 15, 1916	559
		03 F. Rosenberg to Alexander von Staël-Holstein, Oct. 21, 1916	563
		04 F. Rosenberg to Alexander von Staël-Holstein, Nov. 29, 1916 此信結尾寫在第二頁頂端。	567
		05 F. Rosenberg to Alexander von Staël-Holstein, Mar. 4, 1917	571
		06 F. Rosenberg to Alexander von Staël-Holstein, May 23, 1917 此信結尾寫在第二頁頂端。	579
		07 F. Rosenberg to Alexander von Staël-Holstein, Sept. 19, 1917	584
		08 F. Rosenberg to Alexander von Staël-Holstein, Jan. 25, 1918	586

序號	書信人	信件擬目	頁碼
		09 Alexander von Staël-Holstein to F. Rosenberg, Jul. 7, 1924	590
		10 F. Rosenberg to Alexander von Staël-Holstein, Oct. 11 此信僅署月日，無年代。結尾寫於第一頁頂端。	592

書信人簡介

049 I. V. Gillis（1875—1948）

全名 Irvin V. Gillis，中文名義理壽，美國人。一戰期間任美國駐華公使館海軍武官。曾與人合編《日本姓氏》（*Japanese Surnames*）。曾爲美國建築師葛思德收集醫學古籍，後擴大到珍本古籍，共收集古籍十萬餘册，不乏珍本、孤本，這批圖書後入藏普林斯頓大學，成爲葛思德東方圖書館。

050 Helmuth von Glasenapp（1891—1963）

德國印度學和比較宗教學者。生於德國柏林。早年在德國圖賓根、慕尼黑、柏林、波恩等地學習印度學、哲學和宗教，1914 年獲博士學位。1918—1928 年在波恩和柏林任教。1928—1944 年任教於哥尼斯堡大學印度學系。後任圖賓根大學印度學和比較宗教學教授，直至榮譽退休。1963 年 6 月 25 日因車禍去世。

051 Goette（1896—?）

疑爲 John Andrew Goette，美國新聞記者。1921 年由美國紅十字會派赴中國協助賑灾工作。1923—1926 年任北京中美通訊社經理。1926—1941 年任美國國際通訊社駐華記者。1945 年日本投降後，曾到東京爲國際軍事法庭檢查組作證。

052 V. Goloubew（1878—1945）

戈鷺波，俄裔法國東方學家。生於聖彼得堡貴族家庭。1890—1900 年就讀於聖彼得堡大學自然科學院。1901—1904 年就讀於德國海德堡大學。1905 年定居巴黎。1910 年赴印度考察。曾參加第一次世界大戰。1920 年任法蘭西遠東學院研究員，曾隨該院院長菲諾赴吴哥考古。後參與越南諒山、柬埔寨等地考古。1945 年在河内去世。對印度支那各地古代銅器有很深的研究。著有《印度支那的藝術與考古》等。發表大量論文，代表作爲《東京與安南北部的銅器時代》。

053 Roger S. Greene（1881—1947）

顧臨，美國外交官、社會活動家。早年畢業於哈佛大學，曾任美國駐中國哈爾濱、漢口領事。1921 年任洛克菲勒基金會駐華代表。1928 年任北平協和醫學院校長。曾任中華教育文化基金董事會董事。1935 年回美國。1938—1941 年任“美國不參加日本侵略委員會”主席。1940—1941 年任“援助盟軍保衛美國委員會”副主席。

054 J. Hackin（1886—1941）

全名 Joseph Hackin，譯爲約瑟夫·阿坎，法國東方學家。早年就讀於巴黎大學，師從烈維、阿爾弗雷德·富歇，學習古代東方學。1907 年到吉美博物館工作，1913 年任助理館長，1923 年升任館長。曾參加第一次世界大戰。1928 年任盧浮宮學院印度藝術和考古學教授，1929 年起任盧浮宮學院院長。曾於 1924—1925 年、1929—1930 年、1931 年、1933—1934 年、1936—1937 年多次到阿富汗，對哈達、巴米安、貝格拉姆等地遺迹進行考古學調查，研究古希臘文明對初期佛教藝術的影響。1934 年被任命爲法國赴阿富汗考古隊領隊。1931—1932 年加入法國雪鐵龍汽車公司。1930—1933 年兼任東京日法會館法國學會會長，曾在日本居住。20 世紀 30 年代到過中國。1940 年自阿富汗到倫敦，任自由法國外交顧問。1941 年在西班牙菲尼斯特雷角海上因海難去世。主要著作有《吉美博物館裏的中國繪畫》（*La peinture chinoise au Musée Guimet*）、《插圖亞洲神話》（*Mythologie asiatique illustrée*）、《在巴米安進行的一些新的考古調查》（*Nouvelles recherches archéologiques à Bāmiyān*）、《在貝格拉姆進行的一些考古調查》（*Recherches archéologiques à Begram*）等。

055 Hilda L. Hague

生平不詳。從信箋看，曾任哈佛燕京學社駐北平辦事處秘書。

056 Clarence H. Hamilton（1886—?）

美國佛教學者、博士。曾任康涅狄格州哈特福德布道學院（The College of Missions）教務長、美國東方學會提名委員會會員。從事佛教研究，著有《神秘主義的心理學闡釋》（*A psychological*

Interpretation of Mysticism）、《印度、錫蘭、中國、日本的佛教：閱讀指南》（*Buddhism in India, Ceylon, China and Japan: a Reading Guide*）、《佛教，一種無限同情的宗教：佛教文獻選編》（*Buddhism, a Religion of Infinite Compassion: Selections from Buddhist Literature*）等，譯有《唯識二十論》。

057 Sven Hedin（1865—1952）

斯文·赫定，瑞典地理學家、探險家。生於斯德哥爾摩。1886年就讀於斯德哥爾摩大學地質地理專業，獲碩士學位，1891年入柏林大學。1890年參加瑞典波斯使團到東方。1893—1930年數次來華從事科學考察。1899—1902年曾在羅布泊附近發現古樓蘭遺址。1927—1935年，與中國學術界聯合組建西北科學考察團，任瑞方團長。著有《穿過亞洲》、《1899—1902年中亞考察科學成果》等。

058 Howard Coonley Hollis

生平不詳。曾任克利夫蘭藝術博物館東方藝術部主任。

059 Horstmann

生平不詳。

060 Prof. Hsü

生平不詳。

061 Hu Shih（1891—1962）

胡適，著名學者。安徽績溪人，生於上海。早年在家鄉讀私塾。1904年到上海讀書，入梅溪學堂，次年改入澄衷學堂。1906年考入中國公學。1909年考取庚款留美，入康奈爾大學，學習農科。1912年改入文學院，主修哲學。1914年獲康奈爾大學文學士學位。1915年入哥倫比亞大學，1917年畢業回國，任北京大學教授，兼英文科教授會主任。1926年辭去北大教授職務，赴英國參加庚款咨詢委員會會議。次年歸國，暫居上海。1928年任中國公學校長兼文理學院院長。1930年辭去中國公學校長職務，同年底舉家遷回北平。1931 年兼任北大教授。次年任北大文學院長。1937 年抗戰爆發後，以非官方身份赴美，争取援助。1938 年出任國民政府駐美大使，1942 年離任，還居紐約從事學術研究。1945 年被任命爲北京大學校長，次年歸國就任。1948 年當選中央研究院院士，同年底飛離被包圍的北平。1949 年再度赴美。1958 年回臺灣，就任“中央研究院”院長。1962 年在臺北去世。胡適在哲學、歷史、文學等領域都有開創性的貢獻，主要著作有《中國哲學史大綱》(卷上)、《先秦名學史》、《白話文學史》(上)、《胡適文存》等。

062 Huang Chung Kiang

生平不詳。

063 Arthur William Hummel (1884—1975)

中文名恒慕義，漢學家，美國公理會教士。早年畢業於芝加哥大學。1915 年到山西汾陽銘義中學教英文。1924 年任燕京大學歷史系講師。1927 年回國，任美國國會圖書館首任東方部主任。1957 年與郭秉文創辦中美文化協會(Sino-America Cultural Society)，任首任主席。

064 William Hung

洪業，字鹿岑，譜名正繼，號煨蓮，英文名 William。福建侯官(今閩侯)人。著名歷史學家。1910 年入福州鶴齡英華書院，1915 年赴美留學，1917 年獲美國俄亥俄韋斯良大學文學士學位，1919 年獲哥倫比亞大學文學碩士學位。1920 年畢業於紐約協和神學院，獲神學士學位。1920—1922 年在美國巡迴演講，争取美國友好人士援助中國抵抗日本强占青島。1923 年受燕京大學之聘，協助哈里·盧斯爲燕京大學在北平西郊建造新校舍募得巨款，同年返回北京城，參與新校舍建設，并任燕京大學歷史系教授。後歷任燕京大學文理學院院長、歷史系主任、圖書館館長、研究院文科主任等職。1925 年赴哈佛大學講學。1930 年回國，任燕京大學國學研究所所長兼導師。1933 年、1940 年先後獲得美國俄亥俄韋斯良大學名譽文學博士和名譽神學博士學位。在燕京大學期間，曾任哈佛燕京學社北平辦事處執行幹事，兼任哈佛燕京學社引得編纂處總編輯。1937 年獲巴黎茹理安(儒蓮)獎金。1941 年 12 月太平洋戰争爆發後，與陸志韋、趙紫宸、鄧之誠等人被日軍逮捕入獄，次年出獄後拒絶爲日僞工作。1945 年燕京大學復校，仍任歷史系教授。1946 年赴哈佛大學講學，1947 年任夏威夷大學客座教授，1947—1948 年任哈佛大學東亞語文系客座教授。1948 年起擔任哈佛燕京學社研究員，1963 年退休。主要論文有《引得説》、《利瑪竇的世界地圖》、《禮記引得序》、《春秋經傳引得序》、《杜詩引得序》、

《蒙古秘史源流考》(英文)、《史通點煩篇臆補》、《再論杜甫》(英文)等。著作有《中國最偉大的詩人杜甫》(英文專著)、《洪業論學集》等。

065 Mrs. Hussey

生平不詳。

066 J. H. Ingram (1858—1934)

全名 James Henry Ingram，中文名盈亨利，美國公理會傳教醫師。1887 年來華，任職於通州公理會所屬醫院。1913 年任教於北京協和醫學校。1917 年美國對德宣戰後，加入美國紅十字會，赴西伯利亞協助捷克俘虜返國。1920 年回北京，1934 年在北京西山別墅被土匪槍殺。

067 K. Ito

伊東教順。生平不詳。

068 A. L. Lvanov (1878—1937)

全名 Aleksei Lvanovich Lvanov，中文名伊鳳閣，漢學家、蘇聯外交官。1901 年聖彼得堡大學東方語言學系漢滿語專業畢業。1902 年來華學習漢語，任譯學館俄文教習。1904 年回國，次年以編外副教授的身份講授中國文學。1922 年隨蘇聯遠東全權代表飛到中國，次年受聘爲北京大學研究所國學門導師。1924 年任蘇聯駐華大使館首任漢文參贊。1927 年回國。伊鳳閣是首位注意到俄國探險家哥司羅夫在喀喇和托古城發掘的西夏文書的俄國學者。1909 年發現西夏文、漢文雙解詞典《番漢合時掌中珠》，據此發表《西夏語研究》。1923 年曾在北大《國學季刊》上發表《西夏國書説》。著有《王安石及其變法》、《華語初級讀本》、《漢語口語初級讀本》、《中國哲學資料：法家，韓非子》等。

069 Prof. Jackson

生平不詳。

070 Nelson Trusler Johnson（1887—1954）

美國外交官。1907 年來華，任美國駐華領事館翻譯。1909 年任美國駐奉天副領事。後歷任哈爾濱、漢口、重慶、長沙、上海等地領事。1926—1929 年任美國國務院遠東司司長。1929—1935 年任駐華公使，1935 年升格爲大使，1941 年卸任。1941—1945 年任美國駐澳公使。1945 年任美國遠東委員會秘書長。

071 Kam？

生平不詳。

072 Mr. Keller

生平不詳。

07 F. S. Kershaw

生平不詳。曾任美國東亞學會秘書。

074 Kungpah T. King（1878—1926）

金鞏伯，名紹城，一名城，鞏伯爲其字，又字拱北，號北樓，又號藕湖。浙江吴興南潯人。1902 年留學英國倫敦大學，學習法律。1904 年任上海公共租界會審公廨會審官，1905 年辭職。後任編訂法制館協修、大理院刑科推事、民政部咨議。1911 年，以中國代表身份參加美洲萬國監獄改良會。中華民國成立後，歷任内務部僉事、衆議院議員、國務院秘書、蒙藏院參事等職。在繪畫方面有相當造詣，1920 年在北京創辦中國畫研究會。1926 年突患傷寒去世。

075 Sohtsu G. King（1886—1949）

金紹基，字叔初，浙江湖州南潯人，金紹城三弟。1902 年赴英國留學，入皇家學院，習電氣學。

1905 年畢業歸國，任教於高等實業學堂，次年任北京商務委員會所屬技術學校電氣科教授，後任清政府商部交通委員會委員。1911 年在郵傳部郵務總局任職。1928 年參加組織北平博物學協會及博物學研究所，後任北平美術學院副院長、北平博物學協會會長。曾兼任北京大學教授、華洋義賑會執行委員、中華教育文化基金董事會董事等職，爲中國經濟學社社員。曾參與建設靜生生物調查所和中國地質調查所，與秉志合作靜生生物調查報告《香港介類第一部分》、《香港之軟體動物》等，著有《北戴河貝殼》、《華北海岸常見貝殼》。因經商致富，從事文物、書畫和古董的收藏。

076 Kazuo Kitamura

生平不詳。

077 Nobuji Kitamura

生平不詳。

078 Sten Konow（1867—1948）

挪威印度學家。1891 年畢業於奧斯陸克里斯蒂安尼亞大學。1893 年獲博士學位。1894—1896 年任柏林皇家圖書館助理館員。1896—1899 年任克里斯蒂安尼亞大學講師和助理教授。1906—1908 年在印度研究碑銘學。1910 年重返奧斯陸，任克里斯蒂安尼亞大學印度語文學教授。1914 年任漢堡大學印度歷史與文化教授。1919 年回奧斯陸任印度語言教授。曾當選德國東方學會、英國皇家東方學會、法國巴黎東方學會榮譽會員，柏林學院通訊會員。

079 Dr. Kotvicz

生平不詳。曾任前蘇聯利沃夫大學（University of Lvov）教授。

080 Robert Keen Lamb

1935 年畢業於哈佛大學，獲哲學博士學位。曾任哈佛大學經濟學講師。從書信内容看，曾供職於哈佛大學對外宣傳辦公室(Publicity Office)。

081 Charles R. Lanman (1850—1951)

查尔斯·兰曼，美國梵文學者。生於美國康涅狄格州諾威奇。1873年獲耶魯大學博士學位。畢業後赴德，游學於柏林大學、圖賓根大學、萊比錫大學。1886年回國，任教於約翰霍普金斯大學。1880年受聘爲哈佛大學梵文教授，并執掌印度—伊朗語言系，1926年退休。1889—1990年到印度旅行，收集了很多書籍和500種手稿。1888年出版《梵文讀本》(*Sanskrit Reader with Vocabulary and Notes*)，長期任《哈佛東方叢書》(*Harvard Oriental Series*)編輯，并英譯、注釋了印度詩人Rājaśekhara十世紀寫的戲劇*KarpūraMañjarī*列在叢書的第四種出版。曾任美國語言學協會主席，美國東方學會副主席、主席等職。爲美國人文與科學院、英國皇家亞洲學會、法國亞洲學會、哥廷根社會科學院、法蘭西銘文與美文學術院等學術機構榮譽會員。

082 K. S. Latourette (1884—1968)

全名Kenneth Scott Latourette，中文名賴德烈。美國中國學、日本學、世界基督教學學者。生於美國俄勒岡州。1904年獲俄勒岡林菲爾德學院(Linfield College)學士學位。畢業後入耶魯大學，1909年獲哲學博士學位。畢業後任學生海外傳教志願者運動(Student Volunteer Movement for Foreign Missions)秘書。1910年來華，任教於長沙雅禮學校，1912年因健康原因回國。1916年任教於俄亥俄州丹尼森大學(Danison University)。20年代初再度來華。1921年任耶魯大學神學院宗教系教授，1938年任耶魯大學宗教學系主任。1953年退休。1928—1937年任美國學會理事會中國研究促進委員會委員。1934—1939年任雅禮會和湘雅醫學院理事。1938年獲中國政府翡翠勛章。1968年因車禍去世。著有《中國的發展》(*The Development of China*)、《基督教在華傳教史》(*A History of Christian Missions in China*)、《中國人的歷史與文化》(*The Chinese: Their History and Culture*)、《中國近代史》(*A History of Modern China*)、《基督教擴展史》(*A History of the Expansion of Christianity*)、《革命時代的基督教》(*Christianity in a Revolutionary Age*)、《日本的發展》(*The Development of Japan*)、《基督教史》(*A History of Christianity*)等。

083 Owen Lattimore (1900—1989)

歐文·拉鐵摩爾，美國東方學家。生於華盛頓。幼年隨父來華，12歲起先後在瑞士和英國受中等教育。1920年來華，任職於上海英商安利洋行(Arnold Brothers and Co., Ltd.)，不久任天津《京津泰晤士報》星期周刊編輯。1922年沿絲綢之路赴新疆旅行，1929年出版《通往土耳其斯坦的荒漠道路》（*The Desert Road to Turkestan*），同年獲美國社會科學研究會獎金，到中国東北旅行，研究滿洲移民問題。1931年"九一八"事變後，出版《滿洲——衝突的發源地》（*Manchuria, Cradle of the Conflict*）。30年代初被聘爲北平哈佛燕京學社研究員，後曾訪問延安。1932—1935年任太平洋學會季刊《太平洋事務》（*Pacific Affair*）編輯。1941年7月，以羅斯福總統私人代表身份任蔣介石政治顧問。1942年被召回國，任美國新聞處中國部主任。抗戰勝利後，任約翰霍普金斯大學國際關係學院院長。1952年遭麥卡錫彈劾，被停教職，後經調查無罪，仍任該校教授。1963年，任英國利兹大學漢文教授。在歐美漢學界被譽爲"蒙古通"。著有《高地韃靼》（*High Tartary*）、《滿洲的蒙古人》（*Mongols of Manchuria*）、《蒙古游記》（*Mongol Journeys*）、《現代中國的形成》（*The Making of Modern China*）、《亞洲的局勢》（*The Situation in Asia*）、《中國在亞洲腹地的邊疆》（*Inner Asian Frontiers of China*）等。

084 Dr. Laufer（1874—1934）

全名Berthold Laufer，德裔美籍東方學家、藏學家和人類學家。生於德國科隆。1893年入柏林大學，1894年師從葛禄博（Wilhelm Grube）研究漢學，1897年獲德國萊比錫大學博士學位。1898年移民美國，擔任傑塞普（Jessup）北太平洋探險隊隊長，赴東西伯利亞、庫頁島和黑龍江地區考察。1901—1905年率希夫（Schiff）考察隊到中國考察。1905年任哥倫比亞大學人類學和東方語言學講師。1908—1910年同布萊克斯頓夫人（Mrs. T. B. Blackstone）到西藏考察。1908年任職於芝加哥菲爾德自然歷史博物館，1915年任該館人類學部主任。曾任美國紐約自然歷史博物館人種學助理。1923年再度赴西藏考察。對中國的玉器、瓷器、象牙雕刻、牌樓等都有研究。晚年患憂鬱症，1934年9月13日，在芝加哥跳樓自殺身亡。著作有《漢朝的中國陶器》（*Chinese Pottery of the Han Dynasty*）、《玉》（*Jade*）、《中國的影戲》（*Chinesische Schattenspiele*）等。

085 Madame Lauru（？—1937）

原名Juliet Bredon，中文名裴麗珠，英國女作家。中國海關代理總稅務司裴式楷之女，總稅務司赫德的内侄女。因嫁給曾供職於中國海關的法國人Charles Henry Lauru，故又被稱爲"Madame Lauru"。長期在華居住，熟悉中國風土人情。1937年在舊金山去世。著有《赫德爵士傳奇》（*Sir Robert Hart: the Romance of a Great Career*）、《北京》（*Peking: a Historical and Intimate Description of its Chief Places of Interest*）、《中國風俗節日記》（*The Moon Year: a Record of Chinese Customs and Festivals*）等。

086 F. Lessing（1882—1961）

全名 Ferdinand Diedrich Lessing，中文名雷興，德國東方學家。1925—1927 年任柏林大學東方語言學院中國學教授。1928—1935 年任柏林民族學博物館遠東部主任。1930—1933 年曾參加中國西北科學考察團。1935 年赴美，主持伯克利加州大學東方部工作，曾爲搜集圖書資料赴日本。1946 年起任羅厄爾（Rowell）講座教授。1949 年榮譽退休。主要著作有《漢人和藏人的佛教》（*Chinese and Tibetan Buddhism*）、《喇嘛教》（*Lamaism*）、《雍和宫》（*Yung-ho-kung*）等。

087 Ernst Leumann（1859—1931）

德國東方學家、語言學家。生於瑞士牧師家庭。曾在日内瓦、蘇黎世、萊比錫、柏林等地游學，1881 年獲萊比錫大學哲學博士學位。後到牛津大學學習梵文，曾協助牛津大學莫尼爾・威廉姆斯爵士（Sir Monier Williams）編纂《梵英辭典》（*Sanskrit-English Dictionary*）。1884 年任斯特拉斯堡大學梵語學教授，1919 年起任弗萊堡大學教授。主要從事從梵文翻譯各種經典，研究耆那教和梵文語言史，并對中亞細亞發現的粟特語進行解讀研究。曾將于闐文《彌勒下生經》譯成德文。

088 Sylvain Lévi（1863—1935）

法國東方學家，主要從事印度語言和佛教研究。生於巴黎。巴黎大學文學博士，通曉漢文、藏文和庫車語，注重梵文和藏文佛典的研究。曾任法蘭西學院教授、法國亞細亞學會會長。法國漢學家戴密微、伯希和的老師，美國東方學會榮譽會員。1905 年到尼泊爾搜尋佛典。1907 年發表研究《天業譬喻經》著作。1911 年出版庫車語佛經殘片。1912 年出版《法句經》修訂本。1923 年冬曾率法國考古隊到雲南調查，次年四月到北京，在北京大學和中法大學作學術演講。曾與俄國謝爾巴茨柯伊、比利時蒲辛合作，共同校勘與翻譯佛經，校訂敦煌本稱友《俱舍論釋》第一章、《唯識二十論》及世親的釋文、安慧《唯識二十論釋》、《大業分別論》等。法譯《俱舍論疏》、《大乘莊嚴經論》等。與日本高楠順次郎合編法文佛教辭書《法寶義林》（未完成）。

089 Lin Li Kuang（1902—1945）

林藜光，佛教學者。福建思明人。精通英、法、德、日多國文字，對梵文、巴利文、藏文有專門的研究。早年畢業於厦門大學哲學系，後留校任教，與時任教厦大的法國漢學家戴密微過從甚密。1929 年應鋼和泰聘請到北平，任哈佛燕京學社中印研究所研究助理，并隨鋼和泰學習梵文、藏文，編有《大寶積經迦葉品梵漢引得》。1933 年赴法國，在巴黎國立東方語言學校講授中文，并隨烈維學習梵文、巴利文，後遵烈維之囑從事梵文寫本《諸法集要經》的校訂工作。1936 年因母親病故回厦門，曾應中國佛教學會厦門分會之邀，作"關於歐洲人士研究佛學之一斑"演講，同年回巴黎。1945 年病逝。

090 H. C. Hua-jin Lin

生平不詳。

091 Francis C. Liu

中文名字、生平不詳。從信箋看，曾任中國文化經濟協會執行秘書辦公室秘書。

092 H. Lüders（1869—1943）

全名 Heinrich Lüders，譯爲海因里希·呂德斯，德國東方學家、梵文學者。早年先後在慕尼黑大學學習德國語言和文學，在哥廷根大學學習印度學。1894 年獲博士學位。1895—1899 年任教於牛津大學印度學院。1903 年被羅斯托克大學（Rostock University）聘爲副教授，1905—1908 年，任該校印度語言學教授。1909 年任柏林弗里德里希—威廉大學古代印度語言文學教授，同年當選普魯士科學院正式會員。陳寅恪留學德國時曾受業於呂德斯。1931—1932 年任柏林大學校長。1935 年退休。曾先後當選法國亞洲學會、美國東方學會、英國皇家東方學會榮譽會員。

093 Herbert M.

生平不詳。

094 Ma Heng（1881—1955）

馬衡，字叔平，别署無咎，號凡將齋主人，浙江寧波人。金石學家。1901 年畢業於南洋公學。1917 年任北京大學附設國史編纂處徵集員。1918 年任北京大學文學院國文系講師，兼教體育。1923 年任史學系教授，兼研究所國學門導師、考古研究室主任。1923—1929 年任北京大學圖書館古物美術部主任。1925 年任故宫博物院古物館負責人。1929—1931 年任北京大學圖書館館長。1934 年任故宫博物院院長，1949 年後仍任故宫博物院院長、北京市文物整理委員會主任委員。1953 年因病休養，兩年後逝世。馬衡先生畢生致力於金石學的研究。1927 年在日本東京帝國大學講“中國的青銅時代”，開創了青銅器的斷代。1928 年任燕下都考古團團長，發掘老姥臺遺址。1930 年在西北科學考察團發現“居延漢簡”的工作中，起過重要作用。被譽爲中國近代考古學的前驅者和奠基人之一。主要著作有《中國金石學概要》、《凡將齋金石叢稿》、《漢石經集存》等。

095 MacMurray

生平不詳。

096 H. F. MacNair（1891—1947）

全名 Harley Farnsworth MacNair，中文名宓亨利，美國遠東史學家。1912 年來華，任上海聖約翰大學歷史學和政治學教授，兼任《密勒氏評論報》特約編輯、《教務雜誌》編輯部執行委員。1926 年回美，歷任華盛頓州立大學、芝加哥大學遠東史教授。著有《中國近代史選讀》（*Modern Chinese History Selected Readings*）、《華僑志》（*The Chinese Abroad, their Position and Protection*）、《革命中的中國：對民國時期政治活動和軍閥政治的分析》（*China in Revolution: an Analysis of Politics and Militarism under the Republic*）、《遠東國際關係史》（*Far Eastern International Relations*）、《近代遠東國際關係史》（*ModernFar Eastern International Relations*）等。

097 Mrs. Mamen

生平不詳。

098 Georges Margouliès

中文名馬古烈，生卒年不詳，俄裔法國漢學家。早年留學法國，師從伯希和，獲巴黎大學文學博士。曾任教於巴黎東方語言學校。1930 年受法國政府派遣到中國考察教育。著有《〈文選〉辭賦譯注》（*Le "Fou" dans le Wen-Sinan, étude et textes*）、《中國騈文演進史》（*Évolution de la prose artistique chinoise*）、《中國文學史》（*Histoire de la Litterature Chinoise*）等。

099 Prince Mdivani

生平不詳。

100 Father Mostaert（1881—1971）

全名 Father Antoine Mostaert，中文名田清波，比利時傳教士、蒙古學家。青年時期在天主教修道院學習，19 歲起，用五年時間學習哲學和神學，同時學習漢語文言文和蒙文。1905 年來華，被派到到鄂爾多斯南部的城川傳教，直至 1925 年，致力於蒙古語言學的研究，同時對鄂爾多斯宗教儀式、民俗、文獻等進行了調查研究。1925 年被派到北京整理研究在鄂爾多斯收集的調查資料，并繼續從事研究。1948 年離開北平遷居美國弗吉尼亞州阿林頓，研究蒙古語著作所用的中期蒙古語。主要著述有《鄂爾多斯（南部）蒙古方言》、《鄂爾多斯志》、《鄂爾多斯蒙語詞典》等。

101 Herbert Mueller（1885—1966）

米和伯，德國漢學家、藝術收藏家。1908 年畢業於波恩大學，獲博士學位。1909—1912 年任職於柏林博物館遠東部。1912 年到中國，曾參與考古發掘。後定居北京，主要從事藝術品收集和貿易，曾任萊比錫印刷及相關藝術國際博覽會駐遠東代表，德國通訊社北京分社負責人。1930 年在紐約出版《松林中國藝術和考古收藏：展覽目録》（*The Sunglin Collection of Chinese Art and Archaeology*：*Catalogue of Exhibition*）。

102 G. K. Nariman（1873—1933）

東方學家、語言學家。生平不詳。著有《梵文佛教文學史》（*Literary History of Sanskrit Buddhism*），譯有《伊朗對穆斯林文學的影響》（*Iranian Influence on Moslem Literature*）等。

103 Mr. Nixon

生平不詳。

104 Y. Obala

生平不詳。

105 B. I. Pankratoff

全名 Baris Ivanoviter Pankratoff。生平不詳，曾在鋼和泰主持的中印研究所工作。

106 Willys R. Peck（1882—1952）

美國外交官。生於天津，父親爲美國公理會駐天津傳教醫師。1907 年開始進入美國駐華領事界工作。1914—1919 年任駐青島領事。1923—1928 年任駐華使館漢文參贊。1928—1935 年任使館參事。曾兼任清華學校和北京美國學校董事會董事。1941—1942 年任美國駐泰國公使。

107 Paul Pelliot（1878—1945）

伯希和，法國漢學家。生於法國巴黎。中學畢業後就讀於斯塔尼斯拉斯學院，獲文學士學位。後入法國漢學中心學習漢語，又入巴黎國立東方語言學校學習。是法國漢學家沙畹、烈維等人的得意弟子。1899 年被選爲法國印度支那古迹調查會的寄宿生。1901 年受聘爲法蘭西遠東學院教授。1900—1903 年三次到中國考察。1904 年回國。1906 年率中亞考察隊從巴黎啓程，在新疆各地考察之後，於 1908 年 2 月到達敦煌，挑選佛教大藏經未收的文獻、帶有題記的文獻和非漢語文獻 6000 餘卷運回巴黎。1911 年任法蘭西學院中亞歷史考古學講座主講，一戰期間應徵入伍，後出任駐北京武官。1921 年當選法國金石與美文學院院士。1935 年任法國亞細亞學會主席，1939 年被聘爲中國中央研究院歷史語言研究所研究員。曾主編著名漢學雜誌《通報》，1945 年在巴黎去世。伯希和精通漢、滿、蒙、藏、阿拉伯、伊朗等東方語言，主要研究中西交通史，被公認爲 20 世紀最權威的漢學家。著有《敦煌千佛洞》（*Les Grottes de Touen-houang*）、《馬可波羅游記校注》（*Marco Polo*）等。

108 W. B. Pettus（1880—1959）

全名 William Bacon Pettus，中文名裴德士，美國傳教士。生於美國阿拉巴馬州莫比爾，先後畢業於密蘇里大學和哥倫比亞大學。1914 年來華，任北京基督教青年會幹事。1916 年起任北京華北協和華語學校校長，1941 年底被日軍羈押，1945 年復職。1959 年在美國加州去世。

109 Mr. Plomp

生平不詳。

110 Lucius C. Porter（1880—1958）

博晨光，美國學者。生於天津。1897 年回美國威斯康辛州就讀其祖父創建的比洛特學院（Beloit College），1901 年畢業。1906 畢業於耶魯神學院。1909 年受美國海外宣教團派遣，任教於通州華北協和大學，1916 年兼任校長。1917—1919 年任華北公理會幹事。1918 年協助司徒雷登創辦燕京大學，1922 年任男科主任，1923—1941 年歷任文學院哲學系副教授、教授、系主任等職務。其間於 1922—1924 年被聘爲哥倫比亞大學丁龍漢學講座教授；1928—1939 年任哈佛燕京學社北平辦事處總幹事；1928—1929 年、1931—1932 年，在哈佛大學講授中國哲學。1943 年被日軍逮捕入獄，關入山東濰縣集中營。1949 年返回美國。著有《中國對基督教的挑戰》（*China's Challenge to Christianity*）。

111 Alan Priest（1898—1969）

普愛倫，東方美術史家。就讀於哈佛大學時，對中國藝術產生興趣。1925 年到中國學習語言和藝術。回美後任職於美國大都會藝術博物館遠東藝術部。20 世紀 30 年代曾再度到中國，與琉璃廠古董商合作，將龍門石窟《帝后禮佛圖》偷運至美國。著有《中國繪畫面面觀》（*Aspects of Chinese Painting*）。

112 Przyluski（1885—1944）

全名 Jean Przyluski，譯爲普祖魯斯基，法國東方學家、印度學家。早年曾任印度支那地方官吏。1926 年任法國高等研究實驗學院佛教語文學研究導師。主要從事佛教經文的梵、藏、漢文本對勘，同時研究宗教歷史和考古。曾與法國女藏學家瑪賽爾・拉露合作研究。曾任法國遠東學院院長、主編《佛教書目學》雜誌。著有《阿育王的傳説》等。

113 Reid（1899—?）

疑爲John Gilbert Reid，中文名李約翰，美國外交史學者。美國來華傳教士李佳白（Gilbert Reid）之子。1921年畢業於漢密爾頓大學，不久來華，在北京和上海協助李佳白，任尚賢堂（The International Institute of China）幹事，直至1928年。1922—1924年曾任英文《北京導報》副編輯。1928年回國，就讀於加利福尼亞大學，1931年獲碩士學位，1934年獲博士學位。1935—1936年任賓夕法尼亞大學彭菲爾德獎金研究員。1937—1939年任華盛頓州立大學史學助理教授。1939—1946年任美國國務院國際關係副研究員。1946—1958年任歷史處遠東組組長。1958年後任教於加利福尼亞大學。曾任美國歷史協會會長。著有《清帝的遜位與列强（1908—1912）》（*The Manchu Abdication and the Powers*）等。

114 John D. Rockefeller（1874—1960）

全名John D.Rockefeller Jr.，譯爲小洛克菲勒，老洛克菲勒的獨生子。1897年畢業於布朗大學，獲文學士學位。畢業後進入美孚石油公司紐約總部，擔任老洛克菲勒助理。1901年創辦洛克菲勒醫學研究所。1910年辭去美孚石油公司副總裁和董事、美國鋼鐵公司董事職務。1913年創立洛克菲勒基金，任第一任總裁。1921年小洛克菲勒曾來華出席洛克菲勒基金會投資建立的北京協和醫學院的落成典禮。

115 Rolf

生平不詳。

116 F. Rosenberg

生平不詳。

THE GEST CHINESE RESEARCH LIBRARY

McGILL UNIVERSITY LIBRARY

MONTREAL

ROBERT DE RESILLAC-ROESE, PH.D.
ASSISTANT CURATOR

GERHARD R. LOMER, M.A., PH.D.
UNIVERSITY LIBRARIAN

I.V. GILLIS, PEKING, CHINA.
COLLABORATOR

Peking
June 15th, 1928

RECEIVED from Baron A. Staël-Holstein the sum of twenty dollars ($ 20) local currency in payment for making photostat printes of a Tibetan book.

(I V Gillis)

THE GEST CHINESE RESEARCH LIBRARY

McGILL UNIVERSITY LIBRARY

MONTREAL

ROBERT DE RESILLAC-ROESE, PH.D., ASSISTANT CURATOR

GERHARD R. LOMER, M.A., PH.D., UNIVERSITY LIBRARIAN

I.V. GILLIS, PEKING, CHINA. COLLABORATOR

Peking
June 18th, 1928

Dear Staël:-

I am desirous of obtaining for the Library a good copy of the work entitled "T'ung Wên Yün T'ung" (同文韻統).

I understand that this book contains a syllabic comparison between the Sanscrit and Tibetan vocables, the sounds being expressed in Chinese by means of the well-known system of initials and finals.

The work was published in 1750 by Imperial order I believe.

I would appreciate it very much if you could help me out in this matter, and I presume that it could be obtained through one of your many friends interested in Tibetan and Sanscrit.

Yours very sincerely,

I V Gillis

THE GEST CHINESE RESEARCH LIBRARY

McGILL UNIVERSITY LIBRARY

MONTREAL

ROBERT DE RESILLAC-ROESE, PH. D.,
ASSISTANT CURATOR

GERHARD R. LOMER, M. A., PH. D.,
UNIVERSITY LIBRARIAN

I. V. GILLIS, PEKING, CHINA.
COLLABORATOR

葛思德華文藏書庫

September 6th, 1929

RECEIVED from Baron A. Staël-Holstein the amount of thirty dollars local currency ($ 30), in full payment for making sixty (60) photostat prints.

The Gest Chinese Research Library
per I. V. Gillis

THE GEST CHINESE RESEARCH LIBRARY

McGILL UNIVERSITY LIBRARY

MONTREAL

ROBERT DE RESILLAC-ROESE, PH. D., ASSISTANT CURATOR

GERHARD R. LOMER, M. A., PH. D., UNIVERSITY LIBRARIAN

I. V. GILLIS, PEKING, CHINA. COLLABORATOR

葛思德華文藏書庫

Peiping
February 11th, 1930

Dear Staël:-

Herewith I am sending to you a photostat print of a sample page of a collection of Mongol sutras that I have discovered and am considering buying.

Would you be so good as to glance at this and let me know if this is the same collection as that that we have under consideration to buy for Harvard.

Do not bother to reply, for I shall come down to see you on Thursday forenoon about eleven o'clock or a little after, and you can give me the information then.

Yours very sincerely,

I. V. Gillis

THE GEST CHINESE RESEARCH LIBRARY
McGILL UNIVERSITY LIBRARY
MONTREAL

葛思德華文藏書庫

ROBERT DE RESILLAC-ROESE, PH. D., ASSISTANT CURATOR | GERHARD R. LOMER, M. A., PH. D., UNIVERSITY LIBRARIAN | I. V. GILLIS, PEKING, CHINA. COLLABORATOR

September 16th, 1930

Dear Staël:-

Herewith my check for the $ 250 for the preliminary expenses of the two men going to Jehol, and please instruct them to keep a detailed account of these expenses and let them understand that this is not pay.

Also, it should be made clear to them that thay are <u>not authorized to close any deal</u>, but are to go to Jehol to investigate the position, inspect and check up on the Kanjur in as much detail as possible within the time and under the circumstances, ascertain whether the monks will sell and for what price, and if they will sell then to take steps to obtain a huchao when the time comes to bring ~~them~~ the books to Peking. In other words, make preliminary arrangements only but as full as possible, and then come back (after not more than ten days at Jehol) and report results.

Yesterday you may have thought that I was somewhat too liberal with Petro, but I wished to make certain of his keen assistance and tie him up with us, for when he mentioned the French expedition that he is apparently connected with I envisaged the possibility of his negotiating with them.

Yours very sincerely,

I. V. Gillis

上熱河來往路費單

來往汽車票錢	大洋	貳拾柒元
路上吃飯錢	大洋	伍元
住二十天房飯	大洋	六拾伍元
請關係人吃飯錢	大洋	拾伍元
給兩個關係人錢（每人拾伍元）	大洋	叁拾元
零費	大洋	捌元

共計大洋壹佰伍拾元正

十月二十二日

梁莘軒具

My dear Gillis

Will you be so kind as to photograph the ~~st double~~ pages 44 to 55 of the Divyāvadāna and pages 11b to 14a of the Chinese book? ~~2 4 ff~~ ~~You~~ ~~?~~ May I have a ~~black on~~ white on black and a black on white copy of each page? ~~There will be altogether 1x six 12 white on black sheets of the Divyāvadāna and three white on black sheets of the Chinese book, because two pages~~

~~Two pages will~~ There will surely be enough ~~roo~~ room for two pages on each of your photographic sheets, and there might be even enough room for four pages (two Divyāvadāna and two Chinese pages ~~sheets~~ on each sheet).

55
43
12 Seiten
also 6 Aufnahmen

11b - 12a
12b - 13a
13b - 14a
3 Aufnahmen

I enclose a cheque for the amount of your bill dated March 31st 1930.

With many anticipated thanks

Yours sincerely

AStaëlHolstein.

THE GEST CHINESE RESEARCH LIBRARY

McGILL UNIVERSITY LIBRARY

MONTREAL

葛思德華文藏書庫

ROBERT DE RESILLAC-ROESE, PH. D., CURATOR

GERHARD R. LOMER, M. A., PH. D., UNIVERSITY LIBRARIAN

I. V. GILLIS, PEKING, CHINA. COLLABORATOR

November 7, 1931

Dear Staël:-

Last night after you left I thought things over and there is a most important point that we did not discuss, - the exact moment of delivery.

They must understand most clearly that actual delivery must be made to us, and that their responsibility does not cease until then. The arrival of the books within the walls of Peking cannot be considered delivery by any means, for the books may be confiscated after that and even before we ever see them.

Delivery is to be understood as when the books are in our actual possession; either delivered to our own trucks or carts, or to some place mutually agreed upon.

Also, during the night I thought of a friend (foreign) who is perfectly trustworthy, who has himself a motor truck, and for whom I at one time did a very considerable favor. I will see you Monday forenoon and talk this over with you.

Yours sincerely,

I. V. Gillis

Baron A. Staël-Holstein,
ex-Austrian Legation,
Peiping.

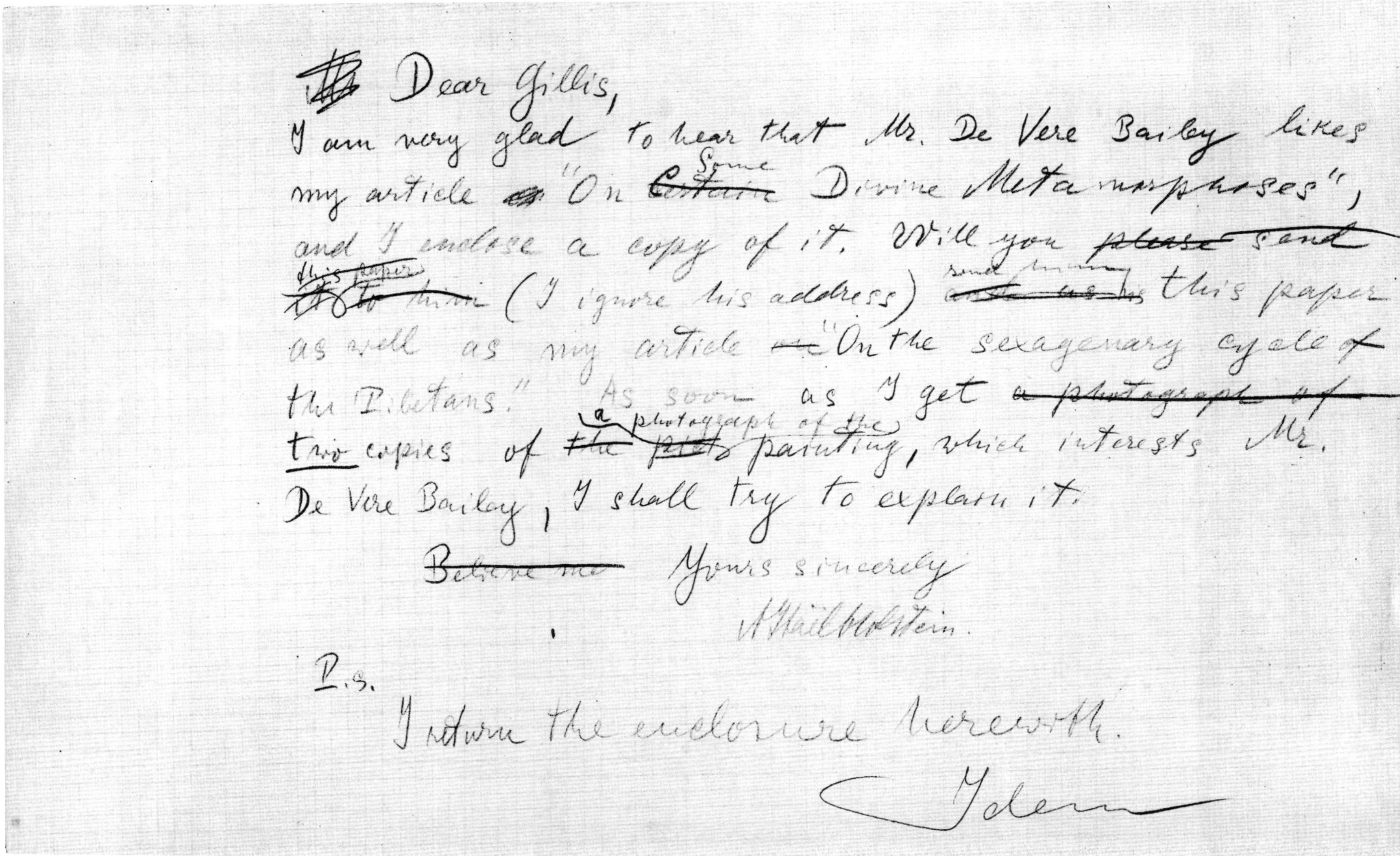
Dear Gillis,

I am very glad to hear that Mr. De Vere Bailey likes my article ~~as~~ "On ~~Certain~~ Some Divine Metamorphoses", and I enclose a copy of it. Will you ~~please send~~ ~~this paper~~ ~~to him~~ (I ignore his address) ~~as well as~~ send him this paper as well as my article ~~as~~ "On the sexagenary cycle of the Tibetans." As soon as I get ~~a photograph of~~ two copies of ~~the~~ a photograph of the ~~pict~~ painting, which interests Mr. De Vere Bailey, I shall try to explain it.

~~Believe me~~ Yours sincerely

A. Staël Holstein.

P.S.

I return the enclosure herewith.

Idem

REPUBLIC OF CHINA

GOVERNMENT TELEGRAPHS

RUNNING NO

CHARGES	TELEGRAM NO	CLASS	WORDS	SENT TO	DATE
$	OFFICE FROM	DATE	H M	TIME	
By	REMARKS			BY	

NOTHING TO BE WRITTEN ABOVE THIS

PLEASE WRITE DISTINCTLY

Chase, Harcol, Cambridge (Massachusetts U S of A 美國

staelveyuk	peglabijoz	harvard	cytazdoncy
mongolian	kanjur	ebkipfiezy	sinoindian
buddhistic	ipujyogost	unique	kuogydoncy
akmymuvyat	fikyndozje	mifudepyuj	odvadpawbo
		Gillis	

Staël urgently request(s) us (me)(to) buy for Harvard complete(s) copy Mongolian Kanjur. Absolutely essential for Sino-Indian Buddhistic investigation (of). Practically unique; no copy in America, two in Europe. Will (would) cost about $ 3000 gold dollars. Please(s) reply immediately. (signed) Gillis

I request that the above telegram may be forwarded according to the Electrical Communications Act of the Republic of China, the Rules and Regulations of the Ministry of Communications for the acceptance and transmission of telegrams and the International Telegraph Convention and the Service Regulations attached thereto, by which I agree to abide.

I V Gillis — Sender's Signature | Peiping — Address | January 30, 1930 — Date

Königsberg i. Pr. Münz Str. 4
am 1. Februar 1933

Hochverehrter Herr Baron.

Empfangen Sie meinen herzlichen Dank für die liebenswürdige Übersendung Ihrer drei wertvollen Abhandlungen. Ich habe sie mit größtem Interesse gelesen und viel aus ihnen gelernt. Sie sind mir gerade im Augenblick insofern noch von ganz besonderem Wert, als ich gegenwärtig mit einer Gesamtdarstellung des Buddhismus beschäftigt bin, für welche ich durch diese Artikel wichtige Anregungen erhalten habe. Bei der Lektüre dachte ich an die schönen Stunden, die ich in Ihrem gastfreien Hause verleben durfte u. der schönen tibetanischen Bilder, die Ihr Haus ausschmücken. Ich bin inzwischen Ihrem Vorbild gefolgt u. habe meine kleine Wohnung hier mit den Bildern geschmückt, die ich in Peiping erwarb, so wirkt mein Arbeitszimmer jetzt als eine verkleinerte Ausgabe Ihres prächtigen Salons.

Ich bin inzwischen wieder viel gereist. Im vorigen Jahr war ich in Australien, Neuseeland, Rarotonga, Tahiti, Fiji, Hawaii u. zweimal in Amerika, das ich einmal via Salt-Lake City - San Francisco - Vancouver u. einmal von ~~Vancouver~~ San Francisco, Los Angeles - Santa Fe - New Orleans durchfuhr. Ich habe mich etwas mit den Problemen der asiatischen Einwanderung beschäftigt u. viel Material gesammelt.

Aus Ihrer alten Heimat höre ich ab u. zu. Stcherbatsky schrieb mir mehrmals, er ist von erstaunlicher Arbeitskraft, trotz der wenig erfreulichen äußeren Verhältnisse. Dieser Tage war Baron Engelhardt (Reval) hier u. hielt einen interessanten Vortrag über den deutsch-baltischen Bildungsgedanken.

Hoffentlich geht es Ihnen u. Ihrer Familie gut, trotz aller politischen Unruhe, die allerdings auch bei uns ziemlich groß ist. Indem ich Sie bitte, mich Ihrer Frau Gemahlin zu empfehlen u. alle unsere gemeinsamen Peipinger Freunde zu grüßen, bin ich

stets in Verehrung Ihr ganz ergebener

Helmuth v. Glasenapp

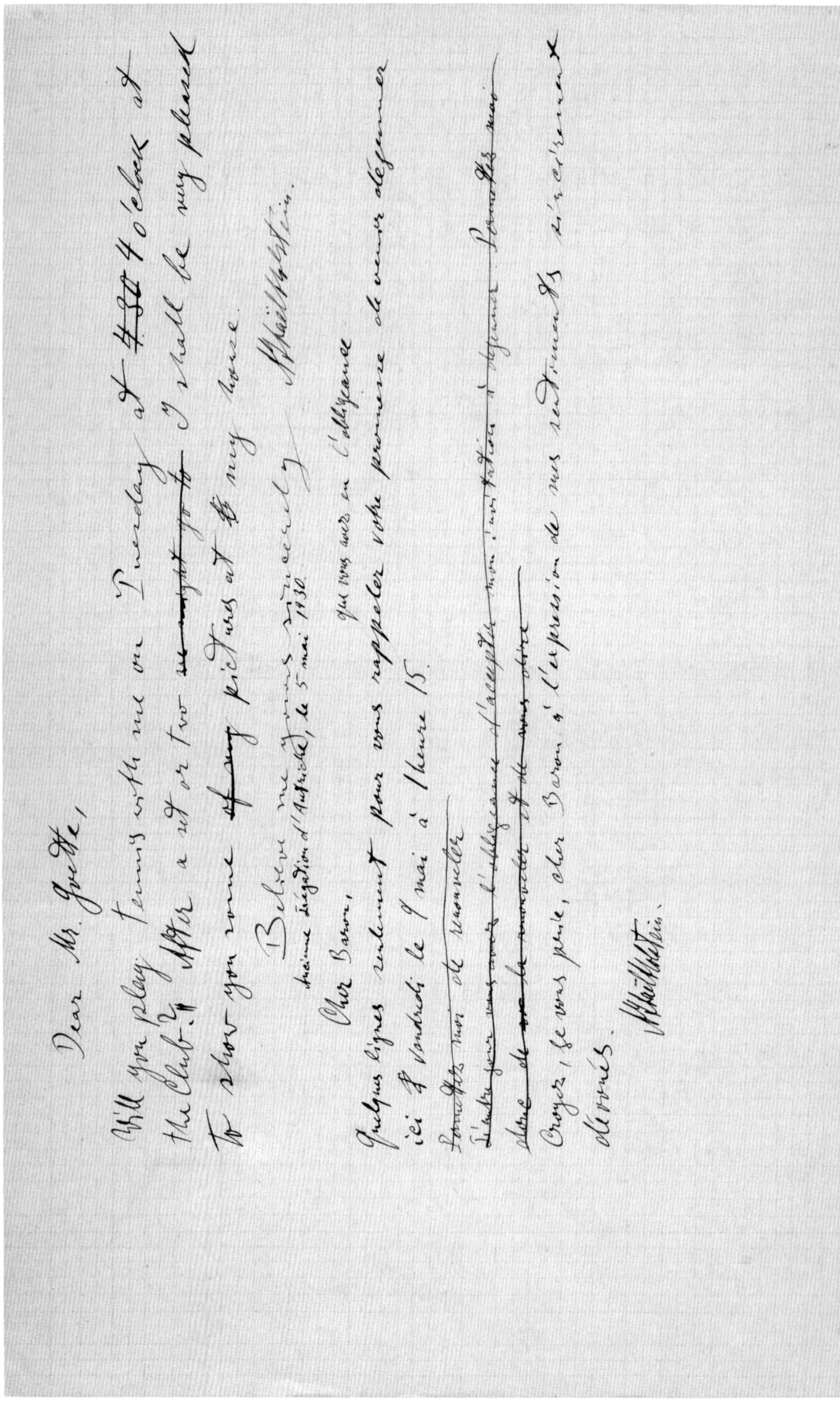

Dear Mr. Goette,

Will you play tennis with me on Tuesday at ~~4.30~~ 4 o'clock at the Club? ~~If~~ After a set or two ~~we might go to~~ I shall be very pleased to show you some ~~of my~~ pictures at ~~[illegible]~~ my house.

Believe me yours sincerely A. Staël-Holstein.

Ancienne Légation d'Autriche, le 5 mai 1930.

Cher Baron,

Quelques lignes seulement pour vous rappeler votre promesse de venir déjeuner ici ~~[illegible]~~ vendredi le 9 mai à 1 heure 15.

~~Permettez moi de renouveler~~

~~l'autre jour vous avez l'obligeance d'accepter mon invitation à déjeuner. Permettez moi donc de [illegible] la renouveler et de vous dire~~

Croyez, je vous prie, cher Baron à l'expression de mes sentiments sincèrement dévoués.

A. Staël-Holstein.

ÉCOLE FRANÇAISE
D'EXTRÊME-ORIENT

GOUVERNEMENT GÉNÉRAL DE L'INDOCHINE

Hanoi, le 24 septembre 1929.

Cher Monsieur et Collègue,

Permettez-moi tout d'abord de vous présenter tous mes hommages et toutes mes félicitations à l'occasion de votre mariage et de souhaiter à vous ainsi qu'à la Baronne de Staël-Holstein de longues et belles années de bonheur.

Je vous remercie infiniment de votre lettre du 2 septembre ainsi que de votre notice sur le Chu Fo P'u Sa Shêng Hsiang Tsan.

Vous avez lu dans le Bulletin de 1927 le compte rendu de vos travaux. Nous envisageons pour plus tard la publication des documents lamaïques que vous avez bien voulu nous confier.

Pour ce qui est du "Comparative Calendar for Chinese, European and Mohammedan history", nous ne possédons pas cet ouvrage et nous croyions que ce dernier a été édité par vos soins. Nos libraires anglais sont Luzac (46, Great Russell Street) et Probsthain (41, Great Russell Street) à Londres.

Vous verrez sans doute à la fin de l'année mon jeune camarade E. Gaspardone, membre de l'Ecole française d'Extrême-Orient, qui se rend en Chine et sera très heureux................

reux de faire votre connaissance. Je le recommande à votre cordial accueil, sachant d'avance que vous ferez pour lui tout le possible afin de lui faciliter ses études et recherches. M. Gaspardone est un sinologue distingué qui a devant lui certainement un grand avenir. Il est élève diplômé de l'Ecole des Langues orientales, où il a travaillé avec M. Vissière.

Je regrette infiniment de ne pouvoir me rendre moi-même en Chine; mais je reviens de Java où j'avais pris part au 4e Congrès du Pacifique, et ne puis songer pour l'instant à une nouvelle absence prolongée. Du reste je m'apprête à profiter du congé auquel j'ai droit, et me rendre en France au début de l'année prochaine. Ma santé morale et physique a grand besoin d'un séjour en Europe, et il serait imprudent d'attendre trop longtemps.

En vous demandant, cher Monsieur et Collègue, de bien vouloir transmettre mes respectueux hommages à la Baronne et en vous renouvelant toutes mes félicitations et tous mes voeux, je reste bien cordialement,

Votre très dévoué,

V Goloubew

(V. Goloubew)

Сердечный привѣтъ!

[illegible]

Monsieur le Baron A. de Staël-Holstein,
Ancienne Légation d'Autriche, Pékin.

of this opportunity if offered to him.

Dear Mr Greene:

~~Replying to~~

Many thanks for your letter. ~~Dr. Ostrom~~ Mr. Gordon ~~he~~ Bowles whose name has been mentioned to you by Mr. Ostrom, was my pupil during ~~the second~~ one semester at Harvard last year. He read some Chinese Buddhist texts with me and showed ability as well as serious application ~~to~~ in his studies. I consider him entirely worthy to receive the Willard Straight Fellowship for Chinese Studies. His father is a missionary in Japan and cannot assist his son in his studies to any considerable extent financially. I like Mr Bowles personally and I ~~think he~~ am sure he will make good use

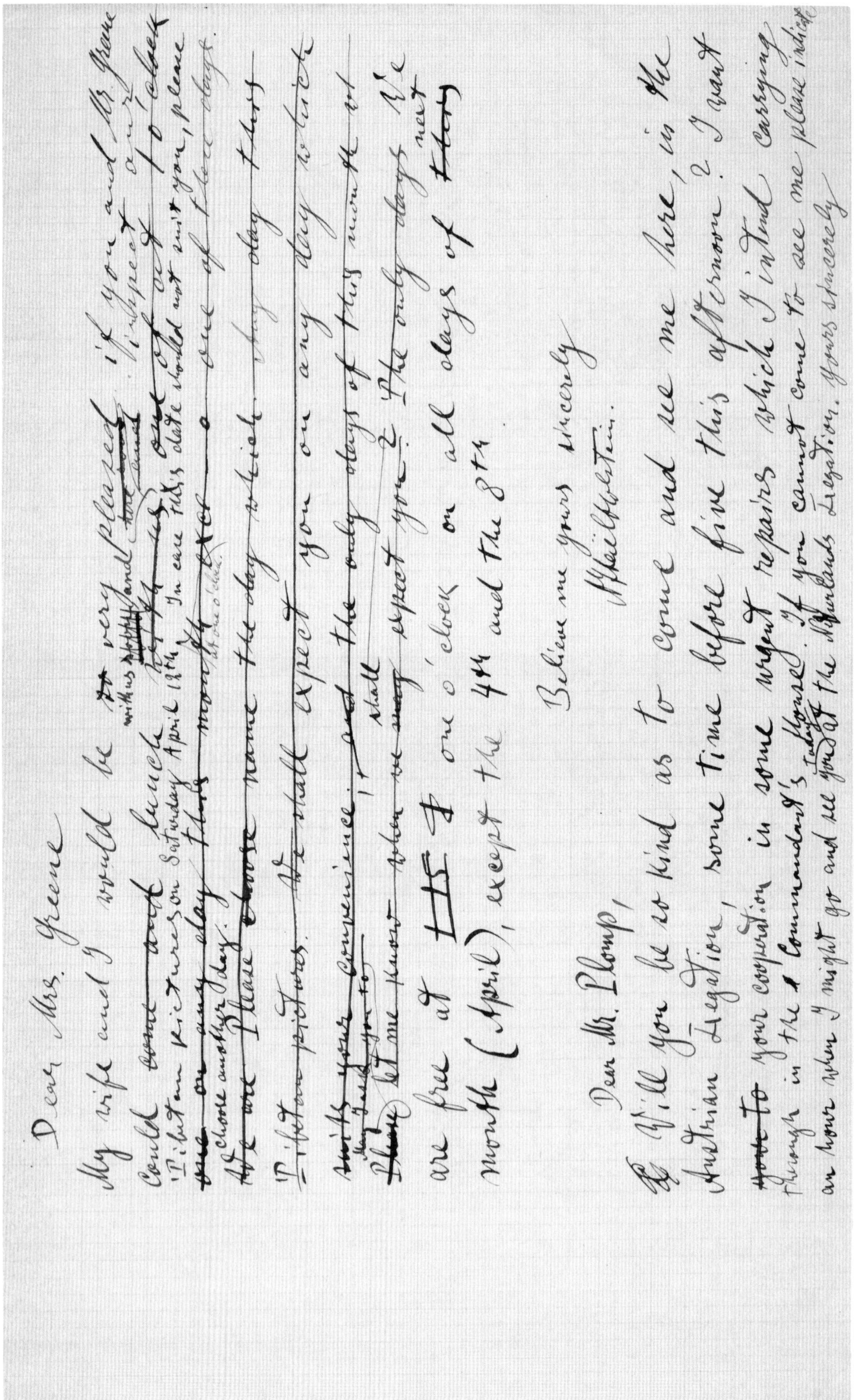

Dear Mrs. Greene

My wife and I would be ~~so~~ very pleased if you and Mr. Greene could ~~come and~~ lunch with us ~~[illegible]~~ and ~~here and~~ inspect our Tibetan pictures on Saturday April 12th at one o'clock. ~~with us one of at 1 o'clock one on any day this month exce a one of these days.~~ In case this date should not suit you, please choose another day.

~~We are Please choose name the day which. Any day this Tibetan pictures. We shall~~ expect you on any day which ~~suits your convenience. and the only days of this month at~~ ~~Please~~ ~~May I ask you to~~ ~~let me know when we shall expect you?~~ ~~The only days~~ We are free at ~~1.15 &~~ one o'clock on all days of ~~this~~ next month (April), except the 4th and the 8th.

Believe me yours sincerely

A. Hoeltelstein.

Dear Mr. Plomp,

~~W~~ Will you be so kind as to come and see me here, in the Austrian Legation, some time before five this afternoon? I want ~~your to~~ your cooperation in some urgent repairs which I intend carrying through in the ~~C~~ Commandant's House. If you cannot come to see me today please indicate an hour when I might go and see you at the Netherlands Legation. Yours sincerely

私立北平協和醫學院
PEIPING UNION MEDICAL COLLEGE
PEIPING, CHINA

OFFICE OF THE DIRECTOR.

January 13, 1932

Dear Baron von Stael Holstein:

I see from a report presented at the meeting of the Trustees of the Harvard Yenching Institute on November 9th, 1931, that your work on the "Eight Hundred Buddhas" is approaching its final stage. Whether this refers to the editorial work or to publication I am not sure, but presumably the former.

You may have heard this from some other source, but I am writing you in order to be sure that you know that your work is receiving attention.

Yours sincerely,

Roger S. Greene

Baron von Stael Holstein
Ex-Austrian Legation
Peiping

RSG:RP

89 L

私立北平協和醫學院
PEIPING UNION MEDICAL COLLEGE
PEIPING, CHINA

OFFICE OF THE DIRECTOR

April 24, 1933

TELEGRAPHIC ADDRESS
"MEDICAL, PEIPING"

Dear Baron:

I have just received a letter from Professor Chase containing the following paragraph, which seems to dispose effectually of your fear that you would be asked to return to Cambridge at an early date:

"I am very glad to have your letter of February 20th and to have such direct evidence of the value placed on Baron von Stael-Holstein's presence in Peking. All of us here have had the impression, I think, that he was doing excellently and certainly adding to the reputation of the Institute. There has been no definite discussion of when we should ask the Baron to spend another year or half-year in Cambridge. It certainly was not in our minds to invite him next year, largely because of the need for economy, and certainly we ought not to ask him to come until he is in good health again. The Educational Committee will be very much interested in everything you have said, and I am sure will agree with me in the whole matter of the Baron's work."

With kindest regards, I am,

Yours sincerely,

Roger S. Greene

ROGER S. GREENE.

Baron Von Stael-Holstein
Ex-Austrian Legation
Peiping

RSG:RP

89 I.

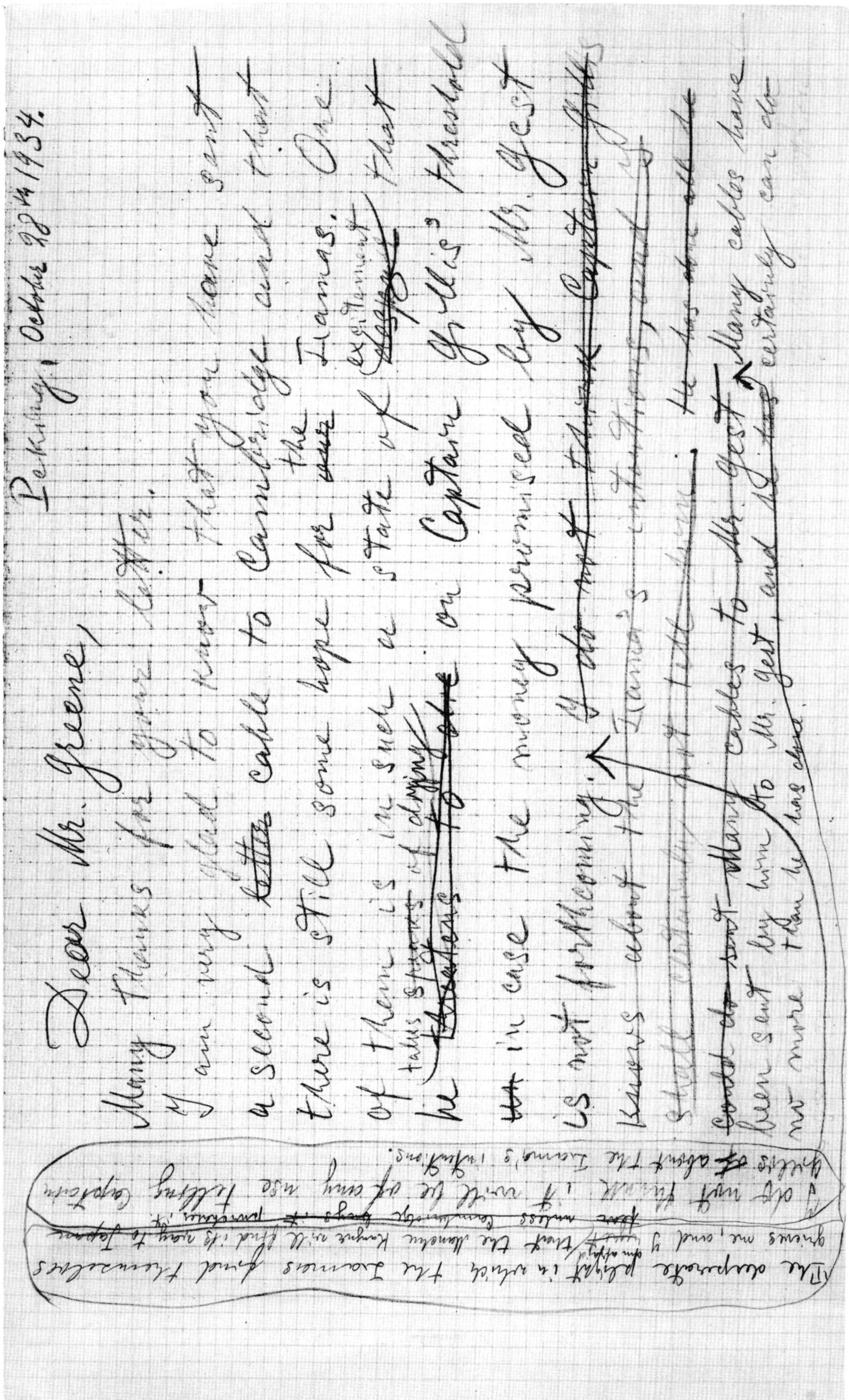

Peking, October 28th 1934.

Dear Mr. Greene,

Many thanks for your letter.

I am very glad to know that you have sent a second ~~letter~~ cable to Cambridge and that there is still some hope for ~~our~~ the Lamas. One of them is in such a state of ~~despair~~ excitement that he ~~threatens to die~~ talks ~~speaks~~ of dying on Captain Gillis' threshold ~~in~~ in case the money promised by Mr. Gest is not forthcoming. ~~I do not think Captain Gillis knows about the Lama's intentions, and I shall certainly not tell him. He has done all he could do sent Many cables to Mr. Gest.~~ Many cables have been sent by him to Mr. Gest, and he ~~has~~ certainly can do no more than he has done.

The desperate plight in which the Lamas find themselves grieves me, and I ~~fear~~ dreadfully fear that the Manchu Kanjur will find its way to Japan ~~soon~~ unless Cambridge buys ~~it~~ purchases it. I do not think it will be of any use telling Captain Gillis ~~of~~ about the Lama's intentions.

~~Note to line 32~~ Note.

~~The Lamas have returned to their native steppes and it will be a long time before they return to Peking.~~

Nov. 27th 1934.

Dear Mr. Greene,

I have ~~just~~ learned from a trustworthy source that the Manchu books, ~~we wanted~~ which Mr. Gest ~~wanted to buy & have been taken~~ could not pay for owing to the depression, are no longer for sale. ~~have been taken to~~ sent to ~~the South~~. The Peking personage in question would not wait any longer, and ~~all hope of buying them & must be abandoned, because~~ has sent them South ~~(whether to~~, probably with a view to presenting them to the Nanking government. In any case the books ~~are no longer~~ have already ~~been~~ left Peking, ~~So has the Lama, who~~ and all hope of seeing them again here must be abandoned.

Believe me yours sincerely, N. Staël Holstein

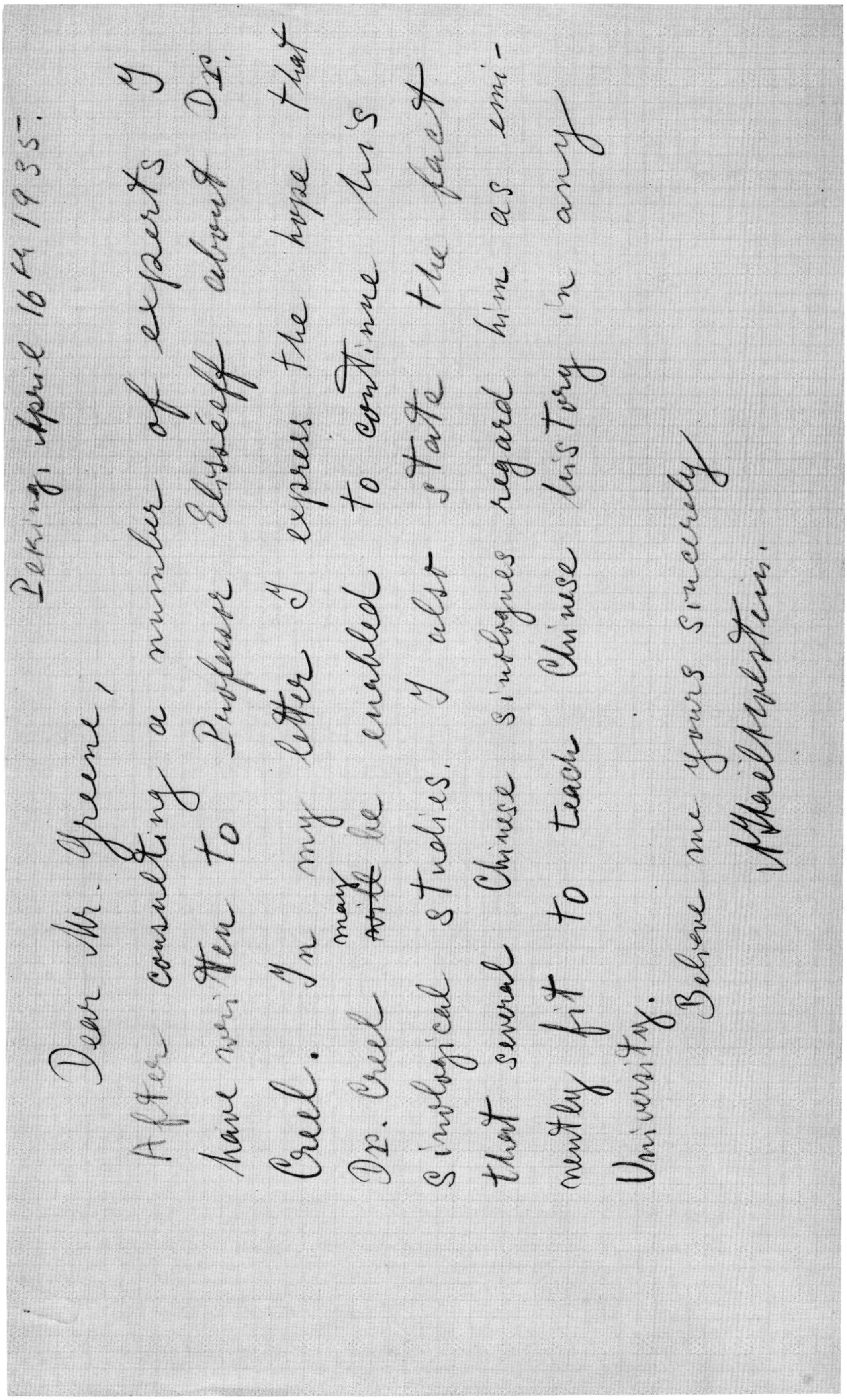

Peking, April 16th 1935.

Dear Mr. Greene,

After consulting a number of experts I have written to Professor Elisséeff about Dr. Creel. In my letter I express the hope that Dr. Creel ~~will~~ may be enabled to continue his sinological studies. I also state the fact that several Chinese sinologues regard him as eminently fit to teach Chinese history in any University.

Believe me yours sincerely

A Staël Holstein.

Peking, June 22nd 1935.

Dear Mr. Greene,

I am very much obliged to you for sending me Mr. Putnam's circular letter. ~~I find~~ ~~survey~~ ~~The list~~ The list ~~of the Indic collections~~ of American collections containing Indic manuscripts ~~is~~ ~~very interesting~~ ~~of great interest. It may~~ highly interests me. I never knew that such quantities of this material could be found in the United States.

Believe me yours sincerely and gratefully

A. Staël-Holstein.

Dear Mr. Greene,

In ~~a~~ my letter dated November 18th 1931 I wrote the following ~~[illegible]~~ words to Professor Woods: "As to the latter [i.e. the English text] Mr. Roger Greene promised me not long ago ......"

~~May I ask you to let me know who~~ ~~Could~~ ~~Will you be so kind as to let me know who will to appoint some~~ Please to let me know ~~whom you will appoint~~ who will ~~be your~~ act as your deputy (during your absence) as far as our books are concerned. ~~during your absence?~~ ~~As soon as~~ In a month or two some ~~[illegible]~~ of our editions will be ready for final approval. I may add that ~~your deputy will not have there will be only I your deputy will not have~~ our editions will contain ~~[illegible]~~ comparatively little English text and that your deputy will not have much work ~~[illegible]~~ to do in connection with our proof sheets.

Kindly excuse me for bothering you again and believe me yours sincerely

Dear Mr. Greene,

~~Very many~~ Many thanks for sending me Mr. Chorley's address! I am very glad to be able to thank him ~~for~~ once more for the interest which he took in the Lama temples.

Believe me yours sincerely

A. Staël Holstein.

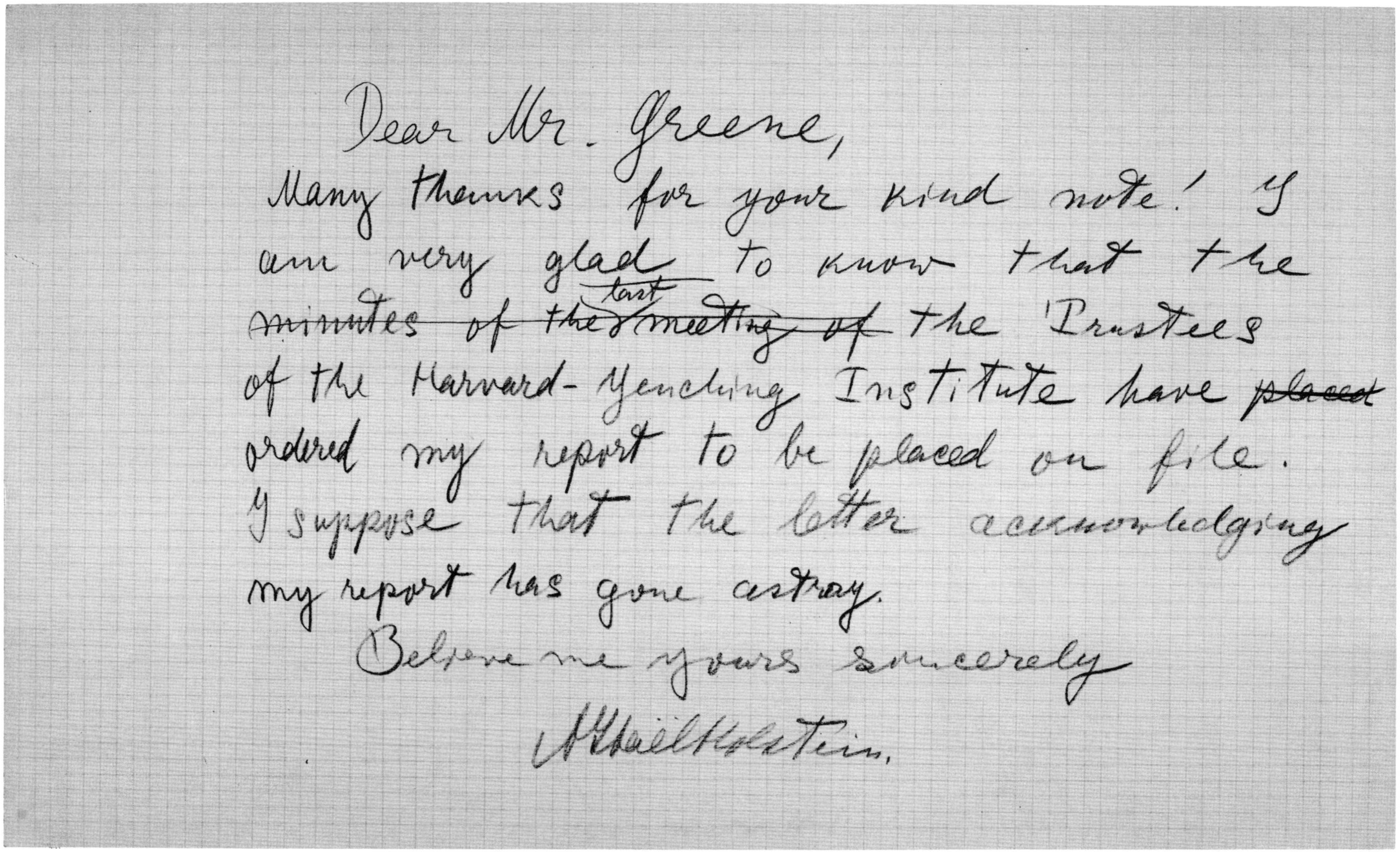

Dear Mr. Greene,

Many thanks for your kind note! I am very glad to know that the ~~minutes of the last meeting of~~ the Trustees of the Harvard-Yenching Institute have ~~placed~~ ordered my report to be placed on file. I suppose that the letter acknowledging my report has gone astray.

Believe me yours sincerely

A. Staël Holstein.

Dear Mr. Greene,

A great weight has been lifted off my mind by your kind note. I am delighted to know that I shall be able to stay here for some time to come, and I feel extremely grateful to you for having written to Dean Chase.

Believe me yours sincerely

Hôtel des Wagons-Lits, Peking, November 2nd 1929.

Dear Mr. Greene

I approve your suggestion about the method of payment to Baron de Staël.

I find that he consents to the procedure which you outline. The western foreigners (at present: Pankratoff and Behrsing) will receive Yenching cheques, but none of the Asiatics who will be paid directly by Baron de Staël ~~in cash,~~ (out of his own pocket,) in the customary way, without consultation with any one. At the end of every month (or quarter) Baron de Staël will send Mr. Porter a statement enumerating the payments made by him to his Asiatic assistants and will then receive a single Yenching cheque covering all those payments. This cheque to be made out to Baron de Staël. And the details of the expenditure to be left to him.

Afterwards he will report directly to the Trustees, as

a Harvard professor, and also send a copy of his report
to you and to Mr. Stuart. At any time he is willing
to inform Mr. Porter of any details which might
interest him.

Hotel des Wagons-Lits,
Peking, November 2nd, 1929.

Dear Mr. Greene,

I approve your suggestion about the method of payment to Baron de Stael.

I find that he consents to the procedure which you outline. The western foreigners (at present: Pankratoff and Behrsing) will receive Yenching cheques, but none of the Asiatics, who will be paid directly by Baron de Stael in the customary way out of his own pocket, without consultation with any one. At the end of every month (or quarter) Baron de Stael will send Mr.Porter a statement enumerating the payments made by him to his Asiatic assistants and will then receive a single Yenching cheque covering all those payments. This cheque to be made out to Baron de Stael. And the details of the expenditure to be left to him.

Afterwards he will report directly to the Trustees, as a Harvard professor, and also send a copy of his report to you and to Mr. Stuart. At any time he is willing to inform Mr.Porter of any details which might interest him.

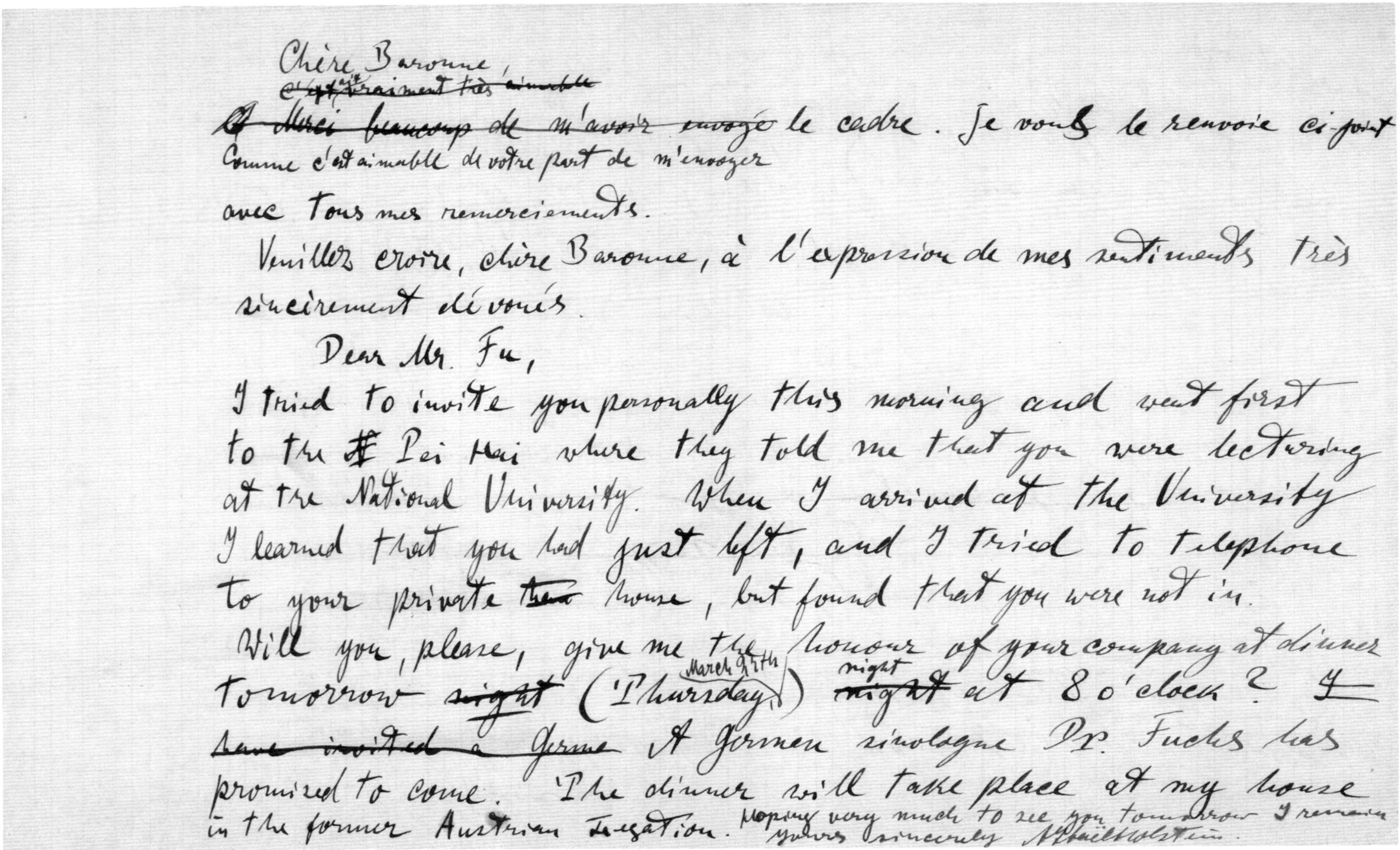

Chère Baronne,
~~C'est vraiment très aimable~~
~~[illegible] Merci beaucoup de m'avoir envoyé~~ le cadre. Je vous le renvoie ci-joint
Comme c'est aimable de votre part de m'envoyer
avec tous mes remerciements.
Veuillez croire, chère Baronne, à l'expression de mes sentiments très sincèrement dévoués.

Dear Mr. Fu,
I tried to invite you personally this morning and went first to the ~~#~~ Pei Hai where they told me that you were lecturing at the National University. When I arrived at the University I learned that you had just left, and I tried to telephone to your private ~~tea~~ house, but found that you were not in.
Will you, please, give me the honour of your company at dinner tomorrow ~~night~~ (Thursday March 27th) ~~night~~ night at 8 o'clock? ~~I have invited a Germa~~ A German sinologue Dr. Fuchs has promised to come. The dinner will take place at my house in the former Austrian Legation. Hoping very much to see you tomorrow I remain yours sincerely A. Staël-Holstein.

Hochgeehrter Herr Doctor,

~~Ich~~ ~~Die~~ ~~Das~~ Die beiliegenden Photographien [stellen] ~~von~~
~~zwei~~ ~~mir gehörenden~~ Statuetten aus meiner Sammlung [dar,]
~~und repräsentieren~~
~~repräsentieren sind~~, glaube ich, ganz gut ~~e~~ ~~Repräsentan-~~
~~ten der~~ [die] Tibetische~~n~~ Dämonenwelt. Der auf einer
Ziege reitende Unhold heisst Bdo rje legs und
die Dame ist eine gefährliche Ḍākinī. Näheres
über diese Gestalten können Sie bei Grünwedel (Mythol.,
[pagg. 185-187] ~~Seite 186~~) und bei Waddell (Lamaism, pagg. 26, 371 und 382)
finden.

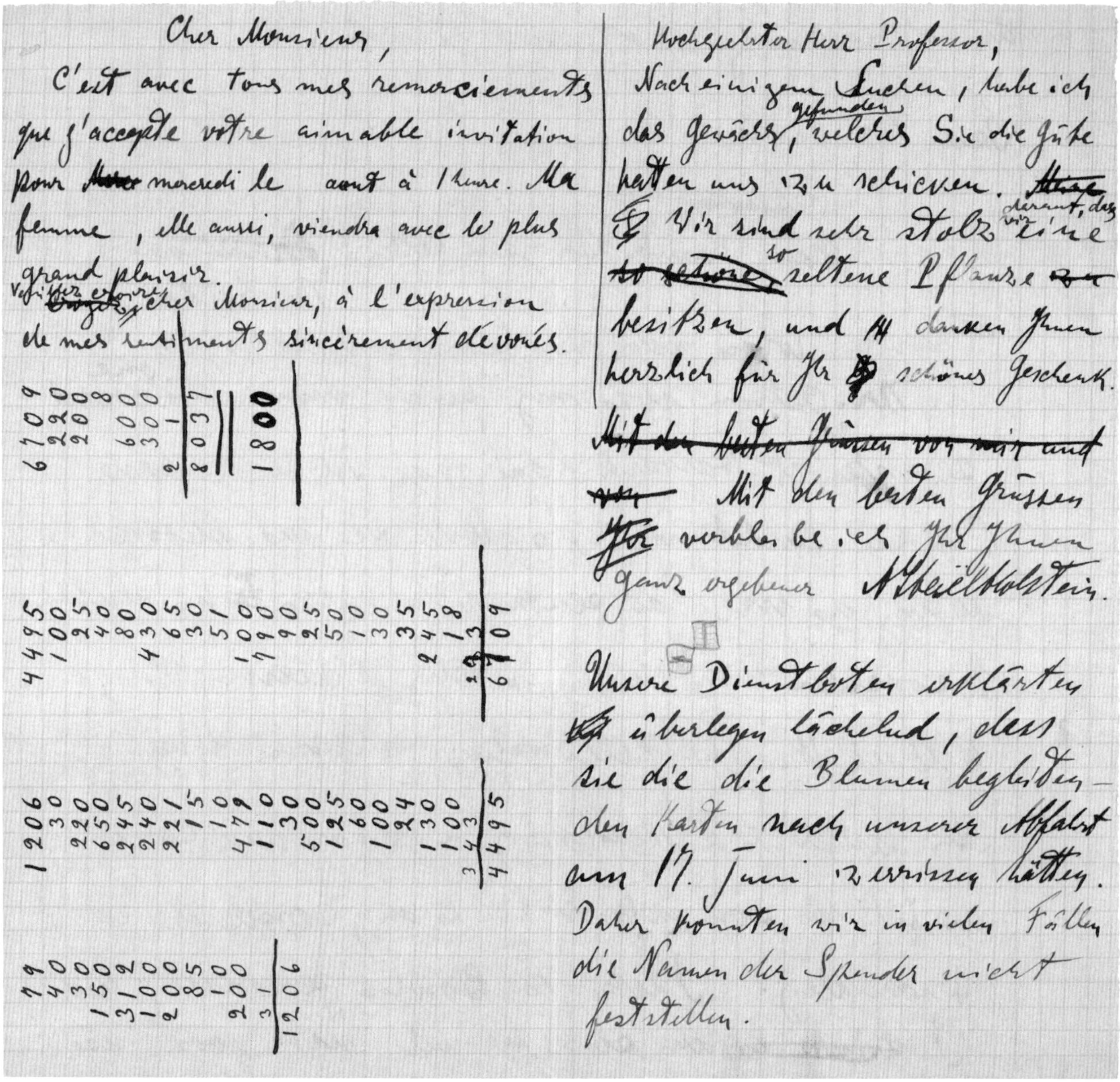

Cher Monsieur,

C'est avec tous mes remerciements que j'accepte votre aimable invitation pour ~~[illegible]~~ mercredi le   août à 1 heure. Ma femme, elle aussi, viendra avec le plus grand plaisir.

Veuillez agréer, cher Monsieur, à l'expression de mes sentiments sincèrement dévoués.

Hochgeehrter Herr Professor,

Nach einigem Suchen, habe ich das Gewächs gefunden, welches Sie die Güte hatten uns zu schicken. ~~[illegible]~~ Wir sind sehr stolz darauf, dass wir eine ~~[illegible]~~ so seltene Pflanze besitzen, und danken Ihnen herzlich für Ihr schönes Geschenk.

~~Mit den besten Grüssen von mir und~~

Mit den besten Grüssen verbleibe ich Ihr Ihnen ganz ergebener [illegible]

Unsere Dienstboten erklärten überlegen lächelnd, dass sie die die Blumen begleitenden Karten nach unserer Abfahrt am 17. Juni zerrissen hätten. Daher konnten wir in vielen Fällen die Namen der Spender nicht feststellen.

DÉLÉGATION ARCHÉOLOGIQUE FRANÇAISE
EN AFGHANISTAN

Kâbul, 16 septembre 1936.

Mon cher Professeur et ami

Il me faut ce court moment de répit entre une arrivée et un départ pour que je trouve le temps de vous écrire, je comptais le faire, il y a longtemps déjà à Paris; mais Paris n'est décidément pas l'endroit où les projets aboutissent facilement. Je préfère encore l'Afghanistan où tout se déroule suivant un rythme moins rapide. Nous sommes arrivés ici il y a quelques semaines et nous repartons bientôt pour le Seistan, où nous comptons mener nos recherches pendant une période de trois mois. Nous aurons ensuite l'embarras du choix car les sites ne manquent pas qui doivent solliciter notre attention. Je vous réserve un exemplaire de notre récent travail sur les fouilles pratiquées au Nord de Kâbul en 1934, par mon collaborateur Carl et par moi-même. Je serais pour ma part très heureux de recevoir de vos nouvelles, ou plutôt de les trouver ici lorsque nous rentrerons à Kâbul en décembre prochain. Nous n'avons, en effet, aucune chance de recevoir des nouvelles durant notre séjour au Seïstân.

Comme je vous l'avais dit c'est Mademoiselle Marcelle Lalou qui s'est occupée des peintures que vous avez eu l'aimable pensée de déposer au Musée Guimet; elle n'a pas poussé son étude jusqu'au point d'être prête à entreprendre une publication détaillée. Les moyens nous font malheureusement défaut d'entreprendre par ce temps d'extrême dépression financière une publication illustrée; les éditeurs spécialisés sont malheureusement en mauvaise posture et nos crédits, très réduits, ne nous permettent pas d'entreprendre sans aide une entreprise comme celle-là. Attendre des temps meilleurs? Sans être pessimiste je pense que cette échéance est encore lointaine. De toute façon vos documents sont conservés chez nous et j'espère pouvoir les montrer au public parisien après notre retour, car il entre dans mes plans d'~~placer~~ organiser une exposition de peintures tibétaines.

Veuillez-vous, je vous prie, mettre mes respectueux hommages aux pieds de la Baronne de Staël. Vous avez les bons souvenirs de ma femme et je vous prie de croire, mon cher Professeur, à mes sentiments de sincère et cordial dévouement — J. Hackin

HARVARD-YENCHING INSTITUTE

ADMINISTRATIVE COMMITTEE IN PEIPING
OFFICE OF THE EXECUTIVE SECRETARY

YENCHING UNIVERSITY
PEIPING, WEST

October 15, 1931.

Baron A. von Stael Holstein,
Austrian Legation,
Peiping.

My dear Baron:

Please accept our apologies for the delay in sending the enclosed cheque. The absence of Mr. Porter and a new secretary in the office were responsible for the mistake made. It will not happen again.

President Stuart wishes me to thank you very much indeed for the addresses enclosed in the note you sent to me this morning.

Very sincerely yours,

Hulda S. Hague

HARVARD-YENCHING INSTITUTE

ADMINISTRATIVE COMMITTEE IN PEIPING
OFFICE OF THE EXECUTIVE SECRETARY

April 2, 1932.

YENCHING UNIVERSITY
PEIPING, WEST

My dear Baron von Stael Holstein:

The treasurer's office has asked me to write and request you to return to them the receipt for their check for $5723.02, issued on February 5. They have no record that you have cashed the check at the bank, and as they have a system of filing the receipts they would like to have the receipt back if you have not lost it.

They received the receipt for the letter in which the check was enclosed, and which was delivered to you by our messenger.

I am sorry to trouble you about this but it seems to be a matter of form here in the treasurer's office.

Very sincerely yours,

Secretary

Peking April 3rd 1932

Dear Miss Hague,

~~It~~ I enclose the receipt, and I humbly ask to be forgiven for the delay.

In a few days I shall send you my expense account for the quarter ending ~~ult~~ on March 31st 1932.

HARVARD-YENCHING INSTITUTE

ADMINISTRATIVE COMMITTEE IN PEIPING
OFFICE OF THE EXECUTIVE SECRETARY

YENCHING UNIVERSITY
PEIPING, WEST

May 6, 1932.

My dear Baron von Stael Holstein:

I enclose a gold draft from the Treasurer's Office as you requested for $250 for the photostat machine as you requested. The Treasurer's Office has asked me to request you when you return the receipt for this to let them know the amount in silver which you receive for the gold draft as this must be reported to New York.

Very sincerely yours,

Secretary

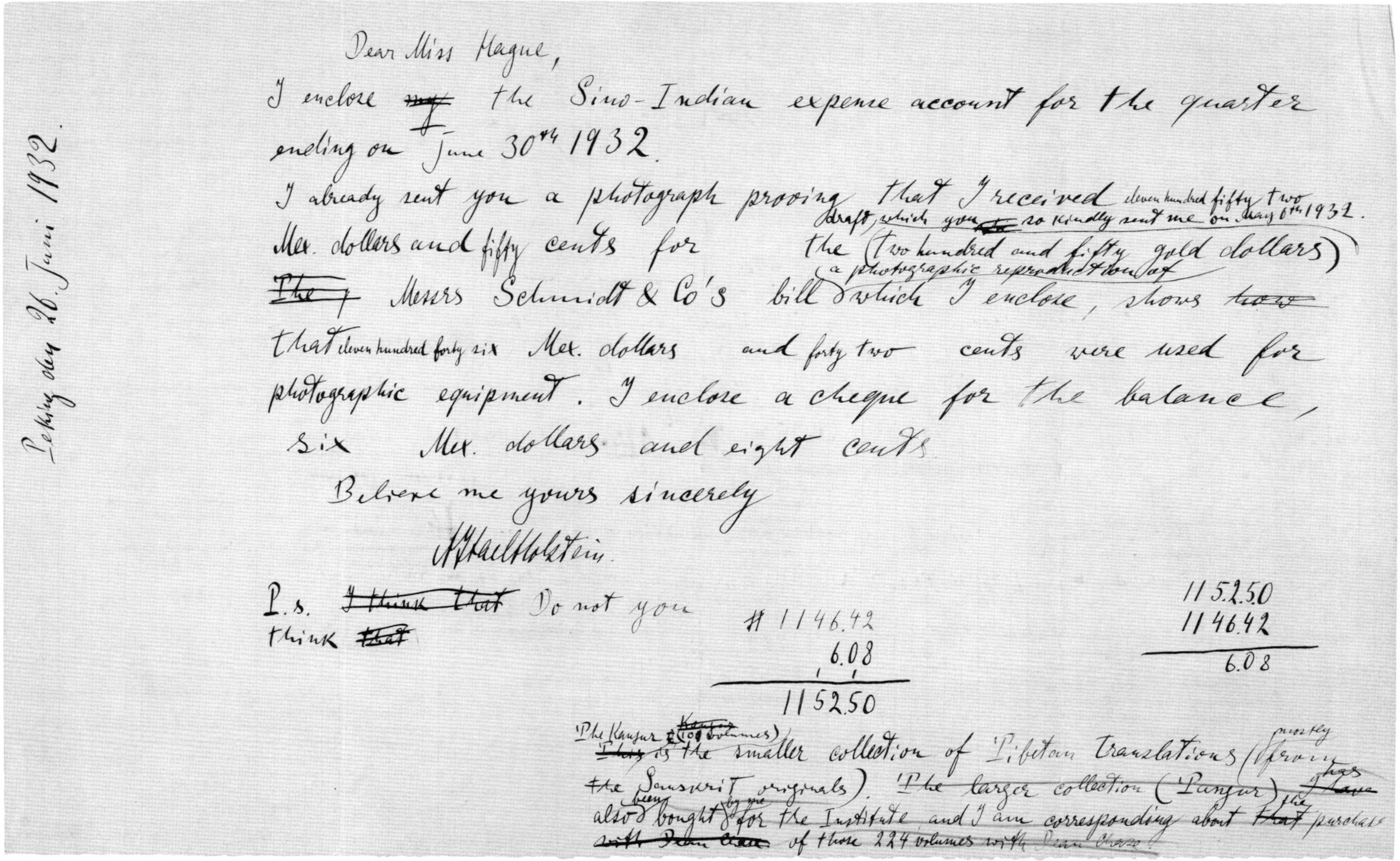

Peking den 26. Juni 1932.

Dear Miss Hague,

I enclose ~~my~~ the Sino-Indian expense account for the quarter ending on June 30th 1932.

I already sent you a photograph proving that I received eleven hundred fifty two Mex. dollars and fifty cents for the draft, which you ~~so~~ so kindly sent me on May 6th 1932. (two hundred and fifty gold dollars)

~~The~~ a photographic reproduction of Messrs Schmidt & Co's bill which I enclose, shows ~~two~~ that eleven hundred forty six Mex. dollars and forty two cents were used for photographic equipment. I enclose a cheque for the balance, six Mex. dollars and eight cents.

Believe me yours sincerely

A. Staël Holstein.

P.S. ~~I think that~~ Do not you think ~~that~~

$ 1146.42	1152.50
6.08	1146.42
1152.50	6.08

The Kanjur (~~Kanjur~~ 108 volumes) ~~This~~ is the smaller collection of Tibetan translations (mostly from the Sanskrit originals). The larger collection (Tanjur) ~~I have~~ has also been bought by me for the Institute and I am corresponding about ~~that~~ the purchase ~~with Dean Chase~~ of those 224 volumes with Dean Chase!

HARVARD-YENCHING INSTITUTE

ADMINISTRATIVE COMMITTEE IN PEIPING
OFFICE OF THE EXECUTIVE SECRETARY

YENCHING UNIVERSITY
PEIPING, WEST

August 30, 1932.

Baron A. von Stael-Holstein,
Austrian Legation.

My dear Baron:

With reference to my previous communication dated June 23, I have now received word from Dean Chase on behalf of the Harvard-Yenching Institute, a copy of which I herewith enclose.

Very sincerely yours,

William Hung

William Hung

HARVARD-YENCHING INSTITUTE

ADMINISTRATIVE COMMITTEE IN PEIPING
OFFICE OF THE EXECUTIVE SECRETARY

YENCHING UNIVERSITY
PEIPING, WEST

September 12, 1932.

My dear Baron:

In the Yenching University Directory which is printed each autumn, we have been listing the names of the members of the Harvard-Yenching Institute. So far, your name is the only one which has appeared under the Sino-Indian Institute. This year Mr. Hung thinks we should list the names of the other members working with you.

Last year your name appeared as in the enclosed slip. I have the following list of members of the Institute as sent to me by you last autumn. Will you please see that this list is correct, and add any other names which should appear. Will you please also give the Chinese name <u>in full</u> of each person. I should appreciate it very much if you could send this to me as soon as possible.

Eduard Erkes
Ferdinand Lessing
Ernst Schieritz
Friedrich Weller

With kind regards,

Very sincerely yours,

Hilda L. Hague

Secretary

Sept. 13th 1932.

My Dear Miss Hague,

~~The list of names which you enclosed. The fr~~

The names mentioned on the list, which was enclosed in your ~~last~~ letter dated Sept. 12th 1932, belong to scholarly friends of mine who happened to ~~be invited~~ attend ~~to~~ a luncheon party at my house together with President Stuart last year. ~~The [illegible] all. All of them have been occasionally consulted by myself~~

The only one of them who ~~may be said to~~ has ever been paid by the Sino-Indian Institute is Professor ~~Friedrich~~ Weller, extraordinary professor ~~at~~ in the University of Leipzig, on leave in Peking. He has ~~he has been here on leave~~

~~I shall pr~~ Owing to the reduced state of our finances I shall, probably, not be able to keep Professor Weller here until the end of the academic year, and I therefore think that his name should not appear in the directory. ~~[illegible] Messrs. [illegible] Messrs.~~ Professor Erkes, Professor Hessing and Schierlitz never had any claim to be ~~[illegible]~~ regarded as members of the H.-Y. Institute.

~~I enclose two articles which~~

Please accept the ~~two article~~ enclosed ~~articles~~ papers, which I recently wrote, as tokens of my respect ~~sincere devotion to you~~ and believe me yours sincerely

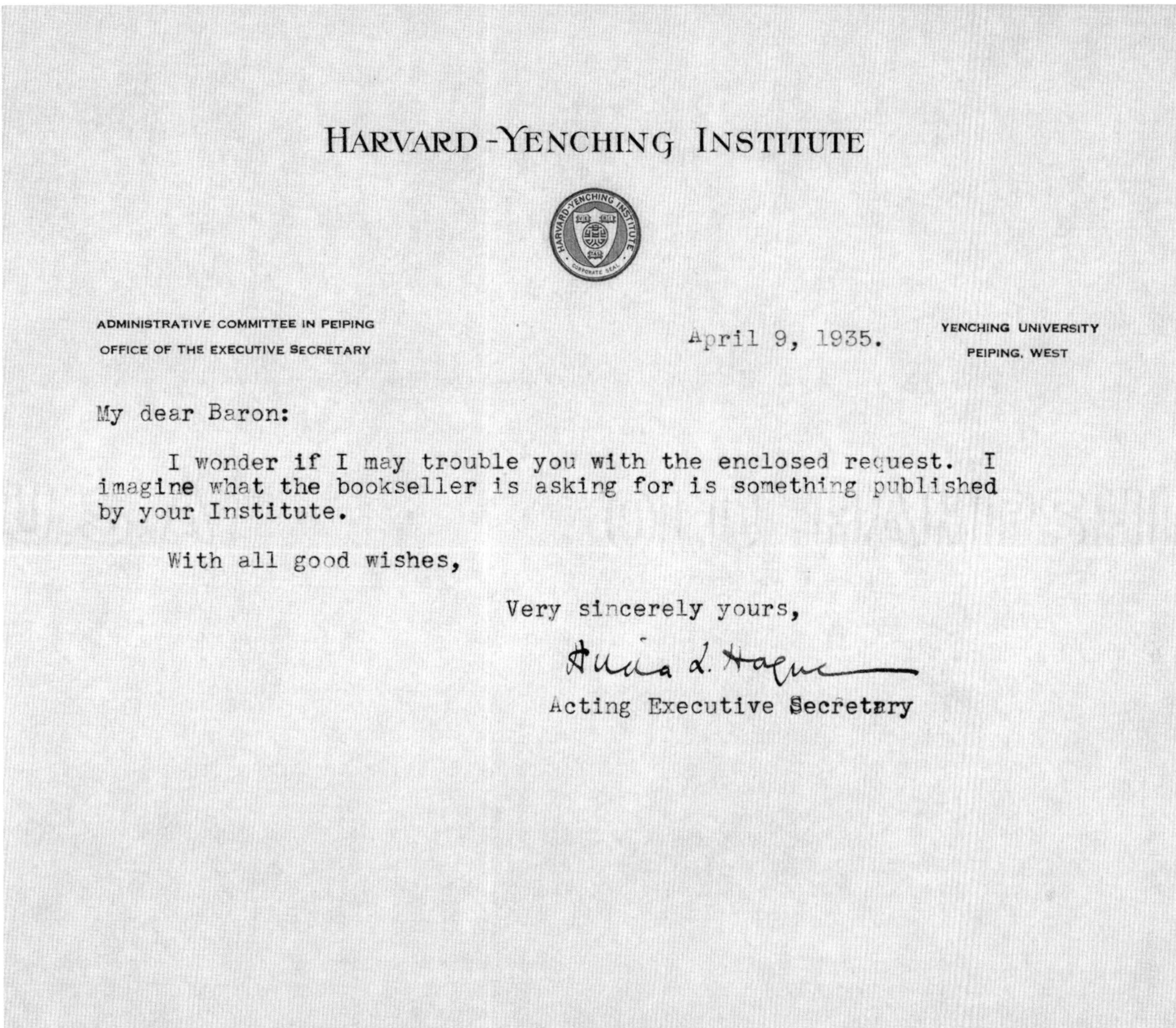

HARVARD-YENCHING INSTITUTE

ADMINISTRATIVE COMMITTEE IN PEIPING
OFFICE OF THE EXECUTIVE SECRETARY

April 9, 1935.

YENCHING UNIVERSITY
PEIPING, WEST

My dear Baron:

I wonder if I may trouble you with the enclosed request. I imagine what the bookseller is asking for is something published by your Institute.

With all good wishes,

Very sincerely yours,

Acting Executive Secretary

HARVARD-YENCHING INSTITUTE

Yenching University,
Peiping, April 11, 1935.

Baron von Stael Holstein,
Austrian Legation,
Peiping.

My dear Baron:

Many thanks for your prompt reply to my note. I have sent the book to London this morning. I have also sent to Mr. Hung your note for him.

With regard to the price of the book. Our custom here when such books are sent abroad is to charge half the Mexican price in gold and send the books postage free. That is to say I have charged for your book U.S.A.$ 3.00, and have asked the publisher to remit this amount directly to you. If this is not the way you wish the transaction handled then please let me know at once how your Institute wishes the matter to be handled.

We are continually having requests for a list of our publications. So far we have only had such a list prepared in Chinese. I am now preparing a little booklet in English which will list each book with a paragraph or two describing the contents. The Sinological Index Series will be included, and I have been wondering whether it would possible to include the publications issued by your Institute.

The booklet will contain a brief foreword giving the history and aims of the Harvard-Yenching Institute which will be followed by a list of its publications, giving the price of each, when and where published, author, etc. and the brief description of the contents referred to above.

Very sincerely yours,

Hilda J. Hague

Acting Executive Secretary

II

Peking April 14th 1935.

Dear Miss Hague,

At the request of Dean G. H. Chase a hundred copies of the first volume of the Harvard Sino-Indian Series have been sent to ~~the Harvard University Press~~ ~~which is~~ Cambridge Mass., and they ~~Harvard University Press~~ are being sold there now. ~~This arrangement is very convenient and I like~~ this arrangement ~~I am very glad that I think that this is quite sufficient and that we need not mention in any printed publication that copies can also be obtained at in Peking.~~

~~I like the arrangement because very much. Please do not mention the fact that copies may also be obtained here in any printed publication.~~

I think I must not interfere with the sale of the book at Cambridge Mass. by advertising the fact that copies of ~~it~~ may also be obtained here.

With many thanks for your ~~kind~~ note I remain yours very sincerely

A. Staël-Holstein.

HARVARD-YENCHING INSTITUTE

哈佛燕京學社

OFFICE OF THE EXECUTIVE SECRETARY
幹事辦公處

PEIPING OFFICE
北平辦公處
YENCHING UNIVERSITY
燕京大學
PEIPING, WEST
北平西郊

April 18, 1935.

Baron von Stael-Holstein,
Austrian Legation,
Peiping.

My dear Baron:

Many thanks for your note in reply to mine. I am afraid I did not make myself very clear as to the reasons why I wanted the information about the publications of your Institute. We have no thought whatsoever of selling them here in Peiping. In Mr. Porter's absence I find I know very little about your Institute, and I was not aware that your publications were sold at the Cambridge end. I assumed that they were all sold by your office.

I have really two reasons for making the enquiry:

1) We are, as I mentioned, planning to issue a statement in English of the books published by the Institute. I am only planning to give the titles of books that can be obtained here in China. If your publications are all handled at Cambridge, then it would be quite simple to state that all publications of the Sino-Indian Institute are handled through the Harvard Office, and it will not be necessary to give a list of titles. But I should like ~~to~~ you to tell me whether only certain of your publications are so handled, or all of them.

2) We are constantly receiving requests for information regarding the Harvard-Yenching Institute, its organization, activities, professors, publications, etc. As you know, every year in China a number of handbooks are issued which give information about the important educational institutions and institutes of the country. Would you have any objection to such a statement as the following appearing:

"In 1929 the Sino-Indian Institute of a Peiping merged with the Harvard-Yenching Institute. It ~~and~~ is ~~now the~~ centre for research in the history ~~and philosophy~~ of Buddhism, ~~and its transmission to China,~~ and offers opportunity to properly qualified scholars for advanced instruction in Sanskrit, and the T~~x~~ibetan and Mongolian languages. The Institute is under the direction of Baron A. von Stael-Holstein, ~~and its publications are obtainable through the Harvard Office."~~ Ph. D. etc.

The publications of the Sino-Indian Institute are obtainable through the Harvard University Press, Cambridge Mass. U.S. of America.

Please make any corrections that may be necessary.

2

I am sorry to trouble you with these matters but hesitate to have anything appear in print which might be incorrect or distasteful to you. To make a statement about the Harvard-Yenching Institute and to make no mention of the Sino-Indian Institute and its activities would appear to be very misleading, for whatever statement is issued will include the activities of the Harvard Office.

If Mr. Porter were here I should probably not have to trouble you with all this. He appears to be enjoying his stay in Szechwan very much indeed. We expect him back about the first of June. I wonder if you have heard that Mr. Ware of the Harvard Office is planning to be in Peiping this summer arriving some time in June.

With all good wishes,

Very sincerely yours,

Acting Executive Secretary

Peking, April 27th 1935.

Dear Miss Hague,

Many thanks for your note. I shall call at Yenching on one of these days in order to discuss the paragraph about the Sino-Indian Institute with you.

Believe me yours very sincerely

A Staël Holstein.

HARVARD-YENCHING INSTITUTE

ADMINISTRATIVE COMMITTEE IN PEIPING
OFFICE OF THE EXECUTIVE SECRETARY

May 3, 1935.

YENCHING UNIVERSITY
PEIPING, WEST

My dear Baron:

I have just been talking with Prof. Hung about Dr. Liebenthal's article for the Yenching Journal. He tells me that he saw Prof. Jung Keng yesterday and asked him to send you word as soon as possible about the pagination, so you will not doubt hear from the latter within a few days.

Very sincerely yours,

Hilda L. Hague

Secretary

HARVARD-YENCHING INSTITUTE

ADMINISTRATIVE COMMITTEE IN PEIPING
OFFICE OF THE EXECUTIVE SECRETARY

YENCHING UNIVERSITY
PEIPING, WEST

May 4, 1935.

My dear Baron:

Mr. Jung Keng has asked me to let you know that the first page of Dr. Leibenthal's article for the Yenching Journal will begin with page 179.

Very sincerely yours,

Hilda L. Hague
Secretary

HARVARD-YENCHING INSTITUTE

ADMINISTRATIVE COMMITTEE IN PEIPING
OFFICE OF THE EXECUTIVE SECRETARY

May 29, 1935.

YENCHING UNIVERSITY
PEIPING, WEST

Baron A. von Stael-Holstein,
Austrian Legation,
Peiping.

My dear Baron:

I have been asked to make enquiries from you regarding Dr. Liebenthal's article for the Yenching Journal. The Journal is now ready for binding and the printing office would like to have the article as soon as possible. Will you please let us know when we may expect to receive it. We would also like to know the exact pagination as another article will follow it.

The parcel can be sent out by the University Bus service if left at the bus office 司法部街北口 大陸汽車行

Very sincerely yours,

Hulda L. Hague

Acting Executive Secretary

Peking July 2nd 1935.

Dear Miss Hague,

I am awfully sorry to learn (from your letter dated June 29th) ~~to Mr. P'an)~~ [to Mr. P'an] that eighteen copies of Dr. Liebenthal's article are missing. I enclose a letter from the Imprimerie des Lazaristes, who are quite certain that they sent more than 1012 copies to Yenching. ~~I possess only one copy which~~ ~~'They have no more copies left.~~ ~~I~~ 'The only copy I possess I send ~~you~~ along. ~~Please accept it as my~~ ~~And ask~~ Please ask the Yenching printing office to accept it as a modest gift from myself.

Believe me yours sincerely

AStaëlHolstein.

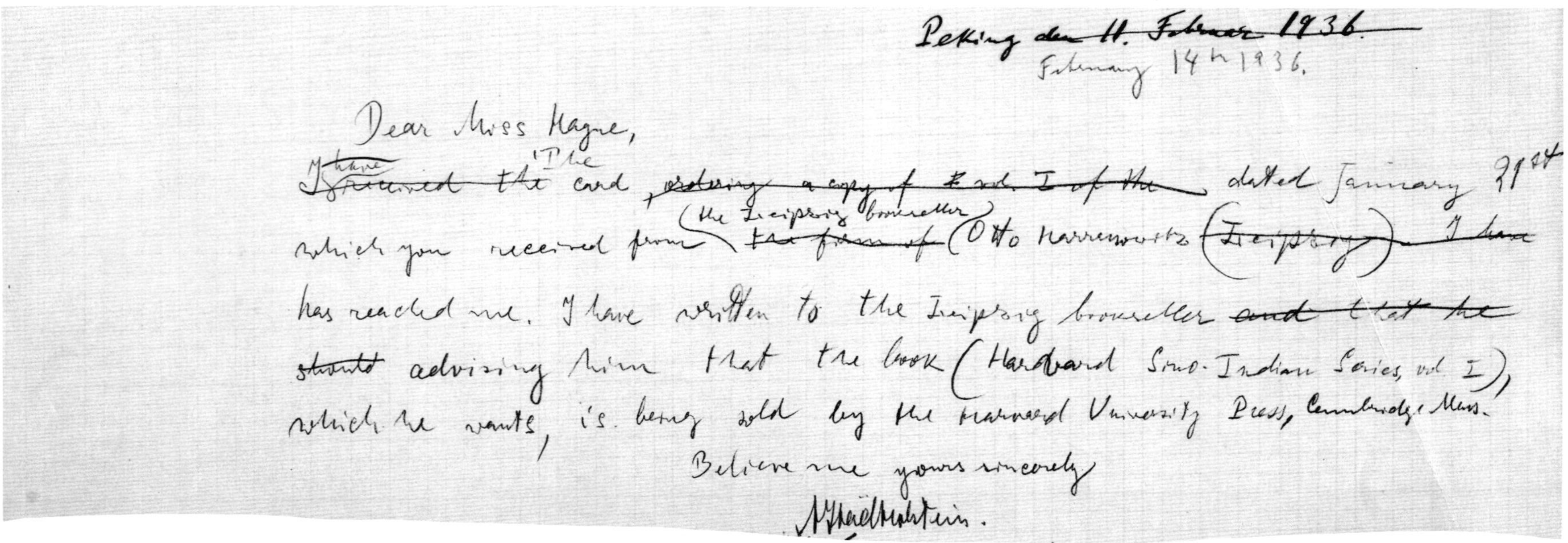

~~Peking den 11. Februar 1936.~~
February 14th 1936.

Dear Miss Magie,

~~I received~~ I have ~~the~~ The card, ~~ordering a copy of the vol. I of the~~ dated January 31st which you received from (the Leipzig bookseller) ~~the firm of~~ (Otto Harrassowitz ~~(Leipzig)~~ ~~I have~~ has reached me. I have written to the Leipzig bookseller ~~and that he should~~ advising him that the book (Harvard Sino-Indian Series, vol. I), which he wants, is being sold by the Harvard University Press, Cambridge, Mass.

Believe me yours sincerely

A. Staël-Holstein.

YENCHING UNIVERSITY
PEIPING.

Monday

My dear Baron:

Many thanks for your note. As it happens I must come to town two or three mornings this week, and again next week, to the dentist.

So, it would be much easier for me to drop in at your house, than to have you come away out

here about so small a thing.
I will bring in what I have
written and show it to you
for your approval.

In haste,

Andie L. Hague

YENCHING UNIVERSITY
PEPING, CHINA.

Tuesday

My dear Baron von Staël-Holstein

Very many thanks for your reply to my note, which was received this morning.

We are having spring holidays in the University this week, but the offices will all be open again this coming Monday. Mr Hung is in the hills now, and I am going away for a few days tomorrow. This is just to let you know in case that should

be a delay of a day or two in
sending in the check for your
statement, should it arrive
before Monday.

Very sincerely yours,

Hudin J. Hagner

HARVARD-YENCHING INSTITUTE
哈佛燕京學社

OFFICE OF THE EXECUTIVE SECRETARY
幹事辦公處

PEIPING OFFICE
北平辦公處
YENCHING UNIVERSITY
燕京大學
PEIPING, WEST
北平西郊

June 29, 1935.

Dear Mr. P'an:

When you sent out the printed copies of Dr. Walter Liebenthal's article for the Yenching Journal of Chinese Studies, we found there were short 18 copies.

Will you please furnish these missing copies as soon as possible, as we cannot complete the publication of the Journal until we have these in hand.

Very sincerely yours,

Hilda L. Hague

Secretary

The larger collection (Tanjur) has also been bought ~~—~~ for the Institute with money I received by me long ago, and I am corresponding with Dean Chase about the purchase of those 224 volumes.

Dear Mr. Nixon,

Kindly excuse ~~me for not having~~ this late answer. ~~The charact~~ I think that ~~the char~~ the centre of the cross is occupied by an ~~The character ā generally takes the form 丮 ?? I still — My assistant Professor Weller (Leipzig Univ.) does not agree~~ Indian character (āḥ) which takes the following form in Lamaistic books 丮: ; 𢀡 āḥ is one of the most powerful ~~charms~~ mystic syllables used by the Lamas. Believe me yours sincerely A. Staël-Holstein.

Lieber Herr Doctor, 华 Kegon repräsentiert die japanische und Huayen die pekingesische Aussprache der Zeichen 華嚴. ~~Die übrigen~~ Alle anderen Fragen, die Ihr Brief ~~aus Peitaiho~~ enthält, sind in einem Memorandum beantwortet, das ich Ihnen einige Tage vor Empfang des Briefes aus Peitaiho in Ihre Pekinger Wohnung sandte. Ich nehme an, dass Sie das Memorandum inzwischen erhalten haben. ~~Ich bin ganz Ich theile Ihre Ansicht die~~ Auch ich bin der Ansicht, dass sich die Banalitäten des Lebens nicht vollständig vermeiden lassen. Hier in Peking verlaufen sie aber doch schmerzloser als in Peitaiho. ~~, wo [illegible] es so schrecklich schwer ist, sich~~ Ich denke daran im Herbst nach Abschluss der wichtigsten Arbeiten eine Ferienreise zu unternehmen~~, nachdem ich~~ Hoffentlich sehe ich Sie noch vorher in Peking. ~~treffen wir uns dann.~~ Herzliche Grüsse von Ihrem ergebenen A. Staël-Holstein.

SIGILLUM COLLEGII MISSIONUM
DISCE UT EVANGELIUM PRAEDICES

The COLLEGE of MISSIONS

[AFFILIATED WITH THE HARTFORD SEMINARY FOUNDATION]

CHARLES T. PAUL, M. A., F. R. G. S., *President*
CLARENCE H. HAMILTON, PH. D., *Dean*

HARTFORD
CONNECTICUT

55 Elizabeth Street,
April 26, 1929.

Professor Baron von Stael
Holstein,
Dep't of Chinese Studies,
Harvard University,
Cambridge, Mass.

My dear Baron Holstein:

It is with pleasure that I recall our brief meeting at the gathering of the American Oriental Society recently. Kindly accept my heartiest greetings and esteem.

I am writing to ask you a question with regard to the Leng Yen Ching (佛說首楞嚴三昧經). I noticed when in China that there was question among some of the Chinese scholars with regard to its authenticity as an original Mahayanist work. At Ou-yang Ching-wu's school at Nanking they seemed to regard it as a forgery, probably of some late Chinese scholar. I remember that in conversation with Dr. Karl Reichelt one day he remarked that you had evidence from Tibetan sources, showing a bona fide Sanskrit derivation of this widely known work. May I ask whether you have discussed this matter anywhere in print? If so I should greatly appreciate having the reference.

Let me thank you again for your suggestions as to books. My copy of Poussin's "Vijñaptimātrātasiddhi" has come. The volumes of Rosenberg and the Japanese Buddhist dictionary are ordered and I am impatient for their arrival.

Yours most cordially,

Clarence H. Hamilton.

Peking d. 23 Febr 1927

Hochverehrter und lieber
Herr Baron

Vielen herzlichen Dank für Ihre grosse Güte sich meiner zu meinem Geburtstag in so überaus liebenswürdiger Weise zu gedenken. Die Karte ist ja hochinteressant und sehr charakteristisch und ich freue mich eine Kopie davon zu besitzen.

Mit wiederholtem Dank
Ihr treu und aufrichtig
ergebener

Sven Hedin.

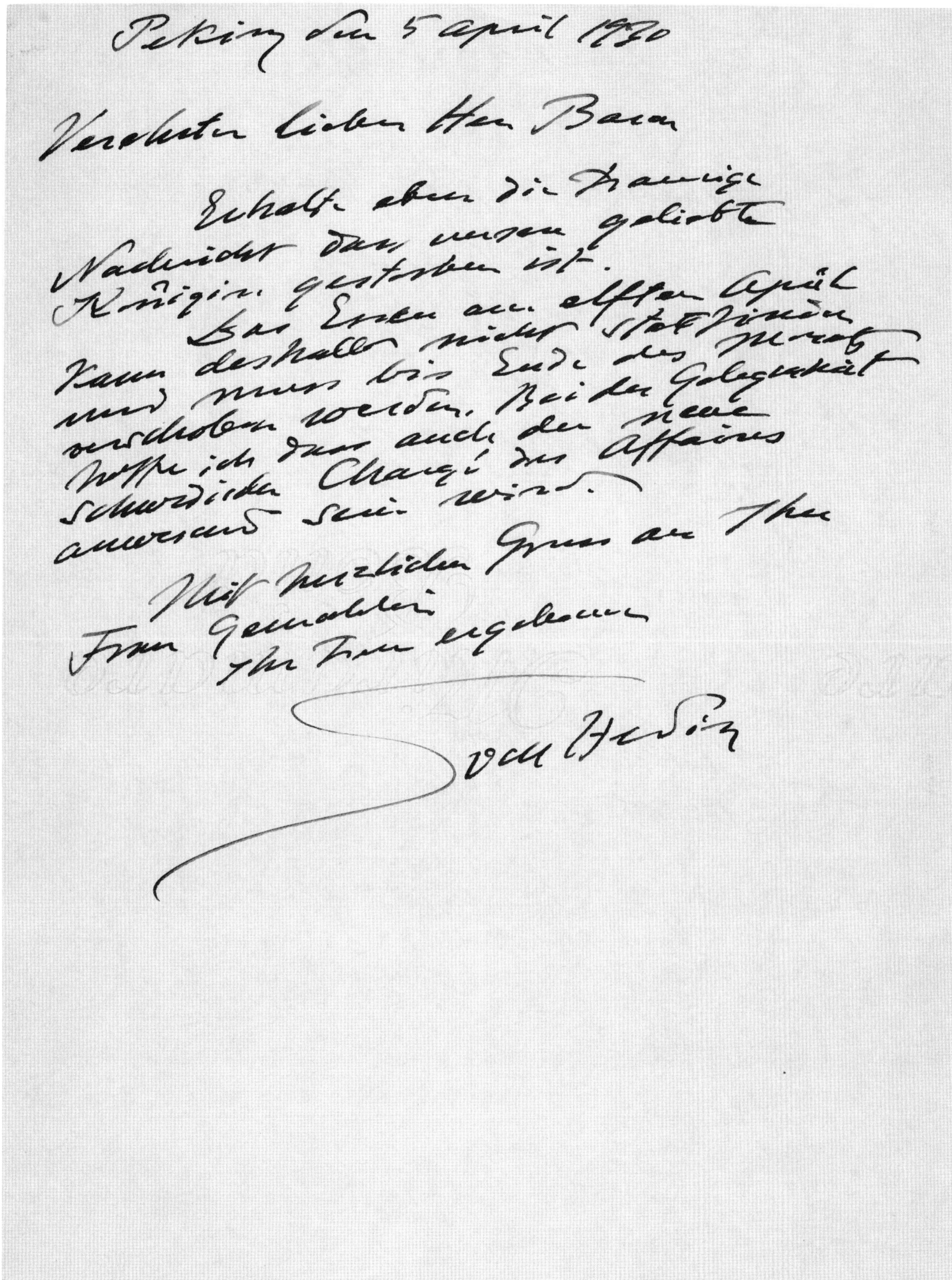

Peking den 5 april 1930

Verehrter lieber Herr Baron

Erhalte eben die traurige Nachricht dass unsere geliebte Königin gestorben ist.

Das Essen am elften April kann deshalb nicht stattfinden und muss bis Ende des Monats verschoben werden. Bei der Gelegenheit hoffe ich dass auch der neue schwedische Chargé des Affaires anwesend sein wird.

Mit herzlichen Gruss an Ihre Frau Gemahlin

Ihr treu ergebener

Sven Hedin

Peking den 4 maj 1930

Sehr verehrter lieber Herr Baron

Jetzt ist der neue schwedische Chargé d'affaires Herr Lagerberg hier und ich und Dr Montell hoffen dass Sie und Ihre hochverehrte Frau uns die Ehre geben wollen bei uns Donnerstag d. 15 Mai, 8.30 zu essen.

In alter Treue
Ihr sehr ergebener

Sven Hedin

Tung Tangtze Hutung
No 25

Peking d. 24 Mai 1930

Hochverehrter Herr Baron

Ich danke Ihnen recht herzlich für Ihren liebenswürdigen Brief und für die wichtige und interessante Mitteilung die er enthält.

Ich habe schon mit meinen Übersetzer davon gesprochen und er wird die betreffenden Dokumente durchsehen und mir berichten.

In der Hoffnung dass Ihnen und Ihrer lieben Frau Gemahlin alles gut geht bin ich

Ihr aufrichtig ergebener

Sven Hedin

Peking den 28 März 1930

Hochverehrter lieber Herr Baron

Sie wissen wohl dass Herr Baron und die Frau Leijonhufvud am d. 12 April Peking verlassen. Am Abend vorher den 11ten habe ich ein ganz kleines Essen im vertraulichen Kreise für sie und es wäre mir eine besondere Ehre und Freude wenn Sie und Ihre hochverehrte Frau Gemahlin mir die Ehre machen wollten bei dieser Gelegenheit zu mir zu kommen.

Dr Montell und ich wohnen jetzt im Herr und Frau Schmidt's Haus, Tung Tang-tse-Hutung 25!

Hoffentlich sind Sie frei! Freitag also den 11. April 8.30 n.M. willkommen!

Mit den besten Grüssen an Ihre liebe Frau Gemahlin

Ihr sehr ergebener

Sven Hedin

Hochverehrter lieber Herr Doctor

Der Gesundheitszustand meiner Frau macht es ihr leider unmöglich, Ihrer ~~gütige Einladung~~ Aufforderung Folge zu leisten, ~~anzunehmen, und die~~ ich aber werde mit dem grössten Vergnügen am 11. April ~~XXi~~ um 8.30 bei Ihnen speisen.

Mit ~~den besten~~ vielen Grüssen von uns beiden und mit dem besten Dank für ~~die~~ Ihre gütige Einladung verbleibe ich Ihr Ihnen ganz ergebener

A Staël Holstein.

Peking d. 16 Juni 1930

Sehr verehrter lieber Herr Baron

Eben bekomme ich einen Brief von Professor J. G. Andersson, Stockholm, der mich bittet Sie zu fragen, was er, nach Ihren Wünschen und Instruktionen, mit Ihrer Sammlung und mit den Kataloge machen soll. Ich hatte ihm nämlich geschrieben, dass ich auf Ihre Sammlung nicht länger reflektieren kann, da wir, seit Ende Oktober 1929, zu einem Verständnis nicht gekommen sind. Inzwischen haben wir so viel gesammelt, dass wir für unsere Bedürfnisse genug haben.

Vielleicht wäre es am besten dass Sie sich an Herrn Professor J. G. Andersson direkt wenden wollten, – sonst bin ich natürlich jeder Zeit bereit mit ihm die Verhandlungen zu führen. Professor Anderssons Adresse ist: Östasiatiska Samlingarna, Sveavägen 65. Stockholm.

Mit herzlichem Gruss
Ihr ganz ergebener

Sven Hedin

GRAND HOTEL DES WAGONS-LITS.
PEKING.

Hochgeehrter Herr Baron

Herzlichsten Dank für Ihre liebenswürdigen Zeilen.

Leider bin ich heute jeden Augenblick in Anspruch genommen, aber wenn es mir nur irgendwie möglich ist komme ich auf ein Sprung Nachmittags etwa nach 4 Uhr zu Ihnen zu kommen. Wenn irgend einen preliminären Entschluss gefasst wird könnte ja die definitive Entscheidung nach meinem Rückkehr erfolgen.

Ihr treu und dankbar ergebener

Sven Hedin

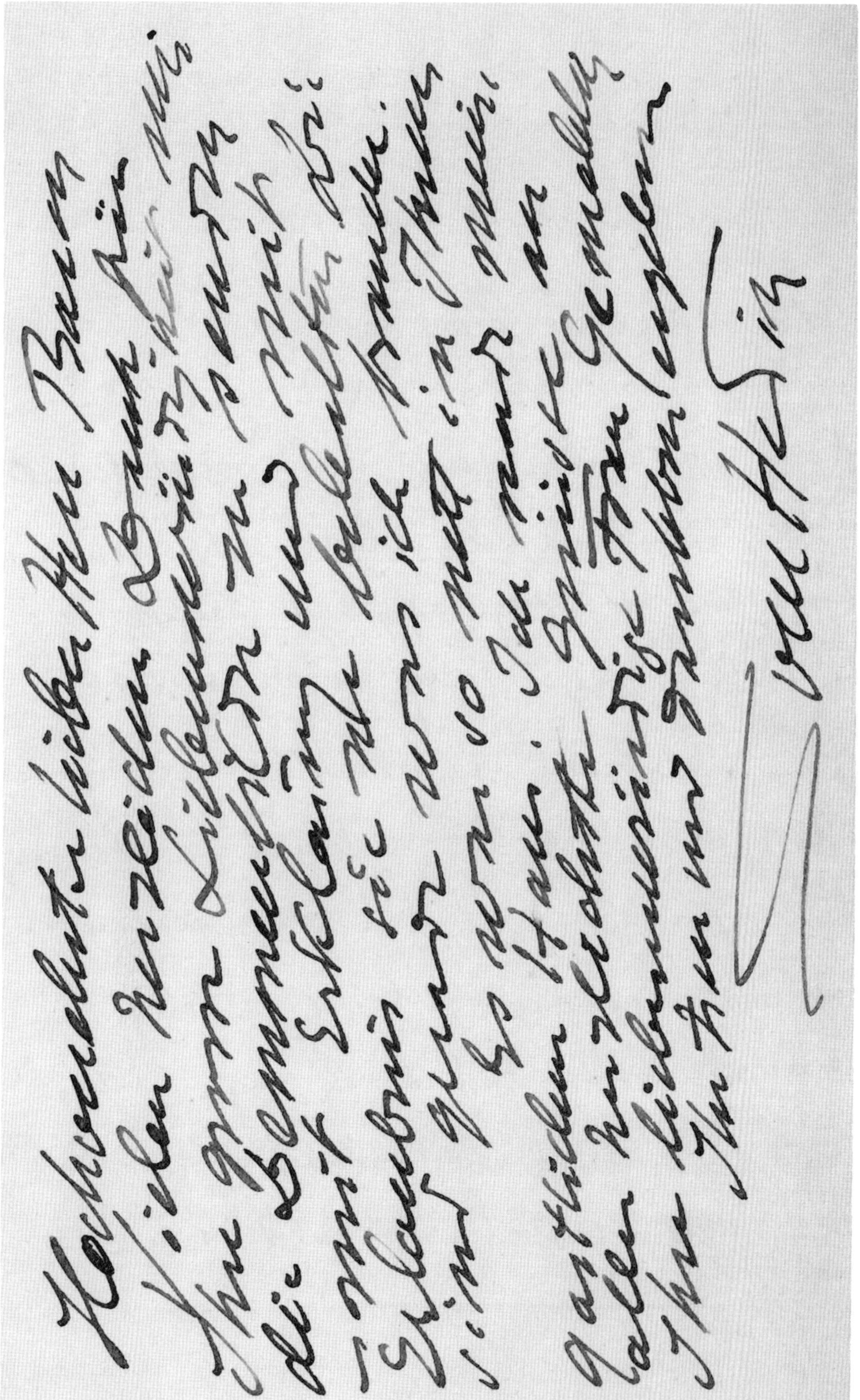

Hochverehrter lieber Herr Baron
Vielen herzlichen Dank für
Ihre grosse Liebenswürdigkeit mir
die [illegible] zu senden
somit Erklärung und mit
Erlaubnis sie zu behalten. Dies
sind gerade was ich brauche.
Es war so nett in Ihrem
gastlichen Haus. Ich sende meine
allen herzlichsten Grüsse an
Ihre liebenswürdige Frau Gemahlin
Ihr treu und dankbar ergebener
Sven Hedin

THE CLEVELAND MUSEUM OF ART
CLEVELAND, OHIO, U.S.A.
STATION E

Frederic Allen Whiting, Director   November 12, 1929   Cable Address: "Musart Cleveland"

My dear Baron de Staël,

First of all, Frances and I wish to join in congratulating you and Madame de Staël. If you will permit me to say so, we think you have both shown very good taste.

About six months ago you wrote asking me to publish a newspaper article for you. I did not answer immediately because, being wholly inexperienced with regard to my task, I thought it would be all over in two weeks, after which I could write you.

~~Please address all communications to *The Cleveland Museum of Art* and not to individuals.~~

TO SHEET 2 DATE

But such, as you know, was not the case.

As soon as I received your letter, I found a collaborator who, I think, is very good at newspaper work, but who, unfortunately, insists on withholding his name. We tried to gather facts from Woods, Clark, and various other sources; and after having spent about three weeks at it, were forced, by the consensus of opinion, not to use them. You see, we were afraid that ~~that~~ the long names of your learned publications would be more apt to frighten than to attract in a newspaper article. Consequently, we finally turned out the unforgivably popular article which I am enclosing in duplicate. I wonder if you have

TO SHEET 3 DATE

seen it already?

When it was finished, I sent it to a man of power on the New York Times, only to have it returned for a signature. As my collaborator would not sign, Professor Woods seemed to think that I was the one to do it. I then mailed it in to the proper department, enclosing plenty of stamps for samples, and soon afterwards departed for Canada.

Returning thence in about a month, and having heard nothing from the Times, what was my surprise to be congratulated by friends on my article. None of them had it, however, nor could any tell me its date. This

TO SHEET 4 DATE

necessitated another delay, but I finally managed to get the information. I then went to my newspaper agency and asked for copies, but they had none. I went in to Boston to the company which acts as distributing agent for all New England, but they had none. At last I wrote again to the Times and this time was rewarded with several copies of the paper. But my difficulties were not over, for they came about four days before I left Cambridge for Cleveland, and I think you will understand when I say that this is the first chance I have had to write you. Please forgive my great delay.

TO SHEET 5 DATE

In the meantime, however, I have received a copy of an Estonian paper that published the article. I am enclosing it for you. I am sending two copies of the Times to Baron Walter Stackelberg also. I do hope it is not too late. I have thoroughly enjoyed "mixing into politics", but I fear that I may have delayed too long.

If there is anything more that I can do, please do not hesitate to call on me, in spite of the fact that I am no longer a member of the Harvard-Yenching Institute.

Please give my kindest regards to Madame de Staël.

Yours very sincerely,

Howard Coonley Hollis

P.S. Please excuse the popular style of the article. Even Prof. Woods agreed that it was best.

ESTONIAN HONORS STILL DUE

Baron von Stael-Holstein's Work Is Cited as Worthy Of His Country's Notice

To the Editor of The New York Times:

Estonia has at last honored Count Keyserling—after the world had acclaimed him as a philosopher and America had fêted him, waiting for the pearls to drop from his mouth in the New York soirées of the Four Hundred. But there is another Estonian scholar, learned and modest and seeking nothing, still outcast, still unrecognized.

Baron Alexander von Stael-Holstein has been an exile in Peking since the end of the war, when his estates were confiscated by the newcomers. Foreign scholars were familiar with his writings on the Buddhist religion and with his comparative texts in Sanskrit, Mongol, Tibetan, Chinese and Japanese. His rambling native house in Peking was known as headquarters for learned Tibetan lamas and distinguished Germans and Russians who were working on their dictionaries and their curious lore.

A House of Wonders.

The caller on Baron von Stael-Holstein had to stumble over the rubbish left by a conflagration, past the gatehouse in ruins and up to the scorched front door. But once there, he was ushered into an apartment which had no like in the West or in the East for strangeness. The gods of Tibetan and Chinese Buddhism were set about the room in orderly profusion. Hells and heavens and purgatories were represented, and the seldom-seen deities of smallpox or of the thunderstorm were there. They had been rifled from some mountain lamasery on the pilgrim road to Lhasa. Cocktails immediately appeared, but as one drank there was a sense that other guests were quietly waiting—or pursuing far different avocations in the next room.

Nothing perturbed the kindly host and nothing was allowed to disturb the welcome of the casual foreigner. Rarely a curtain was lifted, and there, behind it, one saw that there were other guests indeed—red-robed or saffron-robed or clad in black—telling beads, drinking interminable tea and deciphering interminable texts. In short, the tumbledown house in Peking had become by degrees a tiny institute of comparative religions, where ancient wisdom unfolded itself and where the visiting university professor could be sure of catching the correct intonation for the Mongol camel herd's prayer against the dread blizzards, for the herd was there in person and so, too, often was the university professor.

Greasy books in ancient and vile tattered silks were produced from voluminous robes and the professor-Baron might hold the prized volume in his hand for a moment and even copy out a blind text which had puzzled him. Spectacled visitors from Japan came to the room behind the curtain for their studies of Buddhism that is unfamiliar even to them. Russian-trained Buriats from the forests of Siberia who were, in their off moments, members of the great and learned Russian Academy, discussed ethnology with the doctor of the Siamese Legation.

Among them all our host presided, and with them he discoursed on diverse topics in tongues even more diverse. We knew him to be an exile; we knew that his funds were cut off and that the National University of China, which listed his name on its faculty, never paid salaries; but the host never complained nor did he permit sympathy. In fact, he strove to keep up the illusion that he was once more lord of some tens of thousands of ancestral acres and you his honored guest, for the moment condescending to show an interest in his hobby.

He Lectured at Harvard.

For years this strange house and these ancient strange gods and their worshipers have struggled along in Peking, a nucleus of unconsidered learning kept alive by the unflagging scholarship of the Baron. Suddenly, by a turn of the wheel, it was found that Harvard needed courses in the fringes of esoteric Buddhism and in the language in which those fringes are most blindly set down. The Baron accepted the post, came for a season away from his old lamas and his Peking priests, taught in Cambridge and consorted with some of his colleagues who had been familiar with his publications but had never seen his face. It was taken for granted that he could deliver his lectures in English, and he did most pleasantly. He could as well have given them in Russian, French, German, Chinese, Tibetan or his native Estonian.

The year at Harvard is over and the Baron has sailed for the rambling old house in Peking and the delightful companionship of his ragged lama priests. That episode is closed, though in the future an occasional American inquirer may dig him up to sip tea in the great room peopled with gods and to hear the Sanskrit texts intoned from behind the curtain.

What should Estonia, the youngest republic, have to do with outworn lore of distant Asia? Why should she notice the placid scholar who was the first to compile, among other things, a vocabulary of the unknown language of Khotan and point out that it was the very tongue of King Kaniska? That he reconstructed ancient lost Sanskrit texts on a basis of his finds in modern Tibetan and Chinese can mean little to Estonia. True, he was heir to thousands of acres of Estonian soil, but he seems content enough with an exile's life.

Baron von Stael-Holstein adds no single cent to the financial budget of Estonia, but to the budget of Estonian credit in the world market of ideas and in the great system of international values of true worth—what an asset! Even his compatriot, Count Keyserling, does not hold so high a rank among scholars.

HOWARD HOLLIS.

Cambridge, Mass., Aug. 12, 1929.

1/2

ESTONIAN HONORS STILL DUE

Baron von Stael-Holstein's Work Is Cited as Worthy Of His Country's Notice

To the Editor of The New York Times:

Estonia has at last honored Count Keyserling—after the world had acclaimed him as a philosopher and America had fêted him, waiting for the pearls to drop from his mouth in the New York soirées of the Four Hundred. But there is another Estonian scholar, learned and modest and seeking nothing, still outcast, still unrecognized.

Baron Alexander von Stael-Holstein has been an exile in Peking since the end of the war, when his estates were confiscated by the newcomers. Foreign scholars were familiar with his writings on the Buddhist religion and with his comparative texts in Sanskrit, Mongol, Tibetan, Chinese and Japanese. His rambling native house in Peking was known as headquarters for learned Tibetan lamas and distinguished Germans and Russians who were working on their dictionaries and their curious lore.

A House of Wonders.

The caller on Baron von Stael-Holstein had to stumble over the rubbish left by a conflagration, past the gatehouse in ruins and up to the scorched front door. But once there, he was ushered into an apartment which had no like in the West or in the East for strangeness. The gods of Tibetan and Chinese Buddhism were set about the room in orderly profusion. Hells and heavens and purgatories were represented, and the seldom-seen deities of smallpox or of the thunderstorm were there. They had been rifled from some mountain lamasery on the pilgrim road to Lhasa. Cocktails immediately appeared, but as one drank there was a sense that other guests were quietly waiting—or pursuing far different avocations in the next room.

Nothing perturbed the kindly host and nothing was allowed to disturb the welcome of the casual foreigner. Rarely a curtain was lifted, and there, behind it, one saw that there were other guests indeed—red-robed or saffron-robed or clad in black—telling beads, drinking interminable tea and deciphering interminable texts. In short, the tumbledown house in Peking had become by degrees a tiny institute of comparative religions, where ancient wisdom unfolded itself and where the visiting university professor could be sure of catching the correct intonation for the Mongol camel herd's prayer against the dread blizzards, for the herd was there in person and so, too, often was the university professor.

Greasy books in ancient and vile tattered silks were produced from voluminous robes and the professor-

Chinese can mean little to Estonia. True, he was heir to thousands of acres of Estonian soil, but he seems content enough with an exile's life.

Baron von Stael-Holstein adds no single cent to the financial budget of Estonia, but to the budget of Estonian credit in the world market of ideas and in the great system of international values of true worth—what an asset! Even his compatriot, Count Keyserling, does not hold so high a rank among scholars.

HOWARD HOLLIS.

Cambridge, Mass., Aug. 12, 1929.

(局部圖1)

against the dread blizzards, for the herd was there in person and so, too, often was the university professor.

Greasy books in ancient and vile tattered silks were produced from voluminous robes and the professor-Baron might hold the prized volume in his hand for a moment and even copy out a blind text which had puzzled him. Spectacled visitors from Japan came to the room behind the curtain for their studies of Buddhism that is unfamiliar even to them. Russian-trained Buriats from the forests of Siberia who were, in their off moments, members of the great and learned Russian Academy, discussed ethnology with the doctor of the Siamese Legation.

Among them all our host presided, and with them he discoursed on diverse topics in tongues even more diverse. We knew him to be an exile: we knew that his funds were cut off and that the National University of China, which listed his name on its faculty, never paid salaries; but the host never complained nor did he permit sympathy. In fact, he strove to keep up the illusion that he was once more lord of some tens of thousands of ancestral acres and you his honored guest, for the moment condescending to show an interest in his hobby.

He Lectured at Harvard.

For years this strange house and these ancient strange gods and their worshipers have struggled along in Peking, a nucleus of unconsidered learning kept alive by the unflagging scholarship of the Baron. Suddenly, by a turn of the wheel, it was found that Harvard needed courses in the fringes of esoteric Buddhism and in the language in which those fringes are most blindly set down. The Baron accepted the post, came for a season away from his old lamas and his Peking priests, taught in Cambridge and consorted with some of his colleagues who had been familiar with his publications but had never seen his face. It was taken for granted that he could deliver his lectures in English, and he did most pleasantly. He could as well have given them in Russian, French, German, Chinese, Tibetan or his native Estonian.

The year at Harvard is over and the Baron has sailed for the rambling old house in Peking and the delightful companionship of his ragged lama priests. That episode is closed, though in the future an occasional American inquirer may dig him up to sip tea in the great room peopled with gods and to hear the Sanskrit texts intoned from behind the curtain.

What should Estonia, the youngest republic, have to do with outworn lore of distant Asia? Why should she notice the placid scholar who was the first to compile, among other things, a vocabulary of the unknown language of Khotan and point out that it was the very tongue of King Kaniska? That he reconstructed ancient lost Sanskrit texts on a basis of his finds in modern Tibetan and

(局部圖2)

THE CLEVELAND MUSEUM OF ART
CLEVELAND, OHIO, U.S.A.
STATION E

Frederic Allen Whiting, Director February 15, 1930 *Cable Address: "Musart Cleveland"*

Baron A. von Stael-Holstein
Peking Club
Peking, China

Dear Baron von Stael:

I am enclosing a copy of a letter to the Rector of the University of Dorpat which Baron Stackelberg asked me to write. I hope you do not mind my taking this liberty without first asking your permission. Since you told me that Baron Stackelberg was your friend and counsel, I have taken it for granted that any order from him would be agreeable to you. I have suggested to him that letters from other Americans might be useful and if he agrees with me, I intend to ask Woods, Clark, Blake and Langdon Warner each to write one, unless I hear from you that you do not want me to. I think all of them would be only to glad to help, and as Blake is the only one who might not know of the original newspaper article, I do not think it could do any harm to ask them.

Please extend my kindest regards to Madame von Stael.

Yours very sincerely,

Howard Coonley Hollis

Please address all communications to *The Cleveland Museum of Art* and not to individuals

COPY

February 15, 1930

The Rector of the University of Dorpat
Dorpat (Tartu)
Estonia

Dear Sir:

As I have recently learned that Baron Alexander von Stael-Holstein was a former student in your university, I am taking the liberty of writing to you, as the representative of the scholarship of your country, concerning his relation to the Estonian Government. Can it be true, as I have been informed, that he is to receive only an insignificant percentage of the total value of the estate which has been taken from him? Having known Baron von Stael-Holstein for several years not only personally, but also as a profound scholar of Sanscrit, Mongol, Tibetan, and other Far Eastern languages, it is a great shock to me to realize that his native country is less interested in supporting his investigations than are certain scholarly institutions in America. Last year it was my good fortune to be at Harvard University at the same time that Baron von Stael-Holstein was there as Professor of Sanscrit and Buddhist Mythology, and I found that professors and other prominent men were astonished to learn that his work in Peking might have to stop because of lack of funds. May we who work in the Oriental field not be permitted to hope that such scholarship will be supported? It would be a pity if literature and art should suffer because of what seems, at least to an outsider, to be the indifference of Estonia.

In case you care to have information which I am unable to give, his legal adviser is Counsel Walter Baron Stackelberg in your town.

Hoping to hear from you soon that you are willing to use your influence in behalf of Baron von Stael-Holstein, I beg to remain,

Yours very sincerely,

Howard Coonley Hollis
Curator of Oriental Art

HCH:MHB

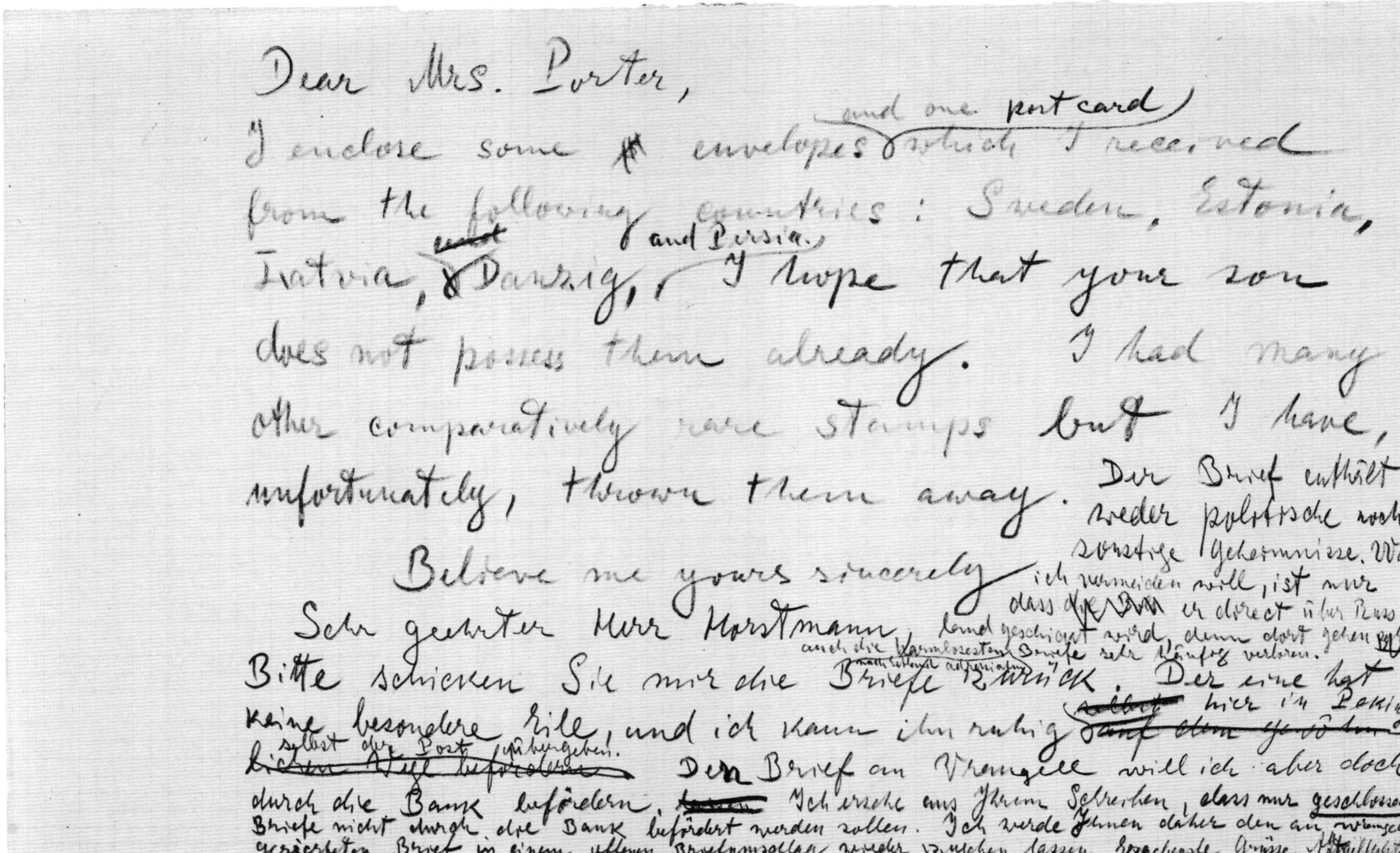

Dear Mrs. Porter,

I enclose some envelopes and one post card which I received from the following countries: Sweden, Estonia, Latvia, Danzig, and Persia. I hope that your son does not possess them already. I had many other comparatively rare stamps but I have, unfortunately, thrown them away.

Believe me yours sincerely

Sehr geehrter Herr Horstmann,

Bitte schicken Sie mir die Briefe zurück. Der eine hat keine besondere Eile, und ich kann ihn ruhig hier in Peking selbst der Post übergeben. Den Brief an Wrangell will ich aber doch durch die Bank befördern. Der Brief enthält weder politische noch sonstige Geheimnisse. Was ich vermeiden will, ist nur dass er direct über Russland geschickt wird, denn dort gehen auch die harmlosesten Briefe sehr häufig verloren. [illegible] Ich ersehe aus Ihrem Schreiben, dass nur geschlossene Briefe nicht durch die Bank befördert werden sollen. Ich werde Ihnen daher den an Wrangell gerichteten Brief in einem offenen Briefumschlag wieder zugehen lassen. Ergebenste Grüsse A. Staël-Holstein.

Peking, March 24th 1932.

My dear Professor ~~Hsü~~ Hsü,

Professor Weller knows much more about Central Asian archaeology, than I do, and I asked him for his opinion about Mr. Li's treatise. ~~He~~ [Professor Weller] expressed ~~it~~ it in German, and ~~I send you~~ [I enclose ~~herewith~~] his ~~the~~ original notes trusting that you will be able to read them yourself, or to have them translated by somebody else. ~~I also Herewith Mr. Li's treatise~~

~~I also return with many Herewith Mr. Li's manuscript I beg to return to~~

~~Believe me yours sincerely~~

~~Please May I ask you to return Mr. Li's treatise which I send you along or together with this~~

I also enclose Mr. Li's treatise.

Believe me yours sincerely

AStaelHolstein.

8 Tuan Ku Hou Hutung,
Nan Chi Tze, City.
March 29, 1919.

My dear Baron Staël-Holstein:

The University Library has the Journal of the Royal Asiatic Society and also the Journal Asiatique. Please let me know, either by writing or by telephone (E. 2429), ~~when~~ on what day you wish to visit the Library. I shall be glad to act as your guide.

With kind regards,

Yours truly,

Hu Shih

Pardon this hastily written letter.
S. H.

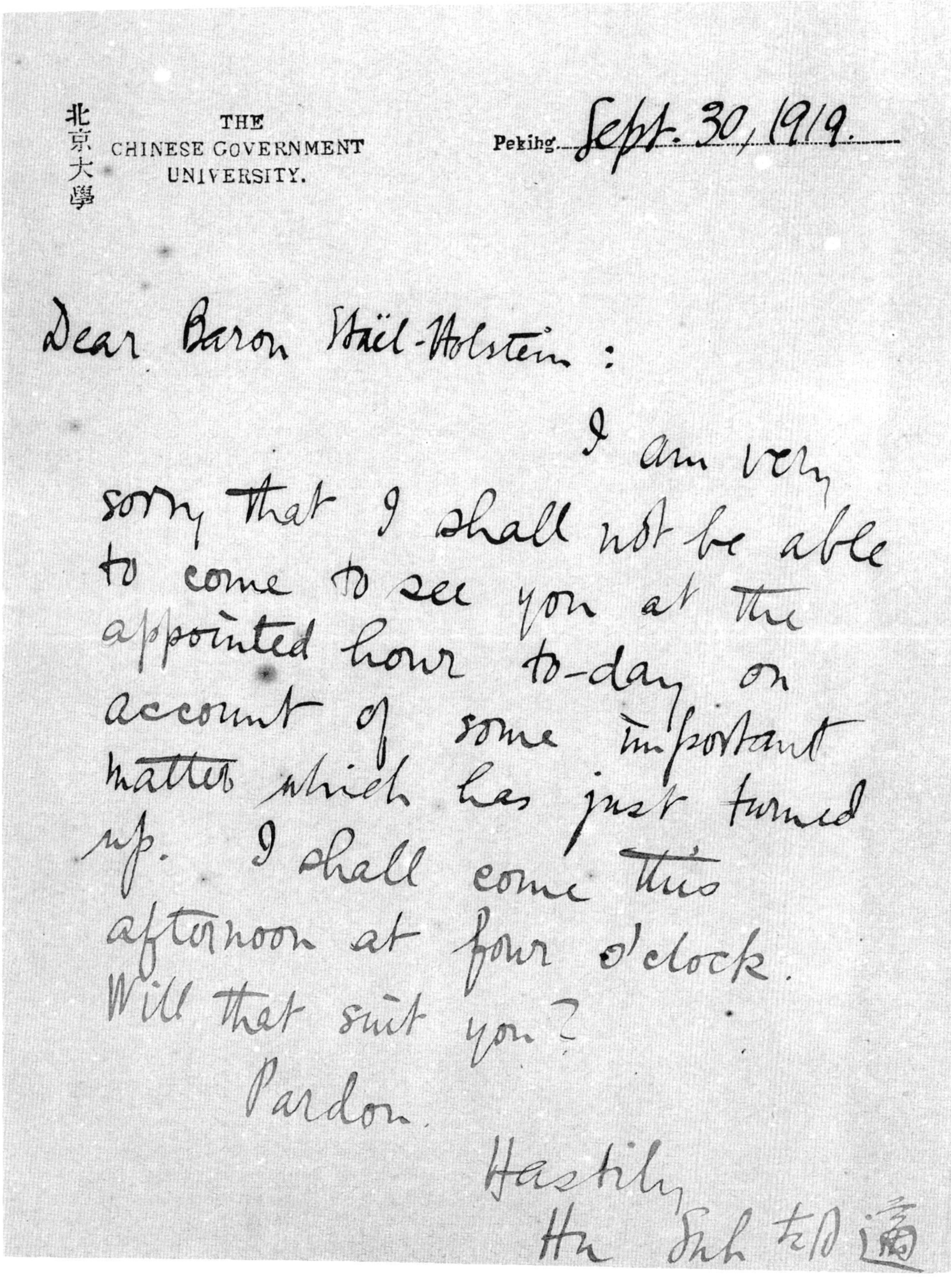

北京大學 THE CHINESE GOVERNMENT UNIVERSITY.

Peking. Sept. 30, 1919.

Dear Baron Staël-Holstein:

I am very sorry that I shall not be able to come to see you at the appointed hour to-day on account of some important matter which has just turned up. I shall come this afternoon at four o'clock. Will that suit you?

Pardon.

Hastily
Hu Shih 胡適

c/o Commercial Press
Hangchow.
September 20, 1923.

My dear Baron:

You will surely be surprised on hearing from me after so unpardonably long a period of silence.

By mere chance, I learned of the death of our friend and your assistant Mr. Huang Chien. I was terribly grieved indeed. For I understand well how he had improved his knowledge of both Sanskrit & Tibetan, and how he had become an invaluable assistant to you in your work. His death was indeed a great loss to society and especially to you at the present moment. And I immediately thought of your lecture course on the history of religions in ancient ~~China~~ India. Whom have you secured for interpretor in this course of lectures?

I then thought of my friend Mr. Kiang Shao-yuan 江紹原 who was once a student in Mr. Lessing's class in Sanskrit and who has recently returned from the University of Chicago where he had specialized in comparative religions. He is now a lecturer in the National University, teaching the History of Religion and a new course of his own device to be known as "Religion & Philosophy: a study of their historical relationship." He will be admirably suited to interpret for your lecture-course. So I took the liberty to write to him asking him to take up this truly pleasurable ~~duty~~ work ~~for~~ with you.

He came to visit me in the hills this noon. He told me

that he would be very glad to take up this work with you. When he was in Peking last month, he called at your house to pay his respects, but you were away that day. He will call again when he returns to Peking this week. I am sure you will find in him a scholar and gentleman whom you will like to work with.

I have not completely recovered my health, but I hope to return to Peking soon after the Moon Festival.

Hoping you have been well since I saw you last, and have received from the Commercial Press all the proof sheets which they promised me to send you,

Yours
as ever,
Hu Shih.

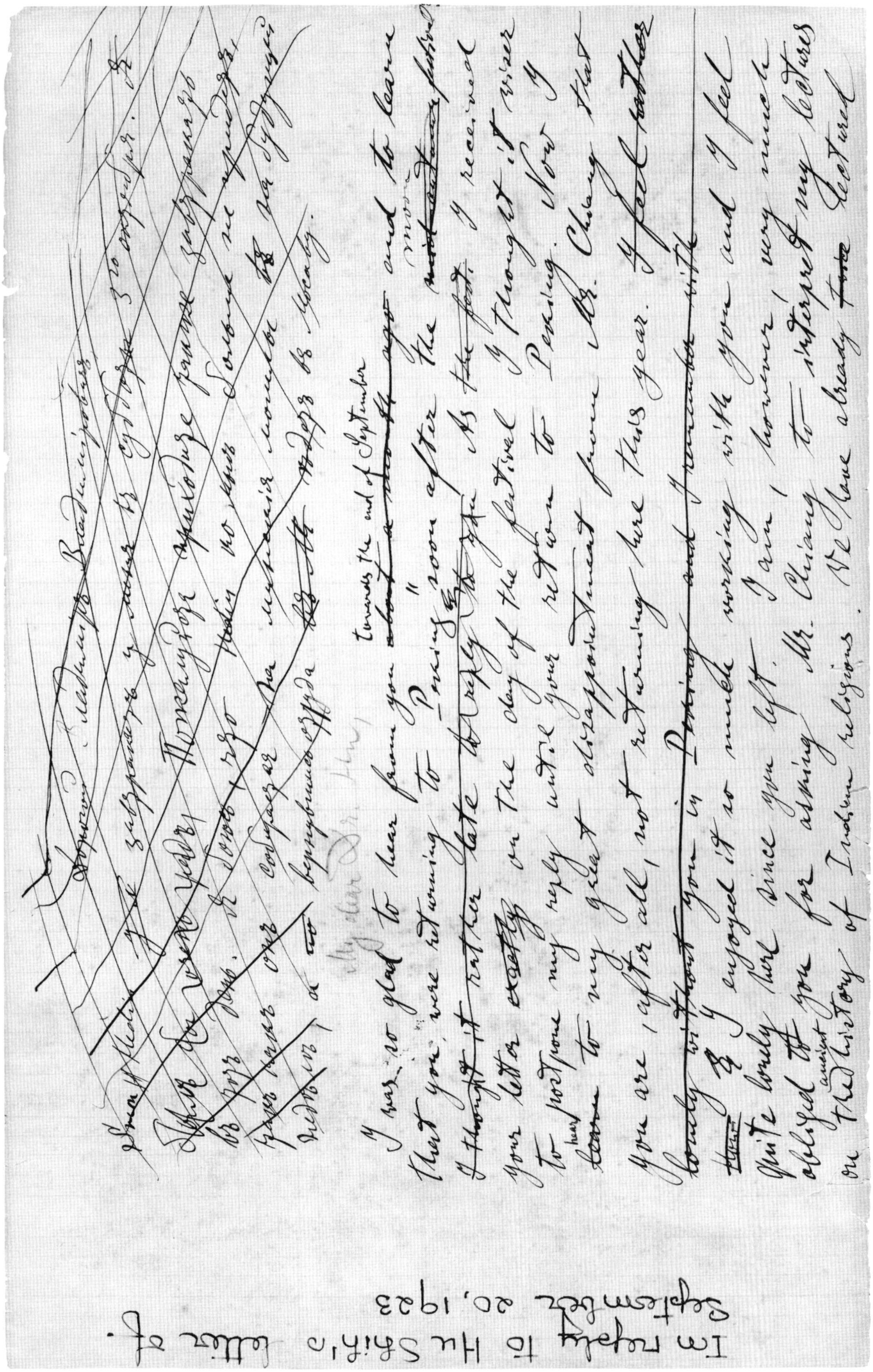

My dear Dr. Hu,

I was so glad to hear from you towards the end of September and to learn that you were returning to Peking "soon after the moon festival". As I received your letter on the day of the festival I thought it wiser to postpone my reply until your return to Peking. Now I hear to my great disappointment from Mr. Chiang that you are, after all, not returning here this year. I enjoyed it so much working with you and I feel quite lonely here since you left. I am, however, very much obliged to you for asking Mr. Chiang to interpret my lectures on the ancient history of Indian religions. We have already lectured

In reply to Hu Shih's letter of September 20, 1923

~~twice~~ together four or five times and he seems to understand all I say and to translate it very well. He has a most attractive personality and I enjoy meeting him very much. We are also studying the 攝大乘論 together and we dream of translating that work which exists in Chinese and Tibetan only into English, a very difficult but fascinating task.

~~Many~~ Already before ~~the~~ the receipt of your letter I knew that you had been ~~urging the Commercial Press to~~ speaking about ~~mentioning~~ my impatience to the Commercial Press because ~~I receive~~ they sent me 45 pages to correct instead of the usual twenty. That is a great improvement and I hope that the edition will appear before ~~the~~ next spring.

Mr. Huang's death ~~has indeed been~~ is indeed a great blow to me. His ~~tired~~ heart and soul were in his Sanskrit and Tibetan work. He ~~had~~ was not only a very successful pupil but had become a real friend. ~~to me.~~ I enclose a copy of my article which appeared in the Kuo-hsio-chi-k'an lately and also my lecture on Hsüan-tsang which you interpreted so splendidly about three years ago when I first appeared at the National University. ~~Hope~~ I hope that you will soon return to Peking for good and that we shall again collaborate in some way or other.

~~In looking forward to so~~ Looking forward to seeing you again, my dear Dr. Hu, I remain yours most sincerely A. Staël Holstein.

My dear Dr. Hu,

~~I have May I introduce~~ I have suggested to Messrs. Chuang and Ch'en, the two students, who want to take up Sanskrit, or rather Indology, as a special ~~st~~ subject, ~~that~~ that they should go and see you. ~~in order to I think they will call at your house ... or one of these days~~. Please excuse me for doing so without ~~any for~~ having ~~first~~ obtained your consent first ~~and give the~~ and receive the young men ~~some advice~~ when they call at your house. I understand that they have to attend classes for about twenty hours a week. That is, I think, a good deal too much for students who want to get a fair knowledge of Sanskrit in three or four years. ~~It takes ... ten years to teach~~ the European scholar Latin — and Latin is much ~~more akin~~ nearer related to German ~~or~~ or English, than Sanskrit is to Chinese. If the students want to be fairly proficient in Sanskrit at the end of three or four years they ought to ~~d~~ devote ~~their~~ the whole, or very nearly ~~their~~ the whole, of their energy to the study of the the language and ~~k~~ of kindred subjects. I venture to suggest, therefore, that these two students should not be <u>forced</u> to attend any classes except mine (6 hours Sanskrit (in consideration of the fact that the Sanskrit ~~class~~ lessons want ~~very much~~ a great deal of preparation at home) and 2 hours history of Indian religious) during next term. If you cannot grant the students' request straightaway yourself, please ~~instruct~~ tell ~~as to the authorities~~ them what ~~to~~ they should do. ~~[illegible]~~ I have mentioned the matter to Mr. Ku. Shall they call on him also?

I do <u>not</u>, of course, suggest that the students should be ~~[illegible]~~ <u>forbidden</u> to attend classes like the Ch'eng-wei-shih-lun.

~~[illegible]~~ Believe me yours sincerely

A. Staël-Holstein.

June 7th 1924.

My dear Dr. Hu

I understand that some of the Soviet representatives will take part ~~at~~ in today's ~~tomorrow's~~ celebration at the National University and that they are very bitter against those Russians of the old régime who do not ~~prop~~ intend registering at the Soviet legation. Professor Ivanoff, Chinese Secretary of the Soviet legation, and many other Russians know that I have been born (Testama near Pernau 1.1.77) and educated in Esthonia, which does not belong to the U.S.S.R, and that the latter cannot therefore regard me as a Russian. ~~On account of the fact that the independ absolute Republic of Esthonia (being quite independent) which has nothing to do with the U.S.S.R is not represented at Peking I have had to use~~

I have, ~~often been telling~~ ~~repeatedly told you~~ ~~told~~ ~~and many other~~ ~~Chinese friends~~ as you know, hardly ever missed an opportunity of telling my Peking friends ~~again and~~, during the last few years that, ~~I never considered myself th~~ although a subject of the Tsar, who was also Duke of Esthonia, I never was a Russian. I hope, therefore, that any measures planned against the Russian "white guards" will not apply to me.

~~I think the case is quite clear~~

~~I think I ou~~

~~May I also ask to inform Dr. Chiang~~

I hardly think that anyone will seriously question my position which has been affirmed so many times, but I think I ought to inform you ~~of the facts they which~~ of the details ~~of~~ which I may ~~might~~ have stated above in order to enable you to reply to ~~possible~~ casual ~~g~~ enquiries.

Believe me yours sincerely A. Staël Holstein.

國立北京大學
THE NATIONAL UNIVERSITY OF PEKING
PEKING CHINA
Department of Indian and Central Asian Philology.
Baron A. von Staël-Holstein, Ph. D. Director of Researches.

My dear Dr. Hu,

~~Many thanks~~ I thank you once more for ~~sending~~ sent me the certificate. I shall try ~~and~~ to obtain the British visum

~~This evening I am leaving for Dairen after having despatched~~

At the end of last term ~~there were~~ no examinations in the history of Indian religions, ~~took place~~ and ~~it is just possible tha~~ I do not know whether any will take place this autumn. No students have so far asked me for the list of questions, but some of them may ~~[illegible]~~ want ~~them~~ it during my absence. ~~As you were so kind as to~~ In view of the facts that you know the subject so well and that you have ~~[illegible]~~ been the ~~de facto~~ real examiner last year, I venture to ~~[illegible] hope~~

send you the questions which I have prepared.

Last year I gave ~~both~~ the students three questions each and asked them to prepare the answers at home. ~~[illegible]~~ I think it is the best plan: to ask the students to reply in <u>Chinese</u>, as experience shows that the English replies are often simply copied out of my book.

Once more many thanks for sending me the certificate! I shall ~~endeavour~~ try and ~~obtain~~ get the British attestation myself. I am leaving today for Dairen. ~~alone~~ later on I intend to go to Shanghai, in order to see the preface of the Ta-pao-chi-ching through the press. I expect to return on October 1st.

Yours sincerely A. Staël-Holstein.

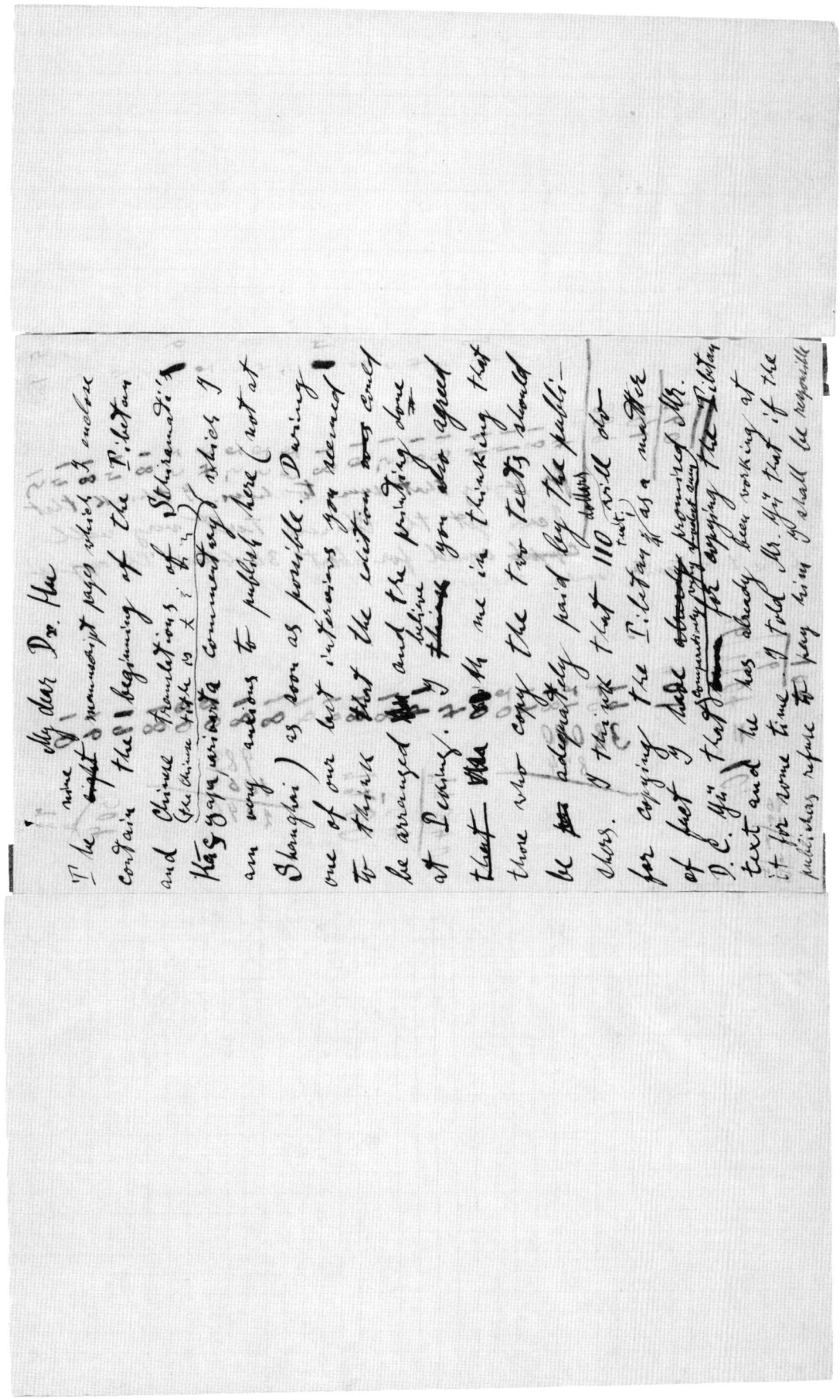

My dear Dr. Hu

The nine ~~eight~~ manuscript pages which I enclose contain the beginning of the Tibetan and Chinese translations of Sthiramati's (the Chinese title is [illegible]) Kāśyapaparivarta commentary which I am very anxious to publish here (not at Shanghai) as soon as possible. During one of our last interviews you seemed to think ~~that~~ that the edition ~~was~~ could be arranged and the printing done at Peking. I believe ~~think~~ you ~~also~~ agreed ~~that~~ with me in thinking that those who copy the two texts should be adequately paid by the publishers. I think that 110 dollars will do for copying the Tibetan text; as a matter of fact I ~~have already~~ promised Mr. D. C. Yü that comparatively very modest sum for copying the Tibetan text and he has already been working at it for some time. I told Mr. Yü that if the publishers refuse to pay him I shall be responsible

15
17
18
17
18
23
34
25
25
23
18
19
15
18
18
17
17
18
4
359
401
760

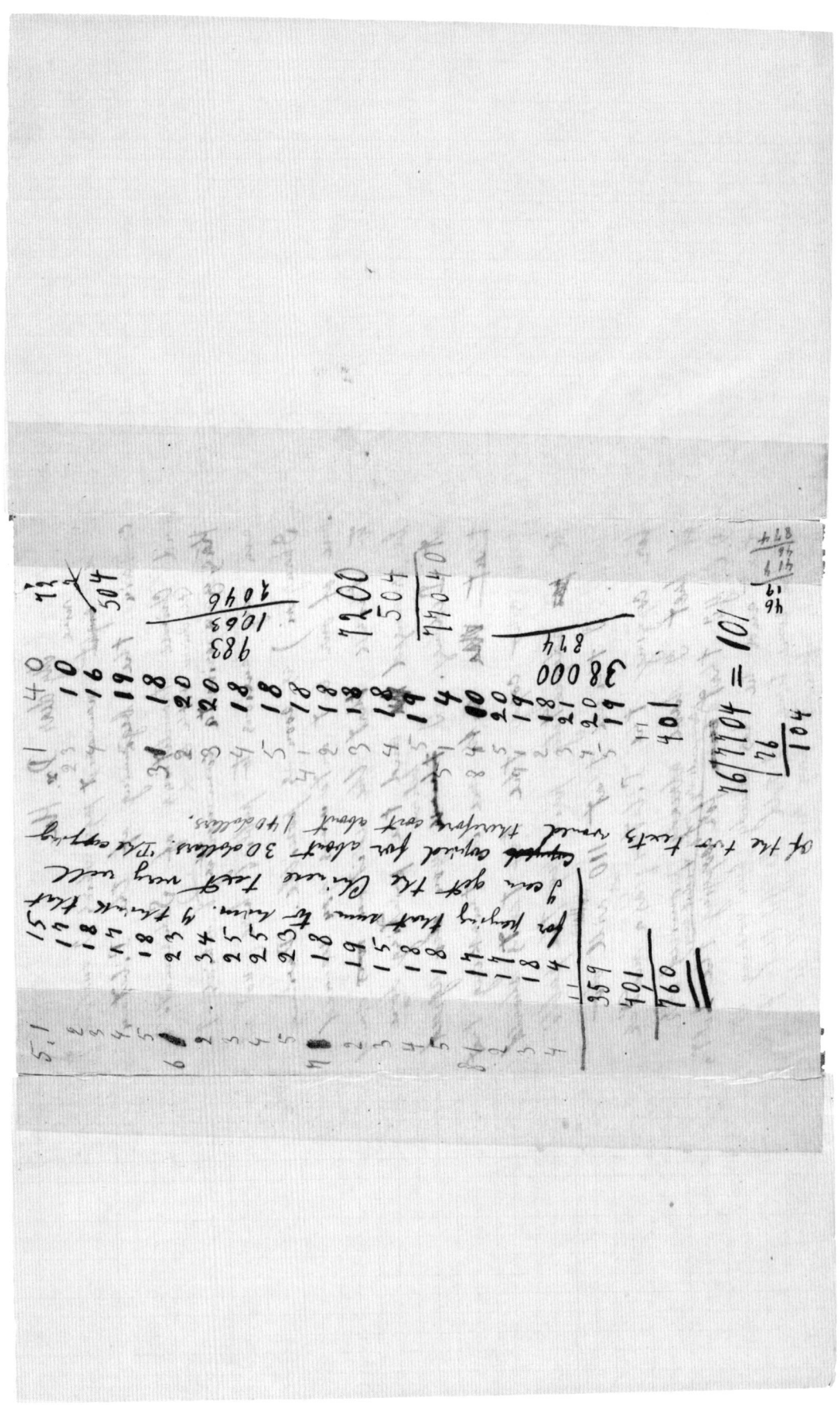

for paying that sum to him. I think that I can get the Chinese text very well ~~copyed~~ copied for about 30 dollars. The copying of the two texts would therefore cost about 140 dollars.

40
10
16
19
18
20
20
18
18
18
18
18
19
4
00
20
19
18
21
20
19
401

38000
874

983
1063
2046

7200
504
7704

504

46
19
414
46
874

16|7704 = 101
76
104

Peking June 19th 1926.

My dear Dr. Hu

I have to thank you for many kindnesses in the past, and I know that you have had to overcome much opposition in maintaining me at the National University. I would therefore not have asked for your assistance in recovering the arrears, if my reasons had not been rather serious ones. Some of those reasons I did not lay before you this afternoon, because I did not like discussing them in the presence of Dr. Porter. The fact is that I am pressed by creditors and that my position will remain uncomfortable, even if Dr. Porter's scheme goes through, unless I get the arrears. Dr. Chiang will perhaps be more amenable to your pleadings if you remind him of the facts:

1) that I had to buy nearly all the books which I wanted for my work, even for my teaching work at the University.

2) that I had to give Mr. Yü some financial assistance.

3) that I must go to Europe for a time, because I have spent ten years in the Far East and have not been out of Peking for more than 50 days all told since 1920 (I could not afford more than a few days' stay at the seaside every year).

4) that I had to pay for the fire, because my landlord had [illegible]

I am awfully sorry to trouble you wit[h] ... but you are my only hope. If you ~~leave China~~ go abroa[d], before ~~this matter~~ the thing is settled, I risk being ~~left~~ left quite stranded here.

Please excuse me and believe me yours sincerely

A. Staël Holstein.

P.S. ~~I know for certain that a group of A group of very influential German professors write to informed me quite unexpectedly that they intended of their intention are trying to obtain a chair for me at a German University and wrote to me quite unexpectedly informed me of their wish~~ Some time ago a quite unexpected letter informed me of the fact, that certain very influential German professors wanted me to fill a chair at a German University. So much is certain; but whether they will ~~succeed~~ ~~to~~ be able to make me a substantial offer in the immediate future ~~[illegible]~~ will not be ~~decided before the month of August~~ known to me before the month of August.

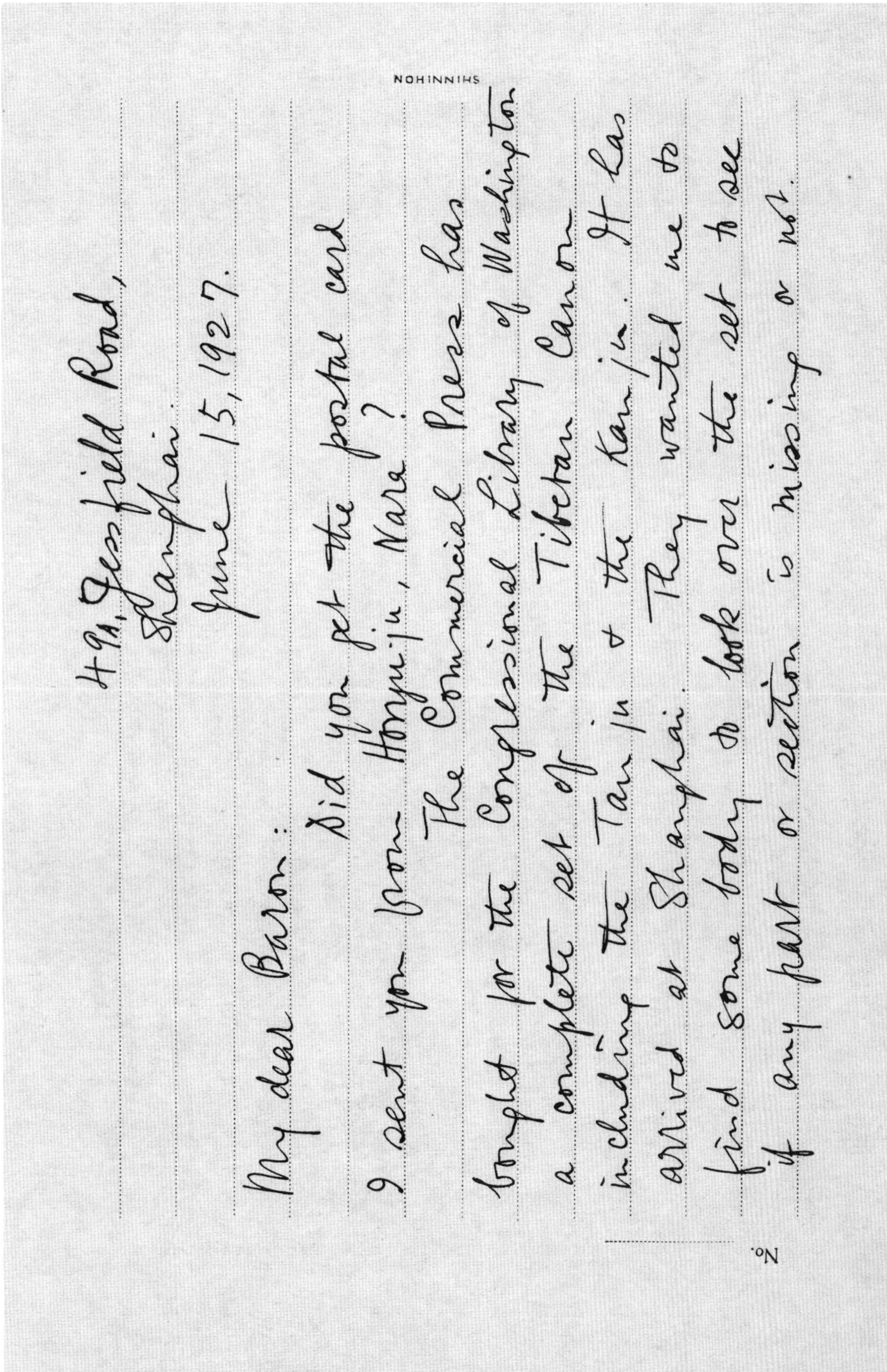

49A, Jessfield Road,
Shanghai.
June 15, 1927.

My dear Baron:

Did you get the postal card I sent you from Horyu-ji, Nara?

The Commercial Press has bought for the Congressional Library of Washington a complete set of the Tibetan Canon including the Tan ju & the Kan ju. It has arrived at Shanghai. They wanted me to find some body to look over the set to see if any part or section is missing or not.

No.

SHINNHON

SHINNHON

I wonder if your assistant Mr. Yü could be persuaded to come down to Shanghai for this purpose? The Commercial Press will pay all his expenses and the expenses of any assistants he may need.

Of course it would be most splendid if you could be in Shanghai some time this summer.

Will you favor me with an answer?

The Commercial Press people wish very much that you could look over this new set of the Tibetan Canon. They also wish to

No.

SHINNIHON

have the ~~K~~ Tanjur volumes (now in your house) shipped to Shanghai.
Their Peking branch will be willing to do the packing and shipping.

I am settling down in Shanghai for the present. I do not take any part in politics, but am trying to do some writing.

With all the best wishes,

Yours truly
Hu Shih.

No.

My dear Dr. Hu,

Many thanks for your ~~card~~ post card from Japan and for your letter from Shanghai. I am very glad to hear that you are well and ~~that you are~~ working hard. I wished you would, after your travels in the 西域, give us a general appreciation ~~of~~ western civilization, and become a ~~"write valuable duplicate" of 之 ...~~ 玄奘 brought up to date. ~~Your~~ articles on those parts ~~subject~~ which I have read during ~~the~~ the last twelve months are wonderfully captivating, ~~splendid~~ but they are too short. We want a good deal more and we are sure that it will be true to sample.

I am extremely ~~very~~ proud to know ~~hear~~ that the Commercial Press want me to ~~come~~ go to Shanghai this summer in order to ~~and~~ inspect their Tibetan books. I am very anxious to go there. But would the Commercial Press be willing to ~~contribute about 300-400 dollars~~ pay my expenses (300 – ~~350~~ 400 dollars Mex.)? Please let me know by wire (Holstein Peking Club Peking). ~~If I receive an affirmative answer I will start at once.~~ I will start for Shanghai as soon as I receive an affirmative answer. The money need not be sent to Peking.

Mr. Ch'en yin ko who has been studying Sanskrit Tibetan and Chinese sūtras at my house for 3 hours practically every week since last October is as keen as I am about retaining the Kanjur and asks me especially to tell you so.

~~[illegible]~~ Looking forward to seeing you again soon at Shanghai I remain yours sincerely A Staël Holstein

&

&

&

My dear Dr. Hu,

~~On June 30th~~ On June 28th I went to the Ching Ch'a T'ing and asked for a passport to Shanghai, because ~~I belong~~ officially I still belong to the ~~[illegible]~~ ~~least favoured~~ nation whose travelling members are specially recommended to the police forces of all countries. I was told by a leading official that the passport would be ready on June 30th. But I waited in vain till Thursday July 14th, when I again met the same official. He told me then that the passport was ready and that it would be sent to me on Saturday (July 16th), but I had to wait until Wednesday July 27th when I finally got the document. On Thursday July 28th I sent you a wire announcing my arrival at Shanghai in about ten days. Please do forgive my not wiring you ~~before~~ earlier, but I could not have given you any definite answer before holding the passport ~~which is~~ in my hands. All Russians tell me that travelling without a passport is impossible.

But now a new difficulty has arisen: the ~~[illegible]~~ Japanese Toho news agency ~~[illegible]~~ reports ~~#~~ on July 23rd ~~that~~ from Shanghai as follows: "The local [Shanghai] authorities being ordered to arrest M. Borodin place under arrest any and all Russians without discrimination." I do not think that a passport issued by the Peking authorities will protect me at Shanghai, but I do not want to ~~give up~~ abandon my trip altogether. Therefore I have decided that I shall ~~[illegible]~~ go to Tsingtao ~~and~~ (leaving here on Tuesday August 2nd) via Tsinanfu and proceed from there by steamer to Shanghai, as soon as I make sure that no arrest awaits me at Shanghai. Perhaps you could inquire at Shanghai and ~~tell~~ advise me ~~[illegible]~~ by wire (my adress: the Strand Hotel Tsingtao), ~~whether~~ what to do. ~~In any case I shall wire you the name of my boat, in case I find it possible to start from Tsingtao to Shanghai.~~

~~A Shanghai passport could might reach Tsingtao in 1-2 days, but an assurance that (typed word) I would be met my boat (name to be wired from Tsingtao) would be met by somebody able to explain my case satisfactorily to the authorities~~

~~If I receive After receiving your telegram~~ I will wire you ~~immediately let you know~~ the name of the boat on which I intend travelling from Tsingtao to Shanghai, ~~as soon as~~ if you suggest that I should go. If you think that I should abandon the trip, you will be able to consult Professor ~~Mr.~~ 陳寅恪 about the Tibetan books. ~~He is due at Shanghai~~ He will leave Tientsin for Shanghai ~~quite independent~~ in any case, on his own account, on August 2nd, and ~~is due~~ his ship (the "Chokei Maru") is due at Shanghai on August 6th. It is true that Mr. 陳 said, that he would be too busy in Shanghai to inspect the Tibetan books, ~~in Shanghai~~ when I told him some time ago, that he should undertake the task. But I am sure that very little persuasion on your part would induce him to change his mind. That arrangement would enable ~~save~~ the Commercial Press ~~to~~ to save a good deal of money. Mr. 陳 is at least as competent ~~to investigate~~ in the matter as I am, and his Shanghai address is: 24F Tongshan (唐山) Road.

I shall be very disappointed, if my Shanghai trip will come to nothing, because I want very much to see you and some other friends in Shanghai, but I must leave the decision in your hands.

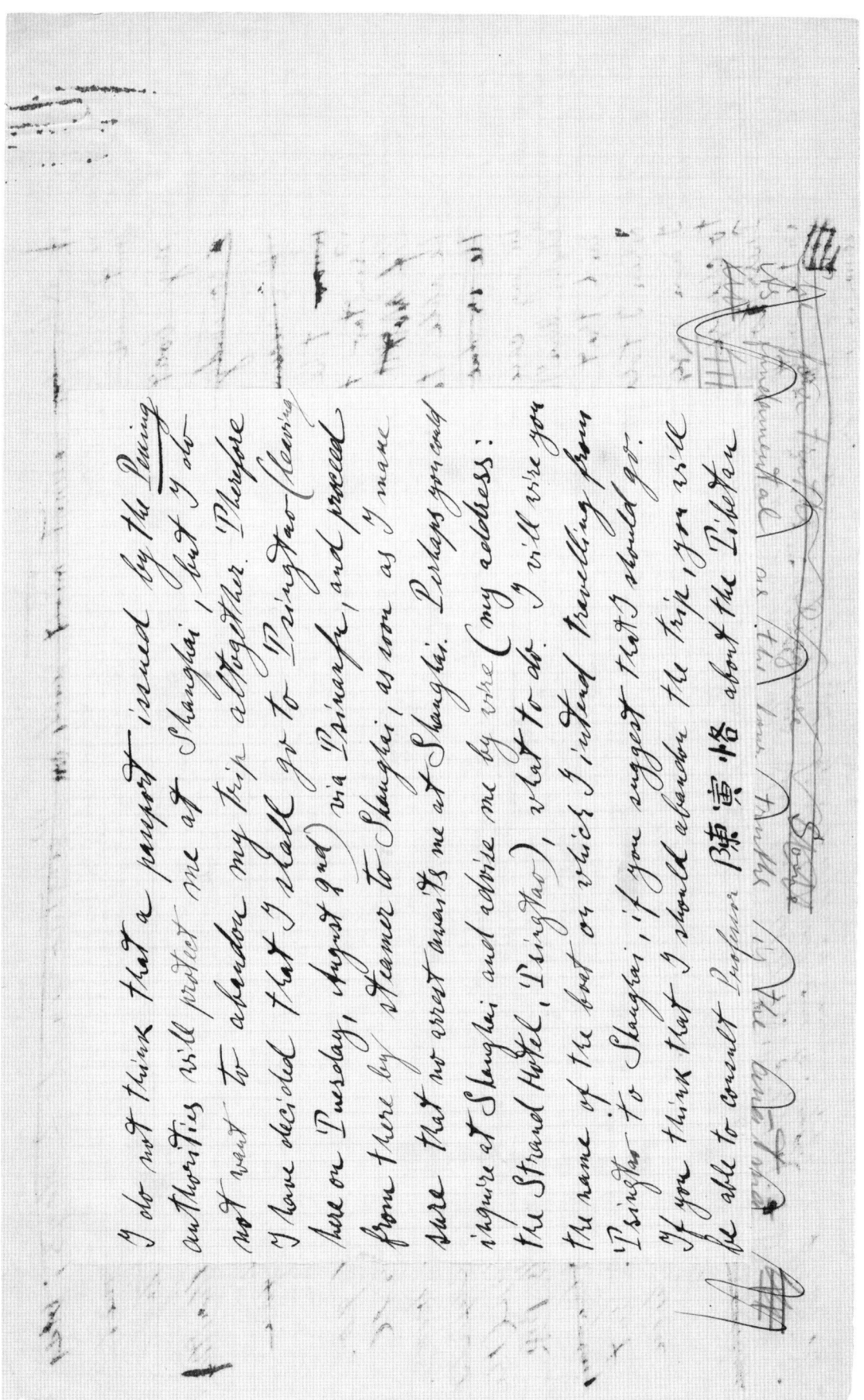

I do not think that a passport issued by the <u>Peking</u> authorities will protect me at Shanghai, but I do not want to abandon my trip altogether. Therefore I have decided that I shall go to Tsingtao (leaving here on Tuesday, August 2nd) via Tsinanfu, and proceed from there by steamer to Shanghai, as soon as I make sure that no arrest awaits me at Shanghai. Perhaps you could inquire at Shanghai and advise me by wire (my address: the Strand Hotel, Tsingtao), what to do. I will wire you the name of the boat on which I intend travelling from Tsingtao to Shanghai, if you suggest that I should go. If you think that I should abandon the trip, you will be able to consult Professor 陳寅恪 about the Tibetan

Another Polo report ~~, dated Shanghai July 28th~~ conforms ~~the forma~~ the former communication in a most striking manner; it is dated Shanghai July 28th and says: "

I believe that my presence in a Shanghai prison cell would be of no use to the Commercial Press or to anyone else and have therefore ~~most reluctantly~~ decided to abandon my trip altogether. ~~I am very I regret very very much that I will not see you this summer, but I feel no compunction about disappointing the Commercial Press, because I think that the Commercial Press will derive nothing but profit from my decision because~~ The Commercial Press ~~But you~~ will be able to consult Professor 陳寅恪 about the Tibetan books. He will leave Tientsin for Shanghai in any case, on his own account, on August 2nd, and his ship (the "Choko Maru") is due at Shanghai on August 6th. It is true that Mr. 陳 said, that he would be too busy in Shanghai to inspect the Tibetan books, when I told him some time ago, that he should undertake the task. But I am sure that very little persuasion on your part ~~would~~ will induce him to change his mind. That arrangement ~~would~~ will enable the Commercial Press to save a good deal of money. Mr. 陳 is at least as competent in the matter as I am, and his Shanghai address is: 24 F Tongshan (塘山) Road.

My assistant, Mr. Yü, has left for Shantung.

~~I am very very sorry that I shall not see you this~~
~~summer~~ I loowed forward very much to seeing you at Shanghai
and to hearing your opinion ~~on the~~ as to the past present and future
of dear old Europe. I also wanted to visit Baroness Ungern
Sternberg, Count Keyserling's sister (c/o Siemens China Co. Shanghai) ~~at Shanghai~~ and I regret very much that I ~~shall~~ shall not be able
to go to Shanghai this year. But is there no possibility
of your coming to Peking? I have found very much
~~material~~ iconographical material absolutely unknown to science
lately and I have had a most successful time since we
last met. How I would like discussing all those things with
you! ~~Mr. V. K. Ting is at Tientsin~~ Have you seen the Croziers?
I gave them your Shanghai address.
Believe me yours sincerely
A Staël Holstein.

My dear Dr. Hu,

I am ~~awfully~~ very sorry to hear ~~that~~ from President Stuart that the Kanjur has to be shipped to Shanghai. ~~But further negotiations~~ We are at present trying to buy another copy which is to replace the one we have been working with, but the negotiations have been interrupted by the Kalgan floods, and whether they will ~~lead to any~~ be successful after the resumption of traffic is far from certain. Therefore I venture to ask you once more to ~~speak to~~ the Commercial Press ~~to through you~~ on my behalf. I can without any inconvenience send them ~~at once~~ forty volumes at once, but I want to keep the remaining sixty odd volumes here, in Peking, ~~until I got the new copy for another year.~~ until July 1st 1930. ~~or not~~. The main purpose of my stay in China is the compilation of an inventory (catalogue raisonné) of the Tibetan as well as the Mongolian Kanjur and of the corresponding parts of the Mongolian Chinese Tripitaka. I am working now with

three assistants paid by Harvard, and soon there
will be seven or eight (of Chinese, Russian, German,
Mongolian, ~~and~~ Tibetan and Japanese nationality). If the whole
Kanjur be shipped to Shanghai at once, that
whole crowd ~~will~~ may be bereft of ~~their~~ its most
important tool for months. Please do ask ~~them~~ the Commercial Press
~~to leave me the sixty~~ to be content with
forty volumes for the time being. My book, ~~publi-~~
~~shed by~~ which the Commercial Press published, ~~has~~ made
the latter known in a number of places
where nobody knew them before and ~~I have not received~~
~~they never paid me for my work~~ that publicity has not
cost them ~~nothing~~ anything except the ~~expense~~ ~~cost~~ price of printing. My
work has been favourably reviewed by Sir Charles ~~Elliot~~ Eliot
~~and~~ as well as by Professor de La Vallée Poussin (in the journal
"le Muséon" of Brussels) and mentioned in many scientific
publications (Journal Asiatique, Paris, etc).

I am glad to hear from Dr. Ting that you are keeping
well and I hope to see you here soon.

Believe me yours sincerely A. Staël-Holstein.

49A Jessfield Road,
Shanghai.
December 21,1929

My dear Baron Stael-Holstein:

Mr.Yuan of the Metropolitan Library has informed me that, because of a sentence in my last letter to you to the effect that 'the transfer (of the Kanjur) is merely formal', you have suggested to retain the Kanjur in your house and asked the Library to send a receipt to the Commercial Press. As this involves a question of responsibility to the Commercial Press on the part of the Library, Mr Yuan and Mr Sun of the Peking Branch of the Commercial Press find this arrangement to be unsatisfactory and have written to me for an opinion.

I quite understand their position and am therefore writing to ask you to deposit the whole Kanjur with the Metropolitan Library so as to enable Mr Yuan to issue a receipt to the Commercial Press. After the transfer, the Library will loan to you or any other scholar any ~~copies~~ volumes of it in accordance with the rules of the Library.

I hope this arrangement may not cause you any serious inconvenience.

With kindest remembrances,

Yours most sincerely,

Hu Shih

I am very ~~pleased~~ much obliged to you for ~~glad to hear~~ ~~that you~~ having written to the Editor of the China Journal who ~~I am very glad to hear that you have written to the Editor of the China Journal, who he will, of course receive your accept your review~~ will, of course, be only too glad to ~~accept~~ print your review. ~~The other day I saw Madame de Warzée, who and~~ Madame de Warzée, whom I meet ~~still~~ occasionally, and myself ~~very much~~ have not given up the hope of seeing you here before long. ~~It would be a~~ ~~It would~~ You will have to pass very near Peking on your way home. It might interest you to inspect ~~that~~ my iconographical material which is absolutely "inédit".

Believe me yours sincerely and gratefully – AStaëlHolstein.

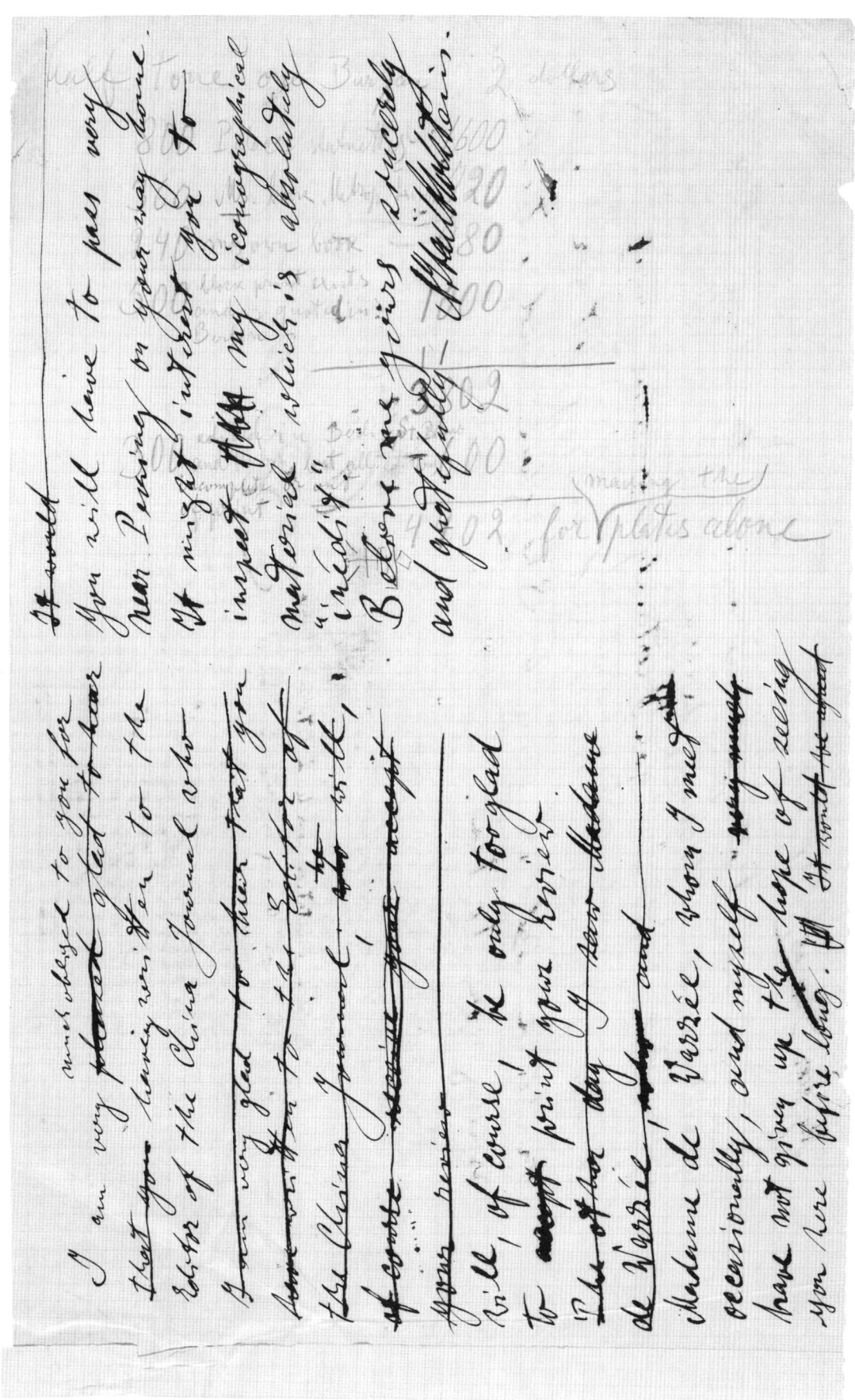

(making the) for plates alone

Peking May 8th 1932.

My dear Dr. Hu,

I am very much obliged to you for sending me your highly interesting ~~new~~ ~~[illegible]~~ treatise on the development of 'Zen Buddhism in China. I am comparing the Sanscrit text of the ~~reading the~~ (Saddharmapuṇḍarīka ~~at present, now, and~~ ~~and comparing it~~ with the ~~Tg~~ Chinese as well as with the Tibetan translations. Dharmarakṣa's translation especially shows many traces of the Taoistic influence which you mention ~~which you mention mentioned~~ in your paper. I am also studying the great T'ien T'ai commentary's (妙法蓮華經句) ~~which~~ attempts at explaining away the evident contradictions and inconsistencies which confront us in the literature of Buddhism. In the commentary ~~又~~ of the Kāśyapaparivarta (大寶積經論) which I am editing (in Tibetan ~~and~~ in Chinese) and which will soon appear (234 pages ~~of~~ out of about 330 ~~are al~~ are already printed) ~~also deals with that question~~, ~~[illegible]~~ the same question is discussed, but a method different from the 判教 is suggested for solving the ~~difficulty~~ difficulties.

~~With kind regards and many thanks~~

~~I remain yours sincerely A. Staël-Holstein.~~

~~We have History does certainly repeat itself.~~

The idea that supreme enlightenment ~~it~~ can not be described or defined ~~by~~ is known in India as well as in China. ~~The pre-Buddhist saint Bāhva replied to was asked by~~ Somebody asked the pre-Buddhist saint Bāhva . . . . .

~~But~~ The ~~old~~ Chinese Zen teachers are evidently ~~certainly~~ more radical than ~~that~~ Bāhva, substituting (as they do) boxes on the ears for silence. We observe the same radical tendencies among certain ~~present day~~ Chinese ~~Bolsheviks~~ Communists. ~~who regard all those who~~ They "out-bolshevik" Moscow by ~~declaring~~ regarding everybody who knows more than 600 characters as a dangerous intellectual and condemning him to death. History certainly does repeat itself.

Dear Dr. Hu

~~On ~~Thursday~~ Saturday July 11th~~ I have arranged a farewell luncheon party for Mr. Roger S. Greene ~~for~~ to take place at my house on Thursday July 11th at 1 o'clock

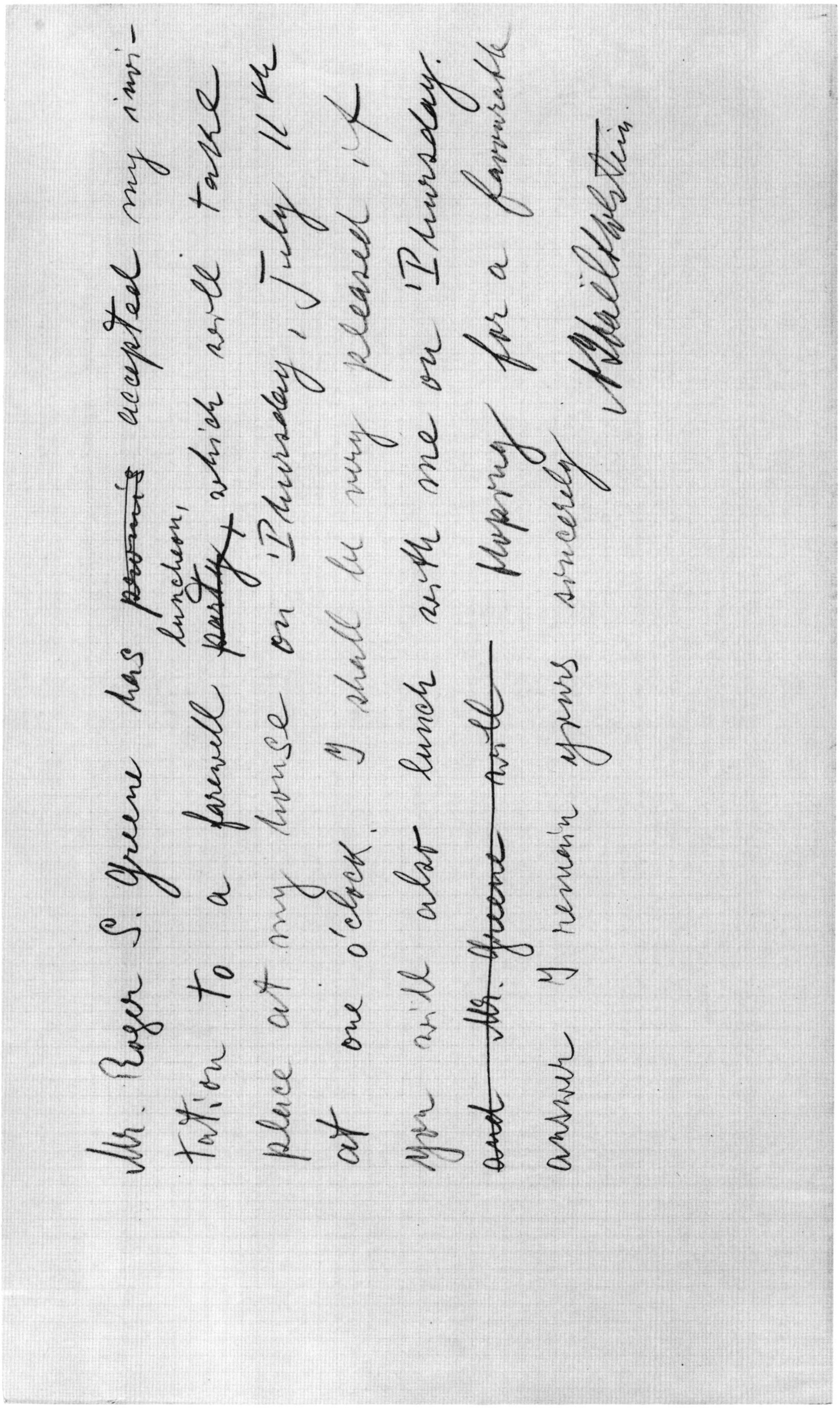

Mr. Roger S. Greene has ~~promis~~ accepted my invitation to a farewell ~~party~~ luncheon, which will take place at my house on Thursday, July 11th at one o'clock. I shall be very pleased if you will also lunch with me on Thursday. ~~and Mr. Greene will~~ Hoping for a favourable answer I remain yours sincerely

A Staël Holstein

Peking, January 31st 1936.

Dear Dr. Hu, ~~by~~

~~I have been asked to consult~~ y

The Harvard people have asked me to consult you about certain questions, which ~~I think will~~ ~~I prefer to, I should rather discuss~~ I should like to discuss viva voce. ~~or Where they~~ Please let me know when I may call on you. I could come and see you at any time, except the forenoon of Saturday.

Believe me yours sincerely

A Staël Holstein.

117.65

Peking, April 8th 1936.

My dear Dr. Hu,

I am very much obliged to you for ~~sending me~~ the two higher ~~enlightening~~ volumes which you so kindly sent me ~~reached me~~ not long ago. ~~I quite I believe~~ I too believe that one must ask for the impossible in order to ~~get~~ obtain the possible, and that the spiritual leaders of the nation ~~should~~ ~~move forward~~ ~~advance a thousand yards if they intend proclaim the news~~ can only succeed in carrying ~~moving~~ the masses a few yards away from their sluggish traditions, if they proclaim ~~they proclaiming~~ the ~~all~~ unqualified adoption of 西化. ~~[illegible]~~ I also greatly admire your enthusiasm for modern science and technology, but I hope that you will allow me to doubt, whether parliamentary democracy as ~~understood in western~~ practised in western

Europe is quite a conditio sine qua non for the civilization, which you recommend. Did not ~~science arise or~~ scientific thought flourish under the ~~absolute~~ practically absolute monarchies of Macedon ~~England~~ (Aristotle) England (Francis Bacon) and France (the XVIII century encyclopaedists)? Did not the ~~modern~~ most perfect protective legislation for labour originate in Bismarckian Germany, which is still abhorred as a hot-bed of dynastic militarism by all ~~well~~ "right-thinking" western democrats?

With many thanks and with kind regards I remain

yours very sincerely

A. Staël-Holstein.

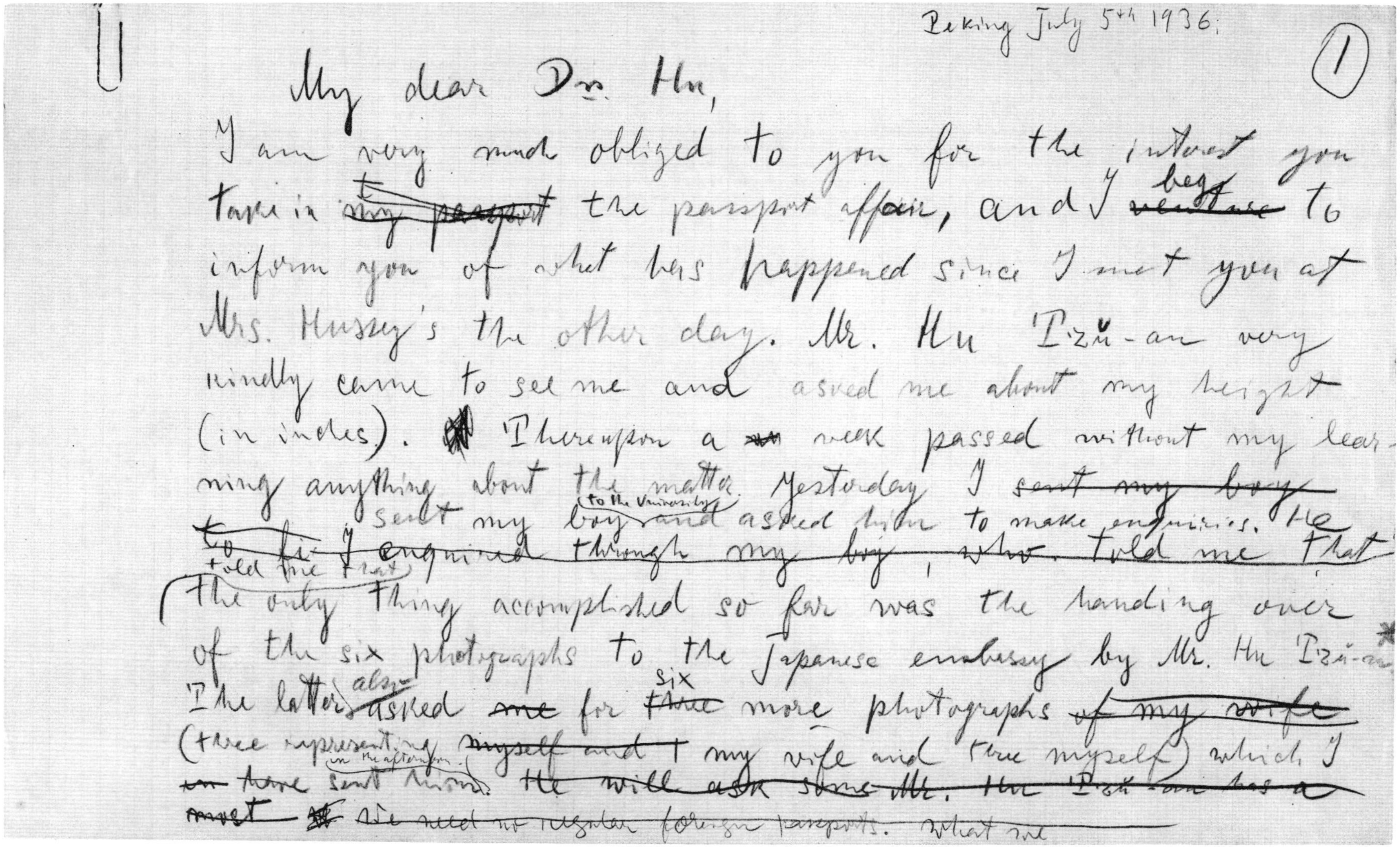

(1)

Peking July 5th 1936.

My dear Dr. Hu,

I am very much obliged to you for the interest you take in ~~my passport~~ the passport affair, and I beg ~~venture~~ to inform you of what has happened since I met you at Mrs. Hussey's the other day. Mr. Hu Tzŭ-an very kindly came to see me and asked me about my height (in inches). Thereupon a week passed without my learning anything about the matter. Yesterday I ~~sent my boy~~ sent my boy to the University and asked him to make enquiries. He ~~I enquired through my boy, who told me that~~ told me that the only thing accomplished so far was the handing over of the six photographs to the Japanese embassy by Mr. Hu Tzŭ-an. The latter also asked ~~me~~ for six ~~three~~ more photographs ~~of my wife~~ (three representing ~~myself and~~ my wife and three myself) which I ~~have~~ sent him in the afternoon. ~~He will ask some Mr. Hu Tzŭ-an has a~~ ~~We need no regular foreign passports. What we~~

(2)

At this rate of progress ~~[illegible]~~ I shall certainly have
to wait for the passports until the summer
~~is past~~ is over and therefore I ~~[illegible]~~ ~~thought~~ of asking
some of my foreign friends in Nanking for assistance. But
~~this course will hardly [illegible] be successful unless~~
~~I personally go to Nanking~~
this course ~~of action~~ involves an intolerable loss of
face. I do not want my foreign friends to know
that after 18 years of residence in China ~~I enjoy~~
I still "enjoy" the status of a Lithuanian or
~~[illegible]~~ Armenian heroine-dealer, who cannot go anywhere ~~in China~~ outside the Legation quarter ~~[illegible]~~
without being liable to arrest and ~~I~~ imprison-
ment for any length of time, unless he can ~~[illegible]~~ show

(3)

a special permit issued by the Chinese police. Such permits I used to obtain without too great difficulties till the new circular was issued, which makes all movements of non-treaty foreigners legally impossible. I think the police should ~~not regard~~ ~~has been is~~ consider me as a tourist, ~~who spends many thous~~ who has to be regarded as ~~assets~~ a financial asset (I spend many thousand dollars of good foreign money yearly in this country) ~~and have never~~ and who should not be ~~subject to~~ ~~chicanery treated as a~~ subject to the regulations devised against the heroine dealers. Mr. Hu Tzŭ-an has a most attractive personality but ~~he has not the personal prestige~~ only a man with great personal prestige will be able to prove to the police officers that a difference exists between the heroine-dealers and myself. Therefore I venture to ask you to intervene personally in the affair. ~~All I~~ ~~I do~~ ~~The document, which I want, need not be a passport to Japan, all~~

(4)

~~require~~ We need not regular foreign passports. ~~What we require~~ All that we require ~~ask for~~ are ~~two~~ permits exactly like those which I obtained last year. Only ~~the~~ our ages (change 37 and 58 into 38 and 59) and the years of the Republic (change 24 into 25) should be amended. I enclose photographs of last year's permits. The ~~permits~~ places mentioned in the permits include 大連 ~~As soon as we~~ which is ~~was~~ rightly regarded (by the Peking police) ~~is considered~~ as Chinese territory. As soon as we reach ~~are in~~ 大連 our troubles are over, because ~~we are under the jurisdiction~~ the Japanese (in temporary occupation of 大連) recognise our Estonian passports. ~~and do not even require a visé for the latter.~~ We can then stay at 大連 or go on to Japan ~~as we li~~ and return to ~~China~~ Peking via 大連. I think that ~~five minutes~~ it will not take you more than five minutes ~~to per~~ ~~person~~ to obtain the permits (from a responsible police official), but I am sure that your personal intervention is necessary. I am ~~certain~~ that a routine letter, which is [what] Mr. Hu Pza-an has contemplated for nearly three weeks ~~contemplates~~, will remain ineffective. Only your personal intervention ~~can save me all the~~ before your departure for America can save us from ~~great~~ further inconvenience and loss of ~~fault~~ face. Believe me yours sincerely A. Staël Holstein.

We intended leaving Peking on July the 7th. This is now, unfortunately, impossible.

Please excuse my [illegible], [illegible]

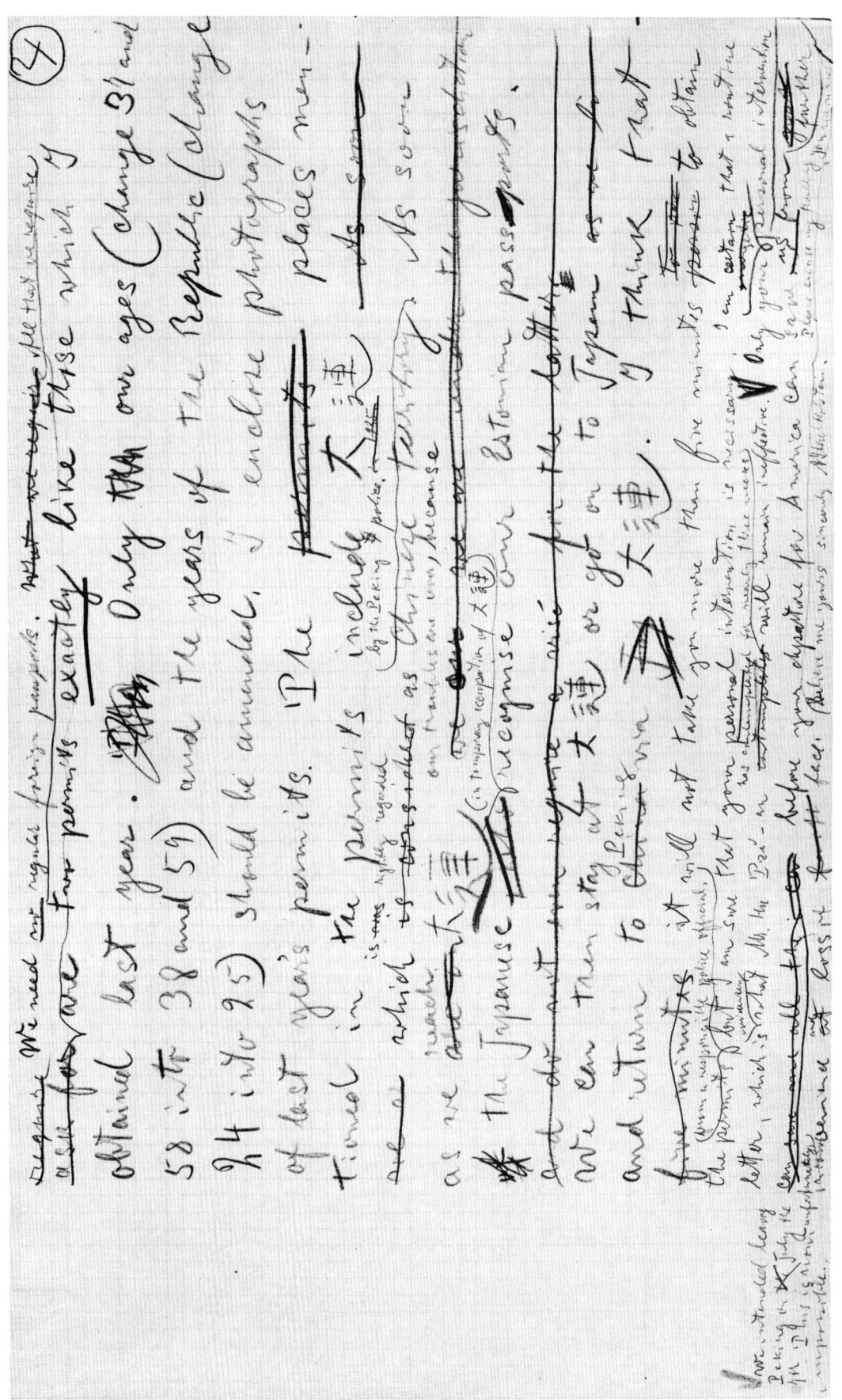

1) This effort was entirely unnecessary. We do not require any (Japanese) visés. ~~A convention~~ According to a Japono-Estonian convention, Estonian citizens travelling in Japan require no visés. I know this from my personal experiences in 1933 and in 1935.

My dear Dr. Hu,

How can I thank you for having acted so energetically in the passport affair? Now everything is O.K., and we ~~shall sail for~~ can set sail on our voyage. I highly appreciate the fact that you have ~~used a part of your~~ found time ~~to spend on our~~ to help us in spite of your impending departure for America.

Wishing you "bon voyage" I remain yours most gratefully

A. Staël-Holstein.

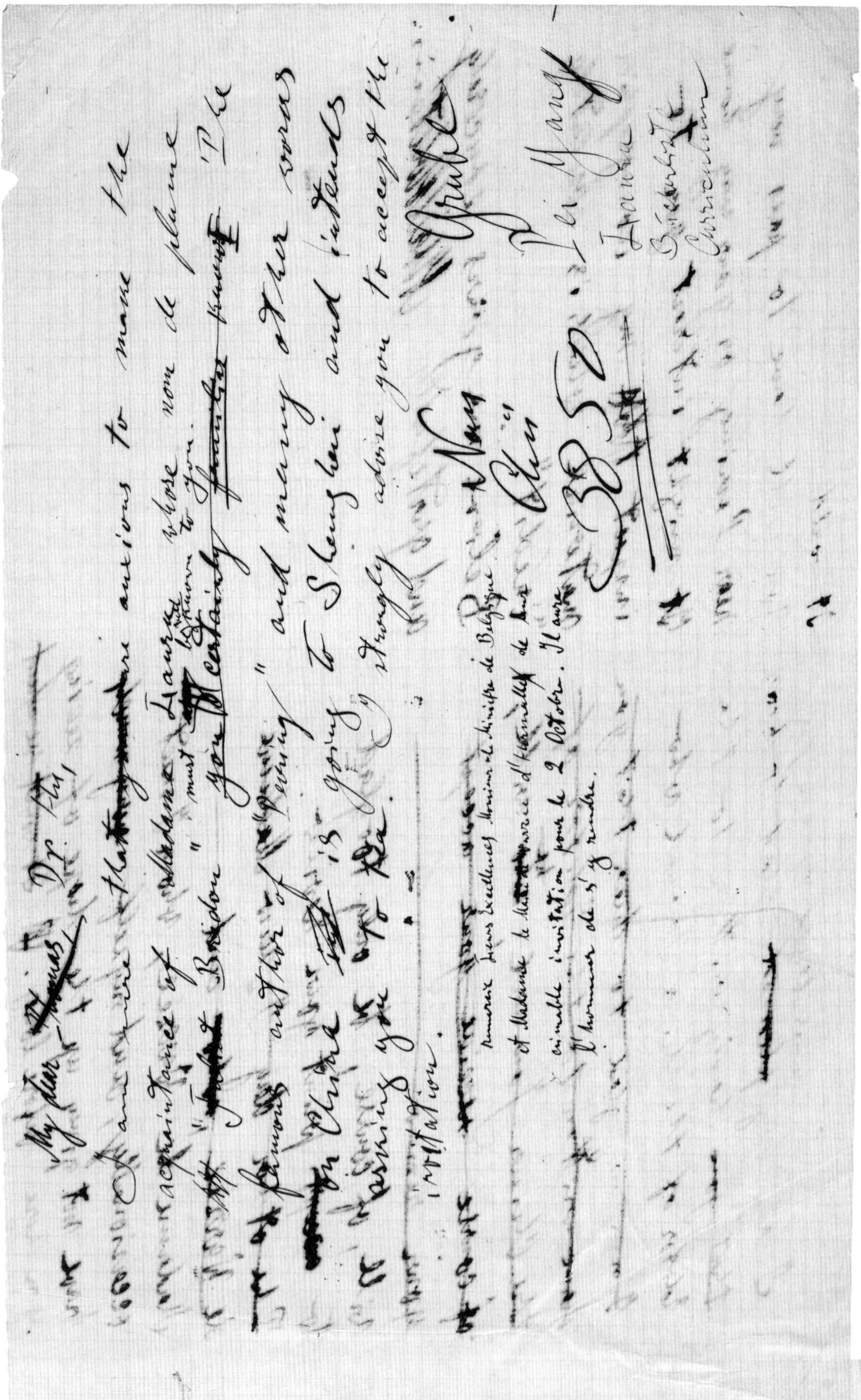

My dear ~~Thomas~~ Dr. Liu,

I am sure ~~that you~~ are anxious to make the acquaintance of Madame Laura whose nom de plume "Juliet Bredon" must be well known to you. ~~you certainly familiar known~~ The famous author of "Peking" and many other works on China is going to Shanghai and intends asking you to tea. I strongly advise you to accept the invitation.

remercie Leurs Excellences Monsieur le Ministre de Belgique et Madame la Marquise d'Hennilles de leur aimable invitation pour le 2 Octobre. Il aura l'honneur de s'y rendre.

Nous

Chü

3850.

Grube

Pei Yang

Laura

Bücherliste

Curriculum

My dear Dr. Hu,

~~Mr~~ Dr. Wu I-t'ai has been a teacher of Chinese at the École des Langues Orientales of Paris for a number of years and M. Demiéville, a professor of the same institution warmly recommends him to me. ~~He is extremely pr.~~ Dr. Wu knows French extremely well, and ~~I venture to I venture to suggest that you get~~ I believe that he would make an excellent professor of French at Tsinghua or ~~he could serve~~ any ~~Peking college,~~ at any other Peking university. ~~which can would appoint him professor of French, will find him extremely useful. He In case He~~ I think that he is also an excellent translator.

Believe me yours sincerely

A. Staël-Holstein.

陸軍交通總司令部
GENERAL HEAD-QUARTERS OF MILITARY TRANSPORTATION
無綫電信處
Radio Department.
personal

Reference No. ....

Peking, April 23rd 1928

鋼男爵,

Dear Baron,

It seems quit a long time since I had the pleasure to meet you in that large temple in the West city.

I like to call on you on Tuesday afternoon (April 24th) at 5.45 together with a friend of mine, Mr. Chao 趙之蘭, who is a faithful follower of Buddhism and knows much about Tibetan Buddhism (密宗) and is also interesting in Buddhas' portraits. I hope it with suit you by that time.

Yours very sincerely
Huang Chung Chiang.

Best regards to Mr. Teng 鄧

LIBRARY OF CONGRESS
WASHINGTON

October 23, 1928.

Baron Stäel von Holstein,
Harvard University,
Cambridge, Mass.

Dear Baron:

The Library of Congress has just sent you from its Chinese Collection the volume of the Dulva from the Tibetan sacred books which the Librarian of Harvard University requested us to send to you. The volume we sent was the Derge edition. It is in 100 vols. and was secured by Mr. Rockhill in 1908.

I may also say that the Library of Congress also has an edition of the Kanjur which was recently purchased by Mr. Rock of the National Geographic Society in Choni just on the border of Kansu and Tibet. This edition has the usual 108 volumes. If you wish a volume of the Dulva from this edition, we can send it to you, I think, upon a request from the Library of Harvard University.

I should also say that we have two different editions of the Tanjur. One of these is the Narthang edition brought to Peking by the Dalai Lama and purchased by Dr. Laufer in 1908. This has the full 225 volumes. According to Dr. Laufer's analysis, it has one volume of index; one volume of Stotra (bstod-pa) of hymns and prayers comprising 58 works; 87 vols. of Tantra (rqyud) comprising 2640 treatises; and 136 sutras (mdo). Besides this edition of the Tanjur we also have an edition from Choni in 225 volumes, but the Choni edition of both the Kanjur and the Tankur were mutilated somewhat in coming from Kansu and therefore need to be collated, and perhaps a few missing pages need to be replaced. But to effect this we shall have to have the services of one who knows Tibetan.

I am glad to know that you are in this country and that you will have a satisfactory year here. Since leaving China or rather since last January I have been in charge of the Chinese Collection of the Library of Congress. We have well over 100,000 Chinese volumes and plan to increase our collection in the coming years. If you come to Washington, I hope you will come to see our Chinese Collection and also our other Tibetan books.

With kind regards, and best wishes, I remain,

Very sincerely yours,

Arthur W. Hummel

Arthur W. Hummel
Chief of the Chinese Division.

The Yung Ho Kung Lamasery of Peking possesses a ~~[illegible]~~ complete copy of the Choni Tanjur. ~~which is said to come from~~ ~~That copy might be compared~~ ~~used to~~
The pages missing in your copy might be ~~[illegible]~~ rotographed at Peking (where we have a photostat). ~~I have a few photostat copies~~

Dear Professor Hummel That would enable you to fill the gaps in ~~your copy~~ the Tanjur lately acquired by the Library of Congress.

I cannot say how grateful I am to you for sending me Vol. II of the Derge Kanjur. Professor Clark of this University prepares (an English a translation ~~an edition~~ of the Pūrṇa 圓, 滿, 氵 story (Comp. Tokyo Trip. Vol. 褱 fasc. 4, page 66. 299.) and of other avadānas. The Sanskrit text is rather corrupt and in order to explain certain passages correctly ~~obtain a correct~~ translation it is necessary to refer to the old translations (Chinese and Tibetan). That is what I am doing at present at the request of Professor Clark. ~~[illegible]~~ In the Narthang edition of the Kanjur the Pūrṇa story occupies the leaves 40–80 of ~~[illegible]~~ Dulva II (comp. Annales du Musée Guimet volume II page 165), but in the Derge edition it ends on leaf 8 of Dulva II. That is why ~~[illegible]~~ the Harvard Library has asked you to be so kind as to send us now ~~[illegible]~~ the volume Dulva I of the Derge Kanjur. I trust that you have already received volume II which I returned to the ~~[illegible]~~ Harvard Library authorities after having ~~studied~~ used it in ~~my private study No 445 of~~ the Library building. I shall be only too happy to inspect the Choni texts lately received by your Library and I could ~~could~~ perhaps ~~[illegible]~~ go to Washington for that purpose. I am very glad to know ~~that you are now occupy the position of chief of the Chinese Division of the United States Government~~ and that you are now a "wohlbestallter Beamter" of the Congress Library and that you direct ~~occupy the pos~~ the Chinese Division.

HARVARD-YENCHING INSTITUTE

HARVARD-YENCHING INSTITUTE CORPORATE SEAL

ADMINISTRATIVE COMMITTEE IN PEIPING
OFFICE OF THE EXECUTIVE SECRETARY

October 13, 1931.

YENCHING UNIVERSITY
PEIPING, WEST

Baron von Stael-Holstein,
Ex-Austrian Legation.

My dear Baron:

I am thinking of a little social gathering possibly to be scheduled in the course of the next few months in which those who are engaged in the various branches of work of the Harvard-Yenching Institute might have an opportunity to get acquainted with one another. I have in mind that the teachers, students and the research assistants may all be invited to this social gathering. I have already made a list of somewhere about fifty, and I am now writing to ask if you would like to have your staff of the Sino-Indian Institute included in this gathering, and if so, may I have a list of the names and addresses.

With kindest regards,

Very sincerely yours,

William Hung

William Hung

Acting Executive Secretary

My dear Professor Hung,

~~Kindly~~ Please do excuse ~~the long~~ me for answering your letter dated October as late as this. ~~Your idea of~~ I quite agree with you in thinking that a ~~Harvard-Yenching convocation~~ meeting of all the Harvard-Yenching scholars etc. should ~~take place~~ meet this winter, ~~but why not and I sugge~~ and I suggest that ~~it~~ (the meeting) might take the form of a tea party at my house which is certainly ~~quite~~ large enough for fifty people. ~~The two parts. Please~~ ~~I possess a number of Tibetan pictures which my Some of the may I could display arrange an exhibition of Tibetan paintings for the occasion. I~~ ~~let me know how you That. I Some of them~~

May I ask to be kindly remembered to Mrs. Hung?

Believe me yours sincerely A. Stael-Holstein.

Some of them will probably be interested in my collections, and I could arrange an exhibition of Tibetan paintings, not usually on view for the occasion.

HARVARD-YENCHING INSTITUTE

ADMINISTRATIVE COMMITTEE IN PEIPING
OFFICE OF THE EXECUTIVE SECRETARY

YENCHING UNIVERSITY
PEIPING, WEST

November 25, 1931.

Baron von Stael-Holstein,
Austrian Legation,
Peiping.

My dear Baron:

It is very kind of you to suggest in your letter of November 7 that you may invite all the persons connected with the Harvard-Yenching Institute to a tea party at your house where they may be given an opportunity to see your fine collection. You stated also that your house is big enough to accommodate fifty persons at such a party. I do think this hospitality of yours will certainly be enjoyed by whomever is invited.

In my letter of October 13, however, I had in mind a gathering on the campus of Yenching University some time this winter whereat the persons connected with the various branches of the Harvard-Yenching Institute work will have a chance to meet each other. The list of names we have at present amounts to 65, and President Stuart has suggested now the date of Saturday afternoon, December 5. The idea tentatively is to have a tea party at the house of President Stuart, and possibly we may also arrange certain exhibits of new acquisitions in the Library, or of the photographs taken during the trip that a few of us took several months ago. While the detailed program is not yet made out, I hasten to write you to find out if the date is convenient for your group. I note that you have given Miss Hague a list of the names connected with the Sino-Indian Institute. This I enclose. Would you want to add more names to this list? Shall I arrange to send individual invitations to each of them in the care of your office?

I think when you and your group have met the other persons at this December 5th party, then we can work out a plan wherein a selected number of these teachers and scholars, not more than 50 might be invited to a tea party at your house, say sometime in the spring or whenever is convenient for you.

Mrs. Hung joins me in kindest regards to you and the Baroness.

Very sincerely yours,

William Hung

William Hung

LIST OF SINO-INDIAN SCHOLARS SUBMITTED BY BARON VON STAEL-HOLSTEIN,
OCTOBER 14, 1931.

Mr. Weller
Mr. Lessing
Mr. Erkes
Mr. Schierlitz

HARVARD-YENCHING INSTITUTE

ADMINISTRATIVE COMMITTEE IN PEIPING
OFFICE OF THE EXECUTIVE SECRETARY

December 1, 1931.

YENCHING UNIVERSITY
PEIPING, WEST

Baron A. von Stael-Holstein,
Austrian Legation,
Peiping.

My dear Baron:

Yenching University is now in the midst of the activities of an intensive patriotic week. This will last until Saturday. It seems desirable that we postpone the party originally scheduled for Saturday afternoon December 5, to the week following.

I am still waiting for the list of personnel from your Sino-Indian Institute to be invited to the party.

With kindest regards,

Very sincerely yours,

William Hung

P.S. Since dictating the above I have received your favor of Nov. 28. Many thanks.
W.H.

My dear Professor Hung,

I shall be delighted to attend the Yenching tea party on Saturday December 5th and I am sure that my German friends (Miss Hayne knows their addresses) will also gladly accept your kind invitation.

~~My wife joins me in sending you and Mrs. Hung~~

My wife and I send you and Mrs. Hung our best greetings.

Believe me yours sincerely

AStaëlHolstein.

~~Über mythologische Evolution~~
Über einige göttliche Metamorphosen.

Sehr verehrter Herr Doctor,

Entschuldigen Sie gütigst, dass ich ~~erst jetzt~~ Ihren Brief vom 14. November erst heute beantworte.

~~Ich werde mit dem grössten Vergnügen Ich fühle mich durch Ihre Aufforderung~~

Ich nehme Ihre ehrende Einladung gerne an, und werde am 8. Januar um 9 Uhr 15 im Deutschen Klub "über einige göttliche Metamorphosen" einen Vortrag halten. ~~Ich nur~~ ~~Nur in Hinsicht bitte ich Sie, freundlichst~~ Es liegt mir aber sehr viel daran, dass ~~möglichst wenige die Presse~~ die Zeitungen von meinem Vortrage ~~vor der~~ im Voraus keine Kenntniss erhalten. ~~Darf ich Sie daher bitten, der Presse Ich will womöglich vor einem rein deutschen Auditorium sprechen~~ Darf ich Sie daher ~~daher~~ bitten, ~~der Presse keinerlei Mittheilungen~~ den Vertretern der Presse nichts über meinen bevorstehenden Vortrag zu verrathen?

Es empfiehlt sich Ihnen hochachtungsvoll Ihr ganz ergebener AStaëlHolstein.

HARVARD-YENCHING INSTITUTE

Yenching University,
January 11, 1932.

Baron A. von Stael-Holstein,
Austrian Legation,
Peping.

My dear Baron:

I am sending you a copy of a notice from our Treasurers Office concerning the coming of a fund of $250.00 for the purchase of a photostat machine for your use. When you have need of the money you may apply directly to the Treasurers Office of Yenching University, or through our office here.

With kindest regards,

Very sincerely yours,

William Hung

William Hung

HARVARD-YENCHING INSTITUTE

ADMINISTRATIVE COMMITTEE IN PEIPING
OFFICE OF THE EXECUTIVE SECRETARY

YENCHING UNIVERSITY
PEIPING, WEST

February 25, 1932.

Baron A. von Stael Holstein,
The Austrian Legation,
Peiping.

My dear Baron:

You will recall that sometime ago you had kindly stated that you would be willing to help in the publication of an index to the authors and titles in the Ta Chen edition of Ta Ts'ang Ching by ascertaining whether the Sanskrit terms inserted by Mr. Hsü Ti-shan are all correct.

We have now finished the making of the cards of all of the volumes of the collection that have been received. Of the few volumes that have not yet been sent from Tokyo, we have provided the cards according to the table of contents, giving the volume, without however the pagination. Mr. Hsü informs me that there are only comparatively few cards from these volumes not received, as they contain generally big treatises.

The cards that have been made amount to a little over 16,000. We are intending to use these cards first to make a title index, and then secondly, to rearrange them so as to provide an author index. Of these cards I understand only about 2,000 have Sanskrit insertions.

Now, before we decide to proceed with the making of the manuscript for printing, I would like to have your expert opinion on several things:

1) Do you think it worth while to have the Hsü Ts'ang Ching authors and titles added? Mr. Hsü seems to think that this is not necessary, but I would like to have your opinion on the matter also.

2) Do you think it advisable to proceed with the printing of the index without waiting for the issuance of the several

-2-

volumes not yet available, and to have the authors and titles in these several volumes indicated in the index without the exact pagination?

3) We do not give the cards to the printers for fear that they might lose some of them, so as a practice we arrange the cards and copy out a manuscript for printing. Now, in order to avail ourselves of your help in reading the proof of the Sanskrit terms, do you think it is better to a) send you all of the cards, b) send you only the cards with the Sanskrit terms, or c) send you the copied manuscript?

4) The titles and authors are arranged in the index according to the Kuei Hsieh arrangement of Chinese characters supplemented by the Wade Romanization and stroke-number indices to the Kuei Hsieh. I am sending you under separate cover a copy of the index to Yi Li, which has recently come off the press. This will give you an idea of the make-up of the index. Do you consider it worth while in the matter of the index to the Ta Ts'ang Ching to add a supplementary index arranged according to the latinized Sanskrit terms?

I shall be very grateful if you will be so kind as to let me have your judgment on these matters at your early convenience.

With kindest regards,

Very sincerely yours,

William Hung

William Hung

P.S. Since dictating the above I have found that Mr. Hsü has not yet inserted the authors' Sanskrit names. Do you think that this ought to be done? W.H.

HARVARD-YENCHING INSTITUTE

ADMINISTRATIVE COMMITTEE IN PEIPING
OFFICE OF THE EXECUTIVE SECRETARY

YENCHING UNIVERSITY
PEIPING, WEST

June 23, 1932.

Baron A. von Stael-Holstein,
Austrian Legation,
Peiping.

My dear Baron:

President Stuart informed me this morning of your enquiry about the amount of money that is on the Harvard-Yenching Institute budget, July 1, 1932 to June 30, 1933, for Y-11, Sino-Indian Institute. I am enclosing herewith a copy of the budget for this period which I have recently received from the Board of Trustees.

You will note on this budget that the figures are given in two columns. Certain of the items are budgetted in gold and the rest are budgetted in silver. It has been the practice of the Trustees to append to the items budgetted in silver a rough estimate of the equivalents in gold. This is done, I presume, chiefly to enable the Trustees to see how the incomes in gold might meet the expenditures in both gold and silver.

According to this budget, the total sum of money that will be at the disposal of the Yenching University Treasurers Office for Harvard-Yenching Institute disbursements, will be L.C. $80,720 and G.$16,500.

Y-11, Sino-Indian Institute, is budgetted as L.C.$14,000 which is estimated to be equivalent to G$3,500. I presume that our Uniersity Treasurer is authorized to pay to the Sino-Indian Institute during the year 1932-33 a total not exceeding L.C.$14,000.

President Stuart has enquired of me whether the Sino-Indian Institute is to receive G.$3,500 or L.C.$14,000, and also, what rate of exchange the Yenching University Treasurer will be able to obtain for the G.$3,500.

So far as I can interpret the budget, the Sino-Indian Institute is budgetted in silver, and therefore, our treasurer will be able to make the payments only in silver. I shall write to the Board of Trustees, however, to ascertain whether this assumption is correct. In the event that we receive definite instructions that Y-11, Sino-Indian Institute, may be paid in gold not exceeding $3,500, we shall immediately communicate with you to ask your judgment as to how the gold might be exchanged into silver. On the latter point may I state that Yenching University Treasurers Office generally secures good exchange rates for gold, which are often slightly better than ordinary counter rates. The practice hitherto has been that when the quarterly payments in gold (for items budgetted in gold) come, the Treasurers Office will consult with the officer for whom each particular payment is intended, on the question of exchange. Should the Trustees instruct us that Y-11 is to be paid in gold, I shall request our Treasurers Office to consult with you on the question of exchange so as to secure the best possible rates.

I hope this communication will answer your enquiries. If it is not clear I shall be very glad to hear from you again.

With kindest regards,

Very sincerely yours,

William Hung

William Hung

Acting Executive Secretary

HARVARD-YENCHING INSTITUTE

ADMINISTRATIVE COMMITTEE IN PEIPING
OFFICE OF THE EXECUTIVE SECRETARY

June 25, 1932.

YENCHING UNIVERSITY
PEIPING, WEST

Baron A. von Stael-Holstein,
Austrian Legation.

My dear Baron:

We are drawing toward the close of the fiscal year, 1931-32. May I suggest that you send in soon your account forthe last quarter of the fiscal year so that I may arrange with our Treasurers Office to have the money paid over to you before they close their accounts.

With kindest regards,

Very sincerely yours,

William Hung

William Hung

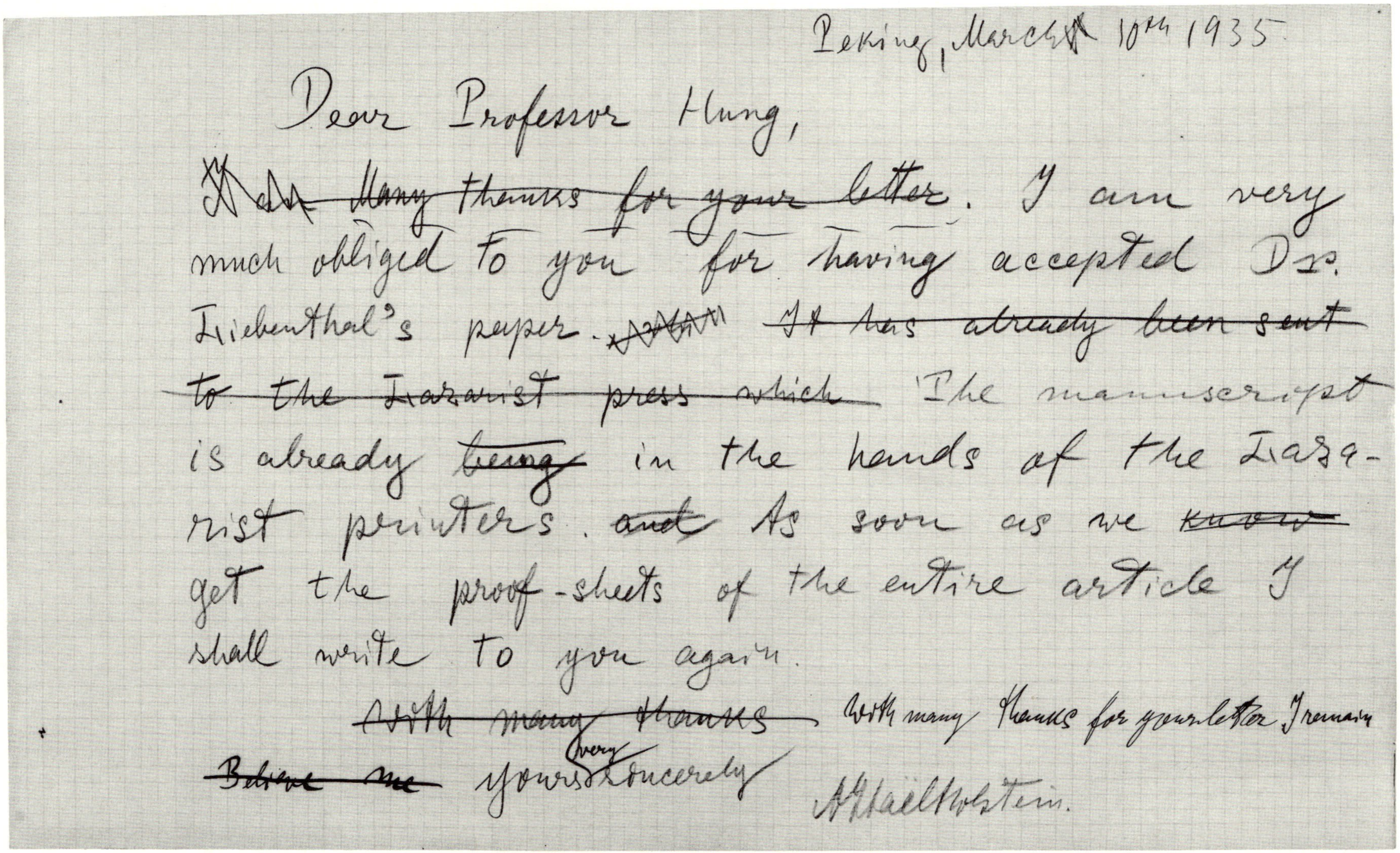

Peking, March 10th 1935

Dear Professor Hung,

~~Many thanks for your letter~~. I am very much obliged to you for having accepted Dr. Liebenthal's paper. ~~It has already been sent to the Lazarist press which~~ The manuscript is already ~~being~~ in the hands of the Lazarist printers. ~~and~~ As soon as we ~~know~~ get the proof-sheets of the entire article I shall write to you again.

~~With many thanks~~ With many thanks for your letter I remain

~~Believe me~~ yours very sincerely

AStaëlHolstein.

54 YEN NAN YUAN
YENCHING UNIVERSITY
PEIPING CHINA

March 28, 1935.

My dear Baron:

I am to leave for a few days' rest in the Hills beginning with to-morrow. I shall be back next week Tuesday or Wednesday. As I have a luncheon engagement in Peiping next Thursday (March 4), may I call on you sometime in the afternoon, between two and three o'clock?

With kindest regards,

Sincerely yours

William Hung

Peking, March 28th 1935.

Dear Professor Hung,

I want very much to see you. ~~May I ask~~ Please ~~you to~~ let me know, ~~at what time you could receive me on Sunday March 31st?~~ In case you ~~prefer court~~ when I may call at your house. I should prefer to do so on Sunday (March 31st) at an hour to be fixed by you, but ~~the~~ any ~~day~~ other day of next week will also do, in case Sunday does not suit you.

Believe me yours sincerely

A Staël Holstein.

燕京大學圖書館
YENCHING UNIVERSITY LIBRARY
PEIPING, CHINA.

April 6, 1935

My dear Baron:

Mr. Jung told me that he would be glad to publish Dr. Liebenthal's article in No. 17 of the Yenching Journal of the Harvard-Yenching Institute.

On account of the special types required and the facility of proof-reading by Dr. Liebenthal, Mr. Jung requests that you may be so kind as to place the manuscript with the same printer who printed your own article.

No. 17 is due to appear in May of this year, therefore it may well to have the article printed as soon as convenient. It may be well to ask the printer not to set the types for the page numbering, for Mr. Jung will later communicate with you the pagination after ascertaining the order of the various articles.

Herewith I am returning the manuscript to you, and I shall appreciate a word from you whether this arrangement is acceptable to you and Dr. Liebenthal.

With kindest regards,

Yours sincerely,

William Hung
WILLIAM HUNG

Baron von Staehl Holstein,
Austrian Legation,
Peiping.

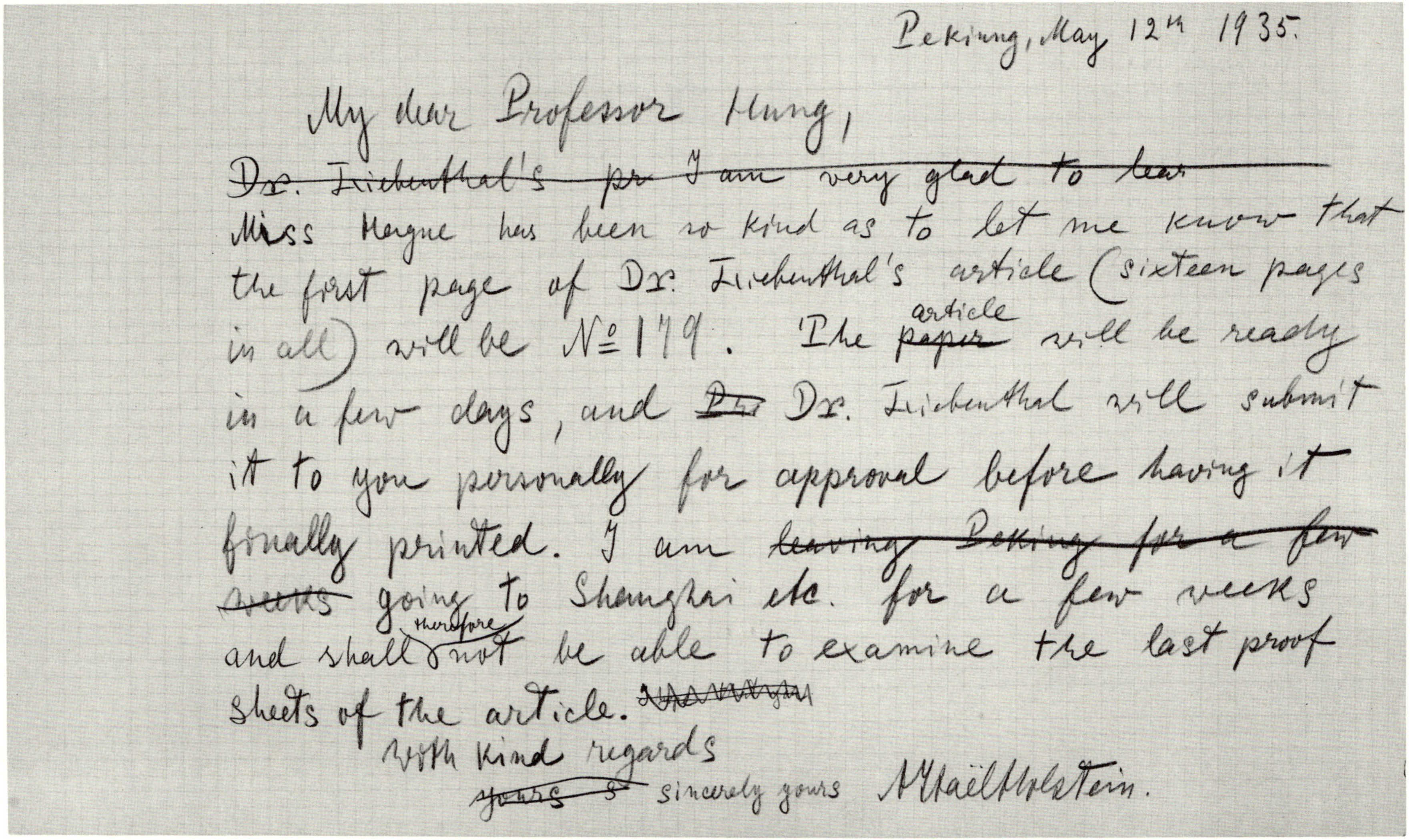

Peking, May 12th 1935.

My dear Professor Hung,

~~Dr. Liebenthal's pr I am very glad to hear~~
Miss Hague has been so kind as to let me know that the first page of Dr. Liebenthal's article (sixteen pages in all) will be №179. The ~~paper~~ article will be ready in a few days, and ~~Dr~~ Dr. Liebenthal will submit it to you personally for approval before having it finally printed. I am ~~leaving Peking for a few weeks~~ going to Shanghai etc. for a few weeks and shall therefore not be able to examine the last proof sheets of the article. ~~[illegible]~~

With kind regards
~~yours s~~ sincerely yours A. Staël Holstein.

My dear Professor Hung,

I shall be delighted to attend the Yenching tea party on Saturday December 5th, and I am sure that my German friends (Miss Hayne knows their addresses) will also gladly accept your kind invitation.

~~My wife joins me in sending you and Mrs. Hung~~

My wife and I send you and Mrs. Hung our best greetings.

Believe me yours sincerely

A. Staël-Holstein.

~~Über mythologische Evolution~~
Über einige göttliche Metamorphosen.

Sehr verehrter Herr Doctor,

Entschuldigen Sie gütigst, dass ich ~~erst jetzt~~ Ihren Brief vom 14. November erst heute beantworte.

~~Ich werde mit dem grössten Vergnügen Ich fühle mich durch Ihre Aufforderung~~

Ich nehme Ihre ehrende Einladung gerne an, und werde am 8. Januar um 9 Uhr 15 im Deutschen Klub "über einige göttliche Metamorphosen" einen Vortrag halten. ~~Ich nur Nur bei Hören bitte ich Sie, freundlichst~~ Es liegt mir aber sehr viel daran, dass ~~möglichst wenige die Presse~~ die Zeitungen von meinem Vortrage ~~vor de~~ im Voraus keine Kenntniss erhalten. ~~Darf ich Sie daher bitten, der Presse Ich will womöglich vor einem reindeutschen Auditorium sprechen~~ Darf ich Sie ~~daher~~ daher bitten, ~~der Presse keinerlei Mittheilungen~~ den Vertretern der Presse nichts über meinen bevorstehenden Vortrag zu verrathen?

Es empfiehlt sich Ihnen hochachtungsvoll Ihr ganz ergebener A. Staël-Holstein.

Dear Mrs Hussey,

~~The~~ The images embroidered on the priest robe, which I return to you with this letter, all represent the Buddha of Long Life. I certainly think that the gift of the robe will be appreciated by Mr. Hamlin.

I have asked one of my "fournisseurs" to show you some small Buddhas.

Believe me yours sincerely

A. Staël Holstein.

華文學校

COLLEGE OF CHINESE STUDIES
(FORMERLY LANGUAGE SCHOOL)
COOPERATING WITH
CALIFORNIA COLLEGE IN CHINA

PRESIDENT'S OFFICE

PEIPING (PEKING) CHINA

Nov. 26, 1932.

Baron Von Holstein,

Dear Barron:- I have been asked to write a review of "The History Of Chinese Medicine", by Drs Wang and Wu. I am inclined to find fault with one cut, it is a Buddhistic image of some Buddha, perhaps Hevajra with his Sakti. The exact name of this Buddah is not in question. This illustration is labled:- "God of Procreation, in the Fa Lun Temple, Mukden."

Do you regard such an immage as the god of procreation?

Yours very cordialy

Begging your pardon for troubling you I

remain Yours

J.H.Ingram. J H Ingram

Ichikawa Chibaken
16th. Nov. 1916.

Dear sir

I read 漢書 (A Chinese history) in Imperial library and there were many interesting
passages, for instance

大月氏國治監氏城去長安萬千六百里不屬
都護.戶十萬,口四十萬勝兵十萬人東至
都護治所四千七百四十里西至安息四十
九日行南與罽賓接土地風氣物類所
有民俗錢貨與安息國同出一封橐駝大
月氏本行國世隨畜移徙與匈奴同俗
控弦十餘萬故彊輕匈奴本居敦煌祁
連至冒頓單于攻破月氏國而老上單于殺
月氏以其頭爲飲器月氏乃遠去大宛西擊
大夏而臣之都媯水北爲王庭其餘小衆
不能去者保南山羌號小月氏國........

In 漢書 there are many passages in
which 月氏 or 大月氏 are contained.
I will tell you the other day.
About Tripitaka I will report to you
in the next post.
When are you coming to Tokyo?
please write to me.

Yours truly K. Ito.

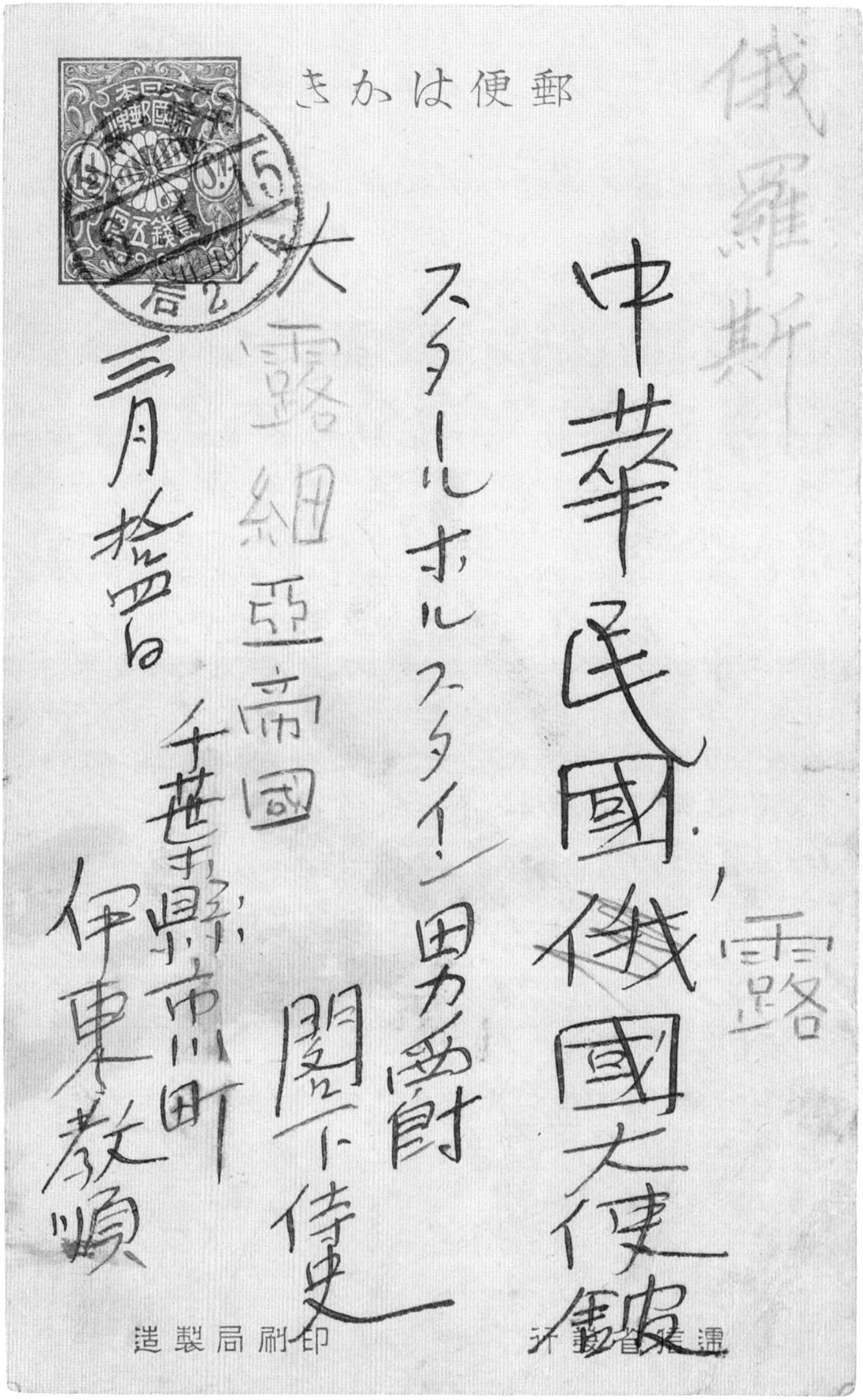

郵便はかき

俄羅斯

中華民國俄國大使館

露路

スタールホルスタイン男爵閣下侍史

大露細亞帝國

千葉縣市川町

伊東敬順

三月拾四日

遞信省發行　印刷局製造

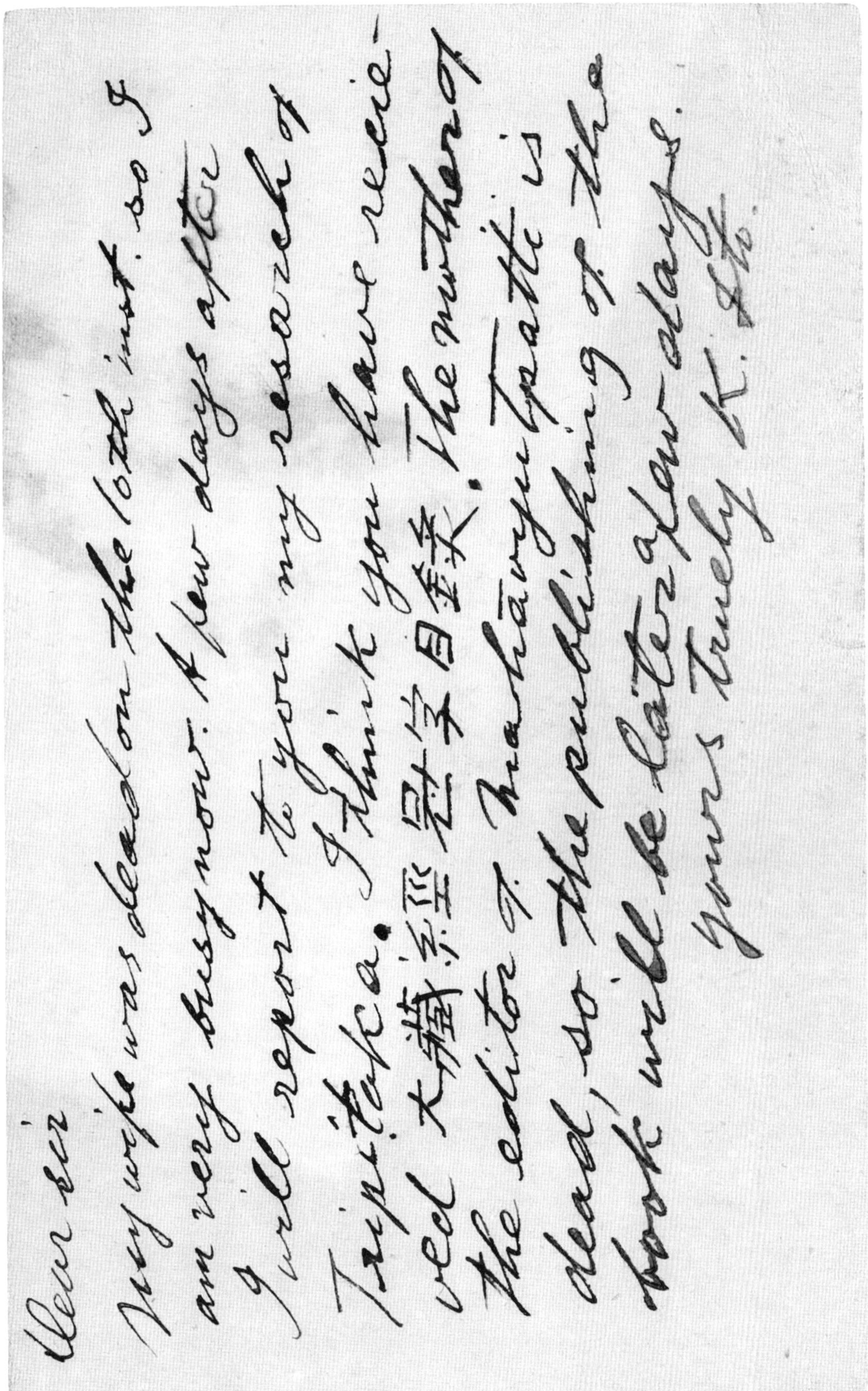
Dear sir
my wife was dead on the 10th inst. so I
am very busy now. A few days after
I will report to you my research of
Tripitaka. I think you have recieved 大藏經君字目錄. The mother of
the editor of Mahāvyutpatti is
dead, so the publishing of the
book will be later a few days.
yours truely K. Ito.

My dear Dr.

29th ~~August~~ July.
Ichikawa Chibaken

I have the honor to send this letter to you.
I think you recieved the book which I sent to you. The book "mahāvyuttpatti was rare in the bookstore because there was few published. I found the book after much trouble.
The reward which you are sending now I hope you will stop from next month till I ask to you, for the ~~a~~ reward which I recieved to this month is sufficient to me for my labor.
But I am continuing my reserches as ever so I will report to you the result after a few days.
I am continuing the reserches as ever and will continue for ever till the items which you wanted to me is reserched up but the reward is sufficient to me for my labor.

When I want the reward I will ask you.

Your's truely K. Ito.

Oct. 16th

My dear sir

I am very sorry for you to write down to you with broken English.

I picked out the items which you wanted to me as pollows por instance

月氏國 牧立. 1063.

and missed the title of books in which the item are contained, so to-day I write down the titles of books.

If you want to translate those passages I will do with broken English and if you want to see me I will go to Nikko whenever you want except Monday, Tuesday. I will write to you again.

I am continuing my resarch and at the end of this month I will see all tripitaka about 350 or 300 volumes.

Your's trully K. Ito.

Ivanoff

Calcutta,

27/VIII/21.

Милостивый Государь,

Господинъ Профессоръ,

Недавно получилъ іюльскій номеръ J.R.A.S. и сегодня, просматривая List of Members, увидалъ Ваше имя. Пишу отчасти чтобы "установить контактъ", а главнымъ образомъ чтобы предложить Вамъ несколько вопросовъ, которые меня очень интересуютъ и отвѣтомъ на которые Вы очень меня обяжете. Я сейчасъ въ Калькуттѣ, какъ видите, изъ Россіи уѣхалъ болѣе трехъ лѣтъ назадъ (16го Мая 1918 г.). Былъ долго въ Персіи, служилъ въ Индійской Арміи (East Persia Force), былъ демобилизованъ въ ноябрѣ прошлаго года, пріѣхалъ въ Калькутту и уже полгода работаю въ Asiat. Soc. of Bengal надъ каталогомъ Перс. и Арабск. рукописей.

Вопросы, которые я хотѣлъ бы предложить Вамъ — чисто освѣдомительнаго характера: есть ли у Васъ что нибудь новое объ Азіатскомъ Музеѣ, объ Университетѣ и о томъ, кто теперь живетъ на Дальнемъ Востокѣ? Мнѣ бы очень хотѣлось знать, какъ живетъ Ѳ.А. Розенбергъ, Алексеевъ и Владимірцевъ. Одинъ Буддійскій монахъ здѣсь, въ Калькуттѣ, Срамана Ванъ Хуй, говоритъ, будто младшій Розенбергъ, спасаясь самъ, погибъ, при попыткѣ перейти въ Японію или что-то въ этомъ родѣ (онъ толкомъ не могъ объяснить мнѣ это). Это было бы чрезвычайно печально.

Вы навѣрно знаете, что Елисеевъ (японистъ) въ Парижѣ, Н. Марръ тоже былъ недавно тамъ, но вернулся въ Петербургъ. Sylvain Lévi устроилъ Щербатскому лекціи въ Collège de France и онъ (Щерб.), по моимъ послѣднимъ свѣдѣніямъ (отъ В. Ѳ. Минорскаго), сидитъ въ Прагѣ, возясь съ [illegible]. С. Ѳ. Ольденбургъ будто-бы живъ и здоровъ, а Бартольдъ будто бы профессоромъ въ Египтѣ (я въ этомъ не увѣренъ).

Я писалъ безчисленное множество разъ въ Россію, но до сихъ поръ, болѣе трехъ лѣтъ, отвѣта не имѣю. Спасибо Минорскому, что пишетъ изъ Парижа.

Я буду радъ, если Вы отвѣтите. Несомнѣнно, я всегда къ Вашимъ услугамъ для всякихъ порученій здѣсь, въ Калькуттѣ.

Желаю Вамъ всего самого лучшаго, здоровья и благополучія и счастья,

искренно уважающій Васъ

В. Ивановъ.

W. IVANOW
c/o Asiatic Society of Bengal,
1, Park street, Calcutta.

1/XII/22.
Calcutta.

Многоуважаемый

Александръ Александровичъ.

Въ моемъ прошломъ письмѣ я невольно ввелъ Васъ въ заблужденіе, написавъ, что Peterson'овское изданіе Nyayabindu здѣсь не имѣется. Я дѣйствительно не могъ отыскать его въ здѣшнихъ каталогахъ. Въ томъ печатномъ спискѣ, к. я послалъ Вамъ, это изданіе помѣчено среди тибетскихъ текстовъ, но это ошибка, т.к. это тибетскій текстъ Nyayabindu съ комментаріемъ Vinitadeva или что-то въ этомъ родѣ. Однако я все-же старался отыскать, и, послѣ долгой возни, добился того, что мнѣ нашли где-то случайно сохранившійся экз. Nyayabindu, к. я и посылаю Вамъ одновременно, отдѣльнымъ пакетомъ.

Какъ я писалъ Вамъ уже, здѣшнія библіотеки всѣ одинаково безпомощны для справокъ. И иногда случайно бываютъ открытія! Книга пострадала отъ червей, но другого экземпляра не было.

Отъ Zucker'а я имѣлъ письмо изъ Агры. Теперь онъ уже вѣроятно давно на пути въ Египетъ.

Новаго у меня пока ничего не накопилось. Я все жду, что Вы сообщите новыя сведения о России. Я также не могу пока добиться ответа из Музея и думаю, что это все-еще небезопасно для музейских переписываться съ за-границей, опасно и молчать. Мне вчера писал из Парижа Минорский, но у него никаких известий тоже.

Итак, пока по-прежнему всё хорошо. Надеюсь, что будете писать о себе. Будьте здоровы и бодры.

В. Иванов.

Влад. Алекс.

W. IVANOW.

c/o Asiatic Society of Bengal,

1, Park Street, Calcutta.

3/2/23.
Calcutta.

Многоуважаемый Александр Александрович.

Получил Ваше письмо от 10/12 — около, как видите, почти двух месяцев. Я очень виноват перед Вами в том, что задержал отправку книг. Записка Ваша нашлась вскоре после того, как я отправил Вам Nyayabindu. Если бы я знал, что книги нужны Вам спешно, я бы послал сейчас-же.

Сегодня-же дал Бабу список книг, к. Вам нужны, и завтра пошлю их. Сегодня посылать было бесполезно, т.к. пароход идет только 6го.

Я не знал, что Лемм умер. Его не особенно уважал, но жалко, конечно. Я получил письмо от А.И.; к сожалению, в нем было не очень много сведений, т.к. если я и знаю что нибудь, то главным образом из Парижа. А.И. советует ехать в Россию. Но не рано-ли? Если тихий, никому никогда не сказавший резкого слова Крачковский сидит в тюрьме, то что-же ждет меня, с моей резкостью и раздражительностью. Да и ехать-то не на что, а там, в Петербурге, все эти музеи 'гнилых камней' и т.п. кажутся довольно таки 'лишними пустяками'. Ведь теперь, когда всякими 'реквизициями' Россия обобрана до-чиста, трудно придумать, откуда будут взяты деньги когда выйдут суммы, полученные за награбленное в церквах золото. Я не осуждаю С.Ф. и других, кто укрепляет все эти музеи и институты. Я понимаю хорошо, что здесь действует главным образомъ стремленiе спасти остатки интеллигенцiи. Но ясно, какъ день, что всякое прикосновенiе свѣжаго воздуха и здраваго смысла къ этой заколдованной области, напримѣръ Россiи нашихъ дней, заставитъ все это превратиться въ прахъ и грязь.

Здѣсь въ Индiи чрезвычайно трудно и тяжело. Всюду сокращаютъ, урѣзываютъ, упраздняютъ и т. д., и жизнь становится все тяжелѣе. И никто не можетъ предсказать, когда это все кончится. Хоть бы война какая нибудь случилась на Востокѣ, — все таки заработокъ бы нашелся.

Со Nyaya-Bindu др. Peterson'омъ въ спискѣ вышла большая путаница, какъ я уже Вамъ писалъ своевременно. Одно и то-же названiе относилось къ Тибетскому и Санскритскому тексту. Но все-же я нашелъ и послалъ то, что Вы хотѣли.

Никакъ не могу добиться свѣдѣнiй объ Алексѣевѣ и Владимiрцовѣ. Т. к. они оба близко относятся къ интересующей Васъ области, б. м. Вы слыхали о нихъ что нибудь? На дняхъ хочу написать большое письмо С. Ө. Я очень боюсь, однако, не можетъ ли это его скомпрометировать.

Книги, какъ Вы писали, отсылаю сiю минуту. Изъ Вашихъ 15 рупiй израсходовано (2/-8, 3/-/10/-4/-6 и пересылка 1-3) — 11 рупiй 11 ана. Укажите, какимъ способомъ лучше всего возвратить Вамъ остающiяся 3/-5. Быть можетъ, Вамъ надо еще какую нибудь книгу?

Шлю Вамъ самыя лучшiя и сердечныя пожеланiя успѣха.

Н. Ивановъ.

Адресъ пока-прежн.-же.

P.S. Простите, что отниму еще немножко Вашего времени. Только-что получил письмо от Sir Aurel Stein'a, который просит узнать для него нижеследующее: ..... anything about the ground crossed to the north and N.W. of Barkul (on the Tien-Shan) by Potanin in 1876-7, and Przhevalsky in 1879-80. I mean the desert hills and plain of Dzungaria for about 200 miles distance beyond Barkul. The briefest abstract concerning the general character of this ground would suffice.

Как Вам известно, я очень мало знаю о Средней Азии, т.е. о той ея части, о которой спрашивает Stein. И я боюсь, что здесь я не найду подходящих матеріалов для того-чтобы дать исчерпывающий ответ. А так как Вы специалист как раз в этой области, то я беру на себя обратиться к Вам со просьбой указать, где я могу найти необходимыя сведѣнія, и имеется ли что-нибудь в Изв. И.Р.Г.О. Конечно, это только в том случае, если исполненіе этой просьбы не потребует никакой траты времени и других усилий. Вы очень обязали бы меня Вашими указаніями, особенно [illegible], т.к. мне хотелось бы "облагодарить" Стейна за его постоянную ко мне любезность. Не знаю, переписываетесь ли Вы с ним? Он сейчас работает над своими матеріалами последних двух экспедицій, и сидит почти безвыездно в Кашмире. Я так и не видался с Бухары, 1915 г., хотя до сих пор приходится довольно часто обмениваться с ним письмами.

Простите за длинное посланіе.

[signature]

21/IX/23.
Calcutta.

Многоуважаемый

Александръ Александровичъ.

Очень благодаренъ за Ваше милое письмо отъ 7/VIII. Я очень радъ, что на этотъ разъ я могъ быстро и удачно исполнить Ваше порученіе: хотя книга, которую Вы спрашивали, и разошлась давно, и уже долгое время обѣщаютъ выпустить новое изданіе, но мнѣ повезло, и я случайно досталъ одинъ экземпляръ. Она состоитъ изъ двухъ частей, которыя отдѣльно не продаются. Пошлю Вамъ её обязательно завтра-же.

Я слышалъ, что С.Ѳ. и Алексѣевъ были на празднованіи 100-лѣтняго юбилея RAS, и потомъ поѣхали въ Парижъ.

Оріенталистъ въ Индіи вырождается еще больше въ частности, чѣмъ въ Китаѣ. Я сейчасъ печатаю свой каталогъ Персидскихъ рукописей Аз. О-ва. Набрано уже болѣе 400 страницъ, всего-же, видимо, будетъ за 1000. Приходится спѣшить, а потому иногда печатаютъ больше 100 страницъ въ мѣсяцъ, и меня иногда совершенно забрасываютъ корректурами. Работаю до 14-16 часовъ въ сутки. Какъ это ни странно, несмотря на всѣ дефекты Baptist Mission Press, они прилагаютъ очень мало хлопотъ съ діакритическими знаками. Я бъ сказалъ, что эта сторона дѣла обстоитъ очень хорошо. Я не знаю той Шанхайской печатни, о которой Вы пишете, но вполнѣ допускаю возможность многихъ непріятностей, а потому искренно сочувствую.

Что слышно объ Ѳ. А. Розенбергѣ? Мнѣ никакъ не удается завязать съ нимъ переписку, а вѣдь мы были когда-то друзья. Правда, я не сочувствовалъ многимъ его идеямъ, какъ и онъ не одобрялъ кое-что въ моихъ, но въ общемъ мнѣ какъ-то больно видѣть, что всѣ мои попытки остаются безъ послѣдствій. Или, быть можетъ, пока еще такая 'роскошь', какъ частная переписка не допускается въ свободной пролетарской странѣ? А очень жаль.

Очень прошу передать мои комплименты А. И. Иванову. Быть можетъ Вы будете такъ любезны и не найдете затруднительнымъ передать ему прилагаемую записку? Если это почему-либо Вамъ доставитъ неудобства, то просто порвите ее.

Пока пожелаю Вамъ всего хорошаго, всяческаго успѣха и удачи. Не буду повторять, что я всегда къ Вашимъ услугамъ для всякихъ порученій по части индійскихъ и тибетскихъ книгъ. Мнѣ всегда большую помощь въ этомъ дѣлѣ оказываетъ J. van-Manen, голландецъ, давно живущій въ Индіи, занимающійся Тибетомъ (онъ теперь General Secretary въ Аз.-мъ О-вѣ).

Итакъ, еще разъ всего хорошаго.

Искренно преданный Вамъ

В. Ивановъ.

23/VII/24.
Calcutta.
c/o Asiatic Society of Bengal,
1, Park Street.

Многоуважаемый

Александръ Александровичъ.

Очень благодарю Васъ за Ваше любезное письмо отъ 23/VI, которое я получилъ вчера. Я радъ, что Вы живы и здоровы, и продолжаете научную дѣятельность.

Вы справедливо жалуетесь на своихъ корреспондентовъ. Я тоже былъ въ очень хорошихъ отношеніяхъ со Ѳ. А. Розенбергомъ. Когда я былъ въ Бухарѣ, онъ писалъ мнѣ почти каждую недѣлю. А теперь я также и не имѣю отвѣта ни на одно изъ моихъ многочисленныхъ писемъ. Я думаю, есть причины, которыя дѣлаютъ писаніе писемъ за-границу не очень безопаснымъ предпріятіемъ. Все пишутъ рѣдко: Бартольдъ, Алексѣевъ, и др.

Я тоже думаю, что въ письмахъ изъ Россіи, и даже въ открытыхъ [illegible] кто оттуда пріѣхалъ, много недоговореннаго, и что всяческія неопредѣленности скорѣе всего обычны. Мнѣ бы очень хотѣлось вернуться, мнѣ безконечно надоѣла Индія, или, вѣрнѣе, Калькутта. Но я совершенно не представляю, что меня ждетъ.

Мой каталогъ еще не вышелъ. Онъ представляетъ настоящій 'рекордъ' въ смыслѣ 'быстроты изготовленія' и особенно печатанія, небывалый случай въ Индіи — 960 стр. убористаго шрифта въ 14 мѣсяцевъ!

Конечно, эта нелепая [illegible] и спешка (основанная на уродливых расчетах 'философских' и 'идеалистических' церковных скотов) страшно повредила всей работе. Но что делать! $3\frac{1}{2}$ года я работаю по 10–14 часов в день, без какого бы то ни было отдыха, даже воскресений. Плата мизерна, конечно. И если я работаю, то только потому, что это была редкостный случай практики, возможность на деле, а не в виде теоретических соображений, пройти через все фазы этой сложной и трудной операции. Надеюсь, что второй каталог, над которым я теперь начал работать, если удастся довести его до конца, будет много лучше, хотя эта коллекция хуже первой.

Если увидите А. И. Иванова, передайте ему мои самые лучшие пожелания.

С. Ѳ. Ольденбург написал мне несколько строк из Парижа, обещая написать большое письмо из Германии. Но он так и вернулся в Россию, не сделав этого, и я так и не получил письма. Видали-ли Вы брошюрку о 'Востоковедении в Петрограде'? Картинка довольно 'пышная', но, в сущности, вся это только 'фарс'. Вся публика, эти '53 персоны', просто не имеют времени 'заседать' во всех этих многочисленных учреждениях, не только работать. А жаль будет, если умрут наши великолепные русские традиции в Оріенталистике.

Я мечтаю, что мы с Вами увидимся в Петербурге, куда Вы рано или поздно вернетесь. Скорее-бы!

Всего хорошего, желаю Вам благополучно дожить до лучших дней, которые должны настать. Пишите; если есть порученія, не откладывайте сообщить их. Всего хорошего.

В. Иванов.

Dear Professor Jackson,

A few days ago I met ~~I came~~ Dr. Lucius Porter ~~told me it~~ and was very glad to hear from him that he had seen you not long ago ~~at~~ in New York and that you were as active and as flourishing as always.

~~At~~ A year or two ago I met another American friend of yours (I forget his name) and we sent you a "Bierkarte".

I wonder whether you ever received it?

LEGATION OF THE
UNITED STATES OF AMERICA

Peking, March 17, 1933.

My dear Baron:

With further reference to our conversation of last evening, in the course of which I expressed my interest in the fact that, after receiving from you the reprint of your article "On two Tibetan pictures representing some of the spiritual ancestors of the Dalai Lama and of the Panchen Lama" printed by the Bulletin of the National Library of Peiping, I noted in my copy of the Journal of the American Oriental Society, on pages 338 et seq., your article "Notes on two Lama paintings":

You have now given me for perusal the copies of the declaration which you have asked the American Oriental Society to publish in this Journal explanatory of this situation. I have read the letter which you received from Mr. Jayne dated December 10th, as well as the telegram which you received from him dated December 28th asking for permission to publish in the Journal of the American Oriental Society. I also have the photograph of the certified copy of your telegram to Mr. Jayne dated December 31st requesting him to inform the American Oriental Society that you could not let them have the article because it had already been published.

It seems to me that you did everything that you could do under the circumstances to inform those responsible at home of the situation here. As far back as December 10th Mr. Jayne was endeavoring to get the article returned to you. Now, I do not know when the American Oriental Society's Journal, Volume 52, No. 4, for December, 1932, went to press, although the cover

indicates

Baron de Stael Holstein,
Ex-Austrian Legation,
Peiping.

- 2 -

indicates that it was published on December 30, 1932, two days after Mr. Jayne sent his telegram requesting permission to publish. My copy of the Oriental Society's Journal came to me about two weeks ago. If the date on the cover of the Journal has any significance at all, the articles published therein must have been set up and ready for the press very shortly after December 30, 1932, if not before, and it seems therefore that you have a very reasonable complaint against the Journal for having put you in a somewhat embarrassing position by publishing your article without your permission.

Very sincerely yours,

Nelson Trusler Johnson

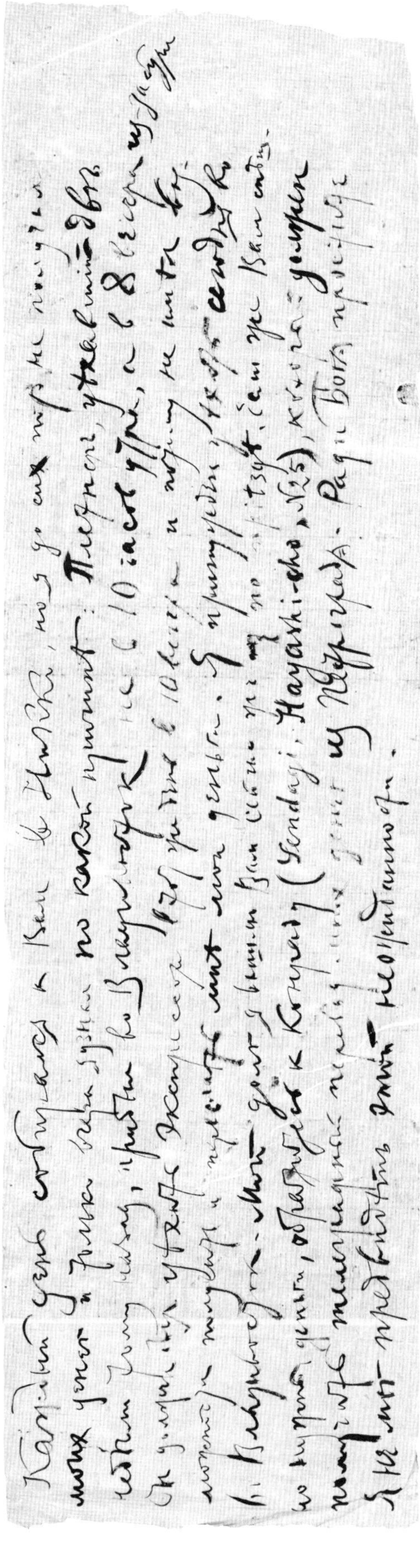
Каждый день собираюсь к Вам в Никко, но я до сих пор не получил
моих денег и только вчера узнал по какой причине: Плетнер, уехавший две
недели тому назад, прибыл во Владивосток не в 10 часов утра, а в 8 вечера из-за бури.
Он должен был уехать экспрессом, который уходит в 10 вечера и поэтому не имел возможности получить и переслать мне мои деньги. Я принужден [illegible] сегодня во
Владивосток. Мой долг я вышлю Вам сейчас [illegible] по [illegible]. Если же Вам спешно нужны деньги, обратитесь к Конраду (Sendagi, Hayashi-cho, №25), который должен
получить телеграфный перевод моих денег из Петрограда. Ради Бога простите
я не мог предвидеть этой неожиданности.

Словарей, въ которыхъ бы были полностью Го-он, Кан-он, То-ин, не существуетъ. Приходится сделать сводку изъ нѣсколькихъ словарей. Возьмите словарь Нотри (本富). Изъ старыхъ словарей могу указать 字A (прилагаю бумажку); ихъ найти можно у продавцовъ старыхъ книгъ. Но самая полная сводка его Вы можете получить у Гото Асатаро (Goto Asataro) 後藤朝太郎 съ которымъ Вас может познакомить Фудзиока.

Ваш Е. Поливанов

Oct. 22nd 35

My dear Mr. Keller,

~~Kindly~~ Please ~~do~~ excuse this late reply to your letter. I do recall the wonderful dinner, to which you invited Pelliot and myself about seven years ago, and I remember ~~[illegible]~~ very well how much we both enjoyed the evening.

~~[illegible] "The translation [illegible] of "Don Quixote" should of course be done by a native~~

~~The chronology of Sarat Chandra Das~~

Sarat Chandra Das is responsible for a great number of the mistakes, which Professor Pelliot rectifies in his article. The latter has, however, not received all the attention, ~~it~~ which it deserves. ~~[illegible]~~ Some of the erroneous dates due to Sarat Chandra Das have become ~~have been are have been~~ almost classical, and are constantly repeated even in the most modern ~~publications. The statement that Con-kha-pa died in 1417, for instance, is found in [illegible] Sarat Chandra Das' translation of the Rehu-mig~~ (1882) as ~~well as in (Journ. of the As. Soc. of Bengal 18~~

of the article, however, ~~is~~ contains an examination of of a number of (European and Indian) treatises on Tibetan history, in which Professor Pelliot discovers an almost incredible number of chronological miscalculations. ~~Most~~ The majority of ~~most of which are due~~ these mistakes are originally due to an arithmetical error on the part of ~~the~~ Csoma de Körös, ~~who~~ the famous Hungarian scholar, who ~~composed wrote~~ + published a Grammar of the Tibetan Language and many other learned works about a hundred years ago.

~~Among the~~ Among the authors criticized by Professor Pelliot we find Georg Huth and Sarat Chandra Das, whose historical works are full of ~~historical~~ chronological mistakes. The fact that the erroneous Christian dates founded on the ~~miscalculati~~ miscalculations of these writers are evidently still regarded as correct by a number of modern authors seems to justify the publication of ~~chronological tables, which are me give more details than the papers~~

I hardly venture to hope that Tibetan writers
will ever consult my tables, I regard ~~but~~ ~~I do not think~~ the possibility
that some Chinese writers on Tibet may do so
~~does~~ as less remote. If the Emperor Ch'ien-lung
~~had had~~ ~~[illegible] Tibetan~~ had had carefully prepared Sino-Tibetan
chronological tables at his disposal he ~~might have~~ would probably have placed
~~fixed placed~~ Tsoṅ-kha-pa's birth in the year
~~[illegible]~~ 13 , instead of affirming that the great refor-
mer was born in ~~[illegible]~~ 14 .

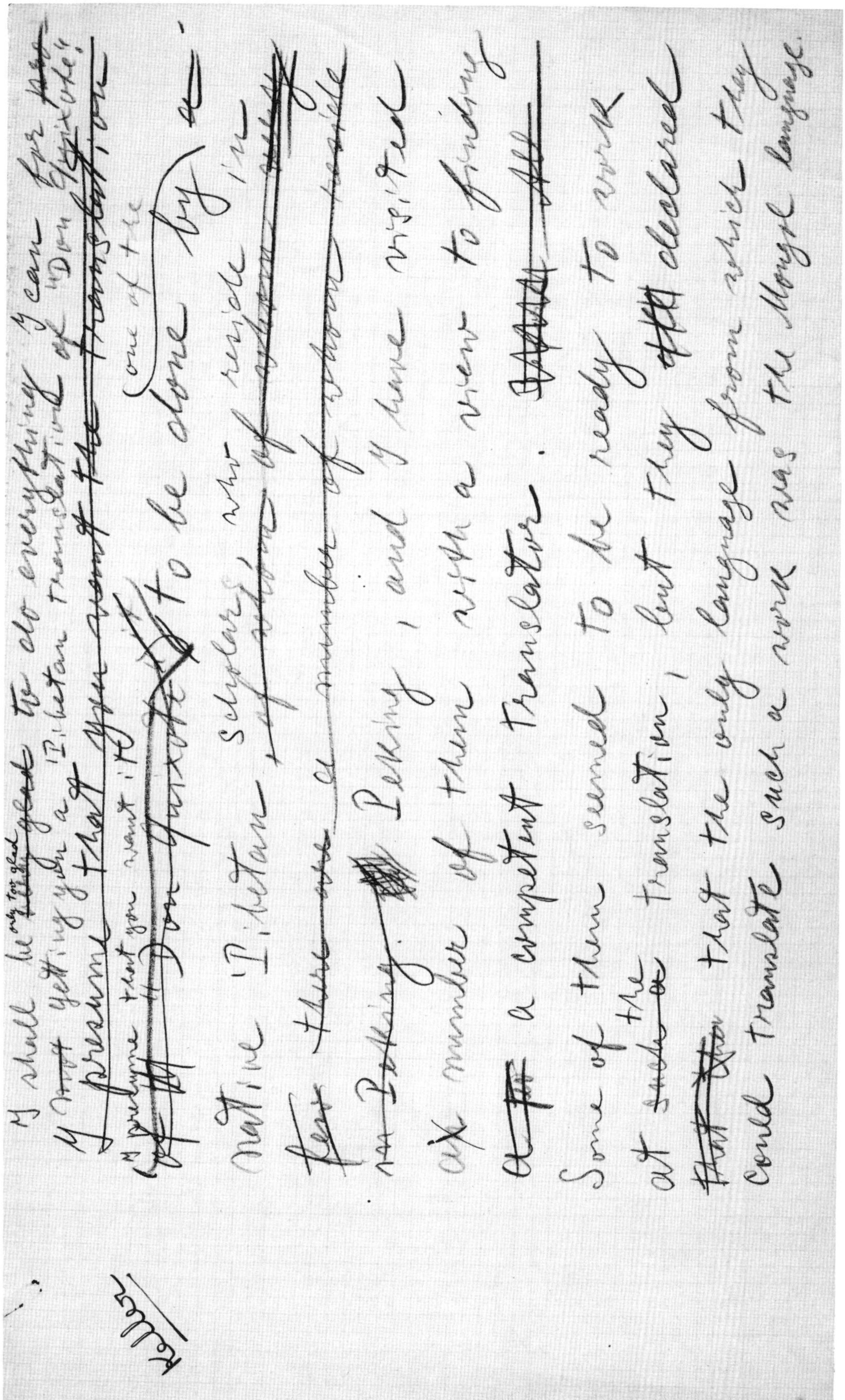

Keller

I shall be only too ~~very glad~~ glad to do everything I can for ~~pro-~~
I ~~root~~ getting you a Tibetan translation of "Don Quixote".
~~I presume that you want the translation~~
I presume that you want it ~~of the "Don Quixote"~~ to be done by one of the ~~a~~
native Tibetan scholars, who reside in ~~, of whom of whom very~~
~~few there are a number of whom reside~~
~~in Peking.~~ Peking, and I have visited
a number of them with a view to finding
~~a to~~ a competent translator. ~~All~~
Some of them seemed to be ready to work
at ~~such a~~ the translation, but they ~~all~~ declared
~~that the~~ that the only language from which they
could translate such a work was the Mongol language.

Therefore I looked for ~~tried to find~~ a Mongol translation of "Don Quixote". As I did not succeed in finding one, I decided to wait until Mr. ~~Owen~~ Lattimore returned from his journey into the interior, before answering your letter. Mr. Lattimore tells me that he knows of no Mongol translation of Don Quichote, but that he ~~will~~ will try and have one prepared for you. As soon as I get a Mongol translation, I will again approach the Tibetans.

~~I am a~~ I am very proud to hear that "all of the trustees who know me wished ~~that~~ I should again make a visit to America". I had a ~~wonderful &~~ splendid time in Boston in 28/29 and ~~[illegible]~~ I shall certainly accept the invitation when it comes, although .... Dr. Ware, who spent a couple of months here this summer, will better be able to explain to you viva voce ~~what~~ the dots stand for, than I could do in a letter.

With many thanks for your kind note and with my best wishes I remain yours very sincerely

A. Staël Holstein.

Note

One of the writers, whose chronology Professor Pelliot criticizes is Sarat Chandra Das, ~~other~~ the author of a transl

Note

Professor Pelliot's ~~discovery~~ discoveries have not received all the attention, which they deserve, and some of the authors, whose ~~chr~~ chronology has been entirely discredited in the article quoted above, are still regarded as authorities. ~~by so~~ Some of Sarat Chandra Das' erroneous dates, for instance, have found their way into quite modern publications. Comp. Sarat Chandra Das' article in the Journal of the Asiatic Soc. of Bengal for 1882, pages 21–22, and ~~page 174 of the Asiatic Mythology (London 1932)~~ Professor Hackin's article on ~~the~~ the Mythology of Lamaism (Asiatic Mythology, London 1932, page 174). ~~which state that Mkhas~~ Both ~~the~~ papers state that Mkhas-grub, Con-kha-pa's famous pupil, died in 1439. The correct date seems to be ~~1438 (Ea~~ ~~1438 (Earth Horse)~~ 1438 (Earth-Horse, Rehu-mig page 279b). Comp. also note 15 ~~in~~ of my article on two Tibetan ~~paintings~~ pictures (Bulletin of the National Library, Peiping 1932).

Peking, February 27th 1936.

My dear Mr. Keller,

Many thanks for your letter dated November 21th 1935. I have obtained a copy of Ho Yü-po's translation of Don ~~Q~~ Quixote into Chinese, and Mr. Lattimore has found a Mongol, ~~(his own secretary)~~ who is able and willing to ~~will~~ translate the Chinese text into his own language for one hundred U.S. dollars. I think we shall easily find a Lama, who will translate the Mongolian translation into Tibetan. Mr. Lattimore is going to America in March and will report to you personally as soon as he reaches Boston.

I am very glad to hear that ~~the~~ ~~you like the~~ ~~Tanjur~~ ~~wh~~ ~~volu~~ (Kanjur and Tanjur) Tibetan volumes which I bought here some years ago.

I do not think that the expected changes in the status of Peking will interfere with my work in any way.

I infer from your letter that ~~you do~~ Chiang Jui-ching's translation of Don Quixote is unknown in Boston. May I ~~enclose a copy of~~ present you with a copy of Chiang Jui-ching's translation?

With many good wishes ~~for~~ I remain yours very sincerely

A. Staël-Holstein.

My dear Mr. Keller, Mitte Juli 36 abgesch.

Many thanks for your letter dated June 5th ~~193~~ 1936. The Sino-Mongolian translator of "Don Quixote" has left Peking to spend ~~[illegible]~~ the hot months in his native steppes. As soon as he returns I shall get into touch with him and report to you how his translation work progresses. ~~I suppose I shall have to consult I do not~~ I shall also consult him as to the price of printing ~~of printing~~ the Mongolian and the Tibetan versions. You will, I think, find that the printing charges are astonishingly low. The hundred U. S. dollars, which you sent me, ~~I shall keep [illegible]~~ I shall have to keep — for the present. I do not know ~~what kind of a~~ the details of the contract, which ~~Mr. Lattimore~~ has concluded with ~~the~~ Mr. Gombozhap (Mgon-po-skyabs), the Sino-~~Indian~~ Mongolian translator. It is very kind of you to enquire about my health. It has given me no great trouble during the ~~last~~ few months, ~~I The only~~ but I still must refrain rigorously from drink. I could

not now enjoy a banquet like the one to which you so
kindly invited ~~me~~ Pelliot and myself in 1928.

ADDRESS OF THE SECRETARY IS
MUSEUM OF FINE ARTS, BOSTON

EAST ASIATIC SOCIETY
OF BOSTON

9 April 1929

Dear Baron de Staël-Holstein,

On behalf of the President and Council I have the pleasure of extending to you an invitation to become a non-resident member of the East Asiatic Society of Boston. The responsibilities of members are not onerous: they attend the meetings if they care to; and non-resident members pay an initial fee only. That is $5.-

As the Society was founded to promote the study and the discussion of subjects relating to the Far East, we very heartily hope that you may be interested to join it.

Very sincerely yours,

F. S. Kershaw

Secretary

Baron Alexander de Staël-Holstein
8 Sherman Hall,
Soldiers' Field P.O.
Boston

8 Sherman Hall, April 10th 1929

Dear Mr. Kershaw,

I highly appreciate the honour of being a non-resident member of the East Asiatic Society and I thank you as well as the Council very much for ~~this~~ your invitation. I also enclose a cheque for the amount of my initial fee ($5).

~~I hear that there will be another East Asiatic dinner on Monday April 22nd. May I attend that dinner and will you be so kind as to let me know ~~where~~ to whom the subscription is to be paid?~~

Believe me yours very sincerely A. Staël-Holstein.

Fong Tchai Yuan

Friday 22nd June

Dear Baron Stahl,

Just a line to inform you that I have made arrangements for my friends to meet you here at my house at 3 o'clock in the afternoon on the 27th inst. (Wednesday next) There will be three gentlemen coming and

I dare say they will be able give you some information about what you wanted to find out.

As it is not easy to get them all come together I hope you will not fail to come

Looking forward to the pleasure of seeing you again

Sincerely Yours

Kungpah T. King.

13 Chienliang Hutung
Tungsze Pailou
Peking 6.6.24.

Dear Baron Von Stahl,

As I have verbally requested you and you have so kindly consented to standardise the pronounciations of a few "Tchou" or charms that my brother has put into romanisation as near as he could make them. I am now sending herewith enclosed a sheet of this Romanized charms. And beg to thank you most profoundly, in advance, for your kindness. With my best regards & with same from my brother

Yours Sincerely
Kungpah T. King.

P.S. I have just come back from Shanghai & will be coming to call on you in the near future.

5th July 1924

Dear Baron Holstein,

Many thanks for your kind reply.

I am getting a copy of the charm made in Chinese & will send same when ready.

Yours sincerely
Kungpah T. King

KUNGPAH T. KING
15 CHIENLIAN HUTUNG
TUNGSZE PAILOU
PEKING

1 - 5 - 25.

Dear Baron Holstein,

I am sending you herewith a copy of the 大悲咒 in its usual version, it starts on the back half of the sixth leaf of the book and finishes at the end of the seventh leaf.

The curious situation is that no one is quite sure of the original dialect this phonetic translation was made in, hence the uncertainty of the pronunciation of the characters. Any enlightenment you may give us will not only be

appreciated by ourselves but also by all
those that wish to say this "Charm" right.

With our best compliments

Yours sincerely

Kungpak T. King

TA 大 PEI 悲 TSEU 呪

NA MO HA LA DAI NU TOU LO YIEH IEH. NA MO UH LI IEH.

PO LU CHI TI SAH POH LA IEH. PU DI SAH TU PO IEH. MO HO

SAH TU PO IEH. MO HO GIA LU NI GIA IEH. EH SAH BEY LA

FA YE. SU DAI NU DAI SI. NA MO SI CHI LI TU IH MOON

UH LI IEH. PO LU CHI DI SAH VAH LA LUN DU PO. NA MO

NU LA GIN SZE. ÇHI LI MO HO BEY TOU SAH MI. SAH PO UH

TU DUH SE BUN. UH SE YIN. SAH PO SAH TOU NU MO PO SAH

TOU NU MO PO GIA. MO FA DUDAI. DAY TZE TOO. AI UH PO

LU HI. LU GIA DI. GIA LU DI. YEE HI LI. MO HO PO DI

SAH TU. SAH PO SAH PO. MO LA MO LA. MO HI MO HI LI

DU YIN. CHE LU CHE LU CHI MOON. DO LU DO LU VAH SER

YIEH DI. MO HO VAH SER YIEH DI. DOO LO DOO LO. DEE LI NI

SAH VAH LA YIEH. TSO LA TSO LA. MO MO VAH MO LA. MO DI LI

IH HI YEE HI. SER NU SER NU. UH LA SUN FOH LA SER LI.

VAH SAH VAH SUN. FOH LA SER ZIEH. HU LU HU LU MO LA.

HU LU HU LU HI LI. SO LA SO LA. SI LI SI LI. SOO LOO

(II)

SSO LOO SOO LOO. PU DE YIEH PU DE YIEH. PU DOO YIEH PU DOO YIEH. MI DI LI MIEH. NU LA GIN SZE. DEE LI SER NI NU. POO IEH MO NU. SO PO HO. SI DOO IEH. SO PO HO. SO DO YEE NY SER BAI LA YIEH. SO PO HO. NU LA GIN SZE. SO PO HO. MO LA NU LA. SO PO HO. SI LA SUN UH MO CHIA YIEH. SO PO HO. SO PO MO HO UH SI DO IEH. SO PO HO. TSER CHI LA UH SI DOU IEH. SO PO HO. ~~NUXXLAXXGINXXSZEX~~ PO DOU MO KI SI TO IEH. SO PO HO. NU LA GIN SZE. BAI GIA LA YIEH. SO PO HO. MO PO LI SUN KI LA IEH. SO PO HO. NA MO HA LA DAI NU TOU LO YIEH IEH. NA MO UH LI YIEH. PO LU CHI TI. SAH BEI LA IEH. SO PO HO. EH SI DIEN TU MAN TU LA PEH DOU YIEH. SO PO HO.

OHTSU G. KING
1 KAKA HUTUNG
TUNGSZE PAILOU
PEKING, CHINA

4th June 1925

Dear Baron Holstein,

Herewith a book of 4 volumes of the collected writings of the Buddist Priest "Yin Kwon" 印光 He is the most revered Priest now, but his writing are chiefly concerned in moral teachings and little concerning discussions of Classics, although undoubtedly he is quitl learned. Please keep the book as I have another set myself.

Yours faithfully
Sohtsu G. King.

SOHTSU G. KING
11 KAKA HUTUNG
TUNGSZE PAILOU
PEKING, CHINA

6th August 1925

Dear Baron Holsteen,

Please pardon this long delay in writing to you, I have been away for some days. I want to thank you very very much for the kindness in giving me the correct pronounciation of the 大悲咒 I fear I have given you an enoamous amount of trouble. Dr. Graban is still at Peitaiho; but I think he will be here in another week's time.

Trusting that you are enjoying

the best of health & thanking you again most heartily

Yours sincerely
Sohtsu G. King.

Dear Mr. Kung,

The English reading of the Roman characters varies too much; therefore I have given you the phonetic value of each Chinese character: 1) according to the French pronunciation (black pencil) and then 2) according to the German pronunciation (red pencil). In many cases I am ~~[illegible]~~ quite sure of the correctness of my indications, but in other cases (where, chiefly, ~~[illegible]~~ magic syllables, without meaning, ~~[illegible]~~ in the ordinary Sanskrit language, occur) I am not. But I have done my best. Please excuse the long delay and believe ~~[illegible]~~ me yours sincerely

Many thanks for sending me Mr. Yin-kuan's (印光) books. I shall read them with great interest.

I

200,Asahicho, Toyohashi,
Aichi-Ken, Japan
10th May,1929

Dear Baron. A von Staël

Excuse me for my long silence. It has already elapsed a year since I had the honour to meet you and Mr. Baron. Ungern with my brother in Kyoto. In that case it is thousand pities to say, we couldn'd to give you any satisfaction with seeing there for my poor guidance.

Since then, certainly, you are enjoying excellent health, we think. Now, we are in a most agreable season. The cerry-blossoms are blooming at their best and birds are singing merry among the trees. The Universe is waking up from a long sleep and seems very happy in this comfortable season.

At the end of last year--November 1928--we had the Emperor's Coronation in Kyoto Capital. So I am going to tell you about the outline of the Imperial Palace which permitted to the public the honour of seeing.

2

These are opened by the Public-Inspection for 5 months- from December I928 to April of this year. Newspaper reported us that the public who had the honour of seeing were 5,339,323 persons, including the Japanese and foreign visitors. The card here-in,the one of His I. M. The Emperor's Carriage passing the Arch for the welcome in front of the Kyoto-Station with His Imperial Procession to perform the Ceremony of Coronation.

Imperial Palace consists of these parts. There are Main Palace which is contained the Shishin-Den, Shunkoden, Sento-Palace which is contained Daijyo-Kyu, Two Assembling Hall and the Banquet Hall.

First of all, passing through the Gate, we can see the Imperial Porch. Next,through the brilliant-gate and reach the Open Space of Shishin-Den; that which is the place performed the Ceremony of Coronation.

Inside the Shishin-Den there is the Imperial Throne.- (Takamikura-Emperor's Seat, Michodai-Empress's

3

seat) In front of the Shishin-Den there are Banzai Flags, curious drums and bells. The left side of it is adorned with a famous Cherry Tree of Sakon (left side), and the right side a famous Mandanrin Orange Tree of Ukon (right side).

Walking a little, we reach the Shunko-Den. Shishin-Den are coloured brilliantly, but Shunko-Den only white. Because this one is the Holy Place where are enshrined the Sanctuary of the Imperial Ancesters.

Next we come to the Great Assembling Ha-ll, passing the long corridor and reach the Great Banquet Hall. I have never seen such a beutiful Hall. The center of the Hall is a dancing platform used to perform a famous dancing on the Banquet Days, such as Gosetsu, Kume and Taihei Dancings. At the head of this Hall, we see the Emperor's and Emprss's seats. At last we see the Daijyo-Kyu in the Sento-Palace. Here is a very mysterious spot. This is sacred place enshrined the Gods of Heaven and the Earth in order to inherit the ever-unbroken line of Trone.

4

Thus, a multitude from all over the land, after having the honour of seeing the Palace, can not help admireing its magnifience and nobleness.

This is my impression gained by the honour of seeing the Imperial Palace.

I solicit your continual comminucation.

Hoping that you will find this letter in the best of your health,

Yours very truly,

Kazuo Kitamura

I

200, Asahicho, Toyohashi,
Aichi-Ken, Japan.
IIth May I929

Dear. Prof. A von Stäel Holsteine

Excuse me for being my long silent, since I had the pleasure of seeing you in Kyoto with my elder brother; as Proverb says- Time flies like an arrow- a year already has elapsed.

Since then, how are you getting on? In our country, spring is now with us. The cherry-blossoms are blooming at their best and the birds are singing gaily here and there. The Universe are re-covered their vitality after long sleep and full of life.

We, also, are breathing again in this com-fortable season.

Immidiately after you left Kyoto, we had the Highest Ceremony- The Present-Emperor's Corona-tion Ceremony in Kyoto Ancient Palace. The outline of this Ceremony, my elder brother will partly only

2

relate you. Not necessary to use the pleonasm that it was the Great Ceremony with the whole of Nation.

Perhaps, you know quite well the state by newspaper and other means, I assure.

Prof. Ungern gives me lessons in French kindly twice a week. But sorry to say I couldn't to follow his kindly advice for my poor knowledge.

You are always having a good time in your place, I think.

I solicit your continual comminucation. If you permit, I should take this honour as a matter of gratification.

Prof. Ungern are enjoying always excellent health.

In conclusion, hoping that you will find this letter in the excellent health,

Yours very sincerely,

Nobuji Kitamura

PROFESSOR DR. STEN KONOW

~~KRISTIANIA~~ Oslo, Norway
ETNOGRAFISK MUSEUM

4. Nov. 1926

My dear Staël Holstein,

A postcard from you has been lying on my desk for more than two years, to remind me of the fact that I have a dear friend in Peking. And now it is really time to write. I do not know whether the Kāśyapaparipṛcchā has appeared in the meantime, but I am happy to know that you are busy at work. It is such a long time now since we met, and Mrs. Konow and myself long to see you again. Is there any chance of your coming to Europe in a near future? We should all be happy if there were. We had a grand time in India 1924-25, and it is difficult to imagine that almost two years have already passed since then. I have been very busy, but the results of much work often seem rather meagre. I am still at the Kharoṣṭhī inscriptions and have no hope of finishing them before the end of next year. I have had to give up our old theory about Khotanī being the language of the Tokharians. But then I think that the Yüe-chi and the Tokharians were quite different and had different languages. The Yüe-chi were Iranians and became the rulers of the Tokharians, who called their language Ārśi after the designation of their overlords, just as French and Russian have got their designations from alien peoples. And as the other hand classical authors transferred the name of the Tokharians to their Iranian masters. I suppose that you have seen my attempts at settling the chronology of Kharoṣṭhī inscriptions. A new contribution by van Wijk will appear in a near future. He there takes to show that the equal-space system cannot be used in calculating the Kaniṣka dates, and that calculations according to the unequal space system tend to show that the initial date of the era falls about 129 A.D. It seems to me that he must be right. I send you a reprint where I have tried to prove that Kaniṣka cannot be the founder of the Śaka era. Perhaps you have already seen it. But I did not intend to write shop. I wanted to tell you that we attended a meeting of the German Oriental Society in Hamburg last month. We met many friends, and your name was often mentioned, not only the day when we sent you a card. Your numerous friends agreed with us in regretting that you are so far away that we never meet, and we were all hoping for a change for the better. You would give Mrs. Konow and myself great pleasure if you could find time to write a long letter and tell us about your life and your work in far-off China.

With kindest regards and all good wishes

Yours sincerely

Sten Konow

PROFESSOR DR. STEN KONOW

Oslo, Norway, ~~KRISTIANIA~~ Aug. 15th 1927
ETNOGRAFISK MUSEUM

My dear Stael Holstein,

It was extremely kind of you to send me your splendid volume, The Kāçyapaparivarta, and the other two papers. I congratulate you cordially on the completion of these works, the more so because I understand from the slip accompanying the volume how great your difficulties have been. And I thank you heartily for thinking of me in distributing the copies. To us, your friends, however, the chief reason for rejoicing at seeing these works is that we understand that you are well and 'going strong.' We have all been very anxious about you, and we still are. But we may perhaps rest more confident now. I wonder if it would be possible for me to do anything to help you with books or other things. I hope that you will let me know, and it would give me pleasure in case I could do anything. I do not know whether you have seen my journal, the Acta Orientalia, of which the 6th volume is now appearing. Some of the papers might perhaps interest you. I have spare copies of most back numbers, which I could send you. Some few numbers are, however, missing. I could also arrange to send you a copy of future issues in some way. I presume that you would receive them all right. If you want me to do so, kindly let me also know whether everything ought to be registered - sometimes it is safer not to register.

Are you coming to the Oxford Congress next year? In that case you might perhaps go via Oslo where there is to be an international historical congress just before and where you know that you have friends who long to see you. With kindest regards from Mrs. Konow and

Yours sincerely

Sten Konow

August (?) 1927

My dear Konow,

Many thanks for your kind note and for the offer of sending me the "Acta Orientalia". I shall, of course, be extremely happy to have them. So far I have only received occasional reprints. I think it is highly advisable to have the packages registered. Letters and parcels do go astray rather often in these restless days, especially in China. I do not know exactly when I shall be able to go to Europe, but I do hope to see you and Mrs. Konow there before long. Have you received my long letter and the photographs?

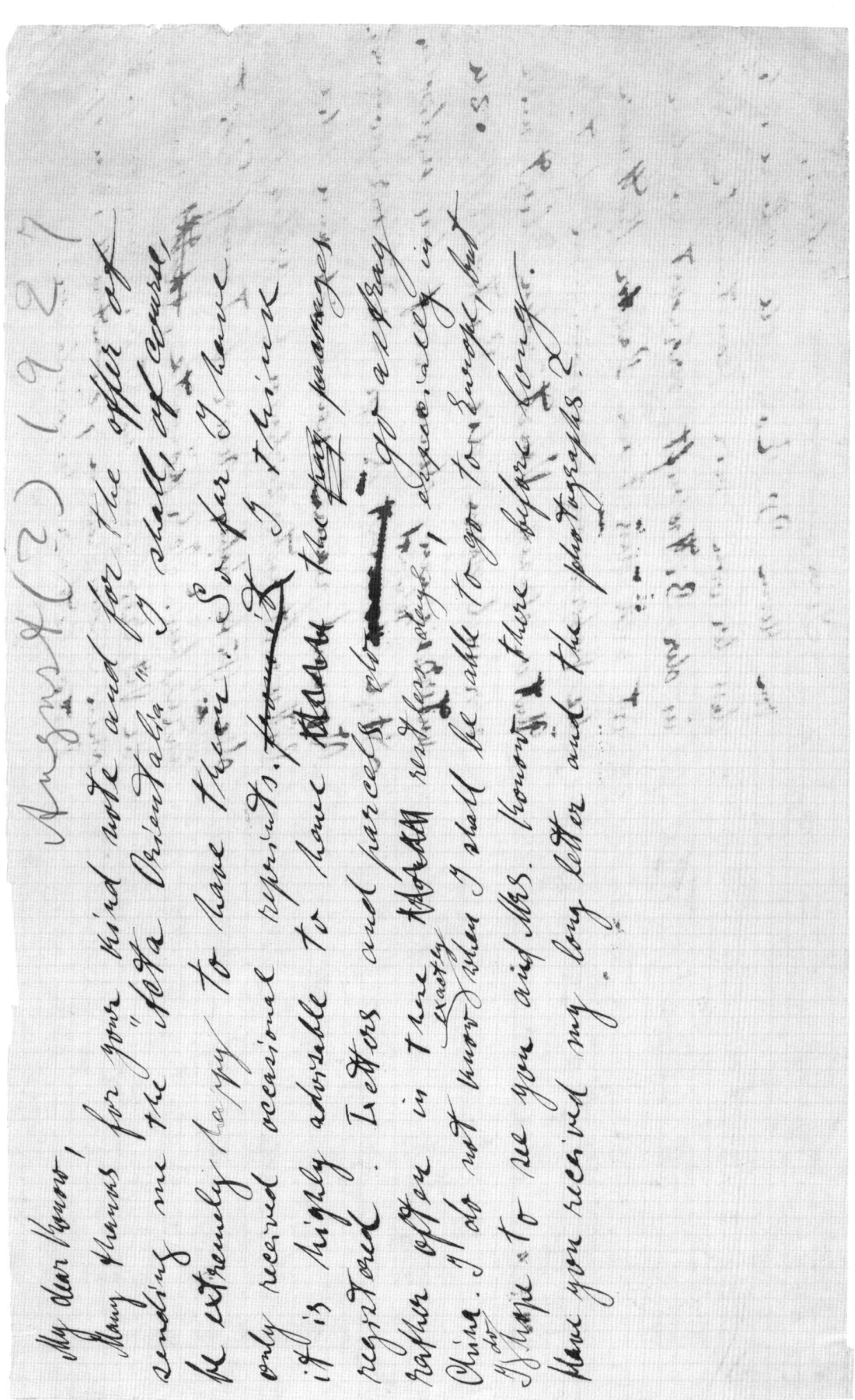

My dear Konow,

Many thanks for your kind letter and for the most interesting article on the eras of the Kharoṣṭhī inscriptions. ~~I note with you~~ I am very glad to see that ~~you Kaniṣka~~ you consider Kaniṣka as a Little ~~Yüe-Chi~~ 月氏 who started on his career of conquest from Eastern Turkestan, and I am sure ~~[illegible]~~ you are right. ~~[illegible]~~ As to the eras I must say that your statements ~~sounds~~ (doubtful reading) appear to me as very plausible, but truly (doubtful reading) I feel rather "out of it" when I read them. ~~All those fascinating problems~~ For want of an adequate library I have had to give up all the fascinating problems connected with the Indo-Scythian period of Indian history and I am now editing Sthiramati's commentary of the Kāśyapaparivarta (Chinese and Tib. only), of which I enclose a few pages.

of Proto-Khotanese ku-ṣi. ~~that~~ ~~that~~ ~~that I must~~
~~say that~~ But why should the ~~P~~ Proto-Khotanese
apply ~~H~~ a name meaning "western mountain" to
a ~~hard riding~~ race who came to Khotan from the
~~East?~~ ~~And why should the Chinese~~ Eastern plains?
I am now editing the commentary of the Kāśyapaparivarta,
of which I enclose a few pages. I have also prepared
indices, a long introduction and part of the entire English translation
of the Kāśyapaparivarta. But the entire commentary must be printed,
before I finish the translation.
I have found ~~much~~ a good deal of ~~[illegible]~~ new iconographical material lately:
1) A bronze pantheon (18th century) consisting of 755 lamaistic statuettes
(practically all different) bearing the names in Chinese only.
All the statuettes have been photographed.
2) A manuscript book ~~containing 300~~ similar to ~~the~~ Pander's Pantheon
des Tschangtscha Hutuktu but ~~more int~~ of greater interest.
The newly discovered book contains 360 images of ~~[illegible]~~ lamaistic

personages, all the names in four languages ~~(Chin~~ (Manchu Chinese Tibetan and Mongolian), and 360 eulogies in Chinese.

3) A book containing 237 coloured ~~images~~ Lamaistic images; ~~[illegible]~~ some of the personages represented belong exclusively to the Red Church. We find Padmasambhava (missing in Pander, in the 755 and in the 360) there, but no representation of Coi-kyong. ~~The book~~ The book was probably compiled ~~very possibly dates from~~ in the 14th century. ~~I propose editing all that material~~ All that material is to be edited by the Sino-Indian Research Institute of Peking, ~~and I have a number~~ which has some other plans besides (a catalogue raisonné of the larger Ratnakuta has already been begun by Chinese Buddhists and Mongolian Lamas under my direction). ~~My friend Professor L. C. Porter, [illegible] who has done to whom the~~ Prof. L. C. Porter, a very active ~~leading~~ member of the group who have hitherto ~~[illegible]~~ financed the Institute tells me that written statements of ~~prominent~~ leading orientalists as to ~~on~~ the necessity etc. of such an Institute would greatly

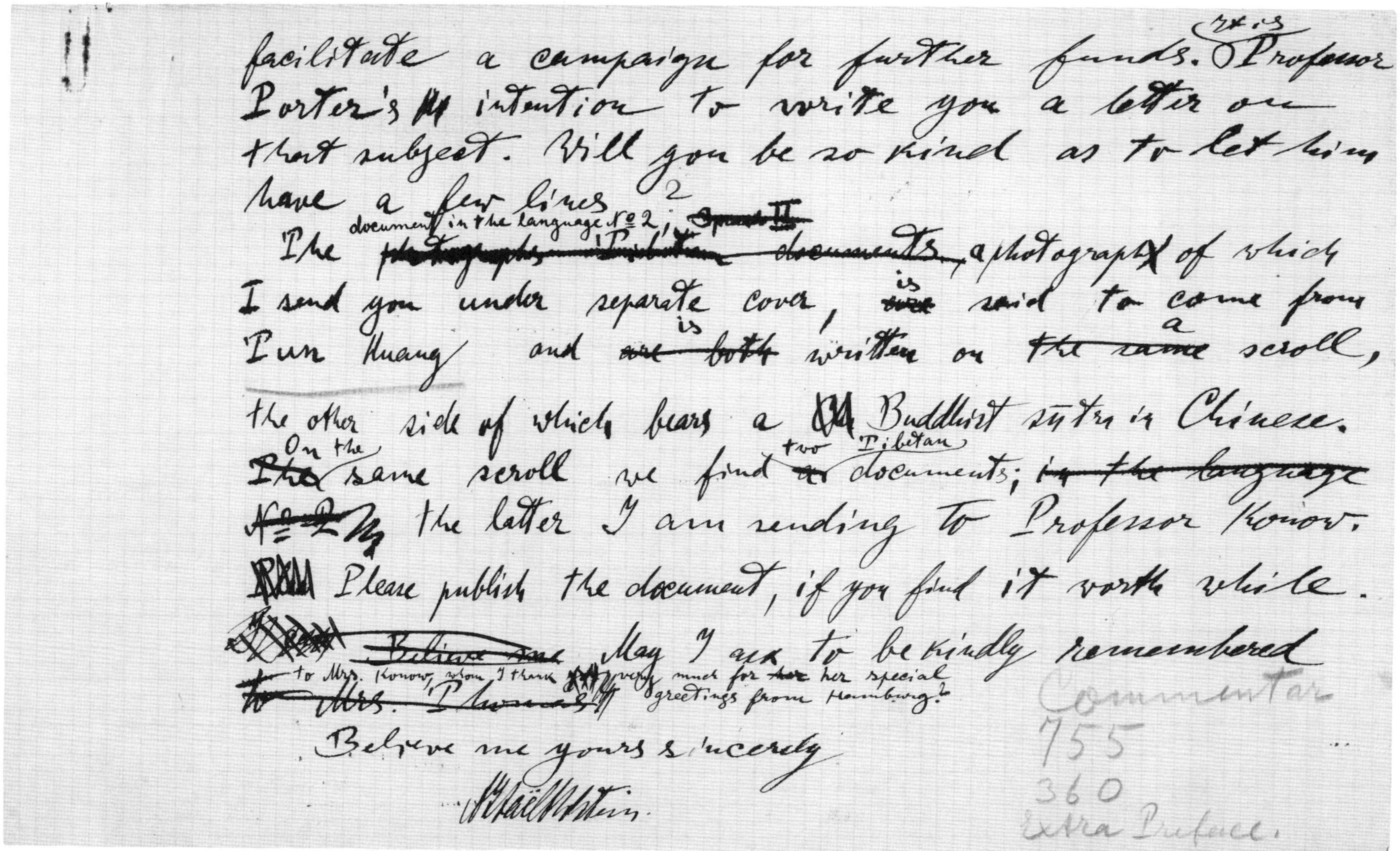

facilitate a campaign for further funds. It is Professor Porter's intention to write you a letter on that subject. Will you be so kind as to let him have a few lines.

The document in the language No 2, a photograph of which I send you under separate cover, is said to come from Tun huang and is written on a scroll, the other side of which bears a Buddhist sutra in Chinese. On the same scroll we find two Tibetan documents; the latter I am sending to Professor Konow. Please publish the document, if you find it worth while. May I ask to be kindly remembered to Mrs. Konow, whom I thank very much for her special greetings from Hamburg?

Believe me yours sincerely

A. Staël Holstein.

Commentar
755
360
Extra Preface.

PROFESSOR DR. STEN KONOW

ACTA ORIENTALIA

OSLO, 14-9-27

ETNOGRAFISK MUSEUM

My dear Stael-Holstein,

Many thanks for your kind letter and for the photographs of iconographical material and of the Saka document. When I have finished the Kharoshthī inscriptions I shall try to find out something about the text, and I hope that Thomas will in the meantime have mastered the Tibetan document. We your friends rejoice at the thought that you are comparatively safe and seem to have your hands full of interesting work. But we should be more happy to know you a little nearer to Europe. Next year there will be an historical congress here in Oslo, in the middle of August, and an oriental Congress in Oxford later on. We all hope that it will be possible for you to come to Europe then, at last. Stcherbatsky has written that it is possible that he is coming here, and if it is in any way possible for you, I hope that you will do so to.

I am convinced that you were right in

thrilling that Kanishka was a little Yüe-chi. The last calculations of Dr. van Wijk seem to show that the epoch of his era was in the year 128/9 A.D. His last recorded year is the 23rd, in the summer, i.e. then A.D. 150-151, and the first of Vāsishka in the summer 152. Was Kanishka dead then, and had he returned to Khotan, as indicated in the Kalpanāmaṇḍitikā (alias Sūtrālaṃkāra).[2] In that case he may be the king Kien (T'ang pronunciation Kian, which may be = Kan, just as Kiap = Kapa, Kadphises) who was murdered in Khotan in A.D. 152 (Hou Han-shu).

I hope to hear from you before long whether you want me to send you the Acta Orientalia. I can do so without any difficulty. Only I cannot send you an absolutely complete copy.

With kindest regards and all good wishes from Mrs. Konow and

Yours sincerely

Sten Konow

Of course I shall be happy to let Prof. Porter have any statement he thinks may be of use, if he wants me to do so.

My dear Konow,

I have known M. Michelet, the Norwegian Minister, for many years, but never did my income constitute the subject of our conversations until a few months ago, when he, quite spontaneously, without the slightest suggestion on my part, told me that his government might perhaps contribute to the upkeep of my Sino-Indian Institute. ~~stated~~ Of course ~~And~~ I jumped at his kind suggestion, because ~~that~~ the Institute has no assured income whatever. The Chinese government have no money, and even my very modest salary as a professor has been in arrears for over thirty months. ~~The French government has~~ I would have died of starvation long ago, if the French ~~government~~ (Ecole Française d'Extrême Orient) and the Americans (the Harvard Orient Institute through Yenching University)

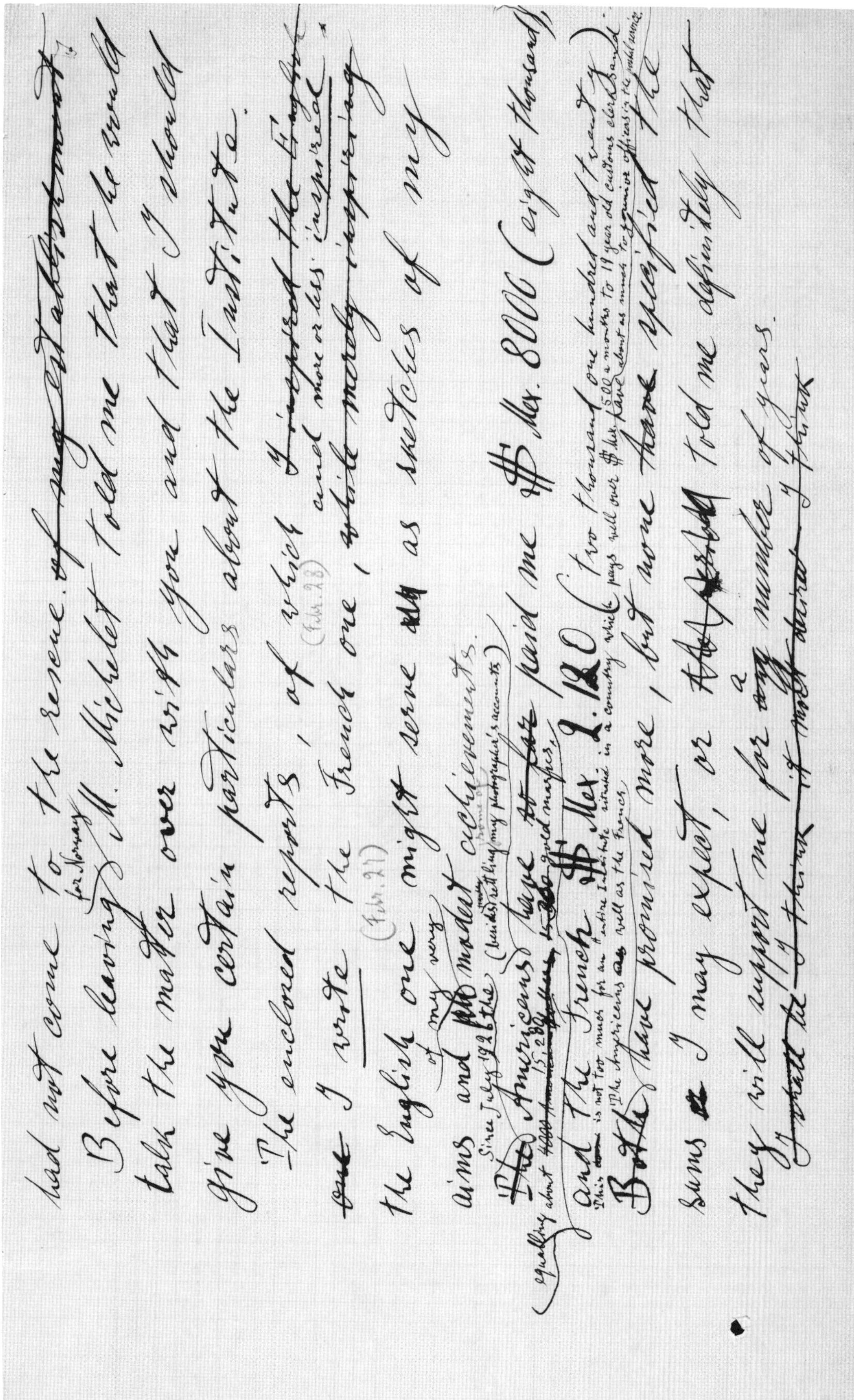
had not come to the rescue. ~~of my establishment~~

Before leaving for Norway M. Michelet told me that he would talk the matter over with you and that I should give you certain particulars about the Institute.

The enclosed reports, of which ~~I inspired the English one~~ I wrote the French one (Febr. 28), ~~while merely inspiring~~ and more or less inspired the English one (Febr. 27) might serve as sketches of my aims and of my very modest achievements.

Since July 1926 the ~~The~~ Americans (besides settling some of my photographer's accounts) have ~~so far~~ paid me $ Mex. 8000 (eight thousand), (equalling about 15,280 gold marks), and the French $ Mex. 2.120 (two thousand one hundred and twenty).

This is not too much for an "entire Institute" situated in a country which pays well over $ Mex. 500 a months to 19 year old customs clerks and about as much to junior officers in the postal service.

~~Both~~ The Americans as well as the French have promised more, but none ~~have~~ specified the sums I may expect, or told me definitely that they will support me for a number of years.

~~I shall be I think it most desired I think~~

I shall be very much obliged to you and to your government ~~if you could guarantee me a certain sum for a number of years~~ for any ~~modest but~~ sum or sums which you might contribute ~~towards the~~ to the funds of the Sino-Indian Institute.

In exchange I could not do very much more than send you our publications (several books and a journal are ~~being~~ printed or are in preparation) and afford you, upon demand, some assistance in buying Chinese, Tibetan, and Mongolian books.

~~May I ask~~ I hope you got my New Year's cards.

May I ask to be kindly remembered to Mrs. Konow?

Believe me yours most sincerely

A. Staël-Holstein.

Norsk Orientalsk Selskap.
Historisk Museum.

Kristiania den 24th May 1928

My dear Staël-Holstein,

I have delayed answering to your letter about the Sino-Indian Research Institute, because I wanted to await Mr. Michelet's arrival. To-day I have met him, and he tells me that you must have misunderstood him when he spoke about the possibility of some support for your Institute from the Norwegian Government. He spoke of the Norwegian Oriental Society. We of the Society are in the most cordial sympathy with the endeavours of the Institute, and we feel confident that it will become of increasing importance for the development of the systematic study of Sino-Indian civilization. When a scholar of your rank is at the head, we are entitled to expect great results, and what we have seen hitherto shows that we are not expecting in vain. We should be very happy if our economical situation could make it possible for us to support the Institute by some contribution. At the present moment we are, however, not so well off that anything can be done. If our circumstances became less difficult in a near future, it will give us great pleasure to reopen the question. And you may rest assured that we shall do our very best, because we are keenly conscious of the importance of the undertaking. To-day we can only send you the last issues of our Acta Orientalia. I think that you have already received P. I of Vol. VI, so that the volume will now be complete.

Is there any hope of your coming to the congress in Oxford in August? If so we sincerely hope that you will include a visit to Oslo in your program.

With kindest regards from house to house and all good wishes

Yours sincerely
Sten Konow

Konow

Peking den 14. August 1934.

Lieber Herr Professor,

Die freundlichen ~~[illegible]~~ Worte, die Sie in den Actis Orientalibus meinen Publicationen gewidmet haben werden sicher auf die Autoritäten der Harvard-Universität einen grossen Eindruck gemacht haben. Ich ~~schreibe habe photographische~~ habe schon vor vielen Monaten eine photographische Reproduction Ihrer Notiz nach Cambridge Mass. expediert und danke Ihnen sehr für Ihre Bemühungen. Bisher ~~bestand~~ ~~meine Institut sind~~ haben wir noch keine weiteren Kürzungen unseres Etats zu beklagen, der im Jahre 1932 um über 40% herabgesetzt wurde.

Ich habe vor Kurzem bronzene Statuetten der zwölf Thiere des ostasiatischen Thierkreises erworben und lege eine Photographie des Bronze-Tigers bei.

Wissen Sie vielleicht, was es mit den Reitern für eine Bewandtniss hat?

~~Ich kann über die tocharische Frage nicht genau verfolgen,~~ Ich habe keinerlei Bedenken gegen die Annahme (Kanishka etc.) (月支 = Yüeh Chih ist eine späte Formbildung) dass die Tocharisch Sprachen. Das hindert mich aber nicht daran, an meiner Ansicht dass die Sprache II das Tocharische ist, festzuhalten. Die einzige der in Betracht kommenden Sprachen, die von a-Stämmen regelmässig den Nominativ auf i (ï) bildet, ist die Sprache II, und, soweit ich mich erinnere, ist der Name des in dem uigurischen Colophon genannten indo-tocharischen Übersetzers Vaibhazaki Aryacintri. Dieses Argument sollte m. E. sehr schwer wiegen. Es scheint mir fraglich, dass ich die tocharische Frage hier nicht genau verfolgen kann.

Mit nochmaligem herzlichem Dank und vielen guten Wünschen verbleibe ich Ihr ganz ergebener A. Staël-Holstein.

PROFESSOR DR. STEN KONOW

ACTA ORIENTALIA

OSLO, Feb. 8, 1935

~~ETNOGRAFISK MUSEUM~~

Gimle Terrasse 5

My dear Staël Holstein,

Some few days ago Mr. Fischer brought me news about you and also a beautiful image, for which I am extremely thankful. I was happy to learn that you are faring well, and also to hear about your bright and handsome boys. We your friends rejoice to know that you are not any more alone but really live in a 'house', i.e. a place where children are playing about. But we also hope that some day we shall meet again in our part of the world. It was also very kind of you to send me your highly interesting reconstructions of Sanskrit verses. Those Chinese characters which are my despair are evidently quite easy to you, and I should feel envious if my admiration did not prevent me from doing so. I suppose that you have read Pelliot's interesting paper about Tokharian. It is excellent but does not carry conviction. I am convinced that 'Tokharian' was not the language of the 'Tokharians', though it was spoken in Tokhari.

stan. I believe that you are right in considering Tokharian proper as an Iranian language, but I do not think that it is Khotani. You have probably seen Leumann's posthumous work, from which we learn that the indigenous name of the language was Hvatana, i.e. Hvadana. Now that designation reminds us so much of the name Khotan, that we are a priori inclined to translate 'Khotani'. But there is one difficulty. At Maralbashi have been found some documents written in the usual 'Tokharian' alphabet, but with a series of unknown signs. I think that I have succeeded in identifying these signs and in reading and translating the documents. They are written in a language which is so closely connected with Khotani that we can only characterize it as a dialect of the same speech. But it can hardly have come from Khotan. Now also here the same Hvadana is used as name of language and people. I am therefore inclined to think that Hvadana has nothing to do with Khotan, but is derived from hva 'Sacas', and is the indigenous name of the Iranian tribe in question. My paper has been sent to press, and I shall send you a copy as soon as it is printed. And then I hope I may look forward to your criticism.

With kindest regards and all good wishes

Yours sincerely

Sten Konow

~~Konow~~ **Konow**

Lieber Herr Professor,

Es ist furchtbar lange her, dass ich zuletzt directe Nachrichten von Ihnen erhalten habe. ~~Sind meine~~ Wie geht es Ihnen und Ihrer Familie? ~~Haben~~ ~~(meine Neujahrswünsche, die ich im December 1932 abschickte, Sie erreicht? in Ihre Hände gelangt?~~ richtig ~~angekommen~~? Sind meine "Neujahrskarten", die ich im December 1932 abschickte, in Ihre Hände gelangt?

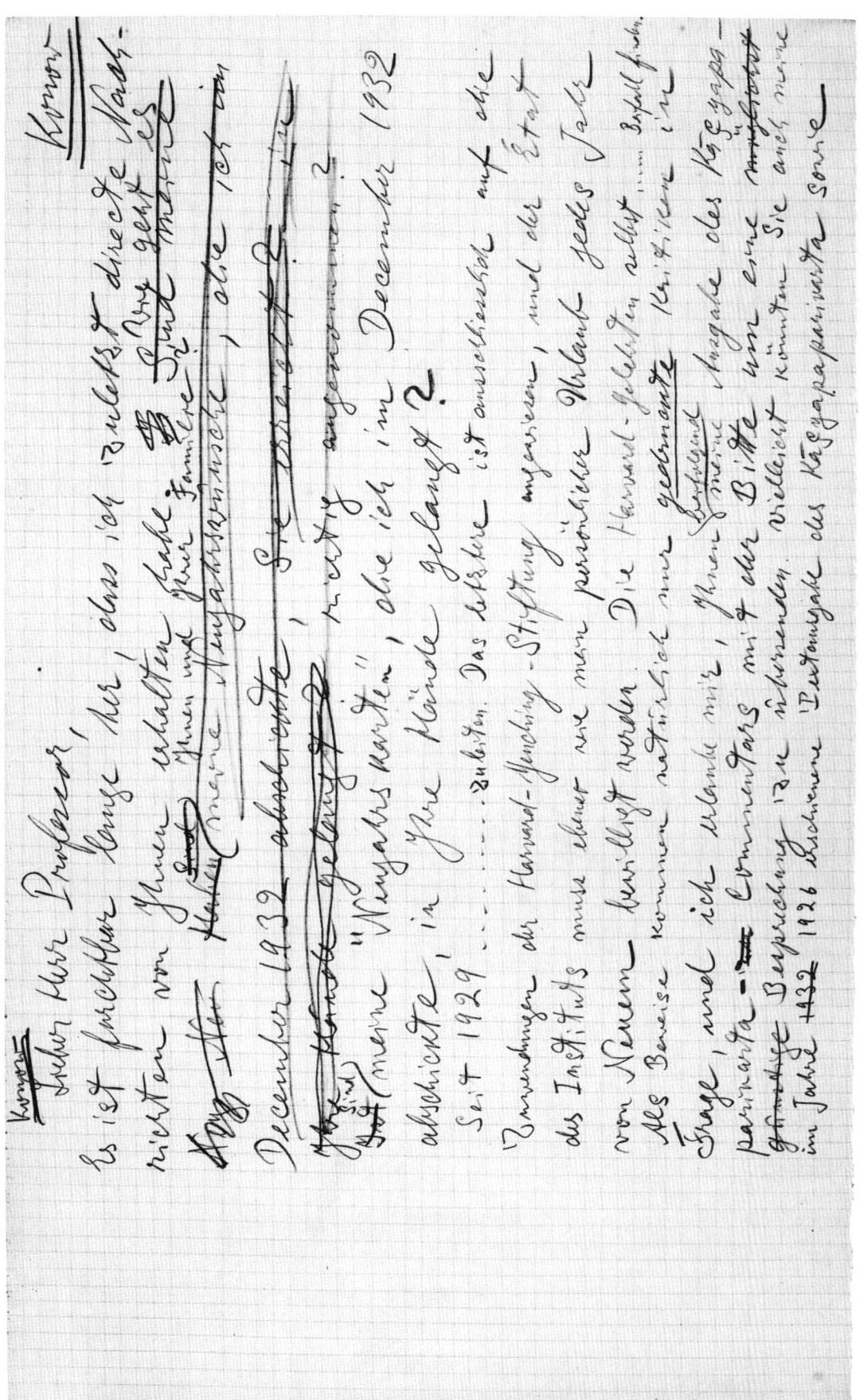

Seit 1929 ....zubilden. Das letztere ist ausschliesslich auf die Zuwendungen der Harvard-Yenching-Stiftung angewiesen, und der Etat des Instituts muss ebenso wie mein persönlicher Urlaub jedes Jahr von Neuem bewilligt werden. Die Harvard-Gelehrten selbst ..... Beifall finden. Als Beweise kommen natürlich nur gedruckte Kritiken in Frage, und ich erlaube mir, Ihnen beifolgend meine Ausgabe des Kāçyapaparivarta-~~C~~ Commentars mit der Bitte um eine ~~möglichst günstige~~ Besprechung zu übersenden. Vielleicht könnten Sie auch meine im Jahre ~~1932~~ 1926 erschienene Textausgabe des Kāçyapaparivarta sowie

meine im Jahre 1932 erschienenen Artikel erwähnen. Ich wäre Ihnen unendlich dankbar, wenn Sie ~~das~~ (auch nur eine meiner Arbeiten besprechen) ~~Ihre~~ wollten.
~~Ich bin sehr Es liegt mir sehr sehr viel an der Verlängerung meines Urlaubes, denn ich will durchaus in Peking (nicht in Amerika) wohnen.~~
~~Ich bin Es wäre sehr schön, wenn Ihre Kritik~~
Die Kritik müsste allerdings, um ~~Erfolg~~ die in erster Reihe erwünschten Resultate zu ~~haben~~ vorzeitigen, ~~noch vor Ende dieses Jahres~~ recht bald erscheinen, denn die nächste amerikanische Sitzung, von der meine Zukunft abhängt, ~~wird~~ soll schon im Frühjahr 1934 abgehalten werden.
Meine Frau ~~wird~~ zieht in diesen Tagen na 八大處 (= Aṣṭamahā-sthāna, nach den acht berühmtesten buddhistischen Stūpas so genannt), ~~wo es~~ wo ~~sie~~ ~~eines der a~~ sie mit den Kindern (Walter und Maria Theresia) die heisseste Zeit in einem der acht buddhistischen Klöster verbringen wird.
Mit der Bitte mich Ihrer Frau Gemahlin empfehlen zu wollen, verbleibe ich Ihr Ihnen ganz ergebener AStaëlHolstein.
Es ist wirklich nicht......

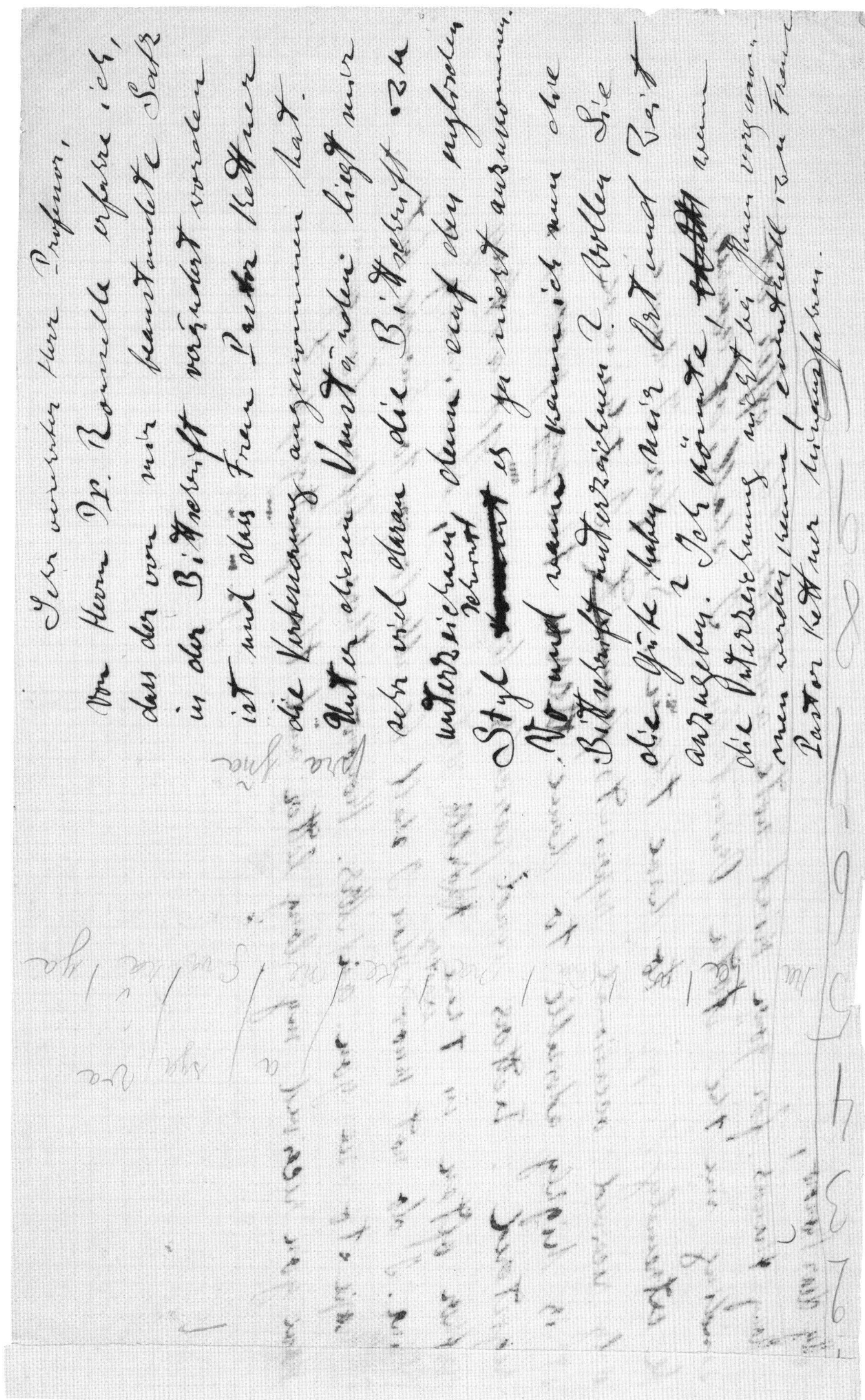

Sehr verehrter Herr Professor,

Von Herrn Dr. Rousselle erfahre ich, dass der von mir beanstandete Satz in der Bittschrift verändert worden ist und dass Frau Pastor Kettner die Verbesserung angenommen hat. Unter diesen Umständen liegt mir sehr viel daran die Bittschrift zu unterzeichnen, denn auf den englischen Styl scheint es ja nicht anzukommen. Wo und wann kann ich nun die Bittschrift unterzeichnen? Wollen Sie die Güte haben mir Ort und Zeit anzugeben? Ich könnte, wenn die Unterzeichnung nicht bei Ihnen vorgenommen werden kann, eventuell zu Frau Pastor Kettner hinausfahren.

October 1, 1933

Lieber Kollega und Freund,

Es hat mich sehr gefreut, endlich einmal seit Jahren von Ihnen zu hören, und ich werde mein möglichstes tun, um Ihnen zu helfen. In meiner Zeitschrift geben wir allerdings nicht lange Anzeigen, ich werde aber eine Notiz schreiben und sie so abfassen, daß sie hoffentlich nützlich sein wird. Da die Zeit etwas knapp ist, und da ich auf den Zeitpunkt der Drucklegung in anderen Zeitschriften keinen Einfluss habe, scheint dies mir die beste Ordnung zu sein. Bitte mir mitteilen zu wollen, an wen ich Abdrücke der Notiz senden soll.

Die letzte Nachricht, die uns von Ihnen zugegangen ist, war die Mitteilung, daß Sie geheiratet hatten, worüber sich auch meine Frau freuen konnte. Seitdem ist sie leider nach sehr schmerzhaftem Krankenlager gestorben, und ich bin schon drei Jahre lang vereinsamt. Sie haben wohl davon keine Nachricht erhalten – die Post scheint nicht immer zuverlässig zu sein.

Vor ein paar Jahren schickte ich Ihnen die Ausgabe der Dokumente, die Sie einmal Thomas und mir zustellten. Keiner von uns hat erfahren, ob Sie die Ausgabe je erhalten haben. Ich habe Ihnen damals auch geschrieben, dass ich gern bereit bin, Ihnen weitere Exemplare zu senden. Da ich aber nichts gehört habe, habe ich nicht weiteres in der Angelegenheit getan. Ich weiss auch nicht, ob Sie sich weiter mit der Saka-Sprache beschäftigt haben. Was Sie darüber geschrieben haben, wird immer seinen grossen Wert behalten. Ich habe persönlich die Ansicht aufgegeben, dass es sich um die Sprache der Tocharer handelt. Ich bin aber geneigt anzunehmen, dass auch das sogenannte Tocharisch nicht die Sprache der Tocharer, sondern die der Yüe-chi ist. Ich habe darüber einen Artikel für die Ostasiatische Zeitschrift geschrieben. Ich weiss aber nicht, wann er erscheinen wird, und ob ich Separatabzüge erhalten werde. Die Zeitschrift selbst aber werden Sie gewiss in Peking sehen.

Es würde uns alle sehr freuen, falls Sie sich entschliessen würden, wieder einmal Europa zu besuchen. An den zwei letzten Orientalistenkongressen haben wir, Ihre Freunde, oft von Ihnen gesprochen, und vielleicht werden wir das nächste Mal die Freude haben, Sie unter uns zu sehen.

Mit herzlichen Grüssen und allen guten Wünschen

Ihr ergebenster

Sten Konow

Ex-Austrian Legation,
Peking, December 24th 1929.

To Dr. Kotvicz,
Professor at the University of LVOV.

My dear Professor Kotvicz,

Some time ago you asked me to send you Manchu documents written with the old Manchu characters without the dots markihg the sounds unknown to the Mongols and peculiar to the Manchu language.

The original of the enclosed photograph belongs to a retired Manchu official who lives in Peking. Please publish the document, if you like. The owner as well as myself will be only too glad if you will do so.

The original of the single Manchu line marked with the characters I discovered under the strip bearing the Chinese line five minutes before I had to return the original to the owner. I could not, therefore, photograph that single Manchu line. But there was time enough to have it copied by hand which one of my Chinese frinds did. Later on I had the Manchu line, hand-copied as it was, photographed and then joined to the photograph of the other 8 lines (seven in Manchu and one in Chinese).
The strip bearing the Chinese characters was pasted over the original Manchu line, but could be detached.

Please

-2-

Please write to me, and let me know about University life at Lvov.

Believe me yours sincerely,

My dear Baron von Stael Holstein,

Please excuse me for troubling you, but for some days now the Harvard Publicity Office has desired a story from you regarding the photographs of The Padmasambhava Codex, the so-called 800 Buddhas, and the Chu Fo P'u Sa Sheng Hsiang Tsan. I shall be very grateful if you will either drop a note or have someone at the Fogg Museum communicate with me at University Hall, Room B, to tell me whether at some time during the next day or two you would be willing to allow me to talk to you on this subject. The Harvard Publicity Office, or the Office of the Secretary to the University for Information, as it is properly named, is concerned with making public the work of the various departments of the University, their recent acquisitions, the lectures of visiting professors, and so forth. It is an official activity of the University to arrange for the publication of such material.

Thank you for any consideration which you may give this note,

Sincerely,

Robert Keen Lamb

(Robert Keen Lamb)

Room B, University Hall.

Manset, Hancock County, Maine, U.S. of America, July 21, 1934

To, Dr. Baron A. von Staël-Holstein, Tsing Hua National University, PEIPING, CHINA: ——————— Honored colleague and friend:

Your beautiful volume, a Commentary to the Kāçyapa-parivarta, edited in Tibetan and Chinese, came safely to hand, and in best of order, on the ninth of May last. Please accept my best thanks for your kind remembrance of me. I feel that I have outlived practically all my Zeitgenossen. Hermann Jacobi of Bonn University is almost the only one now left. But the study of books upon popular astronomy is a great delight to me. It teaches the lesson of humility most effectively. What we call a "terrestrial century" may very well seem to the Neptunians (or Poseidonians) merely a cosmical hour or even a few seconds.——The technical excellence of your book is truly remarkable. But it would be an utterly desperate undertaking to try to produce such a volume here in America.——Indeed, it is amazing to me that any nation of ordinary intelligence should not have abandoned the continued use of any other than a phonetic system of writing long ago. In that condemnation I would include the Indologists, for sticking to the Devanagari characters. Still, you see that our method of writing English is far removed from a scientific one,---as witness din and dean bid and bead, bit and beet, fit and feet, and so on. May be our successors will separate palaeography from knowledge of any language as a system of spoken sounds. We might then hope to know something real and substantial about the civilizations of the past. I hope that your plan includes the work of giving to the Occident a translation of the Kāçyaparivarta. That ought not to be hard to print for one who understands the originals.

Geldner died five years ago last February. And most of the time since then, I have been sick. But I underwent a serious surgical operation (prostate ectomy) a year ago, and recovered from the operation well and promptly. But the dreadfully wet weather of last year laid me low with rheumatic trouble; and this cost me some seven months more. But in April last my native strength re-asserted itself, and I astonished the printers in Goettingen by returning the long unread proofs of the German translation of the Rig-Veda. There are only some sixty pages yet to be set up and printed. So I hope the three volumes (of over 1200 pages) will very soon be out.

I wish I might have the opportunity of a long quiet talk with you, especially about the problematic future of the civilized nations of our tiny globe. I am in my 85th year of life. Things could hardly be worse than they now are in my country. Crime is rampant everywhere. Murders, kidnapping, and banditry, and accidents of every kind connected with our modern ways of living. The fatal accidents of automobiles for one year are now about 37,000 for the U.S.A. And the minor injuries are zahllos. I am quite deaf now, and forced to read the newspapers. But the newspapers have become so degenerate, that they are hardly fit to read. — We are exploring the civilization of the Mayas in Central America, now. It is quite possible that in the course of the last few million years, a good many civilizations have flourished and disappeared from this planet. In short, human history means recorded human history. And what is recorded may be an infinitesimal fraction of the whole.

It appears that the only course left for intelligent and well-meaning people is to keep their courage and be as kindly and generous to others as is possible. --- I wish you health of body and of spirit, and that you may be able to continue some useful work for others as long as you live.

Gratefully yours,

Charles R. Lanman

My address remains 9 Farrar Street, Cambridge, Massachusetts, U.S.America.

YALE UNIVERSITY

KENNETH SCOTT LATOURETTE
PROFESSOR OF MISSIONS AND ORIENTAL HISTORY

1126 YALE STATION, NEW HAVEN, CONN.

October 11, 1928

My dear Professor Von Holstein:

The American Historical Review has asked me to prepare an article on the work that has been done on Chinese history during the last seven years. I am hoping to have the article include what has been done by European, American, Chinese, and Japanese scholars.

I wonder if it would be an imposition if I, a perfect stranger, should request your assistance in getting together the information. I need not trouble you, I think, about the work done in English or in Western European languages. I know, however, no Russian and so know nothing whatever of what is being done by Russian sinologues, especially since the Revolution. I should greatly appreciate it if you could tell me of any centers of Chinese studies in Russia, the names of the principal scholars, and the titles, scope, and scholarly quality of any books or periodicals of the past seven years which seem to you significant for historians.

I should also be grateful if you would give me the same information for China. With the works in Chinese I am, of course, somewhat more familiar and have other sources to which I can go to check up my own information. I may well miss, however, some very significant works and shall be very grateful for a full list of books and periodicals dealing with the history of China during the past seven years which seem to you important enough to notice in a scholarly journal. A brief note about the scope and the scholarly quality of each of the titles mentioned would be of help.

I do not know whether you keep in touch with what is being done in Japan, but if you do I should be very happy to have a similar list of the work of Japanese scholars on Chinese history.

It is a source of real satisfaction to know that you will be in this country and that you and your colleagues at Harvard are engaged in so many important enterprises for those of us who are interested in sinology. I hope to have the honor and pleasure of meeting you before the winter is over.

Sincerely yours,

K. S. Latourette

Peiping, Tuesday April 2nd 1935.

Dear Mr. Lattimore,

We know that you want to be near the Johnsons in the Tung Wang 'P'ang. Our part of ~~that~~ the Temple ~~at~~ is of no use to us in April and May and if you will occupy it during these two months we shall ~~only~~ be very glad. We shall ~~probably~~ want it on ~~than~~ the ~~E~~ first of June.

Believe me yours sincerely

A. Staël Holstein.

Cable: INPAREL, New York

Telephone: PLaza 3-4700

Pacific Affairs

Published Quarterly by
THE INSTITUTE OF PACIFIC RELATIONS
HONOLULU HAWAII

OFFICE OF THE EDITOR
129 EAST 52ND STREET
NEW YORK CITY

21st May, 1936.

Dear Baron,

We have just arrived here in New York and are in the frantic state of trying to get settled down. I have already received a letter from Mr. Keller approving of the projected Mongol and Tibetan translations of DON QUIXOTE. I have asked him to send the cheque for the Mongol translation direct to you for payment to Gombojab as soon as you consider it suitable. In the meantime I have had a letter from Peiping implying that Gombojab may have gone to Kumbum with the Dilowa; but perhaps he has not.

I had only a couple of days in Leningrad, but they were of extreme interest and I was most impressed by the quality of the Mongol and Chinese studies there and by the library and museum facilities which the Academy of Sciences there is able to use. I found Pankratov in better health than I had ever seen him in before and very enthusiastic about his work and the convenience in living quarters and so forth offered to him there. He is, I understand, giving a course in Chinese but also has time for independent work of his own.

Both from what he said and from what he did not say, I had the impression that he left Shanghai much more suddenly than he had ever expected to and probably under considerable pressure. Now that he has got there, however, he feels that he is in a secure position. He told me that he had written a registered letter to you from Shanghai at the time of his departure which you evidently did not receive. The letter, I believe, was given to a room boy at the hotel to post which may account for the fact that it was never received. He was extremely anxious for me to send you and his other friends the most cordial regards and assurances.

After leaving the Soviet Union I had four days in Holland where I stayed with Duyvandak, and ten days in England -- all very rushed but very interesting.

Since we have arrived here just at the beginning of the summer we shall lead an almost nomadic life for the next few months; possibly we shall go to England in September and stay there for two or three months before returning to Peiping. In the meantime, however, the above address may be considered as permanent since a letter will always reach me.

Baron A. Stael Holstein -2- 21st May, 1936.

With the most cordial regards to you and to the Baroness from both of us,

Yours very sincerely,

Owen Lattimore

Baron A. Stael Holstein,
Ex-Austrian Legation,
Peiping,
CHINA.

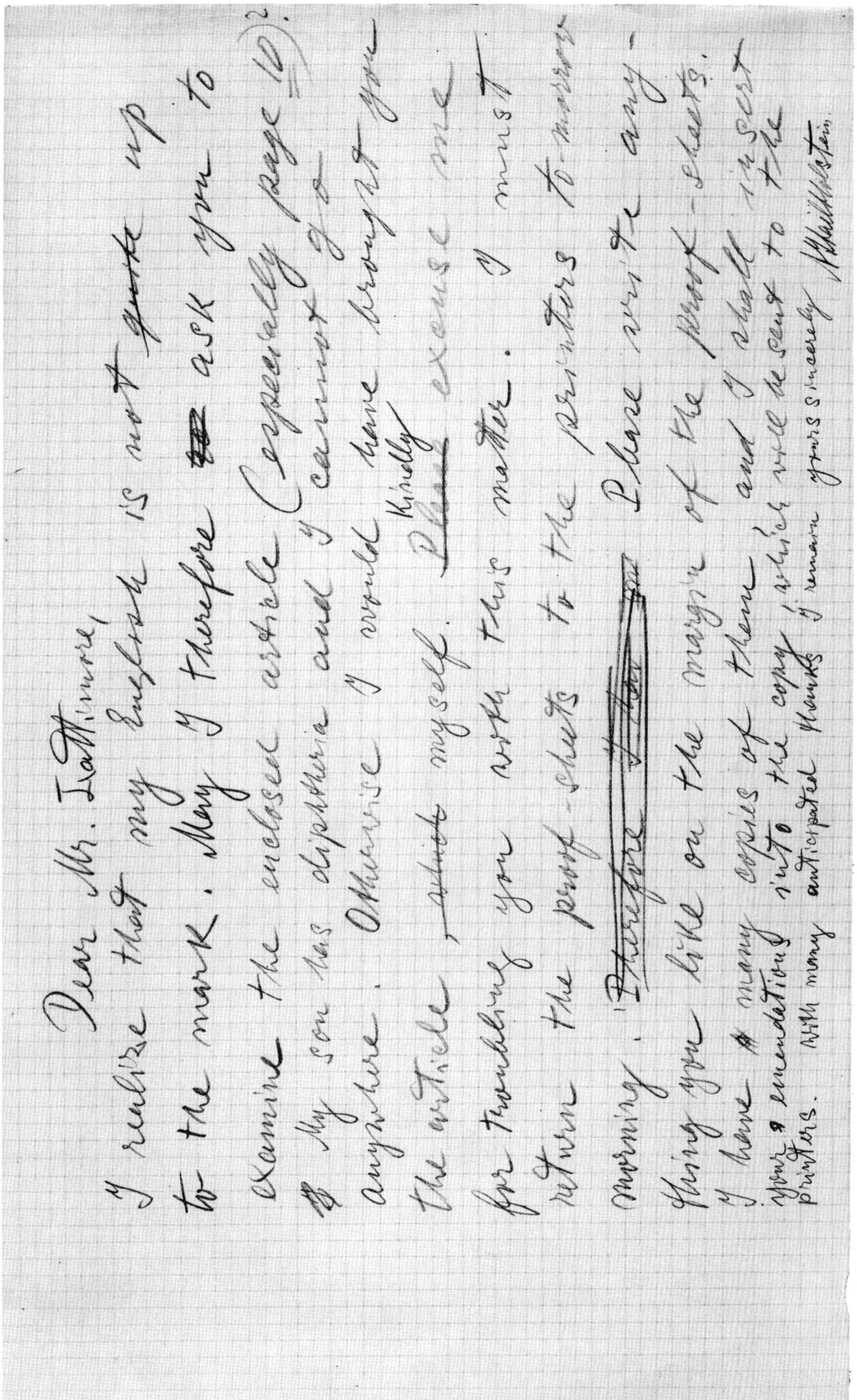

Dear Mr. Lattimore,

I realize that my English is not ~~quite~~ up to the mark. May I therefore ask you to examine the enclosed article (especially page 10)? My son has diphtheria and I cannot go anywhere. Otherwise I would have brought you the article, ~~which~~ myself. Kindly ~~Please~~ excuse me for troubling you with this matter. I must return the proof-sheets to the printers to-morrow morning. ~~Therefore I~~ Please write anything you like on the margin of the proof-sheets. I have many copies of them, and I shall insert your emendations into the copy, which will be sent to the printers. With many anticipated thanks I remain yours sincerely A. Staël-Holstein.

Monday, November 11th 1935.

Dear Mrs. Lattimore,

I am awfully sorry to say that we cannot dine with you tomorrow (November ~~12~~ 29th) as arranged. I ~~have been~~ am quite sick, ~~for the last 2-3 days and can hardly eat anything since Friday evening~~ and my wife ~~refuses to~~ will not leave me. ~~Kindly~~ Please excuse this late notice.

With many thanks for your kind invitation

I remain yours very sincerely

A. Staël-Holstein.

which does not seem to yield any acceptable meaning. I suggest the
ptions have almost all ~~tee~~

Dear Mrs. Lattimore,

It is awfully kind of you ~~that~~ you are ready to examine my proof-sheets. Please do look ~~it~~ them over and write as much on the margins as possible.

Believe me yours sincerely

AStaëlHolstein.

C/o the Fogg Museum, Cambridge Mass, April 4th 1929.

My dear Dr. Laufer,

In the last proof sheets of my ~~###~~ edition of the Kāçyapaparivarta the page (attached, in the Chinese etc.), which now bears the figure VI, ~~used to bear~~ was marked V etc. ~~###~~ Without consulting me the Commercial press changed all the figures (the original ~~#~~ page I became page VI etc) ~~in the "Reindruck" when they~~ before issuing the book. In consequence of this I should have corrected all the references to the preface contained in the preface itself before presenting the book to you. On ~~the~~ page XXVI (with ~~#~~ reference to what etc.), for instance, I refer to pages XVIII and XVI. ~~#~~ XIX and XVII respectively should be read now after the change ~~carried out~~ made by the Commercial Press.

Looking forward very much to seeing you in Chicago in January 1931 I remain yours ~~very~~ most sincerely

A. Staël-Holstein.

Sept. 10th 1934.

Dear Madame Ivanow,

Baroness Ungern-Sternberg (a sister of the philosopher Keyserling) and Countess Lichnowsky (a daughter of Prince Lichnowsky, the [former] German Ambassador in London) will lunch with me on Wednesday at 1.30. I shall be so pleased if you and M. Ivanow will join us. ~~The~~ If you cannot come on Wednesday ~~will you lunch with me (and the ladies~~ please let me know when you will ~~be able~~ [have time] to come to lunch. I may be able to change the date.

Believe me yours sincerely

A. Staël Holstein.

Dec. 5th 1934.

Dear Madame Lawru,

May I present a copy of the Kuo Ch'ao Kung Shih to you? ~~It~~ contains a good deal of useful information about the various palaces of the Forbidden City. This summer ~~Priest~~ Alan Priest asked me to find a Chinese scholar who ~~could~~ assist him in interpreting a certain inscription. I recommended Professor T'êng, and Priest, ~~who~~ worked with T'êng for a number of months told me, when he left for America, that T'êng had proved a great success. Priest ~~pres~~ had made no contract with T'êng, but ~~presented~~ gave the latter one hundred Peking dollars ~~on~~ as a present on the eve ~~of~~

his departure. I hear now that 'Pêng, who ~~has worked with Priest for about~~ has spent about fifty hours in all ~~with~~ Priest, ~~that~~ regards the present as inadequate, but he never told Priest anything about it. Priest left with the impression that 'Pêng was satisfied.

If you still want an English-speaking Chinese scholar to assist you in your researches, please let me know. I think I could recommend one, who worked satisfactorily ~~with~~ than Priest during his last stay ~~here to the latter's satisfaction~~ in Peking.

My son has ~~th~~ ~~dipth~~ diphtheria, and I ~~cann~~ cannot go anywhere. I am ~~ext~~ very sorry that under these circumstances I ~~cann am unable~~ shall not be able to attend Miss Hayes' cock-tail party today.

Peking, December 9th 1934.

Dear Madame Lauru,

Your ~~beautiful~~ splendid present has deeply touched me, and I thank you very much for ~~your~~ me wonderful ~~the~~ book. I highly admire it for its splendid style and for the vivid description of Chinese life, which it contains. You have certainly ~~bott~~ well used the time spent in the village near Heilungt'an. ~~which I remember~~ I shall always ~~cher~~ keep the "Hundred Altars" as one of my most cherished possessions.

Believe me yours gratefully

A. Staël Holstein.

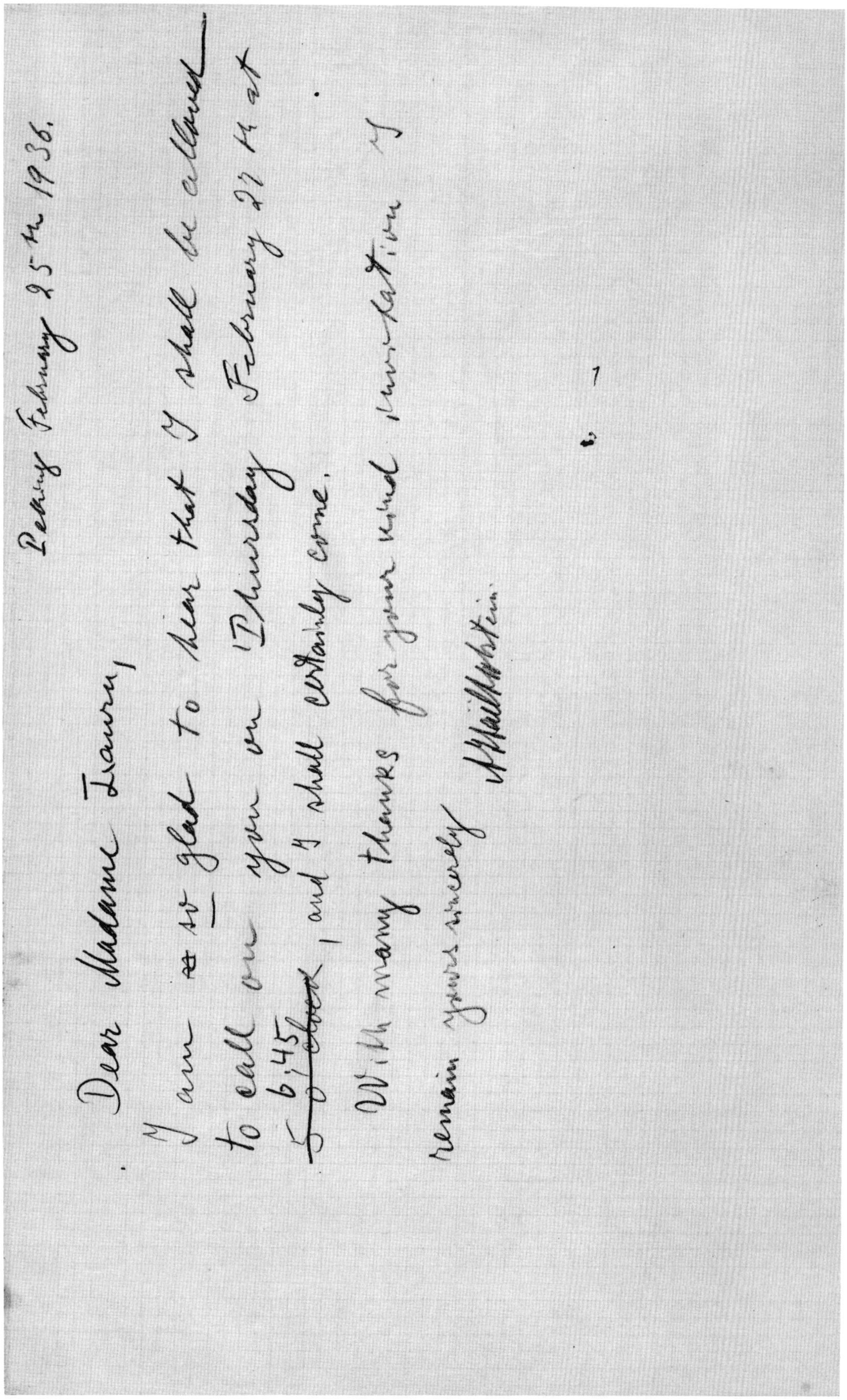

Peking February 25th 1936.

Dear Madame Ivanow,

I am ~~s~~ so glad to hear that I shall be allowed to call on you on Thursday February 27th at ~~5 o'clock~~ 6,45, and I shall certainly come.

With many thanks for your kind invitation I remain yours sincerely

A Staël Holstein.

Dear Madame Liauru,

~~I am awfully sorry to say that~~ I have ~~asked~~ arranged ~~the Mdivanis~~ a cock tail party to meet the Mdivanis, for Saturday and I was just going to write to you in order to ask you to join us when I received your kind invitation. I am so sorry I cannot come to see you and meet Mr. Sitwell on Saturday.

~~Herewith I~~ I return the books (~~Madame Pelliot and~~ verres anciens and la croisière jaune) with very many thanks.

Believe me yours sincerely

A. Staël Holstein.

Dear Madame Lauru,

I have ~~got~~ acquired some ~~pic~~ rather rare pictures and statuettes lately which might interest you. But my Buddhas look ~~well~~ their best only at lunch time. So please do come to lunch and bring Monsieur Lauru with you. I do know that you generally avoid going out ~~do not go out~~ to lunch and that this rule has lately become a principle ~~one of your principles~~. But just as designs which are quite regular are not considered as perfect ~~regarded as unlucky~~ by the Indians I think that principles ~~the~~ become really great only when they are occasionally infringed. May I ask you to fix your own day (all days except Saturdays will do) and to bring Mrs. Councilman also. The latter asked me the other day whether she might come and see my Buddhas. ~~A~~ As soon as I know when I may expect you three I shall ask Percival Landon (a very interesting man who asked me for an interview the other day) to ~~come~~ also.

mgrigs-min disagreement 45
rogs-skyon help and protection
dam-chos-mzad espousing the cause earnestly
zhin-beans-chog-pa may be permitted to feel in mind, i.e. will remember
lha-rzas divine article, i.e. silk scarf
byin-can possessing sanctity 45

Dear Madame Lauwn,

Many thanks for your splendid book which I will always cherish as a most precious possession.

I return to you herewith the document which you bought at the ~~[illegible]~~ Lama temple. ~~It confirms the title~~ It contains four confirmations of the title of viscount granted by three ~~empires of~~ emperors to the following persons:

1) [Wang Chi, son of] Wang Kêng, ~~(Tao Kuang~~ (13th year of Tao Kuang)

2) Kuei P'u ~~(Wang Chi's son~~, son of Wang Chi (7th year of T'ung Chih) [illegible]

3) Tê Yüan, son of Kuei P'u ([24th year of] Kuang Hsü)

4) Tê Hao, [younger] brother of Tê Yüan ~~[illegible]~~ (25th year of Kuang Hsü).

Thanking you once more for your wonderful gift and wishing you a very happy Christmas I remain yours most sincerely

A. Stael-Holstein.

Dear Madame Laury

Until quite recently I thought that ~~I would be quite~~ during the next few ~~f~~ weeks I would have no official obligations to fulfill, but I was mistaken. I ~~shall~~ have [been asked to serve] ~~to give~~ the Swedish ~~Crow~~ Crown Prince, ~~who arrives shortly,~~ ~~a sort o~~ as [a sort of] ~~an~~ instructor in Buddhist iconography and also to make a detailed report on a Tibetan library which a Government institution wants to buy. ~~All this will take me some up much of my time and I shall be unable to leave Peking. I am awfully sorry~~ I shall have a good deal of reading to do ~~for~~ in order to acquit myself creditably of these tasks and can not, unfortunately, leave Peking for the present. I am [I regret] ~~awfully sorry~~ [very much] [under these circumstances] that I shall be unable to accompany you to the "Venerable Prince's" temple next week, ~~where I spent such wonderful days recently~~. I was looking forward so much to seeing the place again where I spent such wonderful days.

Please excuse me for not writing earlier and believe me yours sincerely A Staël Holstein.

My dear Mr.

Let me wish you a ~~nice~~ merry Christmas ~~and a happy new year. I shall be able to~~ now! I look forward very much to wishing you a happy new year personally at your dinner party on the 29th.

My dear Dr. Porter,

Let me wish you and your family a very merry Christmas!

I shall be so pleased if you ~~and Mrs. Porter~~ will come and have lunch at my house on Thursday December 29th at one o'clock.

~~If you would~~ Could you not bring ~~Mr~~ Mr. Hsü, the sanscritist, with you? I want very much to get into touch with him.

Believe me yours sincerely

A. Staël Holstein.

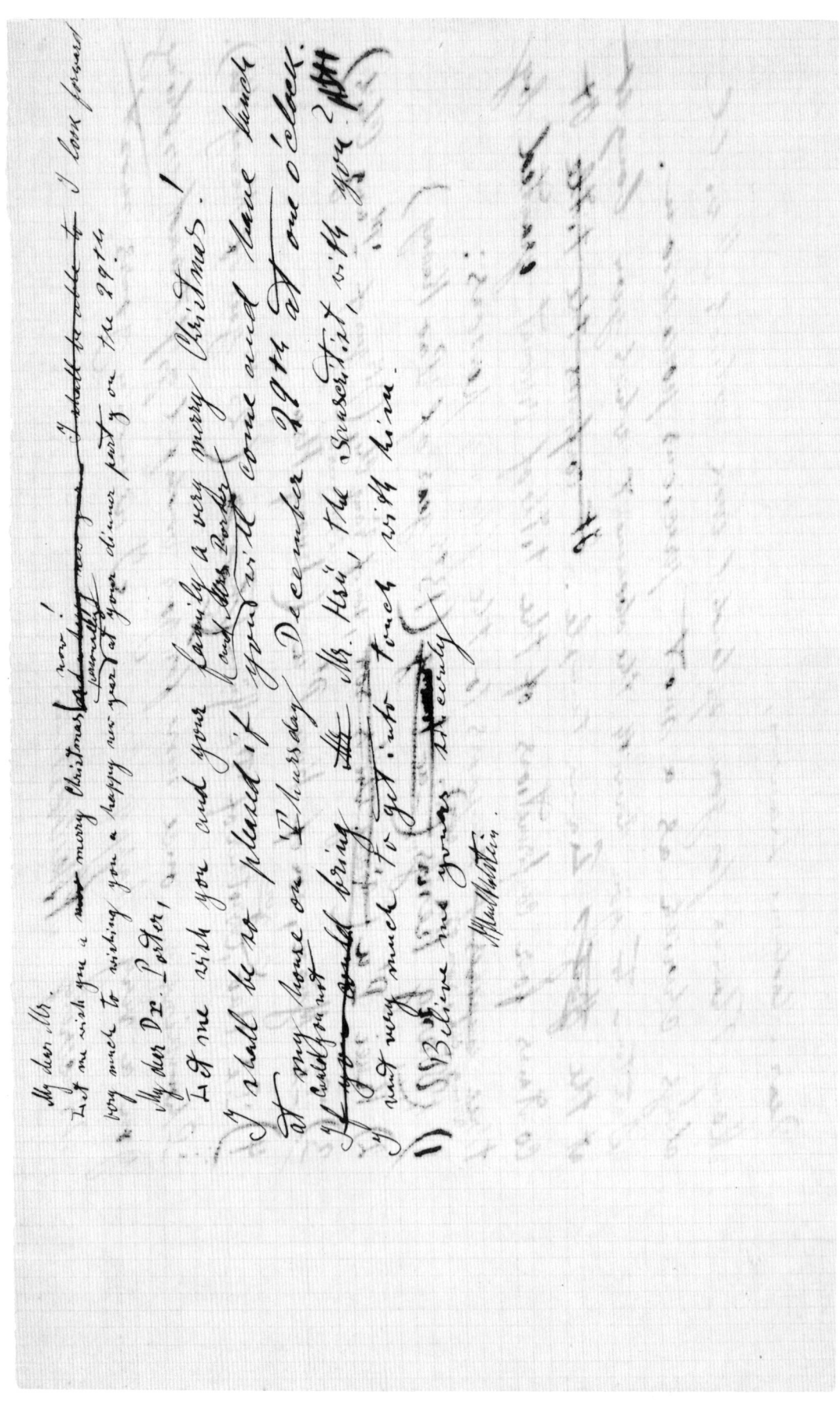

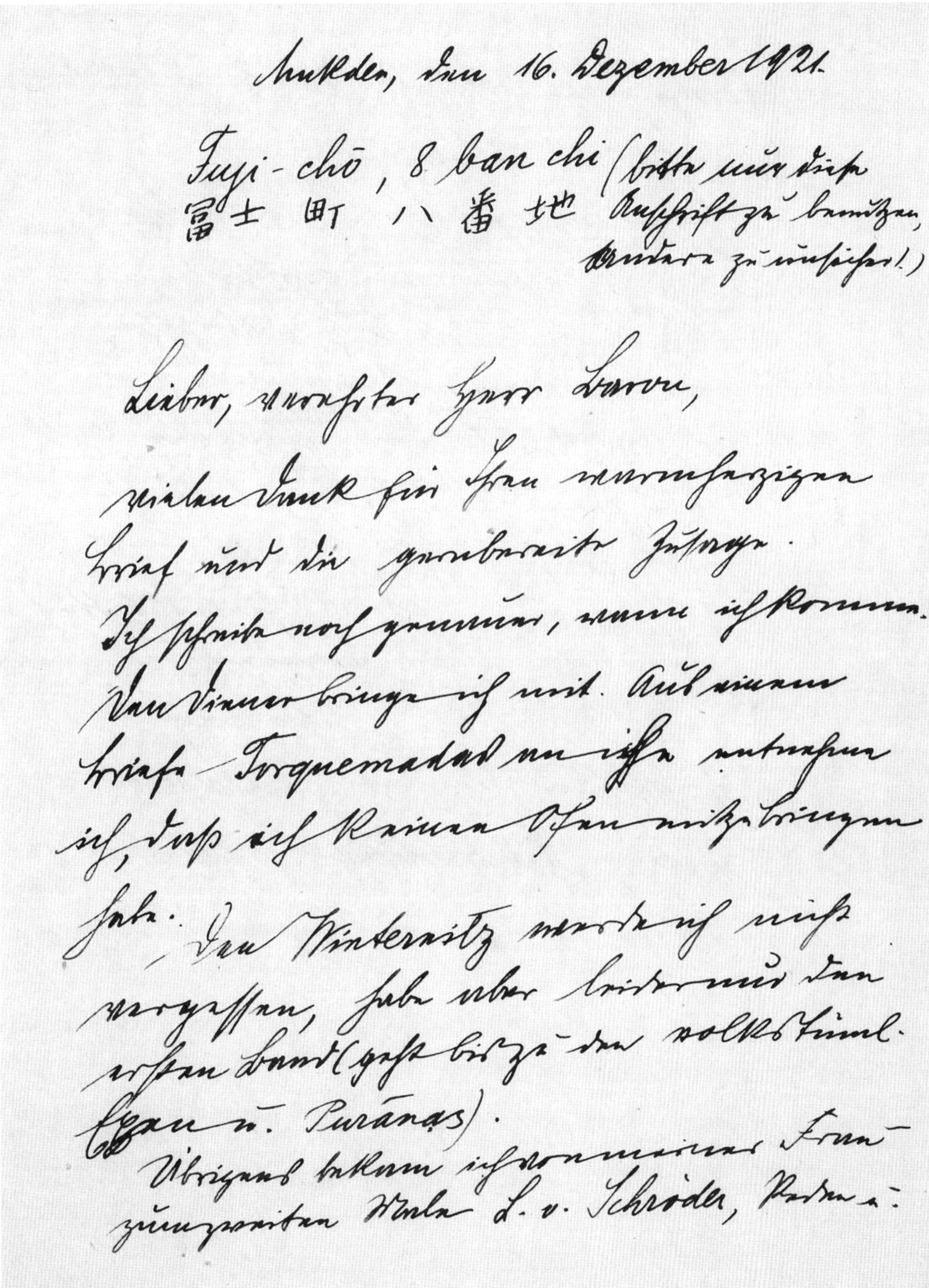

Mukden, den 16. Dezember 1921.

Fuji-chō, 8 ban chi (bitte nur diese
富士町八番地 Aufschrift zu benutzen,
andere zu unsicher!)

Lieber, verehrter Herr Baron,

vielen Dank für Ihren warmherzigen Brief und die gernbereite Zusage. Ich schreibe noch genauer, wenn ich komme. Den Dinner bringe ich mit. Aus einem Briefe Torquemadas an mich entnehme ich, daß ich keinen Ofen mitzubringen habe. Den Winternitz werde ich nicht vergessen, habe aber leider nur den ersten Band (geht bis zu den volkstüml. Epen u. Purāṇas).

Übrigens bekam ich von meiner Frau zum zweiten Male L. v. Schröder, Reden u.:

Aufsätze: Sinesische Kultur u. Literatur

von ihm ist vergriffen.

Einen Vortrag in der 文友會 kann

ich nicht halten – aus verschiedenen

Gründen. – Mit 在黃's Vorschlag

bin ich einverstanden, wenn Ersatz zu beschaffen.

Mit nochmaligem herzlichen Dank

u. freundlichsten Grüßen, lieber Herr

Baron,

Ihr freundschaftlich
ergebenster
Lessing.

Grüßen Sie gelegentl. Zucker,

bitte; seinen Brief erhalten.

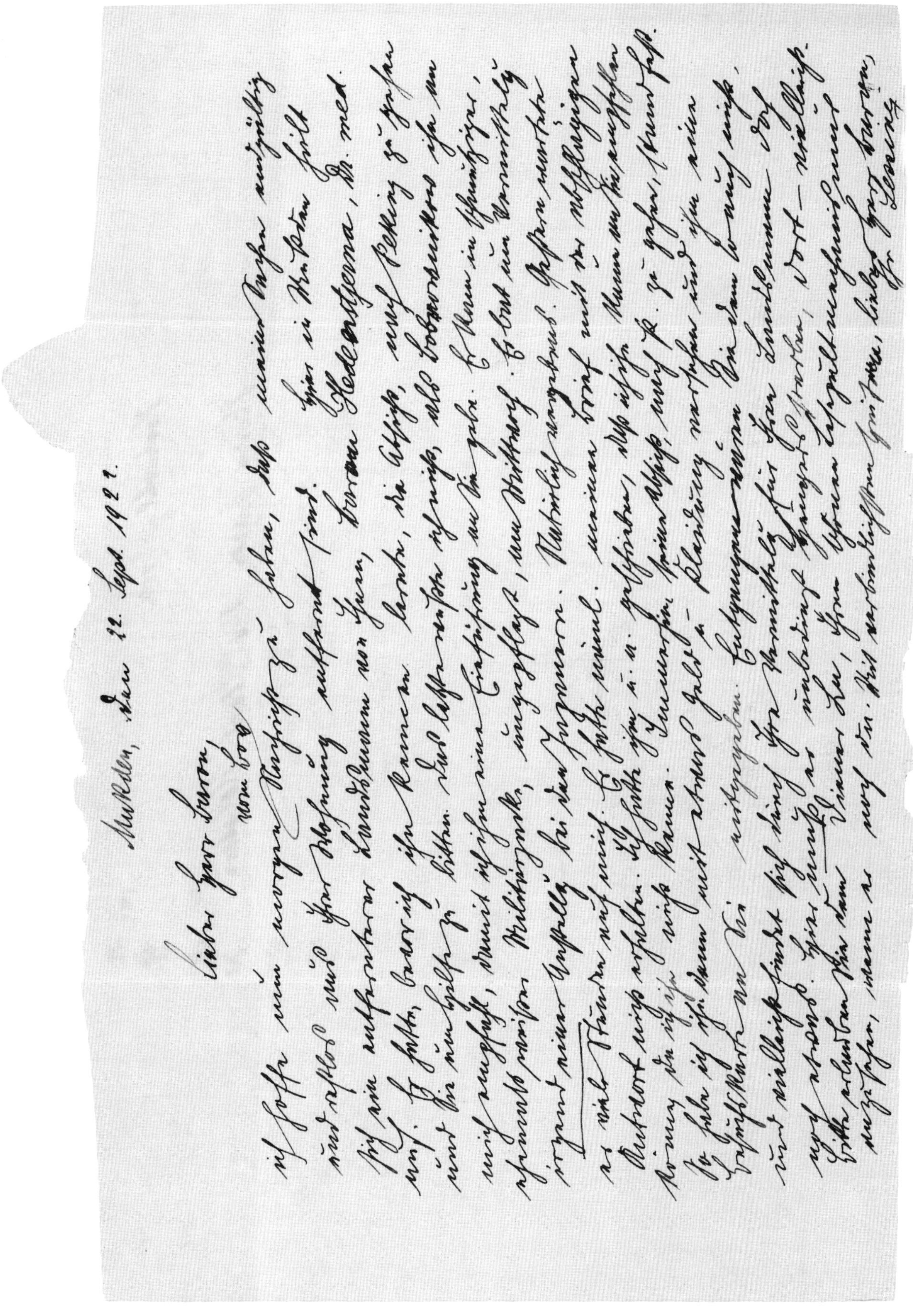

Mukden, den 22. Sept. 1922.

Lieber Herr Baron,

ich hoffe nun morgen vom Boy Nachricht zu haben, daß meine Sachen endgültig und restlos aus Ihrer Wohnung entfernt sind. Hier in Mukden hält sich ein entfernterer Landsmann von Ihnen, Baron Hedenstjerna, Dr. med. auf. Er hatte, bevor ich ihn kennen lernte, die Absicht, nach Peking zu gehen und Sie um Hilfe zu bitten. Das letztere wußte ich nicht, als Gobarewitsch ihn an mich empfahl, damit ich ihm eine Einführung an Sie gebe. Er kam in schmutziger, abgerissener Militärjacke, ungepflegt, am Mittwoch. Er bat um Vermittlung irgend einer Anstellung bei den Japanern. Natürlich vergebens. Gestern wartete er viele Stunden auf mich. Er hatte nämlich meinen Brief mit der abschlägigen Antwort nicht erhalten. Ich hatte ihm u. a. geschrieben, daß ich ihn kaum an Sie empfehlen könne, da ich ihn nicht kenne. Immerhin seine Absicht, nach P. zu gehen, stand fest. So habe ich ihn dann mit etwas Geld u. Kleidung versehen und ihm eine Geschäftskarte an Sie mitgegeben. Entgegen ... Sie dem ... auch nicht. Und vielleicht findet sich durch Ihre Vermittlung für Ihren Landsmann doch noch etwas. Hier muß er unbedingt Hungers sterben, dort – vielleicht. Bitte erlauben Sie dem Diener Lu, Ihnen ... anzusehen, wenn er noch da. Mit verbindlichsten Grüßen, lieber Herr Baron,

Ihr Lessing

Hochwohlgeboren
Herrn Baron A. v. Staël-Holstein
Peking

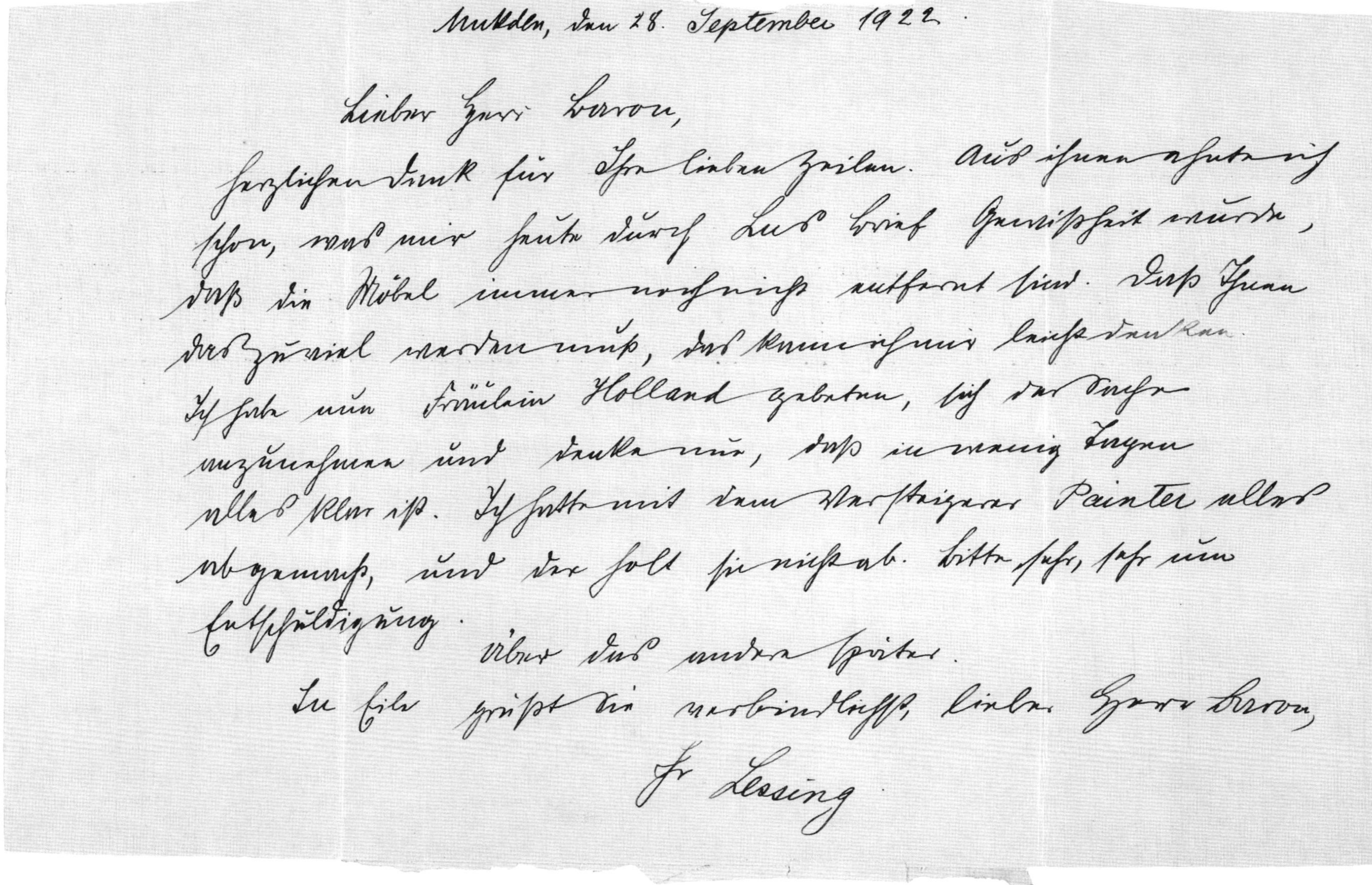

Mukden, den 28. September 1922.

Lieber Herr Baron,

herzlichen Dank für Ihre lieben Zeilen. Aus ihnen ersehe ich schon, was mir heute durch Ihr Brief Gewissheit wurde, dass die Möbel immer noch nicht entfernt sind. Dass Ihnen das zu viel werden muss, das kann ich mir leicht denken. Ich habe nun Fräulein Holland gebeten, sich der Sache anzunehmen und denke nur, dass in wenig Tagen alles klar ist. Ich hatte mit dem Versteigerer Painter alles abgemacht, und der holt sie nicht ab. Bitte sehr, sehr um Entschuldigung.

Über das andere später.

In Eile grüsst Sie verbindlichst, lieber Herr Baron,

Ihr Lessing

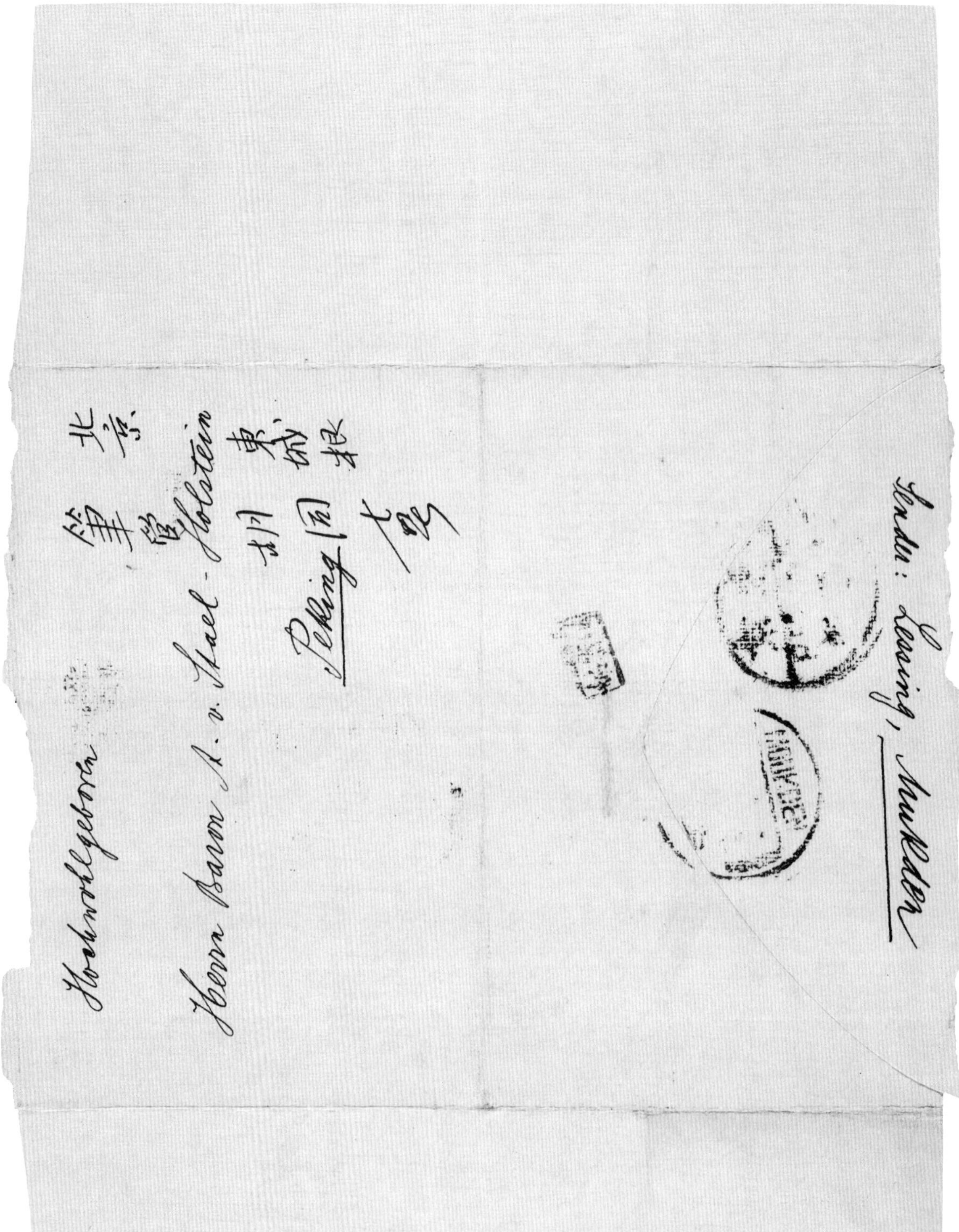
北京東城根
筆管胡同
Hochwohlgeboren
Herrn Baron A. v. Stael-Holstein
Peking

Mein lieber Baron,

ich erlaube mir, Ihnen aus meiner Bergeinsiedelei ~~Sie~~ einen Teil meiner Abschrift zum „Yung-ho-gung" zu senden, in der Hoffnung, daß Sie sie einmal mit dem Werken Ihres प्रज्ञावनुस durchleuchten, wenn Sie Zeit dazu finden möchten. Es ist etwa 1/6 des Ganzen.

Sonnabend abend gedenke ich in die Niederung hinabzusteigen. Ich weiß nicht, ob es Ihre Zeit erlaubt, sonst würde ich um 9 Uhr herum bei Ihnen vorsprechen. Ich komme um 8 Uhr auf dem Bahnhof 西直門 an, könnte also um 9 Uhr in der 筆管胡同 sein.

Wenn es Ihnen ~~nicht~~ irgendwie paßt, dann bitte schreiben Sie mir eine Karte mit nein an die unten angegebene Adresse. Montag gehe ich wieder in die Berge zurück.

Am Sūtrālaṃkāra zu arbeiten, habe ich leider noch gar keine Zeit gefunden.

Bitte grüßen Sie die ~~मह~~ापण्डिता: .

京西八大
處朝陽
庵第七分
局四號

23.7.24.

Herzlichst
Ihr ergebener
Lessing.

Frau Grimm läßt freundlich grüßen.

Lieber Herr Baron,

gestern sandte ich eingeschrieben meinen Dank für den काश्यपपरिवर्त. Heute habe ich schon eine neue Bitte. Könnten Sie mir wohl von der Peking-Leader-Reprints alles, was für mich Interesse haben könnte, – ich nehme an, daß es sich um wohlfeile ~~[illegible]~~ handelt – beschaffen? z. B. 胡適 Our attitude toward Modern Western Civilisation(x). 梁啓超: Archeology in China. (Nr. 25, 1926, 20 Cts.) alles [illegible] je 2 od. 3 Exemplaren. Ferner [illegible] meine Bitte und meinen gestrigen Brief: 金剛般若波羅蜜經六譯 in einem Bande, u. füge hinzu 阿彌陀經 鳩摩羅什譯 u. 玄奘譯 [illegible] 般若波羅蜜多心經, jedes [illegible] 3 [illegible] in 10 [illegible] ganz wie Sie wünschen, [illegible]

(x) Nr. 24, 1926, 10 Cts.

Herzliche Grüße Ihr Lessing.

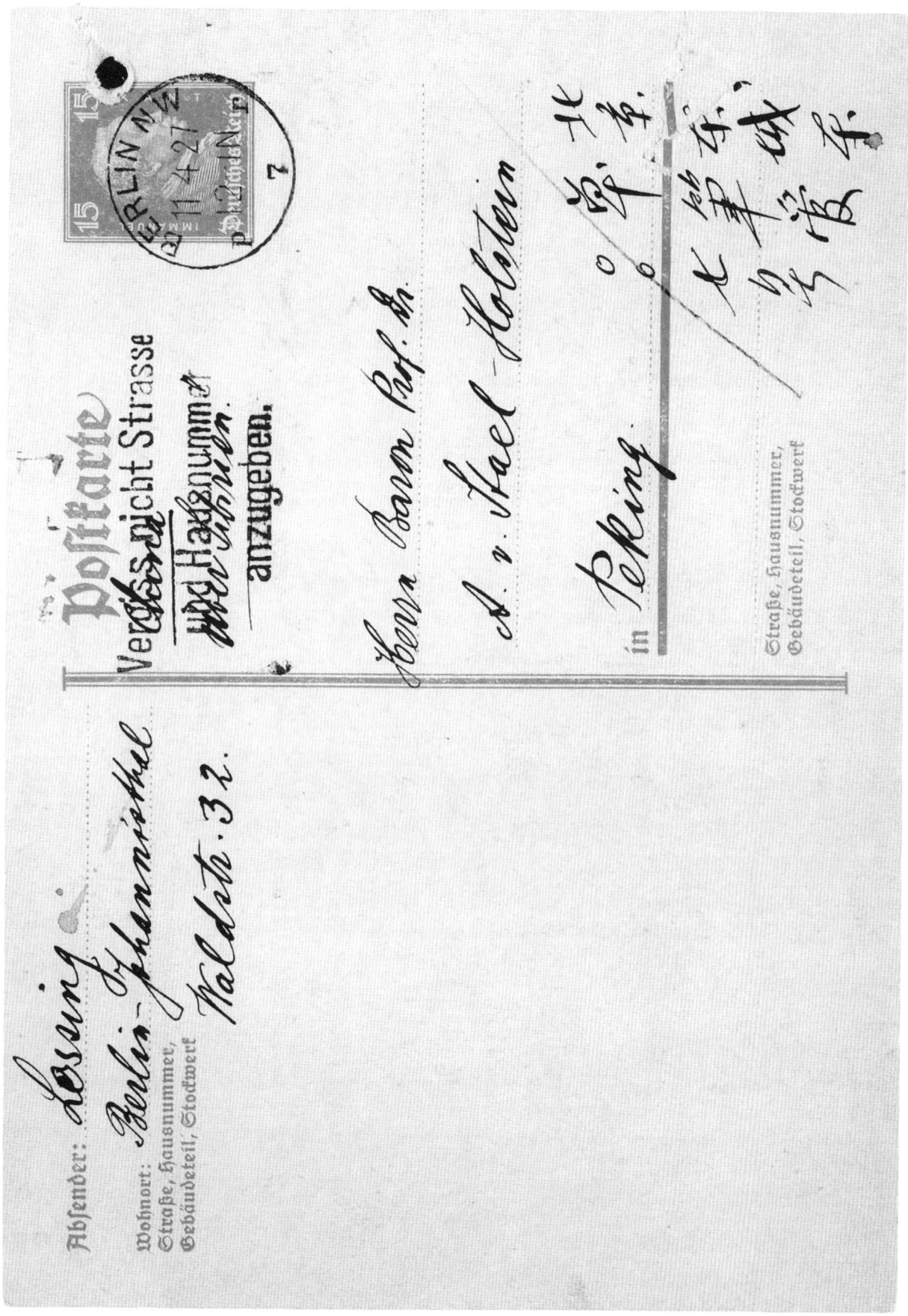
Absender: Lessing
Wohnort: Straße, Hausnummer, Gebäudeteil, Stockwerk
Berlin-Johannisthal
Waldstr. 32.

Postkarte
Vergiss nicht Strasse und Hausnummer anzugeben.

Herrn Baron Prof. Dr.
A. v. Staël-Holstein
in Peking
Straße, Hausnummer, Gebäudeteil, Stockwerk

BERLIN NW 7
11.4.27

Peking, 6/6/31.

Sehr verehrter Herr Baron!

Damit ich Ihnen durch meine Lässigkeit nicht noch unnötige Arbeit mache, beeile ich mich, Ihnen mitzuteilen, dass ich die Photographie od. vielmehr den Lichtdruck der mir anvertrauten "Füllung" gleich gefunden habe. Ich denke, Ihnen Dienstag darüber berichten zu können.

Nachträglich ist mir eine Vermutung eingefallen, die mir die heute besprochene Stelle zwanglos zu erklären scheint. Danach wäre zu lesen ~~statt~~ 以福慧資 statt 以福資慧助於(于?)說聽 und zu übersetzen: mit der mitwirkenden Kraft des puṇya u. jñāna (prajñā) etc.

Solcher "Umstellungen" scheint mir der Text weiterhin gelegentlich noch mehr zu bedürfen, aber man soll dem verantwortlichen Redaktör nicht vorgreifen.

Mit schönen Empfehlungen

Ihr Ihnen stets ergebener

Lessing,

Peking, den 15. Jan. 1932.

才說因緣便打撞碎一石頭

問你那一片[illegible]人能[illegible]

Lieber Herr Baron,

mit dieser Arhat nahm habe ich nachgedacht über das Problem, mit meinem Geld und mit meiner Zeit auszukommen, in beiden Richtungen ohne Erfolg. So muss ich mich bescheiden und beschneiden, die Aufgaben der Aufgaben. Und da ich nun einmal Teil der Schätze des guten Geistes nicht in meinem Sonnenscheingarten bleibt, leider, leider auf seinen Duft verzichten. Es kommt hinzu, dass [Tibetan] bei dem ich [Tibetan] lerne, den Sonnabend Zeit hat. Schade, diese Vorlesungen bei Ihnen hatten mir so gut und waren eine so schöne Abwechslung gegen die allzu künstlerische Lektüre meiner Luxusarbeit. Nehmen Sie meinen herzlichsten Dank für alles. Hitopadeśa. Grüssen Sie bitte Herrn Tschen.

Meine besten Empfehlungen u. Grüsse!

Ihr Ihnen ergebener Lessing

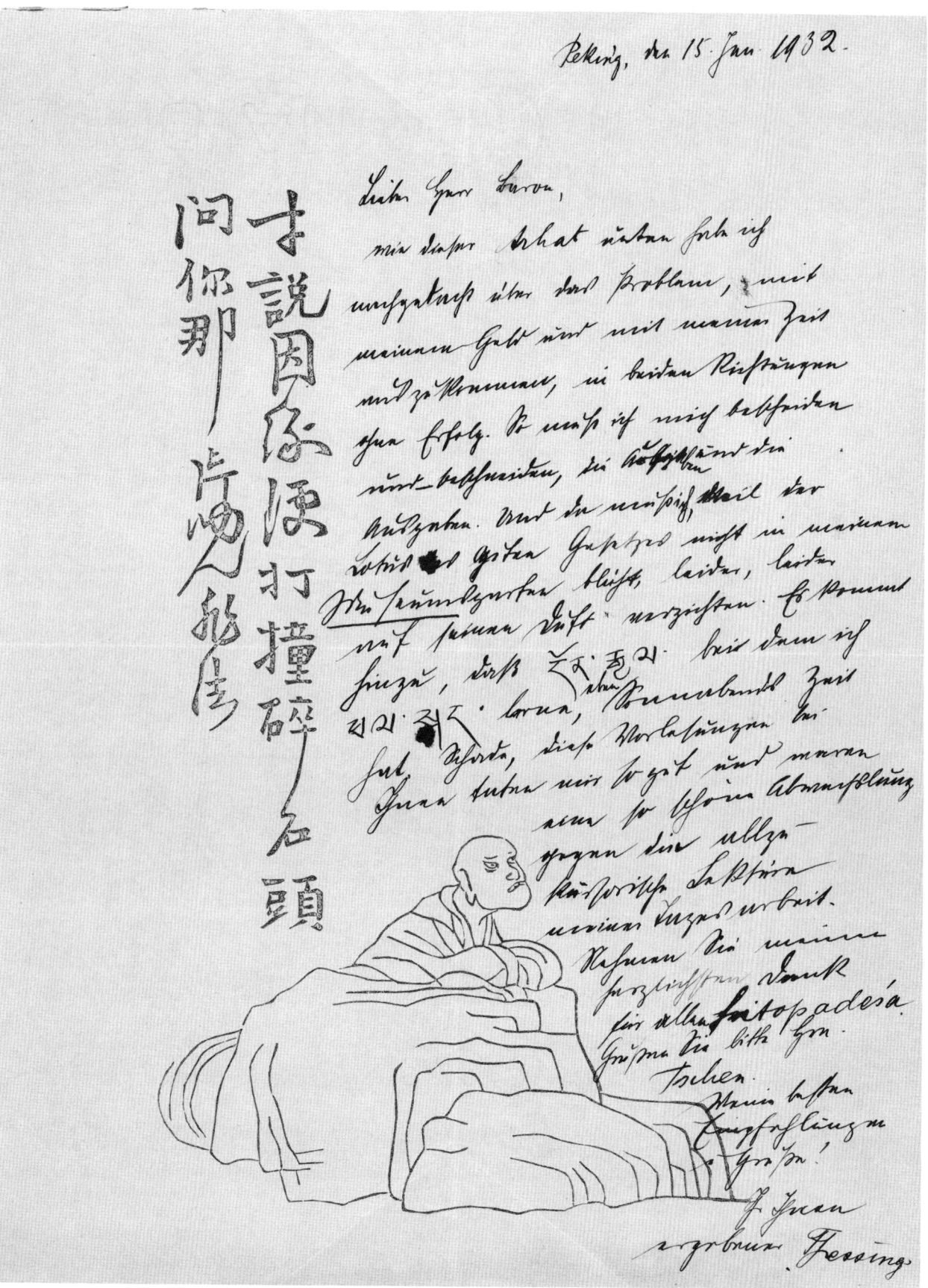

Peking, den 13. Sept 1932.

Sehr verehrter Herr Baron!

Für alle Fälle, obwohl ich glaube, dass Sie es schon selbst gegriffen haben werden, erinnere ich an B. Nanjō №32: 佛說胞胎經 = 大寶積經 13.

青目在假自在動靜分明
即是体態

Gehört 中陰經 № 463 nicht auch hierher? Schriftl. Antwort erwarte ich nicht.

8/10/32.

Lieber Herr Baron,

anbei ein paar Notizen, die leider nicht viel sagen. Wollten Sie sie in dieser Form nicht weitergeben, so würde ich bitten, sie mir nach Gebrauch zurückzugeben. Ich habe keine Zeit gehabt, in der Literatur zu suchen. Hoffentlich genügen sie Ihren Absichten.

Mit herzl. Gruß
Ihr F. Lessing.

1 Photogr.

1

Einige Bemerkungen

zu ~~den~~ der ~~Plott~~ Photographie einer
alten chinesischen Steinskulptur.

Die Skulptur zeigt die ~~gewöhnliche~~ häufige
Zweiteilung des Raumplanes. In dem
oberen, fast rechteckigen Felde ~~Maitreya~~ Buddha /,
auf europäische Weise sitzend, ~~vermutlich~~
~~ohne Schmuck~~, die rechte Hand lehrend
erhoben (?), die linke wahrscheinlich
auf den Knien liegend. ~~Die Tracht bedeckt~~
~~b~~ Das Mönchsgewand bedeckt beide Schultern
Schmuck ~~scheint~~ scheint zu fehlen.
Füsse ruhen auf Lotos.
Rechts und l. von ihm je eine stehende Figur in
anbetender Stellung. ~~Von ihnen fällt die~~
l. von ihm stehende fällt durch ihre
individualisierten Züge auf. In den Ecken
rechts und links je ein Bodhisatva. Der
l. vom Betrachter stehende Bva ist
durch eine Vase (lekythos) in der

2

herabhängenden Hand ausgezeichnet. Ob er einen Buddha im Haar trägt, vermag ich nicht zu erkennen. Avalokiteśvara?

Vor den beiden Bodhisatvas 2 kleine Figuren, auf sitzenden Vierfüsslern, l. (v. Betrachter) auf einem ~~sitzenden~~ Löwen, r. auf einem Tier mit breiter Schnauze u. stehenden Ohren.

Den oberen ~~Abschluss~~ Abschluss dieses Feldes bildet ein Baldachin mit 6 Troddeln, der in einer Volute endigt. Seine Spitze krönt eine Lotosblume.

Die ~~an~~ Anordnung der Gestalten auf dem unteren, grösseren Felde ist wie folgt:

				1	3	5			~~18~~ 24
~~17~~ 23	4	2	6	7				~~14~~ 9	20
	~~10~~ 8	~~6~~ 10	~~7~~ 11		~~7~~ 12	~~9~~ 13			
19									22
			15	~~12~~ 14	16			18	
21	17								

1. Buddha, predigend? Gewand bedeckt beide Schultern. Buddhasitz. ~~L.~~ R. Hand?
   " L. Hand Gefäss.

3

2. Stehende Gestalt im Mönchsgewand(?).

3. " " " in weltlicher Tracht. Individuelle Züge ähnlich der entsprechend. Gestalt im oberen Felde.

4. Stehend. Bodhisatvatracht, Schmuck/ R. Hand hebt stūpaähnliches Gefäss empor. Buddha im Haar? ~~X~~ Guan-yin? S. entsprechende Gestalt im oberen Felde.

5. Stehende Gestalt in Bodhisatvatracht, Schmuck ~~Ähl~~ Ähnlich der entsprechenden Gestalt im oberen Felde.

6. 7. Gestalten ähnlich den Reitern ~~oben~~ im oberen Felde, 7 knieend.

2. Reihe

8. 9. Schwebende Apsaras.

10 – 13. Knieende Gestalten, auf Lotus?

3. Reihe

~~14~~
14. Grosse Mittelgestalt, in "Tänzer"haltung mit stark gebeugtem ~~Knie~~ r. Knie auf ? stehend. Kopf leicht nach l. gebeugt. Buddhatracht.

4.

15. 16. 2 grössere, } Nebengestalten, z. T.
17. 18. 2 kleinere
in lebhafter Bewegung, sitzend.

19 – 22 in Rechtecken am Rande des Steins ausserhalb der das Mittelfeld flankierenden Säulen: 4 gepanzerte Lokapālas, auf verschieden "vāhanas" stehend. über ihnen

23. 24. 2 Apsaras. ~~o~~

An den Säulen je 2 ~~Kinderartig~~ Kindern ähnliche Gestalten. Die Säulen selbst stehen auf (kauernden) Dämonen.

über dem Buddha: Baldachin ähnlich dem über dem oberen Felde.

Ohne einschlägige Literatur und ~~ohne~~ nur auf Grund der Literatur ist es gewagt, ~~über~~ die Szenen näher zu bestimmen. Was ins Auge fällt, ist die ~~Tatsache~~ Ähnlichkeit dieser

5

Darstellung mit lamaistischen ~~Bildern~~ Maitreya-
~~die~~ bildern. Auf diesen erscheint er einmal
als Mönch, lehrend, meist oben auf dem Bildplan,
und darunter auf europ. Weise sitzend, (im "Maitreyasitz") im Tusita-
Himmel. Hier wären,
die Identität der Darstellung vorausgesetzt, die
Felder umgekehrt angeordnet.

Solche Darstellung ~~der~~ einer Gottheit mit ihrem
Parivāra heissen Mandala. Nach dem alten
Schema umfassten sie folgende Ordnungen:

1. San-dsun-hue 三尊會 (1, 4, 5 im zweiten Felde).
2. Hü-kung-hue 虛空會 (23, 24).
3. Bau-lou-go-hue 寶樓閣會 (ajolle).
4. Schu-hia-hue 樹下會 (ajolle).
5. Bau-tschi-hue 寶池會 (8-12?).
6. Li-fo-hue 禮佛會 (2, 3, 4, 5).
7. Wu-yüö-hue 舞樂會 (14-18?).

6.

Vgl. 曼荼羅乃研究 passim,
u. a. Taf. 14.
Wir hätten hier also, soweit erkennbar,
ein ~~siebenteil~~ fünfteiliges Schema.
Zur Ikonographie des Maitreya vgl.
M. Wegner in Ostas. Zeits. 1929 (mir nicht
zugänglich).

Tokio,
Central P. O. B. 58. 17/10/22.

Lieber Herr Prof. Lessing,

Darf ich eine Bitte an Sie aussprechen? In Peking studiert ein junger Japaner, der vorzügliche Anlagen in sich hat und englisch & chinesisch gut spricht. Er hat u. a. auch bei Prof. v. Stael-Holstein "Geschichte der alten Religionen Indiens" belegt. Soweit ich mich erinnere, sagten Sie mir, daß Sie mit Prof. Stael-Holstein gut bekannt sind; würden Sie ihn bitten, den jungen Mann einmal zu sich kommen zu lassen. Findet er ihn gut, so wird sich alles weitere von selbst ergeben. Er kann auf ihn voll vertrauen.

Sein Name ist: Nagamasa Kawakita; er ist in China, um aus dem beengenden Kreise Japans heraus zu sein, & wird wohl im nächsten Jahre nach Europa.

Ich erwarte bald von Dr. Strauss Brief über Tscherbatzkoi etc.

Ich denke gern an die kurzen Stunden in Mukden.

Ihr stets ergebener

[illegible]

Die eigenartige Kürze dieses Briefes werden Sie einem Geschäftsmann nicht übelnehmen.

Freiburg i/Breisgau
Dreisamstr. 35.
April 14. 1928.

Sehr geehrter Herr Kollege!

Vor vielen Wochen sandte mir Kollege Konow (den ich zum letzten Mal 1926 an unserm Hamburger Orientalistentag sah) zuerst ein Transkript und dann auch Ihre Photographie der nordarischen Seite, wie Sie sie ihm einige Zeit vorher geschickt hatten. Ich mühte mich daran ab, so gut ich konnte, und übersetzte den Eingang (den Konow ziemlich anders aufgefasst hatte) für ihn, sandte auch ein noch etwas grösseres Stück in Übersetzung an Thomas, weil Konow wegen des Tibetischen ohne Antwort von ihm geblieben war. Nach längerem Warten kam am 31. März von Thomas eine vorläufige Karte des Inhalts:

Many thanks for your letter and translation. The Tibetan is quite clear, and I will send you a translation shortly. Your rendering of the Khotanī will be most helpful, and we can make an useful publication.

Ich selber hatte von einer gemeinsamen Publikation noch nichts geschrieben, hatte Konow vielmehr empfohlen, das nordarische Dokument in geographischem Sinne zu behandeln, weil der sonstige Inhalt doch nicht deutlich genug sei. Als nun aber am 10. April von Thomas die versprochene 'translation' des Tibetischen ankam, wurde mir nach anfänglicher Unsicherheit (denn das Tibetische hat tatsächlich einen ganz anderen Inhalt als das Nordarische!) die Gesamtsituation klar, und ich schrieb vorläufig – bloß zur allgemeinen Klarstellung – die mitfolgenden fünf Seiten als Anfang einer von Thomas angeregten 'useful publication'. Dieselben fünf Seiten will ich auch Thomas und Konow einsenden (letzterer hat diese Woche den ersten internationalen Linguistenkongreß im Haag mitgemacht und wird wohl erst in einigen Tagen wieder zu Hause sein).

Also Thomas und ich müssen nach der ganzen Entwicklung der Dinge sowohl von Ihnen wie von Konow erst die Erlaubnis für unsere augenblicklich noch ziemlich embryonale Publikation einholen. Denn anscheinend hatte Konow vor, mindestens das Geographische des nordarischen Dokuments zu behandeln — worin er übrigens (auch wenn unser Embryo 'Leumann-Thomas' sich entwickeln wird) unbehindert sein würde. Daß Sie selber ihm in der Sache ziemlich freie Hand gegeben hatten, schien mir aus seinen Briefen an mich hervorzugehen.

Nun fehlen mir aber zur Aufklärung über die nordarisch-tibetische Rolle noch einige Angaben über deren Provenienz, die Sie allein geben können. Meiner in den fünf Seiten dargelegten Auffassung gemäß müßte die Rolle doch wohl in Khotan gefunden worden sein. Andrerseits ist mir bisher nur bekannt, daß aus Tun-Huang antiquarische Funde nach Peking gebracht worden sind. Wie steht es nun tatsächlich mit dem durch Ihre Photographie uns bekannt gewordenen Fund?

Und auch die Photographie selber gibt mir noch Anlaß zu einer Frage. In der elften

Zeile, die mit Tsadikam beginnt, stehen gegen den Schluss hin <u>untergeschrieben</u> die Silben

nā ki chi tti pū u rā hi dra

Die letzte dieser Silben bleibt auf der Photographie unsicher, weil da der Rand der Rolle ein bischen umgedreht ist. Auf der Rolle selber läßt sich gewiss leicht feststellen, ob wirklich dra oder vielleicht dva oder was Anderes gemeint ist.

Von Freund Mironow habe ich lange nichts mehr gehört, während Sie wohl eher mit ihm in Zusammenhang stehen. Er hatte vor ein paar Jahren ein tocharisches (oder nordarisches?) Fundstück, wozu er von mir aus dem Mahāvagga die Parallele wünschte, die ich ihm dann (weil meine eigenen Bücher damals noch in Kisten verpackt waren) nachträglich mit Hülfe von Kirfel in Bonn schicken konnte. Aber ich weiß nicht, ob aus der Sache was geworden ist. — Mit einem Japaner übersetze ich jetzt Mahāvastu; ein größeres Stück ist schon nach Japan abgegangen, um da gedruckt zu werden.

In aufrichtiger Hochachtung Ihr Ernst Leumann.

1

A Khotan King sending political agents to eastern places as far as Śacū (Tun-Huang).

Through the kindness of Dr Sten Konow (Oslo) we have received from the well-known russian orientalist von Staël-Holstein, now residing in Peking, the photographic reproduction of a long roll inscribed on both sides. One side contains, in north-arian language, a report of the political agents mentioned above, describing what places in the east they have visited and what they have done there. The other side of the roll formulates in two versions (a preliminary and a final one) the request written in Tibetan, which those agents submitted to the king of Śacū for surrendering him the presents of their home king and for taking leave before returning to Khotan.

The situation seems to be as follows: Apparently a great many North-Arians (whose central home from old was the town and country of Khotan) had settled eastwards even as far as Tun-Huang (Śacū) and were

2

scattered there inside a heterogenious population which chiefly consisted of Tibetan elements and which, at any rate, were subjects to the tibetan-speaking Kings of Tun-Huang. It appears that the Kings of Khotan entertained connections with those outsiders by sending agents who visited them. At the same time these agents were to bring presents to those outsiders' lords who were residing at Tun-Huang for their allowing the friendly intercourse going on between Khotan and their territory. It seems that permission for this intercourse was not always readily given. For, the request contained in our roll speaks in terms which indicate that the then sovereign of Tun-Huang did not care much to receive personally the Khotanese agents.

Now, the north-arian side of our roll states in a first memorandum that Rrgyadisūmma, the chief agent of the Khotanese King Līn Viśa-saṃbhata, has, on his behalf, seven times inspected the eastern regions up to Ṣacū. Moreover, we read in that memorandum what companions Rrgyadisūmma generally had on his tours and

3

what places were visited. A second memorandum (on the same side of the roll) more explicitely names the persons who formed Rrgyadisumma's retinue on his seventh tour and describes what was acted and learnt on this occasion.

A slight incongruity as to the name of Rrgyadisumma's Khotan sovereign is found between the north-arian portion of the roll and the tibetan one. The former, as was stated before, calls the Khotan King "Lion Vizasambhata". This seems to stand for 'Simha Vijaya-sammata' i.e. the 'Lion taxed Vijaya' which, in ordinary sanskrit, would simply be 'Vijayasimha'. On the other hand, the tibetan request calls the Khotan King shortly 'Lion Majesty' or, more fully, 'Lion Majesty Mun-dmag-tran' where Mun-dmag-tran (literally 'darkness-army') must be meant for Vijaya 'victory' though this rendering is rather inadequate.

Turning again to the first memorandum described before we may infer from it that the Khotan agents, within about a decad of years, have practically travelled through the wole country extending to Ṣacū. The places inspected are enumerated under four heads:

1. 'Towns'. Twenty-three are enumerated; but of these many are, by interlineary notes, declared as 'empty', viz. as containing no north-arian inhabitants.
2. 'Horse towns'; these are perhaps fortified houses (german 'Höfe'). Thirteen are named, and none of these is said to be 'empty'.
3. 'Great towns'. Ten are enumerated, no one 'empty'.
4. This section (comprising lines 25–30) remains obscure.

The second memorandum tells us what the activity of our agents was:

> (they had to settle) much business (among the scattered North-Arians and to show) great amiability (towards them); they helped them in making gardens and pools, and they paid visits wherever the racial feelings tending towards Khotan were kept alive.

In fact the scattered North-Arians were attended to

5

by the Khotan agents as now-a-days a political or clerical diaspora is cared for by emissaries sent out from the home country, or the home church.

One expression, here, is of interest. The places scattered in the east (pūrva-vistarika) which are visited by the agents of the Khotan King appear to him as a field for meritorious action (punya-prayoga) given to his charge through his quality as a godly (viz. kingly) Bodhisattva. And he states that they had also been attended to already by the two (former Khotan) kings Maśiri and Dauṣkara. Maśiri is the king whose name occurs in the Kharoṣṭhī Documents (published by Senart, Boyer and Rapson) under the form Mayiri (y and ś being often interchanged); but the name of Dauṣkara has not turned up yet in the antiquarian remains hitherto investigated.

Freiburg i/B. Dreisamstr. 35.
4. März 1929
Montag.

Sehr geehrter Herr Kollege!

Ihr Brief aus der Harvard University, den ich schon vor zwei Monaten bekommen habe, war mir eine grosse Überraschung. Ich möchte hoffen, dass Sie in Amerika Fuss fassen können. Freilich schreiben Sie, dass Sie Ende April nach Peking zurückreisen wollen. Mittlerweile wird Ihnen Lanman noch mehr, als was unser kurzer Postkartengruss sagen konnte, vom Oxforder Kongress berichtet haben. Ich habe viel Freude an Lanman und an seiner Tochter (die ihn begleitete) gehabt. Er hat mehrmals prächtig gesprochen (in Bonn, wo wir zuerst tagten, und nachher in Oxford). Die Toten-Liste, die er mir schon in Bonn vorwies, mußte er inzwischen um den Namen Geldner's vermehren.

Nun aber herzlichen Dank für für die subtile Nachzeichnung der fraglichen Silben in Ihrem nordarischen Dokument. Dieses wird nun aber durch Konow und Thomas allein herausgegeben, nachdem ich den beiden wenigstens für den Inhalt meine Direktiven gegeben hatte. Ob Sie in Amerika die Bekanntschaft des Geographen Huntington, von dem ich vor Jahren einige nordarische Dinger geliehen bekam, gemacht haben? Aus der Minerva würden Sie wohl ersehen, wo er steckt; er ist irgendwo Professor.

Heute hätte ich noch einmal ein kleines Anliegen, das den Ratnakuta betrifft. Wir haben Ihre Ausgabe, durch die Sie sich ein grosses Verdienst erworben haben, hier noch

nicht bekommen können. So möchte ich
Sie fragen, ob ein Citat aus dem Ratnakūṭa, das ich im Nordarischen habe,
bei Ihnen vorkommt. Das Citat
lautet:
Der Buddha hat im Ratnakūṭa gesagt,
das Denken sei so leer (śūnya) wie
der Ākāśa; er sagte es mit den Worten: O Mahākāśyapa, das Denken
ist in Wirklichkeit bloß vorhanden
im Andern dem Andern gegenüber
[d. h. innerhalb des Einen im Hinblick
auf das Andere], indem es isoliert
vom Andern (pṛthag anyasmāt),
d. h. für sich, nicht vorhanden ist.
Mit freundlichem Gruß und
besten Wünschen Ihr ergebenster
Ernst Leumann.

MAISON FRANCO-JAPONAISE
28 NITCHÔMÉ NAGATACHÔ, KÔJIMATCHI-KOU,
TOKIO
TÉLÉPHONE : GINZA 4906 & 7209

16 juillet 192[illegible]

Mon cher ami

J'ai été très heureux de recevoir votre Kāçyapa. C'est d'abord une nouvelle marque de votre amitié fidèle ; c'est un livre utile, et c'est un beau travail. Et quand on pense aux circonstances où vous l'avez préparé et publié, on est confondu d'admiration. La philologie, elle aussi, a ces héros, discrets et modestes comme les vrais héros. Je ne vous ferai compliment de votre livre qu'en vous parlant de ce qui lui manque encore. Vous annoncez l'intention de publier le commentaire de Sthiramati. Parfait. Mais d'abord et avant tout, donnez-nous les index, l'index, ou mieux encore le vocabulaire sanscrit ; le vocabulaire technique avec les équivalents adoptés pour chaque mot par chaque traducteur, les références à tous les passages, la reproduction de tous les passages qui éclaircissent le sens du mot. La Fédération des Sociétés Asiatiques Interalliées a décidé à plusieurs reprises de publier une série de vocabulaires de ce genre en vue d'un Dictionnaire technique du Bouddhisme sanscrit qui viendra plus tard. J'ai préparé moi-même un

Vocabulaire de ce genre pour la [illegible] que je destinerai à l'impression en rentrant à Paris, vers Pâques. Geuthner a demandé d'être l'éditeur de cette collection. Il y a là un débouché facile de ...

Savez-vous que nous compilons ici, à la Maison Franco-Japonaise, un Dictionnaire de Bouddhisme d'après les sources chinoises et les encyclopédies japonaises, surtout le Daijii et le Daijiten. Le travail a commencé le mois dernier. Takakusu et moi dirigeons; Demiéville, installé ici comme pensionnaire, est rédacteur en chef. Une équipe de cinq Japonais l'assiste, dont deux de nos anciens élèves. Le Comte Otani Sonyu de Nishi Hongwanji fait les frais jusqu'à concurrence de 1.000 yen par mois. Le Dictionnaire sera publié en français et en anglais. Si vous pensez à vous séparer temporairement de la Chine, si vous croyez qu'un séjour au Japon est un stage nécessaire pour l'étude du bouddhisme, dites-le moi. En ce cas, je demanderai au Ministère, à Paris, si on pourrait vous admettre ici temporairement dans la maison comme pensionnaire, tout comme Goloubeff a été admis à l'École Française d'Extrême-Orient quand il était encore Russe. Les pensionnaires ici sont logés, chauffés, éclairés, et ils reçoivent 400 yen par mois comme pension. Il y en a actuellement quatre : Demiéville, Haguenauer (japonisant), Riquier ([illegible], Chambre de Commerce de Lyon), Reclus (géographe, à Kyoto). En outre un membre de l'École Française d'Extrême-Orient, Aubouin, japonisant, qui retournera à Hanoï en septembre, mais qui sera remplacé sans doute par un autre pensionnaire de l'École Française.

Outre le concours de Takakusu, qui vous est tout acquis, on pourrait sans doute trouver des cours à faire, soit à l'Université, soit dans un établissement supérieur libre.

Il est bien entendu que ce n'est pas là une offre positive que je vous fais ; c'est une possibilité à étudier, mais qu'il ne sera utile de mettre à l'étude que si vous ne l'excluez pas au préalable. Votre travail principal serait la collaboration au Dictionnaire : les articles sont au préalable traduits du Daijii et du Daijiten en quasi-français ou quasi-anglais. Il faut alors les reprendre, les refondre, sur un plan établi de façon à grouper les données autant que possible sous des articles d'ensemble.

Nous partons demain pour Gotemba, au pied du Fuji, toute l'équipe ensemble de façon à continuer le travail durant les vacances dans un air moins pénible que celui de Tokyo en été. Je pense revenir ici vers le 15 septembre. Vous avez tout le temps de réfléchir, mais j'espère que vous n'attendrez pas d'avoir pris une décision sur ce point pour m'écrire, et que vous me donnerez de vos nouvelles, de vous et de votre travail, avant qu'il soit trop longtemps.

Ma femme et Demiéville — qui vient de partir pour Gotemba tout à l'heure — se joignent à moi pour vous envoyer toutes nos amitiés.

Sylvain Lévi

Adresse de vacances : Watanabe-besso,
Ninaibashi, Gotemba,
Shizuoka ken.

Cher Maître, 6. 11. 24

Mes remerciement les plus sincères pour votre aimable lettre et pour vos indications concernant ~~le~~ manuscrit syriaque; j'ai ~~aussitôt~~ transmis l'information [illegible] au Musée de l'Université, qui, lui aussi, vous est très reconnaissant.

Je suis ~~aussi~~ également très heureux que grâce a vos bons offices ~~sous peu~~ je serai sous peu membre de la Société Asiatique.

Le commentaire de la Triṃçikā par Sthiramati que vous êtes en train de publier m'interesse extrêmement, parceque j'ai [illegible] beaucoup étudié différents commentaires ~~tibétains~~ par ~~de~~ Sthiramati, ~~traduits en tibétain~~ en traductions tibétaines, surtout celui du Kāçyapaparivarta. Ça ~~[illegible]~~ sera une vraie joie pour

yad (nom. sg. masc. yaḥ, neutr yat, feminine yā) "which" (relative)

~~The following words~~ takes the same terminations as ~~[illegible]~~ tad in all three genders:

~~[illegible] which (relative)~~

katara which (of the two) ?

katama which (of the many) ?

yatara which (of the two, relative)

yatama which (of the many, relative)

anya other

itara different

For example itaraḥ puruṣaḥ "a different man"

itarasmāt puruṣāt "from a different man"

itarābhiḥ pramadābhiḥ "with other women"

yaḥ (masc.) yat (neuter) yā (fem.) are the nominatives sg. derived from the stem yad "which" (relative). This relative pronoun takes the same terminations as etad in all three genders.

yasmin nagare nivasāmaḥ ~~tasmin nagare~~ tasya nagarasya snihyāmaḥ
We like the city in which we live

yasyāṃ senāyāṃ dhīro nṛpo vartate sā senā narāṇāṃ vasu na lumpati
The army in which there is a courageous king does not rob the property of the people

anya "other" (and itara "different") also takes the terminations of etad

kaḥ "who?", "which?"

moi ~~et~~ de pouvoir lire l'original sanscrit d'une de ses oeuvres et j'attendrai le livre avec impatience.

Ivanov habite ~~maintenant~~ maintenant le quartier des légations puisqu'on a reconnu ici les Soviets et il ne vient plus chez moi. Il paraît que la liberté soviétique ne permet pas des visites chez des monarchistes. Quand je verrai Ivanov je lui transmettrai vos "meilleurs souvenirs". J'ai trouvé un excellent élève chinois qui ne fait que du sanscrit depuis cinq mois et dont les progrès sont remarquables, même si on le compare à des étudiants européens.

Veuillez, cher Maître, transmettre mes compliments à Madame Lévi. Mes meilleurs souhaits pour le Nouvel An.

Bien cordialement à vous Staël.

Austrian Legation Compound
Peking, le 8 juillet 1928.

Cher Maître,

Je vous suis infiniment reconnaissant pour votre aimable lettre du 6 août 1927 et également pour votre critique si indulgente de mon édition du Kāçyapaparivarta.

Depuis quelques années je dirige ici un "Sino-Indian Research Institute", que l'Université de Harvard (par l'intermédiaire de la Yenching University) et l'Ecole Française d'Extrême-Orient ont jusqu'ici subventionné. Mais je suis le seul européen, qui travaille régulièrement à cet institut et mes forces ne suffisent pas pour remplir toutes les fonctions, qu'on ne saurait reléguer à des orientaux. Il faut donc que du moins un orientaliste européen collabore avec moi pour que l'institut accomplisse ses différentes tâches. Votre élève, le docteur Rahder, m'a envoyé ses excellentes publications sur les Bodhisattvabhūmis, qui prouvent qu'il s'intéresse aux problèmes,dont s'occupe le S.I.R.I. et qu'il connaît à perfection les langues nécessaires.

Ayant entendu que votre gouvernement est en train d'utiliser le reste de l'indemnité, que les chinois doivent à la Belgique depuis l'année 1900, en subventionnant des oeuvres sino-européennes, je suis allé voir le baron Guillaume, chargé d'affaires de Belgique, et je l'ai prié de réserver une partie de l'indemnité au docteur Rahder.

Je lui ai dit que mille livres sterling par an suffiraient pour assurer au docteur Rahder une existence confortable à Pekin et que j'esperais, qu'il resterait ici du moins pendant deux ou trois ans.

Quelques jours plus tard le baron Guillaume, après

-3-

avoir discuté cette question avec le président de la commission sino-belge, qui dispose de ces fonds, m'a dit " que l'affaire pourrait très bien marcher". Le président (Monsieur Hers) ne peut, évidemment, pas décider la question définitivement sans consulter les autres membres, mais il croit que l'affaire s'arrangera au mois de septembre, quand la commission reprendra ses séances. A présent la commission ne peut pas fonctionner, parce que le gouvernement de Nankin n'a pas encore eu le temps de nommer ses représentants. Je n'ai pas l'honneur de connaître le docteur Rahder et j'ai entrepris ces démarches sans aucune autorisation de sa part, mais je crois que tout orientaliste désire résider en Orient pendant quelque temps.

Le baron Guillaume me dit, que si le docteur Rahder accepte et si vous voulez bien le recommander à la dite commission sino-belge, il faut agir le plus vite possible par les ministères (de l'Instruction et des Affaires Etrangères) à Bruxelles et par la Légation de Belgique à Pekin pour que le dossier soit ici au moment de la rouverture des séances en septembre.

Je n'ai pas écrit au docteur Rahder, l'adresse duquel j'ignore; mon Kāçyapaparivarta que je lui avais adressé "aux bons soins de la société belge d'études orientales" a été renvoyé ici "destinataire inconnu."

Excusez, cher Maître, la hardiesse, avec laquelle j'ai entrepris toutes ces démarches. J'ose vous adresser cette lettre, parce que je sais comment les études sino-indiennes vous sont chères.

Je vous prie de croire à l'expression de mes sentiments respectueusement dévoués.

A. de Staël.

P.S. Le secrétaire de l'Ecole Française d'Extrême-Orient vient de m'écrire que le rapport ci-joint va prochainement paraître dans le Bulletin de l'E.F.E.O. Ce rapport vous donnera quelques renseignements sur le Sino-Indian Research Institute.

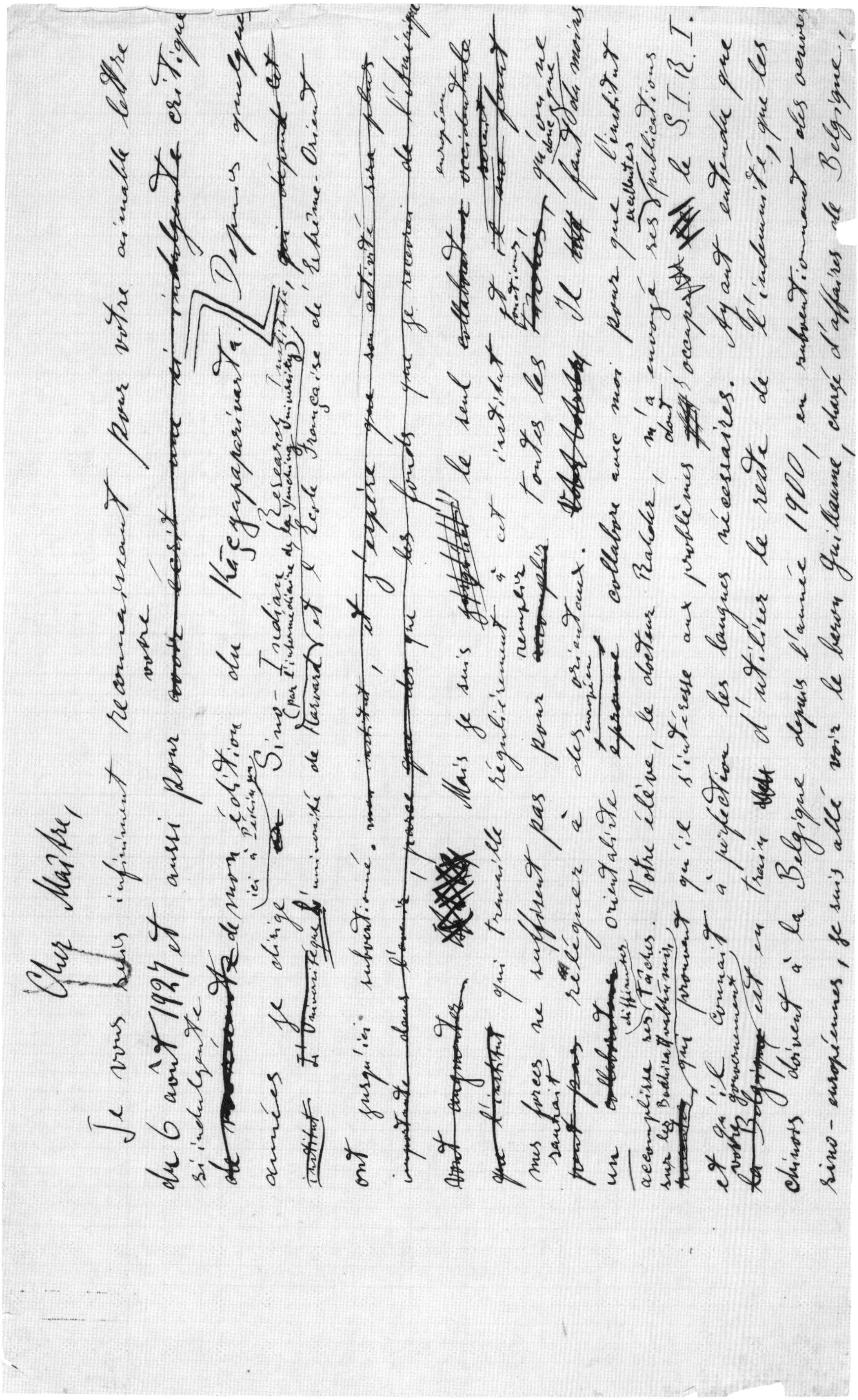

Cher Maître,

Je vous suis infiniment reconnaissant pour votre aimable lettre du 6 août 1927 et aussi pour votre critique si indulgente de mon édition du Kāçyapaparivarta. Depuis quelques années je dirige ici à Pékin un Sino-Indian Research Institute, que l'université de Harvard (par l'intermédiaire de la Yenching University) et l'École Française d'Extrême-Orient ont jusqu'ici subventionné. Mais je suis le seul européen qui travaille régulièrement à cet institut et mes forces ne suffisent pas pour remplir toutes les fonctions, qu'on ne saurait donc que reléguer à des orientaux. Il faut du moins un orientaliste européen collabore avec moi pour que l'institut accomplisse ses différentes tâches. Votre élève, le docteur Rahder, m'a envoyé ses excellentes publications sur les Bodhisattvabhūmis, qui prouvent qu'il s'intéresse aux problèmes dont s'occupe le S.I.R.I. et qu'il connaît à perfection les langues nécessaires. Ayant entendu que votre gouvernement est en train d'utiliser le reste de l'indemnité, que les chinois doivent à la Belgique depuis l'année 1900, en subventionnant des oeuvres sino-européennes, je suis allé voir le baron Guillaume, chargé d'affaires de Belgique, et je l'ai prié ~~d'inviter à Pékin~~ de réserver une partie de l'indemnité ~~Hoey~~ ~~pour le~~ au docteur Rahder. Je lui ai dit que mille livres sterling par an suffirait pour assurer au docteur Rahder une existence confortable à Pékin et que ~~je croyais~~ j'espérais, qu'il resterait ici du moins pendant deux ou trois ans. Quelques jours plus tard le baron Guillaume, après avoir discuté cette question avec le président de la commission ~~savoir~~ sino-belge qui dispose de ces fonds, m'a dit ~~fait connaître, que le président de la commission croyait~~ "que l'affaire pourrait très bien marcher". Le président (~~m~~ Monsieur Hers) ~~est~~ ne peut, ~~naturellement~~ évidemment, pas décider la question définitivement sans consulter les autres membres, mais il croit que l'affaire s'arrangera au mois de septembre, quand la commission reprendra ses séances. À présent la commission ne peut pas fonctionner, parce que le gouvernement de Nankin n'a pas encore eu le temps de nommer ses représentants. Je n'ai pas l'honneur de connaître le docteur Rahder et j'ai entrepris ces démarches sans aucune autorisation de sa part, mais

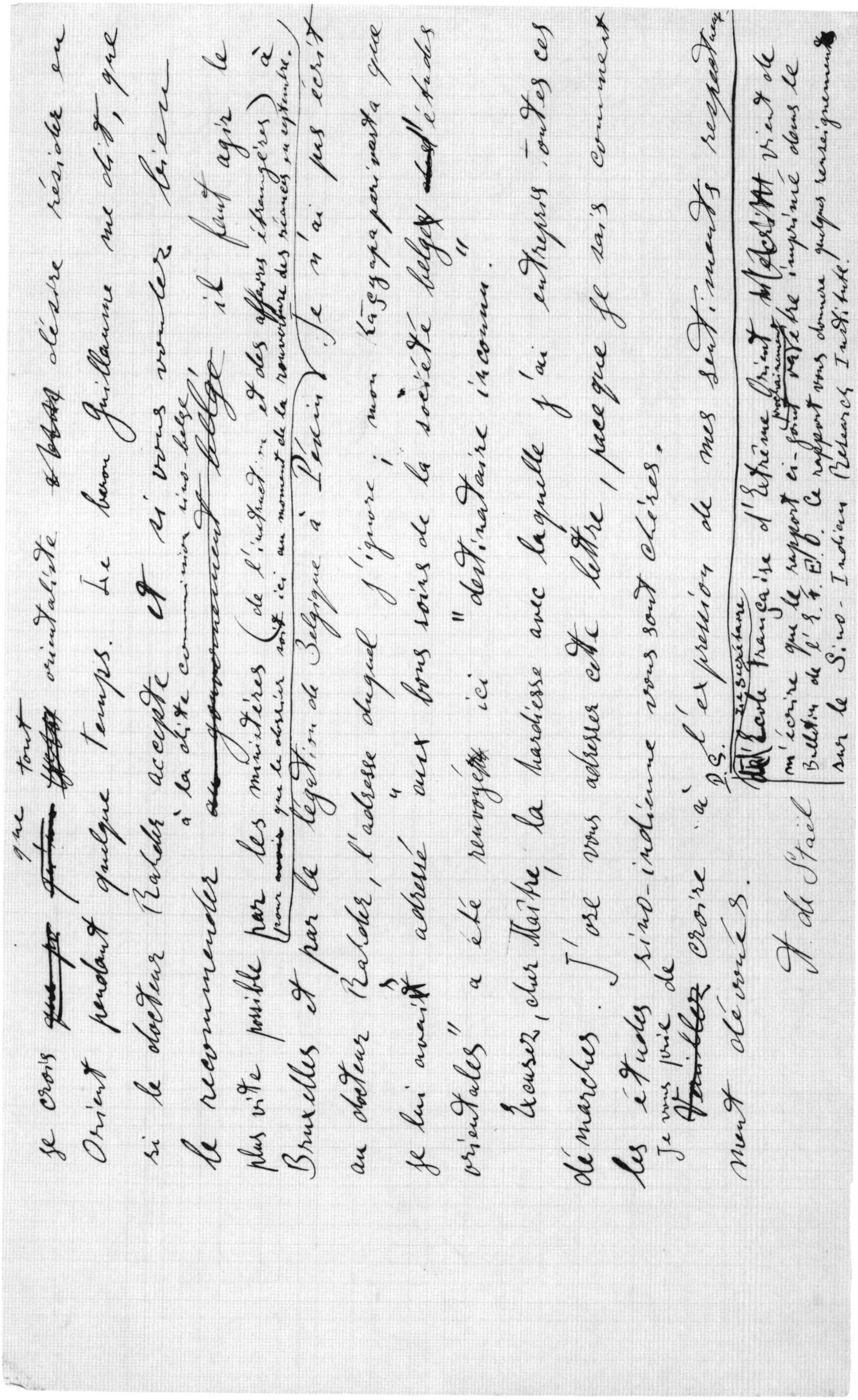

je crois que tout orientaliste désire résider en Orient pendant quelque temps. Le baron Guillaume me dit, que si le docteur Rahder accepte et si vous voulez bien le recommender à la dite commission sino-belge, il faut agir le plus vite possible par les ministères (de l'instruction et des affaires étrangères) à Bruxelles et par la légation de Belgique à Pékin (pour que le dossier soit ici au moment de la rouverture des séances en septembre.) Je n'ai pas écrit au docteur Rahder, l'adresse duquel j'ignore; mon kāśyapaparivarta que je lui avais adressé "aux bons soins de la société belge d'études orientales" a été renvoyé ici "destinataire inconnu".

Excusez, cher Maître, la hardiesse avec laquelle j'ai entrepris toutes ces démarches. J'ose vous adresser cette lettre, parceque je sais comment les études sino-indiennes vous sont chères.

Je vous prie de croire à l'expression de mes sentiments respectueusement dévoués.

A. de Staël

P.S. Le secrétaire de l'École française d'Extrême Orient vient de m'écrire que le rapport ci-joint va prochainement être imprimé dans le Bulletin de l'É.F.E.O. Ce rapport vous donnera quelques renseignements sur le Sino-Indian Research Institute.

Cher Maître,

Je vous suis infiniment reconnaissant de m'avoir fait envoyé les livres par Genthner. Je vous envoie aujourd'hui la photographie d'un manuscrit acquis par l'université de Pékin et aussi la reproduction d'une inscription. On ne sait pas d'où vient le manuscrit. L'inscription a été trouvée à Lo-yang. On me prie de déchiffrer les deux documents. Malheureusement je ne les comprends pas du tout. Peut-être un de vos amis à Paris aimerait il les publier? L'université de Pékin n'en sera que très contente. Ce qu'elle désire surtout c'est d'obtenir aussi vite que possible des indication concernant en langue et le contenu approximatif des deux documents. J'aimerais tellement être membre de la Société Asiatique et je crois que pendant votre séjour à Pékin, dont je garde un si agréable souvenir, vous m'avez promis de me faire membre de la Société. Voulez vous ~~ay m'écrire~~ avoir la grande amabilité de m'écrire que tout est en ordre. Alors je vous enverrai immédiatement la somme nécessaire.

Mon élève Houang est mort quelques semaines après votre départ. C'est très, très triste. Le Gurudeva m'a invité de venir à Çantiniketana après Konow. C'est à vous, mon cher Maître, que je dois cette invitation et je vous en ~~[illegible]~~ remercie de tout mon coeur.

Mes compliments à Madame Lévi.

Croyez moi votre sincèrement dévoué A. Staël Holstein.

Dear Professor Lévi,

In a few days I shall send you my edition of Sthiramati's Kāśyapaparivarta commentary. In note 11 to my preface I ~~have~~ ventured to point out that your translation of certain passages of the Mahāyānasūtrālaṃkāra ~~do not~~ does not agree with Sthiramati's views. I shall be very much obliged to you, if you will kindly send me a few lines and ~~tell me~~ let me know, what you think of Sthiramati's explanations.

I sometimes regret that I have published the Kāśyapaparivarta commentary, because ~~one ought perhaps refrain from~~ a philologist should, properly speaking, refrain from publishing texts, ~~it~~ which he ~~only partly~~ does not thoroughly understand (comp. page of my preface).

The Japanese have, after all, not taken Peking, and we ~~once~~ enjoy ~~complete~~ peace once more after some very exciting weeks. May I ask to be kindly remembered to Madame Lévi? Believe me ~~yours~~ his sincerely and respectfully A. Staël Holstein.

Seeing the commentary edition through the press
was not an easy task, because the Chinese compo-
sitors of the 京華 ~~which is directed by French~~ were entirely unacquainted
with diacritical marks etc. ~~The Lazarist press~~ (The French ~~printing~~ press of the Pei T'ang,) which
printed ~~... my~~ the papers on a Tibetan text and on
two Tibetan pictures which I published in 1932 is
much more efficient.

The Japanese have after all

July 4, 1933.

Dear Baron A. von Staël-Holstein,

I am sorry that I am not able to come to see you to-day. Kindly excuse me. I shall come to see you some other day. I am completely overcomed by the fear that in case I fail to get your permission to go abroad this time, I shall be drowned by the wave of worldly life! There is no way out! With best regards,

Very faithfully yours,

Lin Li Kuang.

August 19, 1933

Dear Baron,

I return herewith $50.00 which you were kind enough to advance for me last May. Thanking you for your kindness.

Very faithfully yours,

Lin Li Kuang.

August 21, 1933.

Dear Baron,

With reference to the manuscripts compiled by myself at the Institute, I write to say that I would be glad to regard the index to the Chinese translations of the Kāçyapaparivarta (on slips) as the property of the Institute, but as the index is already completed on cards, it is only legitimate if my name could be retained as one of the joint authors. As to the Chinese materials for the history of the Tokharians, I hesitate to let you publish it under my name as it is without further and more thorough revision. It is my desire that as soon as I have time at my disposal, I shall rearrange the material and make it more presentable. With best regards,

Very faithfully yours,
Lin Li Kuang.

EASTERN UNIVERSITY
PEKING, CHINA

Room No. 22, China Hotel, Si Chu Shin Kou, Peking.

January 4, 1928.

Herr Stael von Holstein,
7 Pi Kwan Hutung, East City,
Peking.

Sir:

Your great reputation has always been admired by me, so I took the liberty of calling upon you yesterday. Unfortunately I called upon you twice and found that you were not at home. I am very anxious to see you, but for the time being I am rather busy, a few days later when I shall have a little time then I shall beg you to make another appointment for meeting.

With best wishes.

Yours sincerely,

H. C. Hua-jia Lin

安慧三十唯識論釋，解第一頌第二句中段.

ཕྱི་རོལ་གྱི་དོན་མེད་པར་རྣམ་པར་ཤེས་པ་ཉིད་དོན་གྱི་རྣམ་པར་འབྱུང་བ་འདོད་དེ

ཕྱིར་ཤེས་པར་རབ་ཏུ་འཇིན། ཕྱི་རོལ་གྱི་དོན་ནི་བདག་སྣང་བའི་རྣམ་པར་ཤེས་པ

སྐྱེད་པའི་ཕྱིར་རྣམ་པར་ཤེས་པའི་དམིགས་པའི་རྐྱེན་དུ་འདོད་ཀྱི་བྱེད་རྒྱུ་ཙམ་དུ་འདོད

པ་ནི་མ་ཡིན་ནོ། །དེ་མ་ཐག་པའི་རྐྱེན་ལ་སོགས་པ་དང་བྱེ་བྲག་མེད་པར་འཆར་བའི

ཕྱིར་རོ། །རྣམ་པར་ཤེས་པའི་ཚོགས་ལྔ་པ་དག་ནི་བསགས་པ་ལ་དམིགས་པ་སྟེ། དེའི

རྣམ་པ་དང་འདྲ་བའི་ཕྱིར་རོ། །བརྟགས་པ་ནི་ཆ་ཤས་འདུས་པ་ཙམ་ལས་གུད་ན་མེད་དེ།

ཆ་ཤས་དེ་དག་བསལ་ན་བརྟགས་པའི་རྣམ་པའི་རྣམ་པར་ཤེས་པ་མེད་པའི་ཕྱིར་རོ། །དེ་ལས་

ན་ཕྱི་རོལ་གྱི་དོན་མེད་པར་རྣམ་པར་ཤེས་པ་བརྟགས་པའི་རྣམ་པར་འགྱུར་རོ། །རྡུལ་ཕྲ་རབ་བརྟགས་

པ་རགས་ཉིད་ནི་རྡུལ་ཕྲ་རབ་དག་ནི་དེའི་རྒྱུ་ཡང་ཡིན་པའི་ཕྱིར་རོ། །རྡུལ་ཕྲ་རབ་རྣམས་ལ་བརྟགས་པའི་

དུས་ན་ཡང་རང་བཞིན་གྱི་ཐུབ་ཏུ་གྱུར་པ་ཅི་ཡང་མེད་དེ། །དེ་བས་ན་རྡུལ་ཕྲ་རབ་རྣམས་ལ་བརྟགས་པ་

བཞིན་དུ་བརྟགས་པ་ཡང་དམིགས་པར་མི་རུང་ངོ། །གཞན་དག་རྡུལ་ཕྲ་རབ་རེ་རེ་གཞན་ལ་མི་

支那內學院箋

ཐོས་པ་ནི་དབང་པོ་མི་རྟོགས་ཏེ། དབང་པོ་ཡན་ཆད་ཐོས་པ་ནི་དབང་པོས་འབྱུང་བའི་སྐལ་དུ་སེམས་

པ་དེ་དག་གི་ཡང་ཐོས་པ་དང་མི་ཐོས་པའི་དུས་ན་རང་བཞིན་གྱི་ཕྱག་ཏུ་འགྱུར་བ་མེད་པས་དབང་པོ

གཟུང་བ་འམ། དབང་པོས་མི་རྟོགས་པ་ཞིག་ཏུ་འགྱུར་རོ།། གལ་ཏེ་ཡན་ཆད་ཐོས་པའི་རྣལ་ཡུ་

དག་ཉིད་རྣམ་པར་ཤེས་པའི་ཡུལ་དུ་གྱུར་དུ་ཟིན་ན་ནི། དེ་ལྟ་ན་ནམ་པ་དང་རྟག་པ་ལ་སོགས་

པའི་རྣམ་པ་ཐ་དད་པ་མང་ཡིན་པ་དེ་རྣམ་པར་ཤེས་པ་ལ་འབྱུང་བར་མི་འགྱུར་ཏེ། རྣལ་ཡུ་རབ་

དག་དེའི་རྣམ་པ་མི་ཡིན་པའི་ཕྱིར་རོ།། རྣམ་པར་ཤེས་པ་བསྐྱེད་པ་ཡང་གཞན་ལ་ལྟོས་པ་ཡང་རྣམ་པ་

གཞན་དུ་ནི་ཆ་ཤས་ཐལ་བར་འགྱུར་བས་མི་རིགས་སོ།

支那內學院箋

中國文化經濟協會
NATIONAL COUNCIL
OF THE
CHINESE CULTURAL & ECONOMIC INSTITUTE

OFFICE OF THE EXECUTIVE SECRETARY

FU LU CHU, CHUNGHAI, PEIPING.

December 2, 1931

Baron Stael Holstein,
Austrian Legation,
Local.

Dear Sir:-

I have just been informed by Mr. Philip Fugh, general Secretary of our Institute, saying that as he has been under weather rather suddenly, it is impossible for him to visit your art exhibits today.

He was certainly happy to be acquainted with your highness yesterday at the banquet given by Mr. Yi Pei Chi, the head of the Palace Museum.

With best wishes to you for a successful interpretation of your exquisite art display.

Sincerely yours,

F. C. Liu

中國文化經濟協會
NATIONAL COUNCIL
OF THE
CHINESE CULTURAL & ECONOMIC INSTITUTE

OFFICE OF THE EXECUTIVE SECRETARY

FU LU CHU, CHUNGHAI, PEIPING.

December 15, 1931

Baron Stael Holstein,
Austrian Legation,
Local.

Dear Sir:

It is unfortunate that Mr. Philip Fugh, Executive Secretary of our Institute, has been prevented to meet you recently on account of his poor health. As he is now much better and will be able to go around in a couple of days, so he desires to call on you in the very near future.

Will you please let him know when you will be free so that he can carry out his long expected interview with you?

With best greetings to your noble self, I remain,

Sincerely yours,

Francis Liu

Francis Liu
Secretary

中國文化經濟協會
NATIONAL COUNCIL
OF THE
CHINESE CULTURAL & ECONOMIC INSTITUTE

OFFICE OF THE EXECUTIVE SECRETARY

FU LU CHU, CHUNGHAI, PEIPING.

January 26, 1932

Dr. Stael Holstein,
Austrian Legation,
Local.

Dear Dr. Holstein:

May I inform you that Mr. Philip Fugh was sorry to miss your telephone calls this morning? He is busily engaged this afternoon. Will you please call him on the telephone by his home tel. No. 102 West, about ten o'clock tomorrow morning, as he suggested?

He said that he desired very much to have a talk with you. The question that he did not call you up, is because he does not know your telephone number.

With best regards.

Sincerely yours,

Francis Liu

Francis Liu
Secretary

HEINRICH LÜDERS

BERLIN-CHARLOTTENBURG 4
SYBELSTRASSE 19
TELEFON: BLEIBTREU 1411

d.18.März 34.

Lieber Herr Professor,

Anbei sende ich Ihnen eine Abschrift der Anzeige Ihrer Ratnakūtischen Schriften, die in der Orient. Literaturzeitung erscheinen wird, und ich wünsche Ihnen von Herzen, dass Sie weiter die Förderung Ihrer Studien finden möchten, auf die Sie durch Ihre Leistungen Anspruch machen können.

Ich habe, während ich ein Dutzend mal Ihren Namen schrieb, viel an die schönen Zeiten, die wir in dem alten schönen Göttingen zusammen verlebten, zurückdenken müssen, auch an die späteren Petersburger Tage. Wie vieles hat sich seitdem verändert! Nun ist auch Oldenburg dahin gegangen. Als er zum letzten Mal hier in Berlin war, sprach er davon, dass er vor allem andern den in Leningrad liegenden Teil des Karoṣṭhī Dharmapada herausgeben wolle. Krankheit hat ihn doch wohl verhindert, die Arbeit zu beenden. Was wird aus den in Russland liegenden turkestanischen Schätzen werden? Um so mehr freue ich mich, dass durch Sie wenigstens der Ratnakūṭa wieder zum Leben erweckt ist. Dass er als Kāśyapaparivarta wiedergeboren wurde, trübt schliesslich meine Freude nicht.

Nehmen Sie die paar Artikel aus den SBAW. als ein Zeichen des Dankes für Ihre reichhaltige Sendung und als Beweis, dass es meiner Frau und mir selbst gut geht, freundlich entgegen. Vielleicht wird einiges davon Sie interessieren.

Mit herzlichen Grüssen von uns beiden

Ihr H. Lüders.

Die kleine Statuette, die Sie uns durch Frl. v. Gabain zukommen liessen, wacht als freundlicher Genius über den turkestanischen Handschriftenfragmenten auf dem Schreibtisch meiner Frau.

/

The Kāçyapaparivarta. A Mahāyānasūtra of the Ratnakūṭa Class edited in the original Sanskrit in Tibetan and in Chinese by Baron A. von Staël-Holstein, Ph.D., M. Litt.Professor of Sanskrit in the National University of Peking. (Printed in 1926 by the Commercial Press, Shanghai.)

A Commentary to the Kāçyapaparivarta edited in Tibetan and in Chinese by Baron A. von Staël-Holstein. Published jointly by the National Library of Peking and the National Tsinghua University. Peking 1933.

Harvard Sino- Indian Series. Vol.1. Index to the Tibetan Translation of the Kāçyapaparivarta by Friedrich Weller. Published by the Harvard- Yenching Institute. Cambridge Mass. 1933.

Unter den älteren Werken der Mahāyāna-Literatur scheint sich der Kāśyapaparivarta besonderen Ansehens erfreut zu haben. In chinesischen Tripiṭaka sind nicht weniger als vier Übersetzungen erhalten, von denen die älteste aus dem letzten Viertel des 2. Jahrhunderts n.Chr. stammt.Eine zweite Übersetzung entstand zwischen 265 und 42o, eine dritte zwischen 35o und 431, während die letzte von einem Übersetzer herrührt, der in den letzten Dekaden des lo. Jahrhunderts tätig war. Ins Tibetische wurde der Kāśyapaparivarta im 9.Jahrhundert übertragen.

Das indische Original schien verloren zu sein.Aus Ost-Tur-

2

kestan ,diesem Schatzhause der altbuddhistischen Literatur, ist es uns jetzt wiedergeschenkt worden. Vor etwa 4o Jahren fanden einheimische Schatzgräber in der Gegend von Khotan eine nahezu vollständige Papierhandschrift des Werkes. Von den Blättern, deren Gesammtzahl 81 betrug, fehlen nur 8. Die Schrift ist die im Süden des Landes gewöhnlich verwendete Brahmi. Durch den verstorbenen russischen Konsul in Kashgar, Herrn Petrowsky, gelangte die Handschrift in die Sammlungen der Akademie der Wissenschaften in Leningrad. Den Text dieser Handschrift hat vor 8 Jahren Baron A.von Staël-Holstein zusammen mit der tibetischen und den vier chinesischen Übersetzungen herausgegeben. Peinliche Sorgfalt und Genauigkeit, die ein Kennzeichen der Arbeiten des Herausgebers zu sein pflegen, lassen sich auch diesem Werke nachrühmen, obwohl die Drucklegung in Shanghai aussergewöhnliche Schwierigkeiten, besonders auch in typographischer Hinsicht, bereitete.

Die Nebeneinanderstellung des Originals und der fünf Übersetzungen ist eine grosse Erleichterung der kritischen Beurteilung des Textes, und der Herausgeber hat in der Einleitung bereits auf einige Punkte hingewiesen, die sich ohne weiteres aus dem Vergleich der verschiedenen Fassungen ergeben und die nicht nur für die Geschichte des Kāśyapaparivarta selbst von Interesse sind. Es zeigt sich, dass von den 166 Kapiteln, in die der Herausgeber der Übersichtlichkeit wegen den Text zerlegt hat, in der ältesten chinesischen Übersetzung 45 fehlen, in der nächsten 23,in der dritten 22, in der letzten 5, von denen aber, wie eine Notiz besagt, 4 nur deshalb ausgelassen sind, weil ein Blatt in der Sanskrit-Handschrift des Übersetzers fehlte. In der tibetischen Übersetzung fehlt, soweit ich sehe, ein einziges Kapitel.Nun kann gewiss einmal ein Abschnitt aus einem oder dem anderm Grunde später ausgefallen sein- es ist z.B.schwer zu erklären, wie es

3

kommt, dass Kap. 12o in den drei späteren chinesischen Übersetzungen fehlt, während es in der ältesten chinesischen und in der tibetischen Übersetzung erhalten ist- sicherlich aber hat v. Staël-Holstein Recht, wenn er aus dem ständigen Steigen der Kapitelzahlen in den chronologisch geordneten chinesischen Übersetzungen den Schluss zieht, dass der Text des Kāśyapaparivarta im Laufe der Jahrhunderte Zusätze erfuhr, bis er etwa im 8.Jahrhundert den Umfang angenommen hatte, den er in der ostturkestanischen Handschrift, der tibetischen und der letzen chinesischen Übersetzung zeigt. Dieselbe Tendenz, ältere Werke durch Zusätze immer mehr zu erweitern, wie wir sie bei den brahmanischen Epen beobachten können, hat alsoo auch die älteren Mahāyāna-Schriften beeinflusst. Ein anderes Beispiel dafür bietet das Saddharmapuṇḍarīka. Aber auch innerhalb der Kapitel sind offenbar Zusätze gemacht worden.Meist wird in jedem Kapitel zunächst eine Auseinandersetzung in Prosa gegeben und dann, eingeleitet durch die Worte <u>tatredam ucyate</u>, eine Zusammenfassung des Gesagten in metrischer Form. Diese Verse fehlen in den drei älteren chinesischen Übersetzungen stets, während sie in der letzten chinesischen und der tibetischen Übersetzung erscheinen. Man wird aus diesem Sachverhalt nicht ohne weiteres schliessen dürfen, dass die metrischen Teile sämtlich erst später hinzugefügt sind; die älteren chinesischen Übersetzer könnten sie fortgelassen haben, weil sie inhaltlich nichts Neues bieten. Ebenso wenig lässt sich natürlich für die Unursprünglichkeit der Verse die Tatsache verwerten, dass die Zitate aus dem Kāśyapaparivarta in andern Werken, von denen nachher noch die Rede sein wird, fast ausschliesslich Prosastellen betreffen; nur Candrakīrti bringt einmal ein metrisches Zitat, die Strophen von Kap.71. Es kommt aber vor, dass die tibetische und die letzte chinesische Übersetzung Verse bieten, die in

9

dem indischen Texte fehlen (21; 22; 7o), dass der indische Text und die tibetische Übersetzung Verse haben, währendin der ältesten und der jüngsten chinesischen Übersetzung das ganze Kapitel überhaupt fehlt (1o7), dass anderseits die letzte chinesische Übersetzung Verse hat, die nirgends anderswo stehen (33; 84; 89), und dergleichen mehr. Das lässt doch darauf schliessen, dass die Verse vielfach erst nachträglich eingefügt sind. Jedenfalls bedarf die Frage der Textgestaltung einer eingehenden Untersuchung.

Der Herausgeber hat dem Werke den Titel Kāśyapaparivarta (Kāśyapa- Abschnitt) gegeben. Das ist der Name, unter dem es im chinesischen Tripiṭaka wie im tibetischen Bkah-ḥgyur geht als Unterabteilung einer 49 Einzelwerke umfassenden Sammlung, die im Chinesischen als Ta-pao-tsi-king (Mahāratnakūṭasūtra), im Tibetischen als Dkon mchog brtsegs pa chen poḥi chos kyi rnam graṅs (Mahāratnakūṭa-dharmaparyāya) bezeichnet wird. Nach B. Nanjio soll diese Sammlung bereits im 8. Jahrhundert bestanden haben und auf indischer Tradition beruhen (Cat. Buddh. Trip. Col. 9; 13). In den Unterschriften der tibetischen und der zweiten und dritten chinesischen Übersetzung (siehe S. VIII) ist das Werk in der Tat als Unterabteilung der Sammlung gekennzeichnet. Sein ursprünglicher Titel aber war, wie v. Staël-Holstein selbst bemerkt, nicht Kāśyapaparivarta.

In Asaṅgas Mahāyāna-Sūtrālaṃkara wird Kap. 24 des Kāśyapaparivarta S. 165,7 zitiert. Sieben Stellen aus ihm werden in Śāntidevas Śikṣāsamuccaya angeführt: Kap. 3; 4 S. 52,12-53,4; 5 S. 148,8-12; 6 S. 55, 3-5; 11 S. 54,11-15; 15 S. 146,4-5; 97-1o2 S. 233,15-234,18 (mit Abkürzungen); 128 S. 196,11-14. Zweimal werden Zitate aus dem Kāśyapaparivarta in Prajñākaramatis Kommentar zum Bodhicaryāvatāra des Śāntideva gegeben: Kap. 11 S. 147,3-7 und Kap. 97-1o2 S. 526,3-527,4 (mit Abkürz

5

zungen). Aber diese Zitette sind nicht selbständig dem Originaltexte entnommen, sondern aus dem Śikṣāsamucaya abgeschrieben. Für das erste Zitat geht das aus der einleitenden Bemerkung āha cātra (nämlich Śāntidevaḥ) hervor, für das zweite Zitat daraus, dass das peyālam zweimal in dem Kommentar und im Śikṣāsamucaya an derselben Stelle steht; in dem Kommentar ist das Zitat nur noch weiter verkürzt. Sechs Stellen werden in Candrakīrtis Kommentar zu den Mūlamadhyamakakārikās angeführt 57 S.358,1o-12, 6o S.27o,7-9, 63-65 S.248,4-249,2, 71 (wo im Sk.nur die erste Hälfte der ersten Strophe erhalten ist) S.156,1-157,4,1o2 S.45,1-4, 138-149 S.47,1-5o,5 und S.336,3-339,2. Im Mahāyāna-Sūtralaṃkāra wird das Werk als Ratnakūṭa bezeichnet, ebenso viermal im Śikṣāsamucaya, aber 146,4 als Ratnakūṭasūtra, in 196,11 und 233,15 als Āryaratnakūṭa. In Prajñākaramatis Kommentar steht 147,3, wie zu erwarten, ebenso wie im Śikṣāsamucaya Ratnakūṭe, 526,3 aber āryaratnakūṭādiṣu. Das ādi kann nach dem, was ich oben über die Quelle des Zitats bemerkt habe, hier nur ungenaue Ausdrucksweise sein. In Candrakīrtis Kommentar wird es ausser in 27o,7, wo die Quellenangabe überhaupt fehlt, überall Āryaratnakūṭasūtra genannt. Es ist ausgeschlossen, dass Ratnakūṭa hier etwa als Name der Sammlung gebraucht wäre, denn wie v.Staël-Holstein selbst hervorhebt, werden im Śikṣāsamucaya- wir können hinzufügen, auch in Candrakīrtis Kommentar- andere Werke, die im chinesischen Tripiṭaka und im Bkaḥ-ḥgyur zur Ratnakūṭa-Sammlung gezählt werden, unter ihrem eigenen Titel zitiert. Auch der Kommentator Sthiramati kennt nur Ratnakūṭa als den Namen des Werkes. Er erklärt, wie v.Staël-Holstein S.XIV f.angibt, im Anfang seines Kommentars, warum dieser dharmaparyāya Ratnakūṭa genannt sei, und bemerkt in dem Schlussverse, dass er einen Kommentar des Ratnakūṭa verfasst habe. Dass in der Unterschrift der tibetischen Übersetzung das Werk dann wieder als Kāśyapaparivarta und

6

Unterabteilung des Sammelwerkes Ratnakūṭa bezeichnet wird, ist dem gegenüber doch völlig bedeutungslos.

Schliesslich wird aber auch in dem Texte selbst das Werk der dharmaparyāya Mahāratnakūṭa oder Ratnakūṭa genannt, so 52,150 iha (in 150 fehlend) mahāratnakūṭe dharmaparyāye, 160 ayaṃ ratnakūṭo dharmaparyāyaḥ. Für dharmaparyāya tritt einige paarmal auch sūtrāntarājan ein; so (in teilweise verderbter Schreibung)157 yāvac ceyaṃ mahāratnakūṭo sūtrantarāja); ito ratnakūṭaṃ sūtrāntarājñād, 159 ito mahāratnakūṭāt sūtrāntarājñā. Der Tibeter bietet in seiner Übersetzung dafür in allen Fällen nur dkon mchog brtsegs pa chan pohi chos kyi rnam grañs, d.i. Mahāratnakūṭa dharmaparyāya, nur in 160 lässt er den Titel fort und spricht nur von chos kyi rnam grañs. Die chinesischen Übersetzungen gehen in der Wiedergabe des Ausdrucks auseinander. Die zweite Übersetzung hat überall(52, 157, 159, 160) pao yen king 'Juwelenschmucksutra', was offenbar nichts weiter als eine ungenaue Übersetzung von ratnakūṭasūtra ist. Die dritte Übersetzung, in der nur die Stellen in 52 und 150 wiederkehren, hat pao tsi king=ratnakūṭasūtra. Die vierte Übersetzung hat in 52, 150, 157 ta pao tsi tschêng fa =mahāratnakūṭa dharmaparyāya, in 159 pao tsi tschêng fa = ratnakūṭa dharmaparyāya, in 160 ta pao tsi king tien und pao tsi tschêng fa king tien, was auf mahāratnakūṭasūtra bzw. ratnakūṭadharmaparyāyasūtra führt, dem im Chinesischen noch ein allgemeiner erklärender Ausdruck wie 'autoritatives Werk' angefügt ist. In der ersten Übersetzung liegt nur die Stelle in 52 vor. Über den dort gebrauchten Ausdruck, der offenbar nicht ganz richtig überliefert ist, hat sich v. Staël-Holstein S. IX ausführlich ausgesprochen. Er kommt zu dem Schlusse, dass er wahr-

---

Bei den chinesischen Texten habe ich mich der freundlichen Hilfe Dr. A. von Gabains erfreuen dürfen.

2

scheinlich mahā(maṇi)ratnakūṭavaipulyasūtra darstelle.

Es kann darnach nicht dem geringsten Zweifel unterliegen, dass der ursprüngliche Titel des Werkes Ratnakūṭa war, der später aus vorläufig unbekannten Gründen auf eine Sammlung von Schriften übertragen wurde. Ob er schon von Anfang an mit dem Zusatz ārya- oder mahā- versehen war, ist eine Frage von geringer Bedeutung, ebenso ob man das Werk als dharmaparyāya oder als sūtra bezeichnete. Der Herausgeber hat, obwohl er den richtigen Sachverhalt erkannt hat, um Verwechselungen zu vermeiden, Kāśyapaparivarta als Titel gewählt, wie mir scheint, nicht mit Glück, denn das Werk wird dadurch als unselbständig charakterisiert, als Unterabteilung einer Sammlung, die zur Zeit seiner Abfassung und wahrscheinlich ein halbes Jahrtausend später noch garnicht existierte.

Für die Entstehungszeit des Werkes bietet vorläufig nur das Datum der ersten chinesischen Übersetzung eine untere Grenze. Für die Heimat des Verfassers gibt vielleicht eine Bemerkung in 49 einen Anhaltspunkt. Dort werden in einem Vergleiche in der Prosa Zuckerrohr-, Reisfelder und Weingärten nebeneinander genannt: yathāpi...yaṃ(lies yo) mahānagareṣu saṃkarakūṭaṃ (lies -kūṭo) bhavati sa ikṣukṣetreṣu śālikṣetreṣu mṛdvīkākṣetreṣu copakārībhūto bhavati. In dem dazugehörigen Verse werden nur die Zuckerrohrfelder genannt: nagareṣu saṃkārur (lies -ru) yathā sucokṣo (lies acokṣo) so ikṣukṣetreṣ' upakāra kurvati. Die tibetische Übersetzung stimmt damit überein, lässt aber in der Prosa die Reisfelder aus: bu ram śiṅ gi žiṅ dag daṅ rgun gyi žiṅ dag la. Von den chinesischen Übersetzungen spricht die dritte, die nach v.Staël-Holsteins Urteil die beste ist, von Zuckerrohrfeldern und Weingärten, die erste nennt stattdessen Reisfelder und Gemüsegärten, die

8

zweite Felder im allgemeinen, die vierte in der Prosa wie in dem Verse nur Zuckerrohr. Es scheint darnach, dass mṛdvīkākṣetreṣu tatsächlich in dem ursprünglichen Texte stand. Weingärten zu erwähnen aber konnte wohl nur einem Bewohner des nordwestlichen Indiens in den Sinn kommen, wo noch heute der Wein gebaut wird. Kalhaṇa, Rāj.1,42, zählt bekanntlich die Traube unter den Dingen auf, die im Himmel schwer zu erlangen, aber in Kashmir gewöhnlich sind.

Der Ausgabe des Kāśyapaparivarta ist jetzt die Veröffentlichung zweier Hilfsmittel zum Verständnis und zur kritischen Herstellung des Textes gefolgt. Der von v.Staël-Holstein herausgegebene Kommentar des Sthiramati, der uns nur in tibetischer und chinesischer Übersetzung erhalten ist, wird sich sicherlich von grösster Bedeutung für die Geschichte der Textgestaltung und die Interpretation des Kāśyapaparivarta erweisen. Die Zeit Sthiramatis ist vorläufig unsicher. Er kann nicht der Sthiramati sein, den Bu-ston als einen Zeitgenossen des Śrīharṣa erwähnt, wann der Kommentar, wie die chinesische Tradition angibt, von Bodhiruci dem Älteren ins Chinesische übersetzt wurde, denn der Letztere lebte schon am Ende des 5.Jahrhunderts. Der Herausgeber verspricht das schwierige Problem der Datierung Sthiramatis später ausführlich zu behandeln. Jedenfalls ist der Text des Kāśyapaparivarta, der Sthiramati vorlag, älter als der in der turkestanischen Handschrift, in der tibetischen und der letzten chinesischen Übersetzung überlieferte. Es kann, wie v.Staël-Holstein bemerkt, kein ~~Zweifel~~ Zufall sein, dass Sthiramati in seinem Kommentar eine Reihe von Kapiteln übergeht, die auch in den drei älteren chinesischen Übersetzungen fehlen. Der Kommentar ist aber auch weiter von Wert, weil er, wie der Herausgeber bereits an einzelnen Beispielen zeigt, für manche in der Mahāyāna- Li-

9

teratur öfter wiederkehrende dunkle oder schwierige Ausdrücke und Phrasen die richtige Erklärung gibt. Was übrigens die von v.Staël-Holstein S.IV, XII f. erörterte Frage betrifft, ob in der Eingangsformel der Sūtras evaṃ mayā śrutam ekasmin samaye bhagavān...viharati usw. die Worte ekasmin samaye zu evaṃ mayā śrutam oder zu viharati gehören, so kann es sich meiner Ansicht nach nur darum handeln festzustellen, von welchem Zeitpunkt an man zu der merkwürdigen Auffassung kam, dass sie mit dem vorausgehenden Satze zu verbinden seien. Dass sie ursprünglich zu viharati gehören, scheint mir selbstverständlich. Im Pāli Kanon finden sich auch genug kleinere Suttas, die mit den Worten beginnen ekaṃ samayaṃ bhagavā... viharati, z.B. Aṅg.Nik.1,274,276,278,279 usw.

Wellers Wortindex zu der tibetischen Übersetzung des Kāśyapaparivarta wird jeder dankbar begrüssen, der sich mit der Wiederherstellung von Sanskrittexten aus tibetischen Übersetzungen zu beschäftigen hat. Der Index ist allerdings kein einfaches Verzeichnis der tibetischen Wörter mit ihren Sanskrit Äquivalenten. Er ist in einer Weise weniger, denn es werden nicht alle Stellen verzeichnet, an denen die tibetischen Wörter vorkommen. Er ist anderseits mehr, denn es werden die einzelnen Wörter im Textzusammenhang vorgeführt. Mir scheint, dass hier des Guten bisweilen etwas zu viel getan sei. Warum z.B. unter dbu mahi lam = madhyamā pratipad die säntlichen Auseinandersetzungen über den Mittleren Weg in extenso gegeben werden, sehe ich nicht ein; ein einfacher Hinweis auf den Text würde hier doch genügt haben. Für die Angaben der Sanskrit Äquivalente der tibetischen Wörter wird über die Textgestalt der ostturkestanischen Handschrift nicht hinausgegangen, doch werden natürlich Textverschiedenheiten angemerkt und Textverderbnisse soweit wie möglich verbessert. In dieser Hinsicht wird

10

in Zukunft noch allerlei zu berichtigen sein, so verlangt z.B. in 90 Metrum und Sinn die Verbesserung von tyaja zu tyajya, nicht tyajan (siehe unter gtoṅ ba) und nad gsor mi ruṅ ba in 118 entspricht nicht dem dīrghaglānya, dīrghagailānya der ostturkestanischen Sk.Fassung, sondern einem acikitsa gailānya oder glānya, wie es in dem im Tibetischen ausgelassenen Kapitel 119 erscheint.

Baron v.Staël-Holstein kündigt weitere Veröffentlichungen an, die im Zusammenhang mit dem Kāśyapaparivarta stehen. Vielleicht ist es nicht unbescheiden den Wunsch zu äussern, er möge uns vor allem eine Ausgabe des ostturkestanischen Originaltextes liefern, der von den zahllosen Fehlern der Abschreiber gereinigt ist und in dem die kleineren, durch äussere Beschädigungen entstandenen Lücken ausgefüllt sind. Mit den Hilfsmitteln, die Weller und v.Staël-Holstein selbst bereitgestellt haben, dürfte das für die Prosateile nicht allzu schwierig sein. In den Versen wird die Entscheidung, ob vom Sanskrit abweichende Formen Fehler der Überlieferung oder Prakritismen sind, nicht immer leicht sein, aber der Versuch, einen lesbaren Text herzustellen, muss doch gemacht werden, so richtig es war, zunächst einfach einen Abdruck der Handschrift zu geben. Die Beigabe einer Übersetzung würde den Wert des Gebotenen erheblich erhöhen. Der Kāśyapaparivarta ist ein für die Geschichte des Mahāyāna-Buddhismus so wichtiges Werk, dass sich die Mühe, die darauf verwandt wird, lohnt, und wir beglückwünschen das Harvard- Yenching Institute, dass es die Reihe seiner Veröffentlichungen mit einer Arbeit, die diesem Werke gewidmet ist, beginnt.

Heinrich Lüders.

HEINRICH LÜDERS

BERLIN-CHARLOTTENBURG 4
SYBELSTRASSE 19
TELEFON: BLEIBTREU 1411 d.28.Juni 1936.

Lieber Herr Kollege,

Den interessanten Knochen,von dem Sie mir Photographien zuschickten, hat Herr Dr.von Soden in Göttingen als Fälschung erkannt. Die Inschrift ist von dem Tonzylinder des Kyros kopiert. Genaueres hat Herr von Soden auf der Rückseite der Photographie, die ich Ihnen wieder zuschicke, selbst notiert.

Ich will aber diesem Fälscher nicht gram sein, da er mir die Freude gemacht hat, wieder einmal von Ihnen zu hören.

Mit den herzlichsten Grüssen, denen sich auch meine Frau anschliesst,

stets Ihr ergebenster

H. Lüders

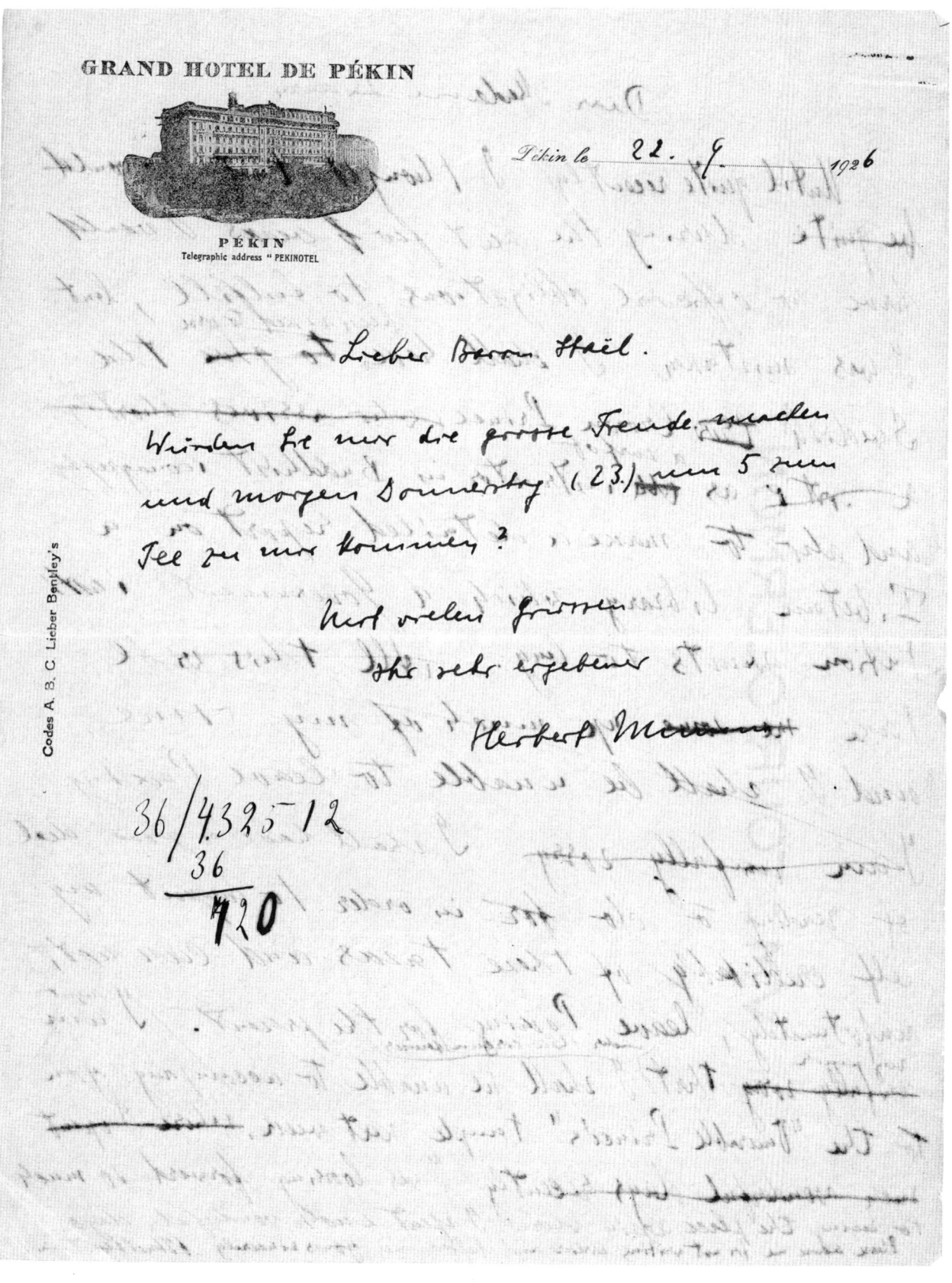

GRAND HOTEL DE PÉKIN

PÉKIN
Telegraphic address "PEKINOTEL"

Pékin le 22. 9. 1926

Lieber Baron Staël.

Würden Sie mir die grosse Freude ~~machen~~ und morgen Donnerstag (23.) um 5 zum Tee zu mir kommen?

Mit vielen Grüssen

Ihr sehr ergebener

Herbert M[illegible]

Codes A. B. C. Lieber Bentley's

36/4325-12
36
720

Peking, August 28th 1933.

Dear Professor Ma,

Mr. Chu (朱) asks me to recommend him to you, and I do so with the greatest pleasure. Mr. Chu has been one of my pupils at the National University of Peking and I know him as a studious and pleasant young scholar.

Believe me yours sincerely

A. Staël Holstein.

Peking, December 27th 1934.

Dear Director Ma,

I am ~~very~~ indeed proud to be a corresponding member of the Palace Museum, and I thank you very much for the new P'in Shu, which I received not long ago. ~~I hope~~ I looked forward very much to meeting you at Mr. Yao's lecture to-morrow, but I shall be unable to be present on account of a bad cold, from which I am suffering.

Believe me yours gratefully

A. Staël Holstein.

Dear Professor Ma,

~~I enclo The enclosed~~ ~~(page)~~ ~~paper contains some references~~
~~The enclosed~~ I venture to ~~present~~ send you a copy of my latest paper (On a Peking edition, etc.) ~~because~~ it describes an ~~hitherto the an~~ edition of the ~~Pek~~ Tibetan Kanjur ✱, a copy of which is still preserved in the Library of the Palace Museum.

自利利他

I am awfully sorry to say that I am unable to accept your kind invitation to ~~the~~ to-day's Palace reception ~~which~~ ✱ because I am not feeling well enough to go out. ~~I rat~~ (Only a few days ago I returned from the German Hospital where I spent three weeks suffering from stomach trouble.) I have not seen you for a long time and I deeply regret missing this opportunity of meeting you.

Believe me yours sincerely A. Staël-Holstein.

My dear MacMurray,

I am ~~sorry~~ indeed sorry to learn of your ~~bereavement~~ irreparable loss and I do mourn ~~your irreparable loss~~ with you.

~~The other day I told you that I had been elected~~

The enclosed document ~~shows that is the only one I received~~ does not ~~contain any~~ mention ~~the Harvard Yenching Institute~~ of Yenching and as a matter of fact ~~according~~ & the original plan (as ~~put before me~~ communicated to me by one of the Harvard members of the Harvard-Yenching Board at Cambridge Mass.) I was to be ~~in the quite independent in my Sino Indian responsible~~ connected to Harvard alone. Later on ~~at the suggestion of~~ other members of the above mentioned Board suggested that there should be some ~~something like a conn some~~ connection with the Yenching staff. Professor Woods of Harvard who is also one of the trustees ~~is~~ will ~~be~~ here in two or three months in order to collaborate in determining ~~my~~ those relations ~~with Yenching which, I hope, will be friendly [illegible]~~

"I shall welcome a
~~Do Pres~~ ~~I do not object~~ ~~in the least~~
~~to object to a~~ connection with President
Stuart and Professor Porter ~~who have~~
to whom I owe a great deal of gratitude.
~~But I do not do at have~~
~~a great aversion against the~~
But I do object to having anything to do with the ~~?~~ new
Chinese Chancellor of Yenching ~~and~~ ~~the~~ with
~~what~~ the "chairman of the Board of Managers",
another Chinese. I have been long
enough connected with the National
University of Peking to know what
Chinese ~~administration means~~. manage-
ment means. In the eyes of ~~all~~ all
Chinese administrators I should be ~~nothing~~
~~but~~ a Harvard professor on special
duty in China and nothing else. I
hope that this point will be made
quite clear when professor Woods
arrives here, but I fear that the whole

thing might be prejudiced ~~by I~~ at tomorrow's meeting of the Administrative Committee of the Harvard Yenching Institute. I do not want to write to President Stuart about it for fear of hurting his feelings; ~~and the t and I venture to~~ ~~But~~ I venture, however, to put the case before you and to ask for your protection in this matter. None of the Chinese available here have any expert knowledge in things Sino-Indian. Why should they interfere with the researches which I am ~~carrying~~ ~~on~~ conducting on behalf of an American University?

The case of the Yenching people is entirely different: they have come to China to teach; ~~not~~ I am here to learn with a view to communicating the results of my studies to the west.

Undergraduate work and research are two different things, qui ne se marient pas, and they should be kept well apart.

I have not, for the reasons given above, mentioned that matter to President Stuart, who should know nothing of this letter, and I trust that your invincible diplomacy will protect me against all Chinese administrators.

If it had not been for your sad bereavement I should have asked for an interview instead of sending you my humble request in writing.

Believe me yours very sincerely

A Staël Holstein.

I am on the best of terms with the Nanking ministry of education, ~~which~~ which appointed me an adviser only a few days ago, and with various other Chinese authorities, but I do not want ~~my~~ to be "registered" ~~as Yenching~~ like Yenching. ~~there as being in charge of a quasi-missionary enterprise.~~ That would be a catastrophy and might change the attitude of the Chinese ~~with respect to my~~ towards my researches. The various native authorities have so far ~~been~~ given ~~me~~ more assistance to me personally than to ~~any~~ all ~~for other~~ foreign ~~I know~~ institution of learning known to me.

Why change that happy state of things? Quieta non movere! [illegible]

ST. JOHN'S UNIVERSITY
SHANGHAI, CHINA.

February 18, 1924.

Baron de Staal Holstein,
Peking.

My dear Baron Holstein:

At the conference of Christian educators held at Nanking a few days ago the Rev. Earl H. Cressy mentioned to me the possibility of your being interested in offering one or two courses of lectures on Oriental Religion and Philosophy. I asked him to write to you at once and bring the subject to your attention, and told him that I would try to get in touch with you immediately. I trust that Mr. Cressy wrote before he left for the United States.

As he may have told you, the Christian colleges and universities of East China are uniting for purposes of advanced instruction during the month of July. The work to be given is of college and graduate grade. Lectures will be given from Monday, July 7th to Friday, August 1st.

I should like very much to have you offer courses for advanced students in the Philosophy and Religion of the East. Our financial resources are limited, and I am not sure whether from that point of view we shall be able to make it worthwhile for you to come. I realize that this is a peculiar method of approach, but will you be so kind as to inform me whether it would be at all possible for you to consider coming to Shanghai for the month of July, and if so, what remuneration would be required? If I hear from you that you are able to consider coming to us, I shall then take up any proposition that you may make with our Summer School Committee, and answer you immediately.

Hoping to hear favorably from you, I beg to remain

Very truly yours,

H. F. MacNair

Dean
Union Summer School

P. S. Any proposition which Mr. Cressy may have made to you will be acceptable to me. Yours, H. F. MacNair

Dear Dr. MacNair,

Many thanks for your kind letter. I ~~am~~ feel indeed honoured by your suggestion that I should lecture at St. John's University in July 1924, but I am afraid that I shall be quite unable to do so this year.

I ~~h~~ am ~~just~~ engaged in editing ~~a~~ the ~~Sanscrit manuscript text of~~ a certain Buddhist Sûtra (the Kaçyapaparivarta) in the original Sanscrit with one Tibetan and four different Chinese translations. The first volume, ~~is~~ ~~pr~~ containing the texts, is practically ready and I shall have to devote the summer months to writing up the notes and to translating part of ~~all~~ the Sûtra into English. ~~I~~ During the ~~winter and~~ Spring I ~~cannot~~ shall not find the ~~a~~ time to do so.

I regret very much that I cannot ~~this year~~ accept your kind offer and I remain yours gratefully

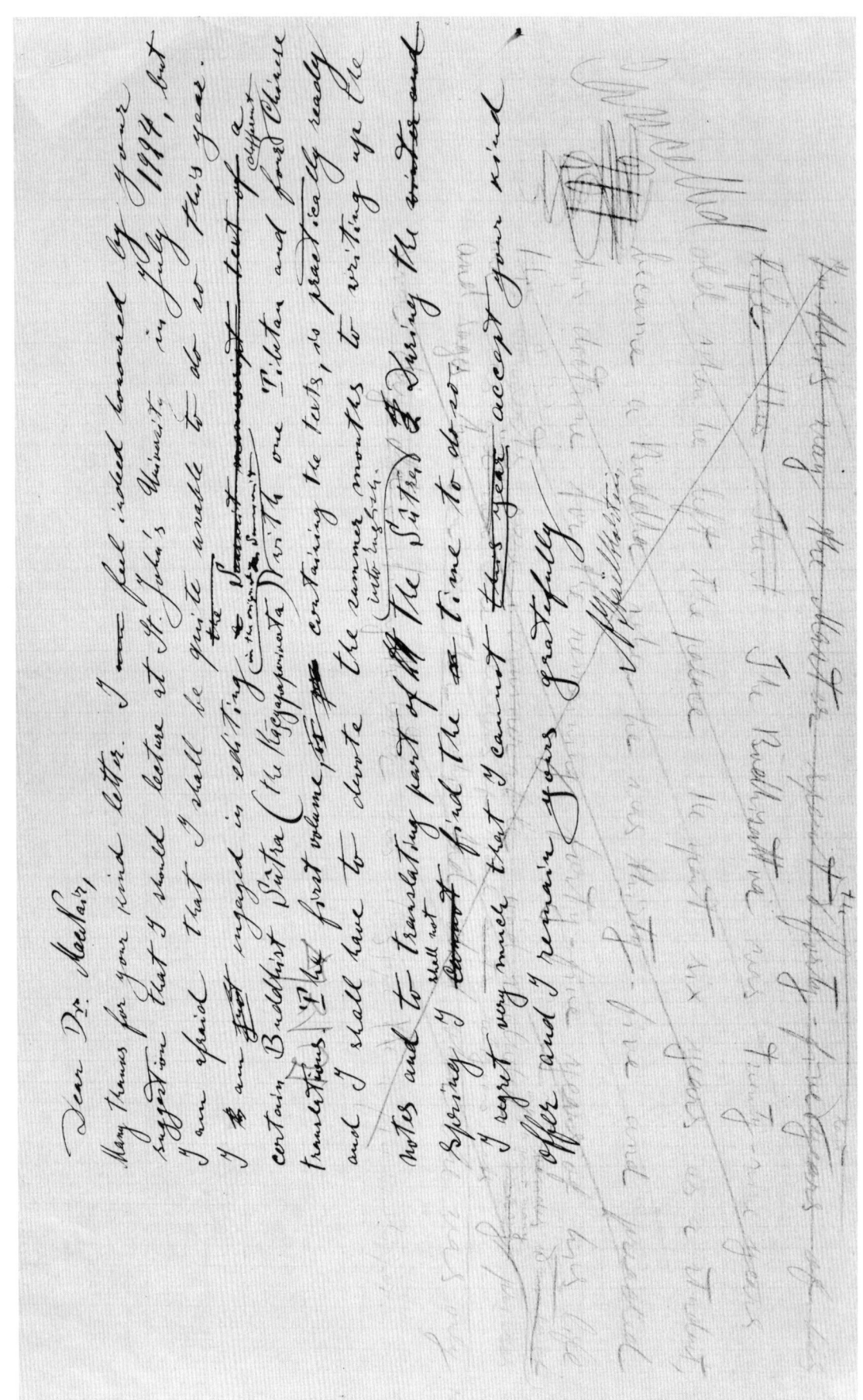

A. Staël Holstein

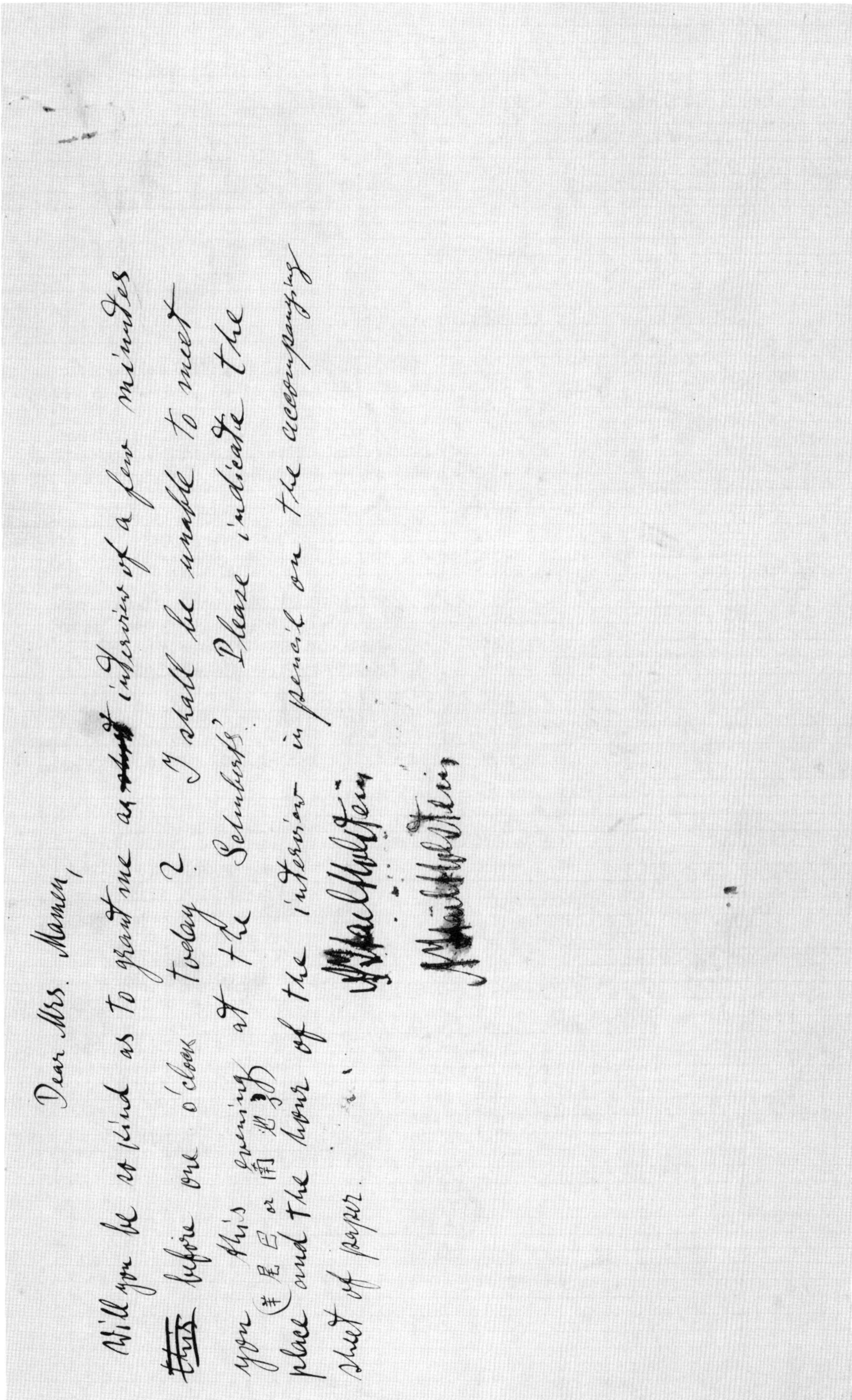

Dear Mrs. Mamen,

Will you be so kind as to grant me a ~~short~~ interview of a few minutes ~~this~~ before one o'clock today? I shall be unable to meet you this evening at the Schuberts'. Please indicate the place (羊尾巴 or 南池子) and the hour of the interview in pencil on the accompanying sheet of paper.

A. Staël Holstein

A. Staël Holstein

G.Margouliès.

98,avenue Klèber.Paris.XVI-e.

3.IV.31.

Monsieur le Baron

A.de Stael-Holstein.

Austrian Legation.

Peking.China.

Многоуважаемый Александръ Августовичъ

Уже немало времени прошло съ того,какъ я покинулъ Пекинъ;передъ отъѣздомъ моимъ оттуда я заѣзжалъ къ Вамъ,чтобы попрощаться,но,къ сожалѣнію,не засталъ Васъ дома.

Въ Парижѣ я все это время былъ занятъ составленіемъ рапорта,а затѣмъ представленіемъ его и обсужденіемъ связанныхъ въ нимъ возможностей.Теперь все это болѣе или менѣе закончено,и я обдумываю свою дальнѣйшую дѣятельность.

Вы меня простите,если я пишу Вамъ такимъ образомъ о своихъ частныхъ дѣлахъ,хотя краткое знакомство наше и не даетъ мнѣ на это права - я надѣюсь,что,какъ китаистъ и,главное,какъ соотечественникъ,Вы меня за это не взыщете.

Для моихъ дальнѣйшихъ занятій мнѣ необходимо,несомнѣнно,снова поѣхать въ Китай и устроиться тамъ на нѣкоторое время.Лично меня интересующая дѣятельность,научная,а также и общественная,по сближенію Китая съ Западомъ и поднятію интереса къ нему,также связана съ Китаемъ.

Я не думаю,чтобы я могъ продолжать работу съ Франціей - они выдвигаютъ вопросъ о принятіи подданства,а я,конечно,не могу отказаться отъ страны,съ которою меня связаваютъ кровь,рожденіе,языкъ и вѣра.

Въ такихъ условіяхъ,для меня ставится вопросъ о возможности работать для Америки - ибо необходимо какъ либо обезпечить свое существованіе,а я личныхъ средствъ не имѣю.

Я подалъ прошеніе о феллоушипъ въ ХарвардъЙенкингъ,но отвѣта еще не имѣю.Вошелъ также въ сношенія,пока,впрочемъ,чисто освѣдомительнаго характера,съ Комитетомъ форъ промошіонъ овъ Чайнезъ Студи,подъ предсѣдательствомъ Гуммеля.

Во всякомъ случаѣ,вопросъ этотъ,устройства для меня возможности работать,въ Китаѣ,или для Китая въ Америкѣ,является для меня кардинальной важности задачею,которую я долженъ разрѣшить въ ближайшемъ будущемъ.

Разрѣшите ли Вы мнѣ просить Васъ,буде Вы,находясь въ Китаѣ,и въ постоянныхъ сношеніяхъ съ Америкой,имѣли какую либо возможность помочь мнѣ въ этомъ совѣтомъ,указаніемъ или же рекомендаціею - не смѣю просить похлопотать - ,не отказаться сдѣлать этаго.

Чрезвычайно буду Вамъ обязанъ,если Вы мнѣ въ этомъ поможете,и заранѣе благодарю Васъ и извиняюсь за безпокойство и свою навязчивость.

Съ искреннимъ уваженіемъ къ Вамъ

Der Kaukasische Fürst Mdivani, der ~~die~~ vor Kurzem die reichste
amerikanische Erbin (Woolworth) geheirathet hat, ist hier
als Tourist eingetroffen und hat mir einen
Brief von Pelliot mitgebracht. ~~Ich werde Das~~
~~fürstliche Paar belastet meine Nerven und~~
~~Die Anwesenheit des fürstlichen Paares kostet ist nerv-~~
~~raubend~~
Neulich waren die Mdivani's bei uns und sprachen
von ~~einer Expedition nach Tibet~~ ihrer bevorstehenden Tibet-Expedition, an
der auch ich theilnehmen sollte.

Herzliche Grüsse an Dich und an Rolf
von ~~Deinem treuen Vetter~~ uns beiden.
Dein treuer Vetter Alec. ~~Alec.~~

~~Olga~~ ~~Laura~~ Olga ssobirait sich schon lange Zeit Dir zu
schreiben, но ~~все~~ никакъ момента свободнаго, weil die
Kinder ~~mit~~ ihr zu viel Sorgen machen. Sie
sind seit Weihnachten fortwährend erkältet.
~~Olga~~ ~~Die Laila~~ Olga hat mir neulich einen grossen philologischen Dienst
geleistet. Sie hat ~~zufällige Verse~~ in einem ~~halb~~ Sanskrit-
buche ~~das~~ zufälliger Verse das~~jenige~~ Argument
gefunden, welches mir ~~noch~~ zum Beweise einer
~~Hypothese~~ [illegible] fehlte. ~~[illegible]~~ !

P.S. ~~[illegible] zufälliger~~

Бывш. Австрійская Миссія (Austrian Legation) 22го февраля 1934 г.

Многоуважаемый князь,

Разрѣшите мнѣ, пожалуйста, напомнить Вамъ о томъ, что я буду ~~Васъ~~ ждать Васъ и княгиню здѣсь въ субботу 24го ~~января~~ февраля въ шесть часовъ на Кокуэ.16.

~~У меня есть нѣкоторыя тибетскія картины, которые~~

~~Такъ какъ Вы интересуетесь археологіей и искусствомъ я собираюсь Вамъ~~

~~показать нѣсколько тибетскихъ картинъ.~~ Я тоже интересуюсь археологіей и мнѣ будетъ весьма пріятно съ Вами побесѣдовать.

Искренно преданный Вамъ А. Сталь.

Его Сіятельству

Князю Мдивани ~~(Mdivani)~~ (Prince Mdivani)

Пекинъ

Ancienne Légation d'Autriche, Pékin le 22 février 1934.

Cher Monsieur,

~~Ma femme et moi serons enchantés si vous pourriez~~

Ne voulez vous pas nous faire le grand plaisir de venir prendre un cock tail chez nous Samedi le 24 février à 6 heures. J'aimerais bien vous montrer quelques tableaux tibétains que vous n'avez pas encore vus.

Veuillez croire, cher Monsieur, à l'expression de mes sentiments bien sincèrement dévoués.

A. de Staël.

Peking, May 24th 1933.

Dear Father Mostaert,

I am very much obliged to you for the copy of the third part of your capital work on the Mongnor ~~dia~~ dialect which you so kindly sent me. I shall always cherish ~~it~~ the book as one of my most precious possessions.

Believe me yours sincerely and gratefully

A Staël Holstein.

Hoping for a favourable reply I remain

yours sincerely

A Staël Holstein.

56 Pei-ho-yen

12.Januar 1928.

Lieber Baron,

mich hatder wissenschaftliche Fimmel gepackt und ich arbeite mal wieder an einer Sache, wegen der ich Sie schon mehr als einmal belaestigt habe und sicher noch mehrmals belaestigen werde: es handelt sich um die Sarira und den Śarira-Kult! Ich habe ziemlich viel Material aus China, eine Reihe von Inschriften auf Reliquiarien und auf Denksteinen ueber die Errichtung von Śarira-Pagoden, endlich auch Zeichnungen und Photographieen solcher Reliquiarien, und neulich habe ich zum ersten Male auch Sarira selber zu Gesicht bekommen, die absolut in ihrer Natur Beschreibungen aus der T'ang-Zeit entsprechen; minimale Stueckchen Achat, Karneol, Krystall und Jade. Vielleicht wird daraus einmal ein kleiner Artikel fuer die Zeitschrift Ihres Instituts, falls Sie so etwas fuer diese Zeitschrift fuer geeignet halten. Was mir voellig fehlt, sind Parallelen aus Indien bezw.Centralsien und die einschlaegigen Stellen aus der buddhistischen Literatur. Sicher giebt es doch Sutren ueber das Verdienst, das man sich durch die Sorge um die Śarira erwirbt. Die Darstellung bei Foucher I, 584-599 habe ich natuerlich genau durchstudiert, das ist aber auch alles und fuer eine wissenschaftliche Behandlung der Materie durchaus nicht ausreichend. Koennen Sie mir zu anderem Material verhelfen? Wie steht es ueberhaupt mit dem Śarira-Kult in Tibet? Giebt es auch dort Śarira-Pagoden und wessen Ueberreste sollen die enthalten, die des historischen Buddha oder auch anderer Buddha's? Ich fand bisher in der chinesischen Literatur Sarira-Pagoden folgender Buddha's erwaehnt:

定光佛	Ting-kuang-fo	=	?
燃燈〃	Jan-teng-fo	=	Dipańkara
釋迦〃	Shih-kia-fô	=	Śakyamuni

und einmal finde ich eine

西天舍利塔 Si-t'ien shê-li-t'a

Einer der eine Sarira-Pagode bergenden Tempel hat den interessanten Namen

梵境寺 Fan-ching-szë. Kann man daraus auf Anwesenheit indischer Moenche dort schliessen oder ist Fan-ching ein terminus technicus des Buddhismus und welchem Sanskrit-Ausdruck entsprechend? Der Śarira-Kult scheint (NB.scheint) in China eng verbunden mit nichtchinesischen Volkselementen. So bin ich bei meinen Studien auf eine Familie des seltsamen Namen's 賀拔 Ho-pa gestossen, deren einzelne Mitglieder so interssante Personennamen haben wie 可泥 K'o-ni, 阿斗泥 A-tou-ni, 破胡 Po-hu. Koennen Sie etwas aus diesen Namen machen?

Ausser Śarira-Pagoden ueber den believed-to-be Uberresten eines Buddha giebt es in China auch solche ueber den Ueberresten von Mitgliedern des Klerus und anscheinend sogar in einem Falle ueber den Ueberresten eines Laien, eines 張筠葬 Chang Yün-tsang, welches doch sicher kein Klostername ist wie etwa 文海 Wen-hai. Oder wuerden Sie letzteren auch nicht fuer einen solchen ansehen?

Sie sehen, es tauchen allerhand Fragen bei dieser Untersuchung eines so kleinen Gebietchens auch auf, und ich fuerchte ernstlich, Sie werden der Fragezeichen dieses Briefes schon muede geworden sein. Bitte, bitte, versuchen Sie mir zu helfen, sie wegzustreichen! Und noch eine - nicht Frage - sondern Bitte: koennen Sie mir einen einer fremden Sprache maechtigen Lettré empfehlen, der mit dem Buddhismus vertraut ist und mir bei der Uebersetzung der Texte zur Hand gehen koennte? Ich finde meinen sonst recht tuechtigen Lettré diesen Dingen gegenueber voellig hilf- und ratlos.

Bei dieser Gelegenheit noch eine andere Frage: ist irgend etwas ueber das erste Auftauchen von Masken bei und ueberhaupt von Mysterienspielen in der buddhistischen Welt bekannt? Manche wollen solche schon auf Gandhara-Monumenten dargestellt finden.

Nun genug und uebergenug! Vielen Dank im voraus fuer alles, was Sie mir sagen koennen.

Mit aufrichtigen Gruessen

Ihr ergebener

Herb. Mueller

DR. HERB. MUELLER
TEL. ADDR. SUNGLIN
56 PEI-HO-YEN TUNG-HUA-MEN
PEKING

17. Jan. 32

Lieber Baron, vielen Dank für Ihre Zeilen. Heute komme ich mit etwas Anderem. Mir ist ein mongolischer Kandjur angeboten, ein sehr schöner klarer Druck. Ich sende Ihnen eine kleine Probe und möchte wissen, ob diese Ausgabe identisch ist mit der Ihrigen und der von Lillis. —

Ich bin von 4 - 5 auf der Bowling Alley und wahrscheinlich noch länger im Club. Wenn es Ihnen passt . . .

Ihr ergebenster

HM

DR. HERB. MUELLER
PEKING

Sonntag. 26/11. 33.

Lieber Baron,

Weitere Beschäftigung mit der Malerei macht es mir sehr wahrscheinlich, dass Tsongkapa's Schüler བྱམས་ཆེན་ཆོས་རྗེ་ gleich zu setzen ist mit dem zu Anfang des 15. Jahrhdts im HuKuo szi residierenden 大國師巴勒丹札什. Ist letztere Gleichung
དཔལ་ལྡན་ བྱམས་ཆེན་
richtig und ist dPal-ldan als Bestandteil des Namens von Byams-ch'en bekannt? Letzterer soll nach Grünwedel 1434 in China gestorben sein. Im HuKuo sze stand früher ein von 1435 datierter Stein – jetzt verschwunden –, bekannt als Ta-kuo-shih (d.h. wie oben) 壽像碑. Mir scheinen die Jahreszahlen darauf hinzudeuten, dass obige Gleichung stimmt und dass der berühmte Compilator des Kandjur und Gründer des Klosters Sera hier gestorben ist. Das eine der 3 Bilder würde also in seine Zeit fallen. Und unter den spirituellen Ahnen des Changchia Hutuktu steht er bei Grünwedel an 9. Stelle. An 13. Stelle erscheint dann der nach Jimme erste Changchia Hutuktu. + 1714.
Dazwischen residierten im Hu Kuo sze:
um 1512: 大慶法王淩戩巴勒丹
大覺法王扎什藏布
um 1543: 藏布嘉勒燦承繼
Sind das bekannte Namen und welches sind ihre tibetischen Äquivalente? Rangieren sie irgendwie im Stammbaum des Changchia H.?

Wäre es möglich, dass schon zur Zeit Dyams-ch'en's auf ihn selber die
Khubilgan-Theorie angewandt wurde und er in Peking selbst 'lebende
Buddhas' als Nachfolger hatte? Oder ist es wahrscheinlicher, dass er in
die Reihe spiritueller Ahnen der ersten Changchia Hutuktu nur (?)
deswegen eingereiht wurde, weil er in Peking (zweimal) lebte und
schliesslich auch hier starb? Vor ihm sind mir keine tibetischen
Namen als mit Pekinger Tempeln verknüpft bekannt. Aber wie
kommt Peking dann schon 1096 zur tibet. Architektur des Pai-ta-szu?
Und wie steht es mit den "roten" Lamas, die sich mit den "gelben" in den Hu-kuo-szu
teilten, die einen im südlichen, die andern im nördlichen Teil wohnend?
Und der Südteil stammt aus der Kin-Zeit!
Und wann ist der Sung-chu-szu zur Residenz der Changchia Hutuktu
geworden? Ich kann über die Geschichte dieses Tempels garnichts finden,
ausser dass er in der Ming Zeit (Name nur!) existierte und dass mit ihm
ein 漢經廠 und ein 番經 | damals schon verbunden waren.
Seit 1808 ist seine Eigenschaft als Residenz der Ch.H. gesichert, durch ein
auch inhaltlich interessantes Edikt, das sich auf die Nachfolge des damals
gestorbenen Träger's der Würde bezieht.
Und so weiter.

Herzlichen Grüsse

Ihr ergebener

Hackmann.

DR. HERB. MUELLER
PEKING

Samstag

Lieber Baron.

Hu-kuo-szu zuerst berühmt geworden unter Khubilai als Residenz des buddh. Mönches 定演 (Fam.-Name 王 aus 三河), der den Titel ~~崇~~ 宗教大師 führte. Älteste Inschrift 1284. Zeitweilig Residenz des 托克托 (oder 託克託) 丞相. 1436 mit 3 andern Tempeln den tibet. Lamas zugewiesen, von denen 450 in Peking. 1512 residierten dort u.a.

大慶法王領占班丹 = 凌戩巴勒丹

大覺 〃 〃 著肖藏卜 = ~~●~~ 扎什藏布

Von 1514 ist das Bild, das Sie zuerst erwähnt. 1515 wurde der Dalai Lama nach Peking eingeladen (Wieger), lehnte aber ab.

Dies zunächst. Vielleicht lässt sich mehr finden.

In Eile mit herzlichen Grüßen

Ihr

HMueller.

收報紙 RECEIVING　中國電報局　本局號數 JOURNAL No. 6690

THE CHINESE TELEGRAPH ADMINISTRATION

局 OFFICE　5690

由 From	CP 17	附註 —REMARKS—	至 To
時刻 Time	14 點 H 35 分 M		時刻 Time 點 H 分 M
簽名 By	J.		簽名 By

原來號數 TELEGRAM NO.	82 13319	等第 CLASS		字數 WORDS	12
發報局 Office from	SHANGHAI	日期 Date	17	點 H 13	10 M

BARON STAEL HOLSTEIN AUSTRIAN LEGATION

PEPING

HERZLICHE GLUECKWUENSCHE ZUM HODRZEITSTAGE

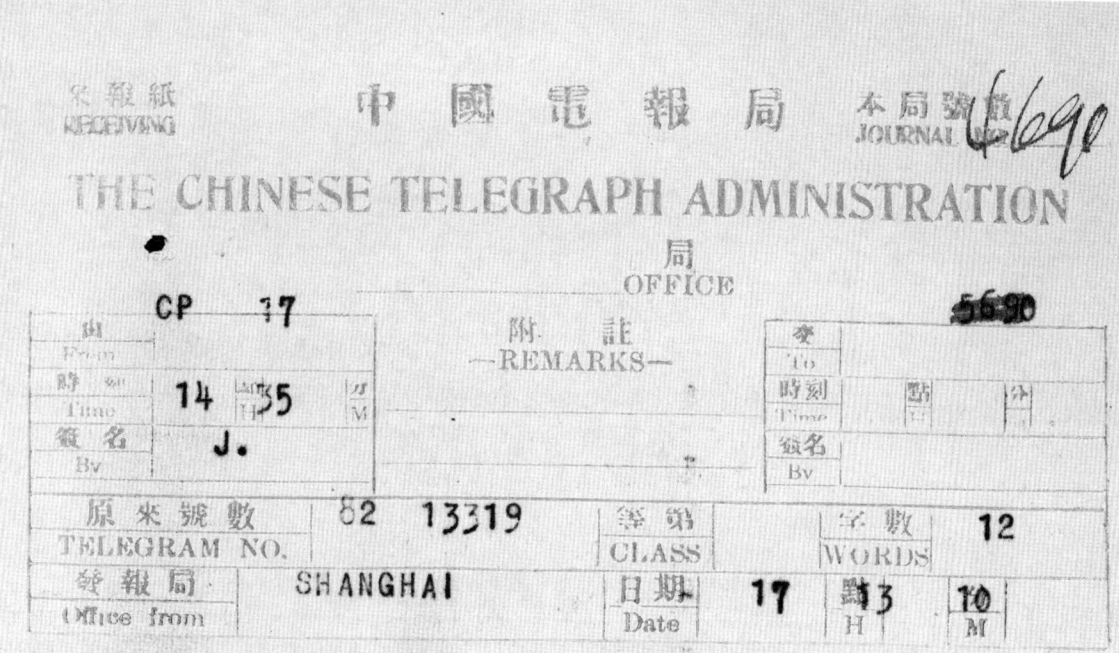

HERBERT MUELLER

G. K. Nariman.
(Journalist.)

3RD VICTORIA CROSS ROAD,
MAZACON,
BOMBAY-10.

2nd January, 1925.

Dear Baron,

I have yet to acknowledge with thanks your appreciation of June 23rd 1924 with the most interesting reprint from the "Kuo-Hsiochi-khan".

I may explain I was away in Persian and have now returned and have great pleasure in replying to your very kind note. It is very flattering to ~~note~~ observe what you say regarding my "Sanskrit Buddhism.", I hope it will be easy for you to introduce the book to any Universities in China. As you note although I have depended largely on Winternitz I have added much from other sources including Russian. It is the first book of its kind in the English language.

Nothing would give me greater pleasure than to receive, whenever your lesiure serves you, copies or notices of the contributions, from your eminent pen, to investigations into Buddhism conducted in any language French, German, Russian or English. Beginning with Wasilief, Russian scho-

-2-

scholars have achieved much in ~~the~~ this direction but much of the labour remains a dead letter to Western Europeans and Americans. I made your acquaintance first in the Bulletin of the St. Petersburg Academy!

With kindest regards
Yrs sincerely
G.K. Nariman

PS: —
Any political notes would be ever welcome
GKN

The larger collection (Pangur) has also been bought for the Institute with money I received by me long ago, and I am corresponding with Dean Chase about the purchase of those 224 volumes.

Dear Mr. Nixon,

Kindly excuse ~~me for not having~~ this late answer. ~~The charact~~ I think that ~~the char~~ the centre of the cross is occupied by an ~~The character à generally takes the form~~ [illegible] ~~My assistant Professor Weller (Leipzig Univ.) does not agree~~ Indian character (āḥ) which takes the following form in Lamaistic books [illegible]; āḥ is one of the most powerful ~~charms~~ mystic syllables used by the Lamas. Believe me yours sincerely A. v. Staël-Holstein.

Lieber Herr Doctor, 華嚴 Kegon repräsentiert die japanische und Huayen die pekingesische Aussprache der Zeichen 華嚴. ~~Die übrigen~~ Alle anderen Fragen, die Ihr Brief ~~aus Peitaiho~~ enthält, sind in einem Memorandum beantwortet, das ich Ihnen einige Tage vor Empfang des Briefes aus Peitaiho in Ihre Pekinger Wohnung sandte. Ich nehme an, dass Sie das Memorandum inzwischen erhalten haben. ~~Ich bin ganz Ich theile Ihre Ansicht die~~ Auch ich bin der Ansicht, dass sich die Banalitäten des Lebens nicht vollständig vermeiden lassen. Hier in Peking verlaufen sie aber doch schmerzloser als in Peitaiho, ~~wo [illegible] es so schrecklich schwer ist, sich~~ Ich denke daran im Herbst nach Abschluss der wichtigsten Arbeiten eine Ferienreise zu unternehmen, ~~nachdem ich~~ Hoffentlich sehe ich Sie noch vorher in Peking. ~~treffen wir uns dann.~~

Herzliche Grüsse von Ihrem ergebenen A. v. Staël-Holstein.

JAPANESE LEGATION
PEKING.

March 14th.

My dear Baron Stael-Holstein,

Will you give me the pleasure of having tiffin with me on Sunday, March 19th, at one o'clock? I am having a small private party on that day, inviting Dr. Sirén, professor of History of Art in the University of Stockholm and few other friends of mine who are interested in Chinese Arts. Thus your joining our party on that day will make the occasion a great deal more delightful and interesting.

Hopping that you can be able to come,

yours sincerely

Y. Obata.

31/III/27

Пекин.

Многоуважаемый

Александр Августович!

Транскрипцию я написал, но прочитать текст как следует, не успел. Сначала я начал писать транскрипцию прямо в Вашу рукопись, но потом, написав все 25 монг. имен, нашел что кое где вкрались неточности и тогда я переписал еще раз на отдельном месте. Следовательно полная транскрипция находится на отдельных местах и имена написанные в рукописи нужно сверить.

Мне кажется, что написал я довольно ясно, может быть только в некоторых местах будет вводить в смущение "гамма" (γ) и q (к-рое я боюсь в моем почерке можно смешать с g). Затем есть еще значек X (взятый также из греч. азбуки). Вот кажется и все.

Уважающий Вас
Панкратов.

Правильная транскрипция.

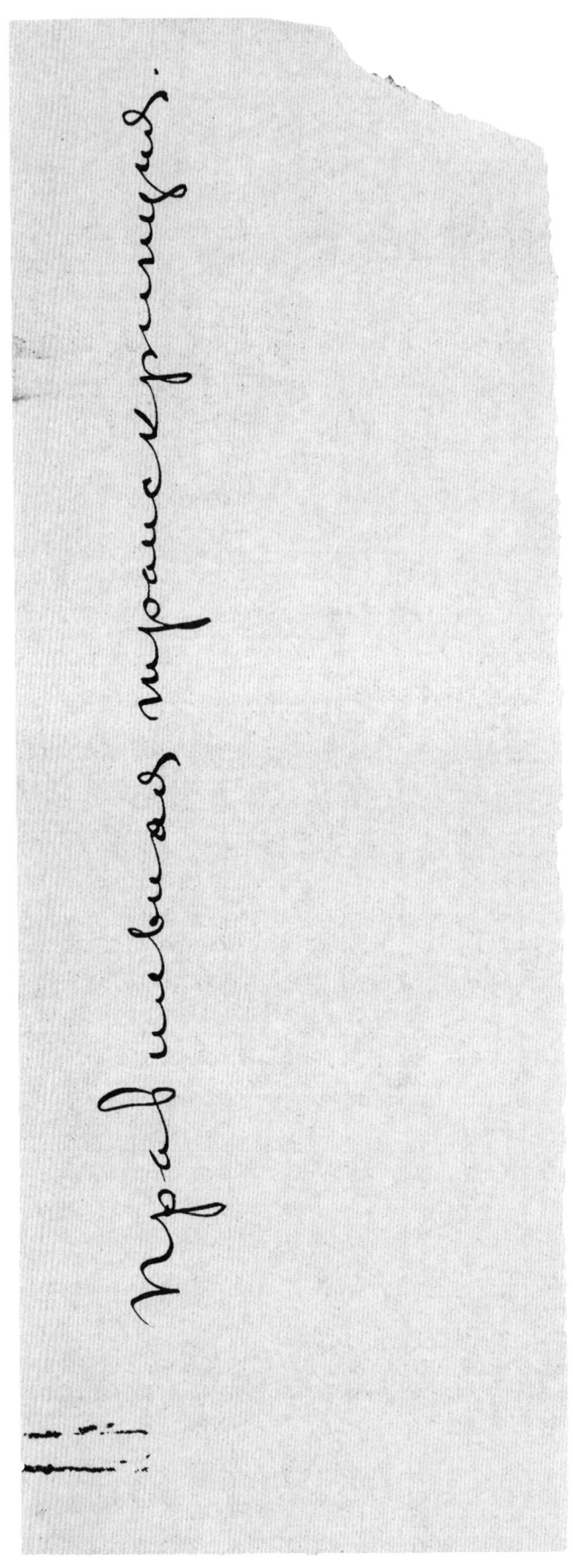

1) Mong. Sigemüni
Manch. sigiyamüni fucihi.

2) Mong. včir ǰirüken iyer sayitur ebdekči.
Manch. vačir efüjen aqu fücihi.

3) Mong. erdeni gerel γarγaqči.
Manch. boobai eldengge fücihi.

4) Mong. luus un erketü qaγan.
Manch. müdüri χani fücihi.

5) Mong. baγatut un ayimaq.
Manch. batürü ayimaqi fücihi.

6) Mong. bayasqulang čoγtu.
Manch. ürgün erdemüngge fücihi.

7) Mong. jal erdeni
Manch. boobai tüva fücihi

8) Mong. erdeni saran gereltü.
Manch. boobai biyai eldengge fücihi.

9) Mong. üǰekseger tusatu.
Manch. sabǖha ele tüsangγa fücihi

10) Mong. erdeni saran.
Manch. boobai biya fücihi.

11) Mong. kkir ügei.
Manch. icihi aqu fücihi.

12) Mong. čoγ i ükgükči.
Manch. toose büre fücihi

13) Mong. ariγun burqan
Manch. bolγonγγo fücihi

14) Mong. ariγun*i ükgükči.
Manch. bolγo be büre fücihi.

15) Mong. usun tegri.
Manch. müke i abqa fücihi.

16) Mong. usun tegri yin tegri
Manch. müke i abqai abqa fücihi.

17) Mong. sayin čoγtu.
Manch. sayin χoronγγo fücihi.

18) Mong. čoɣtu candan.

Manch. dsandan güngge erdemüngge fücihi.

19) Mong. qiǰaɣalal ügei sür ǰibqulaŋtu

Manch. moxon aqu xorongɣo fücihi

20) Mong. čoɣ gerel tu.

Manch. güngge erdemü i eldengge fücihi.

21) Mong. ɣasalang ügei čoɣtu.

Manch. ɣasačün aqu erdemüngge fücihi.

22) Mong. goričal ügei yin kübegün

Manch. büyen aqu i ǰüi fücihi.

23) Mong. čičik ün čoɣtu.

Manch. ilxai güngge erdemüngge fücihi.

24) Mong. ariɣun gerel iyer teyin büget čingger ele medekči.

Manch. bolɣo elden i ümesi sebǰeleme gehün iletü ṣara fücihi.

25) Mong. linggoa yin gerel iyer teyin
büget čingen ele medekči.
Manch. šü ilhai elden ümesi sebjeleme
gehün iletü sara fücihi.

26) Mong. edün čoγtu.

Manch. ülini güngge erdemüngge fücihi.

27) Mong. duratqui yin čoγtu.

Manch. jondoro güngge erdemüngge fücihi.

28) Mong. nere yin čon (ошибка переписчика вместо čoγ) masi uγuγata albarasiqsan (ошибка переписчика вместо aldarsiqsan).

Manch. güngge erdemüngge čolo ümesi algiqa fücihi

29) Mong. erketü yin oqi duvaca yin
qaγan.
Manch. toose i oyo türün i χan
fücihi.

30) Mong. masi teyin büget daruγči
čoγtu.
Manch. füχali gidara ümesi
χorongγo fücihi

31) Mong. bayilduγan ača masi
~~ma~~ teyin büget ilaγuqsan.
Manch. dayin be füχali etehe fücihi.

32) Mong. teyin büget daruqči čoγtu.
Manch. ümesi eteme enggelenžire fücihi.

33) Mong. qamuγa geyigülün joqiyaγči čoγtu.
Manch. gübci be genggiyen i eldebüre fücihi

34) Mong. erdeni lingqoa bar teyin büget daruqči.
Manch. šü ilxai füxali gidara fücihi

1.

35) Mong. aγulas un erketü qaγan
burqan.

Manch. boobai šü ilχa de sayiqan
~~[illegible]~~ tehe sümir alini χan
fücihi.

10 марта, 1929 года.

Пекин.

Дорогой Александр Августович!

Петр Степанович сообщил мне содержание Вашего письма и передал 100 долларов для уплаты жалованья ламе еще 16 февраля и я теперь прошу извинения за то, что не ответил Вам сразу, но на другой же день после посещения П.С. я заболел, слег в постель и пролежал не вставая три недели.

Я затрудняюсь в выражениях, чтобы высказать Вам всю свою признательность за беспокойства по устройству меня в Sino-Indian Institute и могу сказать лишь, что приложу все усилия для оправдания Вашего доверия ко мне своей работой. Что касается Вашего указания на несовместимость работы одновременно в двух учреждениях, то,само собою разумеется, что начав работу в Институте, я отказываюсь от должности в месте теперешних своих занятий.

Ваше поручение относительно составления указателя содержания "Концека" по Монгольскому Ганчжуру пока является чрезвычайно трудным для выполнения. Дело в том, что тот мой знакомый монгол, который раньше доставал для меня несколько томов "Концека" из Махагала-мяо, теперь уехал из Пекина на родину и я остался без связей. Во время своей болезни я поручил нашему ламе завести в Махагала-мяо знакомства и попытаться устроить так, как я это делал прежде: платить ламам определенную сумму за выдаваемый ими том. Не смотря на все дипломатические способности ламы, это поручение ему выполнить не удалось т.к. ламы отказываются дать книги за пределы монастыря даже за плату по 10 долл. за том. Теперь эти дипломатические переговоры я передал в ведение старика Бай-ламы, которому может быть удастся что нибудь сделать. Как только получу первый том, тотчас же сообщу Вам и примусь за работу. Относительно вознаграждения, о котором Вы упоминаете, то о нем не может быть и речи ибо я имею вполне достаточное содержание для того чтобы жить и буду делать обзор содержания "Концека" для собственного удовольствия в свободное от службы время. Весь вопрос заключается лишь в том, чтобы получить Монг.Ганчжур. В связи с этим, я должен Вам сообщить, что в течение 6 месяцев Вашего отсутствия, мною велись и ведутся розыски Монгольского Ганьчжура и Монг.Данчжура, которые можно было бы приобрести. Последнее письмо полученное мною из Внутр. Монголии говорит, что имеется полный и вполне сохранный экземпляр Монг.Данчжура(*), но за него просят безумную цену, а именно 25000 дол. Я в ответе предложил этому монголу торговаться до изнеможения и сообщить мне, когда цена будет более или менее человеческая. Этот же монгол обещает разыскать и Монг.Ганчжур. Я поручил ему, если возможно, найти рукописный экземпляр т.к. по словам Б.Я.Владимирцева, сравнивавшего рукописный Ганчжур Азиатского Музея с печатным - Парижской Библиотеки, текст печатного экземпляра носит следы новейших поправок и изменений, местами совершенно искажающих смысл первоначального текста. Возможно ли будет приобретение указанных Ганчжура и Данчжура для Института?

С ламою дело обстоит плохо. Он заявил, что на днях уезжает в Тибет. Ни уговоры, ни обещания хорошего жалованья, после вашего приезда, не помогают. Он твердит свое, что ему необходимо съездить в Тибет и он непременно вернется осенью этого года, чтобы продолжать работу в Институте. Он заканчивает 3-й том и я пока еще не нашел человека, которому можно будет поручить продолжение его работы.

(*) относительно неполного экземпляра, о к-ром я Вам говорил перед Вашим отъездом, сведений больше не поступало и я не знаю что с ним сделали.

Опасаясь, что Вы могли не получить моего предыдущего письма, посылаю копию его, которая к счастию сохранилась. Пожалуйста сообщите, получена ли теперь Вами бандероль с индексом и 500 бурханов?

Надеюсь, что найду подходящего ламу. С нетерпением жду Вашего приезда.

Искренне уважающий Вас

[signature]

UNITED STATES OF AMERICA

Peking. Sept. 27, 1923

My dear Baron Staël-Holstein:

May I inquire how the translation is getting on? I shall be glad to call on you at any time you find convenient to consult you further about it.

Yours very sincerely
Willys R. Peck.

P.S.
When you write kindly give me your address - I have mislaid it.

~~Dear~~ My dear Mr. Peck,

I beg to present to you my article on a ~~Lamaist~~ Tibetan document written in the cursive script (comp. page 9). I hope you will accept it and ~~conclude~~ believe that it is not mere laziness which prevents me from finishing the translation of your documents. I could decipher them myself but that would take me weeks if not months, ~~Dr Laufer told~~ which I am unable to spare. Dr. Laufer told me in August that the same reason kept him from dealing with your documents. The translation is not difficult — but deciphering the cursive script is. Therefore I have been looking round for a Lama who could transcribe your documents with ordinary characters. I found one and gave ~~them~~ him the documents, but he only transcribed a few lines (rather incorrectly) and then returned the documents to me saying that he could not make out the cursive characters.

When my learned Lama friend (comp. page 4 of my article) arrived here in June I showed him your documents which he could read very easily and he promised to make a transcript of them for me. Unfortunately the learned Lama was called away suddenly and had to leave for Mukden; so the thing had to be postponed until his return. He is due here towards the middle of the 9th Chinese moon, that is to say in a few days and I hope that I shall soon be able to return the documents to you and to let you have a translation. Please do not take the documents away from me before that and excuse the delay.

Peking, October 18, 1923.

My dear Baron de Stael-Holstein:

Replying to your letter of October 17th I beg to say that I appreciate fully the great difficulty you are encountering in translating the Tibetan manuscripts, and am correspondingly grateful for the efforts that you are putting forth. A month ago Dr. Schurman received another letter from Dr. N. Dwight Harris of the Northwestern University, in the United States, asking how the matter was progressing, and Dr. Schurman has replied informing him of the difficulties that you are encountering and of the means taken by you in this connection. He expressed the conviction that the assistance you are so kindly offering affords the only prospect

Baron de Stael-Holstein,
Peking.

\- 2 -

of securing a translation of these difficult cursive manuscripts.

Thank you very much for the reprint of your article, and I am delighted to get it.

Please rest assured that we shall all be only too glad to leave the manuscripts with you and feel great gratitude for the efforts you are making.

Yours very sincerely,

Willys J. Peck.

American Legation
Peking.

Jan. 4, 1924.

My dear Baron de Staël:

Mr. King tells me that his lama friend will transcribe those documents into ordinary characters if we will take them to him at the Yellow Temple tomorrow between 2 and 3 p.m. Will you then accompany me there, if you are at leisure? If you care to do so I will call for you in a motor car at 2 p.m. tomorrow, January 5th (Saturday)

I trust our difficulties are over!

Yours sincerely

Willys R. Peck.

LEGATION OF THE
UNITED STATES OF AMERICA

Peking, December 12, 1924.

My dear Baron Staël:

You will recollect that in connection with the Tibetan manuscripts you so kindly assisted in translating for use in a biography of Mr. W. W. Rockhill you wrote me on May 26, 1924, asking whether you might have photographs of documents 1-18 inclusive for use in a philological journal. You requested, also, that the photographs be prepared in quintuplicate, in black characters on a white background.

I am now in receipt of a letter dated October 29, 1924, from Dr. N. Dwight Harris, Ph. D., of the Department of Political Science of Northwestern University at Evanston, Illinois, U.S.A., acknowledging the receipt of the photostat copies and translations, and asking that I express to you the appreciation and thanks of Mrs. Rockhill and himself for your great courtesy and kindness in taking so much trouble to get the translations made.

Dr. Harris also forwarded to me, to be presented to

you

Baron von Staël-Holstein,

Peking.

- 2 -

you, the photographic copies for which you asked, and he expressed the hope that you would be able to prepare from them a valuable and satisfactory article on Tibetan writing. He begs that you will pardon the delay in sending these copies, which was unavoidable due to his prolonged absence from his post, the necessity of obtaining Mrs. Rockhill's consent, and the time required to have the copies made and delivered to him.

In sending you these copies with the compliments and thanks of Dr. Harris, I beg that you will allow me to express for myself, also, deep appreciation of your courtesy in co-operating so willingly in a work commemorative of my former Chief, Minister Rockhill.

Yours very sincerely,

Willys R. Peck.

Chinese Secretary

Accompaniment:

One parcel containing photographic copies of documents as described.

My dear Mr. Peck,

I beg to express my sincerest gratitude to you, to ~~[illegible]~~ Mrs. Rockhill, and to Dr. Harris for the permission to publish the Tibetan documents in a philological journal, and also for the photographic reproductions of the ~~documents~~ letters ~~which I [illegible] was~~ in quintuplicate, which you so kindly sent to me.

The photographs are beautifully executed, and I shall frame some of them as specimens of Tibetan calligraphy.

The famous Mr. Kawaguchi, who saw them, believes that at least one of the

letters was written by the
Dalailama himself.

With many thanks I
remain yours sincerely

A. Staël Holstein

P.S. I enclose a reprint
of my latest article.

Le baron A. de Staël-Holstein
remercie Leurs Excellences
Monsieur et Madame Cerruti
de leur aimable invitation pour
la soirée du 17 Avril. Il aura
l'honneur de s'y rendre

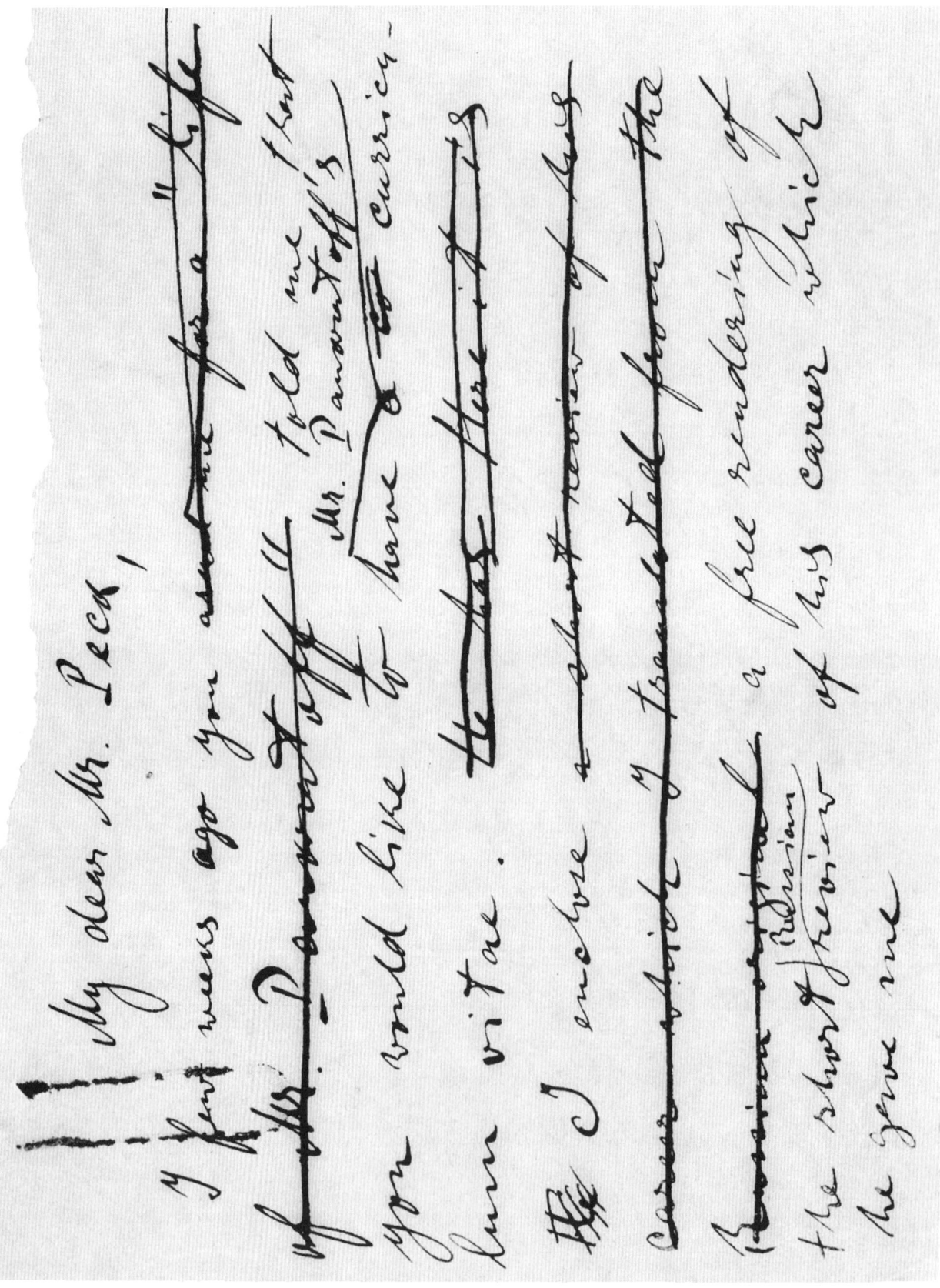

My dear Mr. Peck,

A few weeks ago you ~~asked me for a "Life of Mr. Panaratoff"~~ told me that you would like to have ~~a co~~ Mr. Panaratoff's curriculum vitae. ~~He has Here it is~~ ~~The~~ I enclose ~~a short review of his career which I translated from the Russian original~~ a free rendering of the short Russian review of his career which he gave me

Mr. B. I. Pankratoff's curriculum vitae.

~~I~~ Mr. Boris Ivanovitch Pankratoff, was born on ~~the 29th~~ February 29th 1892 at Kostroma in northern Russia. In 1911 ~~I~~ he ~~got~~ obtained ~~my~~ the maturity certificate ~~of~~ from the Kostroma Higher middle (Realnoye) School, and ~~I~~ matriculated as a student of the Vladivostok High School of Oriental Learning in the same year. In 1916 ~~I~~ he graduated from (the Mongolian department of) that High School ~~and obt was awarded a scholarship the council obtaining at the same time a scholar research scholarship with a view to~~ which at the same time granted ~~me~~ him a ~~special~~ research ~~scholarly~~ scholarship ~~in order to ena to~~ enabling ~~me~~ him to ~~pu~~ continue his ~~my~~ Mongolian studies. ~~[illegible]~~ ~~Since 1917~~ ~~I spent~~ ~~I~~ he spent several years in Mongolia studying the language ~~and~~ but could not, ~~return to~~ on account of the changed conditions, return to Vladivostok.

~~in order to be and become~~
~~a teacher of Mongolian at the~~
~~High School. as according to~~
~~my original~~
~~The High School of Vladivostok~~
~~had in granting me the scholarship~~
~~had intended to appoint me teacher~~
~~of the Mongolian language~~
Instead of teaching Mongolian at
the Vladivostok High School, as
originally intended, ~~I~~ he had to
stay in Peking and teach Russian
at the Russian School for Chinese.
~~I have~~ He has written two treatises (in Russian) which on
account of the revolution etc. could
not be printed
1) "The Solons, their language and literature",
2) "The Dahurs, their language and literature".
~~I have~~ He has also collected much material bearing on the
~~the~~ Tchakhar (Mongolian) dialect. ~~I~~ He speaks: Russian, English, Mongolian and
Chinese. ~~and Manchurian~~ ~~I~~ he can ~~and~~ also read those languages
and Manchurian French and German besides.

Dear Mr. Peck,

Many thanks for sending me the ~~th~~ printing block which I return herewith. The block does not belong to the ~~collection~~ body of ~~t~~ blocks which has been ~~th~~ used for printing ~~the~~ ~~t~~ any complete edition of the canonical works (Kanjur) ~~itself~~ or of the classical commentaries (Tanjur). This is evident from 1) its size; the canonical and classical collections as such were printed in a much larger size 2) ~~from the~~ the fact that ~~the number~~ no number ~~except~~ indicating the volume is found on the page. The page ~~is~~ is the reverse ~~of~~ of leaf № 20 of (Tib. [illegible] Chin. T.) a book called Thugs-rje-chen-po'i-bśags-pa'i ~~[illegible]~~ ~~[illegible]~~ -cho-ga (大悲心懺) or rules of the most merciful one (Avalokiteçvara Chin. Kwan-Yin) for the carrying out of confession. The corresponding Sanskrit title would be Mahākāruṇikadeçanāvidhiḥ.

Pellio t

Mon cher ami,

Il y a longtemps que j'ai reçu votre aimable envoi de livres (deux exemplaires du Mahāyānasūtrālaṃkāra et un ~~exemplaire~~ exemplaire du catalogue tibétain). Je vous suis infiniment reconnaissant pour votre grande amabilité, mais je regrette beaucoup de ne pas avoir reçu de compte. Je ne sais pas combien ces livres~~-~~ coûtent et je me ~~voie~~ trouve dans l'impossibilité de vous rembourser ~~les dépenses~~ ~~que~~ ce que vous avez si aimablement payé pour moi. Voulez vous m'écrire quelques lignes et me donner les renseignements nécessaires? Mon édition du Kāçyapaparivarta n'est pas ~~encore~~ prête. Il n'y a que

朕帝國議會ノ協贊
古社寺保存法
明治三十年六月
法律第四十九號

105 pages d'imprimées. Il ne se hâtent pas à la
"Commercial Press" de Changhaï! Je lis maintenant
"le Mahāyānasūtrālaṃkāra" avec un de mes élèves
chinois et nous étudions les commentaires ~~de Sthira-~~
~~ramati~~ d'Asvabhāva et de Sthiramati, qui
n'existent ~~pas~~ qu'en tibétain (Cordier, tôme III page 376),
en même temps. Nous lisons aussi le Mahāyānasaṃgra-
ha (B.N. № 1247) qui n'existe qu'en chinois et tibétain
et (dont nous possédons) ~~mais il y a~~ deux commentaires (l'un par Vasubandhu et l'autre par Asvabhāva), qui sont très bien traduits en chinois et en
tibétain. Nous espérons de publier bientôt une partie
de nos résultats.

Je viens de recevoir les quatre premier tomes de ~~vous~~ vos "Grottes de Touen-houang". Les magnifiques photographies m'interessent énormément et j'espère que ~~les~~ le texte va suivre bientôt. Est-ce-qu'il y a déja un volume ~~#~~ de texte?

~~Comment va Madame Pelliot~~? Voulez vous avoir l'obligeance de présenter mes respects à Madame ~~Pelliot~~ Pelliot.

A. I. Ivanoff est ici ~~aff~~ avec la mission bolcheviste de Ioffe et continue ses études de ~~Si-sia~~ si-sia. Il possède quelques pièces de si-sia avec transcriptions chinoise et tibétaine!

Encore une fois merci beaucoup pour les livres!

Cordialement à vous

A. v. Staël-Holstein (~~#~~ Mon adresse c/o the Peking Club, Peking).

Pelliot

Mon cher ami,

M. des Rotours m'a dit que vous aviez exprimé le désir d'apprendre mon adresse. C'est malheureusement toujours la même: c/o the Peking Club, Peking. J'habite la ville Chinoise, mais comme il y a quatre Allemands qui portent le même nom que le mien à Pékin, ça vaut mieux d'adresser les lettres au Peking Club. Le travail scientifique est presque impossible ici faute de bibliothèques. Je publie (Commercial Press, Changhai) le Kāçyapaparivarta en sanscrit et en tibétain (en transcription) avec quatre différentes traductions chinoises. Le manuscrit est prêt depuis six mois mais jusqu'ici 17 pages seulement ont été imprimées. Il n'y a pas assez de lettres comme ṅ ṇ etc. (tibétain et chinois). Je pense publier une traduction du texte et d'une partie du commentaire qui n'existe pas en sanscrit. Pourriez vous m'envoyer deux exemplaires du catalogue du Tanjour par Cordier et deux exemplaires du Sūtrālaṃkāra (édition et traduction par S. Lévi)? Je vous enverrai l'argent aussitôt que je saurai le prix.

J'ai tâché d'obtenir ces livres de Londres, mais en vain. Je vous serai infiniment reconnaissant si vous pourriez me les envoyer. Mes compliments à Madame Pelliot.

Bien cordialement à vous

A Staël Holstein.

Mon cher ami,

J'ai reçu le Rosenberg (du Japon) par un de mes amis ~~[illegible]~~ et ~~[illegible]~~ j'espère d'obtenir bientôt le catalogue du Musée de la famille royale de Corée ainsi que le . En attendant je vous n'envoie que le Rosenberg. Mon Kāśyapaparivarta me fait beaucoup de soucis. ~~[illegible]~~ Voilà déjà plus de deux ans que le manuscrit est terminé et la „Commercial Press" n'a imprimé que 143 pages; ~~C'est qu'il~~ il y en aura 260 (textes seuls sans commentaire et sans traduction, qui vont suivre). ~~en tout~~ C'est qu'il sont trop „commercial" et ne veulent pas préparer assez de lettres avec les points etc. diacritiques. Je vous enverrai un de ces jour quelques petits articles que ~~[illegible]~~ j'ai écrits. C'est difficile de travailler ici ! J'ai encore eu le malheur de perdre mon meilleur élève, Houang, qui était ~~mon~~ aussi mon assistant ~~son~~ et chargé [des] ~~de certaines~~ cours (élémentaires) à l'Université. Monsieur Sylvain Lévi connaissait Houang avec lequel il a eu de longs entretiens.

T'sai yuan pei ~~est p~~ après s'être marié est parti pour la Belgique. Hu-shih est malade et va peut être quitter la Chine pour quelque temps. Mazot (Bouillard) et Petithuguenin se portent bien ; je les ~~voi~~ rencontre assez souvent.

J'ai prié Ivanov de vous [envoyer] ~~faire parvenir~~ un exemplaire de ses textes hsi-hsia publiés en 1916 et il m'a promis de le faire. Il est ici en collaboration avec un Monsieur [illegible] et d'autres chinois, mais jusqu'ici rien n'a paru de ses nouveaux matériaux ; depuis un an il me dit ~~que~~ qu'un de ses articles est en train de paraître, mais je n'ai encore rien vu.

Un certain Monsieur I de Sui-yuan a trouvé ~~quel~~ une quantité de cachets ~~hsi~~ hsi-hsia. Il est venu chez moi et je l'ai envoyé chez Ivanov qui me dit qu'il possède des matériaux intéressants.

Veuillez présenter mes respects à Madame Pelliot.

Bien cordialement à vous

Staël-Holstein.

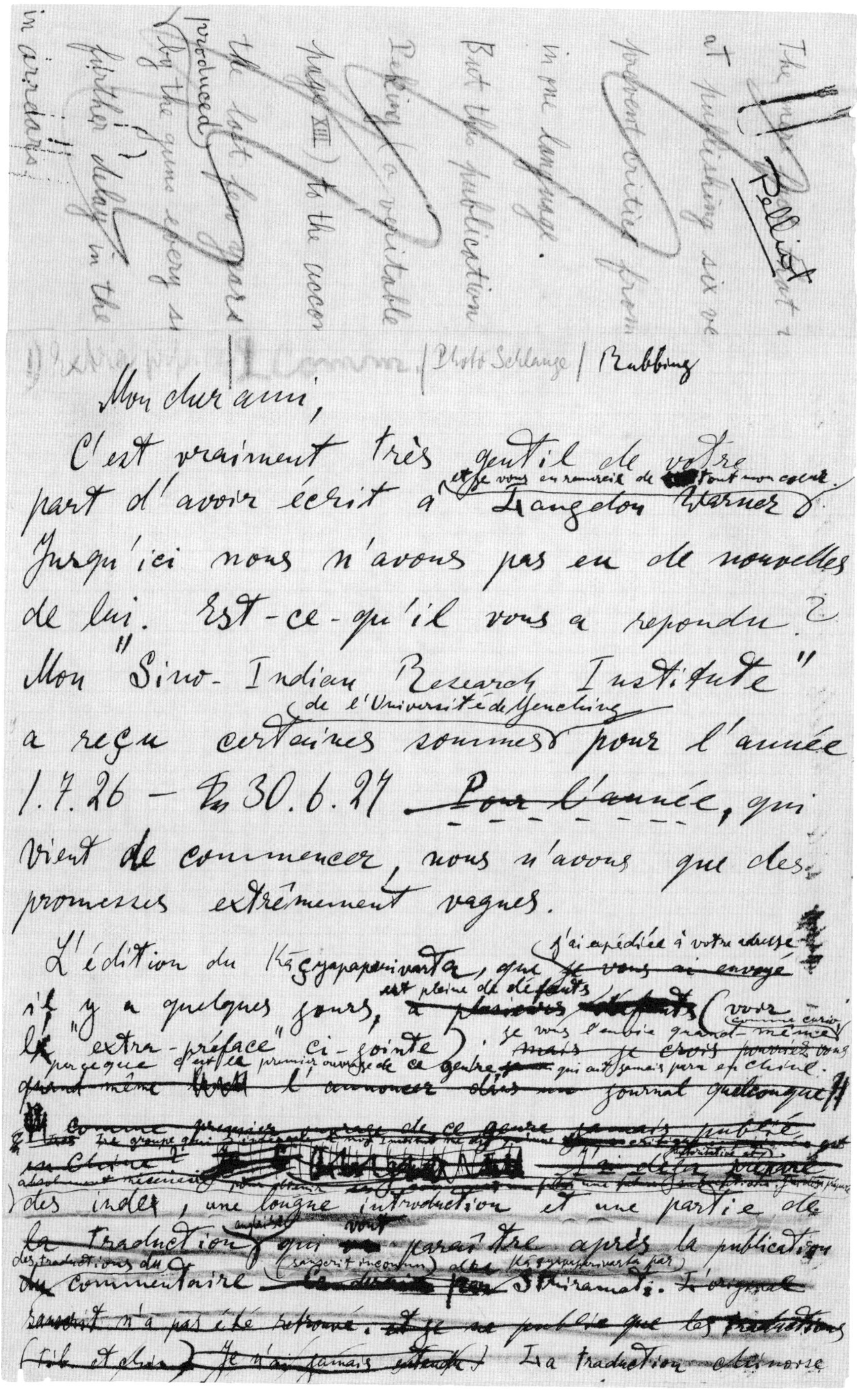

The only ... at publishing six ... different critics from ... in one language. But the publication ... Peking (a veritable ... page XIII) to the ... the last few years ... produced by the game ... further delay in the ... in arrears!!

Extra-preface | Comm... | Photo Schlange | Rubbing

Mon cher ami,

C'est vraiment très gentil de votre part d'avoir écrit à Langdon Warner & je vous en remercie de tout mon coeur. Jusqu'ici nous n'avons pas eu de nouvelles de lui. Est-ce-qu'il vous a repondu?

Mon "Sino-Indian Research Institute" de l'Université de Yenching a reçu certaines sommes pour l'année 1.7.26 – 30.6.27. ~~Pour l'année~~, qui vient de commencer, nous n'avons que des promesses extrêmement vagues.

L'édition du Kāçyapaparivarta, que j'ai expédiée à votre adresse ~~je vous ai envoyé~~ il y a quelques jours, est pleine de défauts ~~a plusieurs défauts~~ (voir l'"extra-préface" ci-jointe). Je vous l'envoie quand même comme curiosité ~~mais je crois pourriez vous~~ parceque c'est le premier ouvrage de ce genre qui ait jamais paru en Chine. ~~quand même ... l'annoncer dans un journal quelconque~~

~~Comme premier ouvrage de ce genre jamais publié en Chine ... J'ai déjà préparé~~ [illegible] des index, une longue introduction et une partie de ~~la traduction~~ qui vont paraître après la publication des traductions du commentaire (sanscrit inconnu) du Kāçyapaparivarta par Sthiramati. ~~L'original sanscrit n'a pas été retrouvé. Et je ne publie que les traductions (tib. et chin.) Je n'ai jamais ...~~ La traduction ... norse la traduction anglaise, qui vont paraître après la publication du Commentaire du Kāçyapaparivarta par Sthiramati. L'original sanscrit de ce commentaire n'existe pas, et je ne publie que les traductions (chin. et tib.). La traduction chinoise abonde en fautes et est en partie tout à fait incompréhensible, ~~Je la publie~~ mais elle nous aide pourtant à corriger quelques fautes, ~~du texte tibétain. Je~~ qui se trouvent dans la version tibétaine. Ce Commentaire (dont quelques pages sont jointes à cette lettre) est en train d'être imprimé à Pékin et on travaille beaucoup mieux ici qu'à Changhai. J'ose donc espérer que la nouvelle édition sera d'un plus grand mérite que celle du Kāçyapaparivarta.

~~Nous sommes en~~ Le Kāçyapaparivarta ~~fait parti~~ appartient au Mahāratnakūṭa dharmaparyāya et je veux faire un catalogue raisonné de toute cette collection; ~~mes assistants ont~~ mes assistants et moi comparons les textes chinois et tibétains. Une grande partie de ce travail a déjà été fait.

A propos de quelques découvertes iconographiques (surtout: une collection de 755 statuettes portant les noms des divinités, une espèce de Panthéon, et deux livres dans le genre du Panthéon de Pander, mais plus intéressants) j'écris à Monsieur Foucher.

Je serai heureux de vous envoyer les livres chinois, dont vous aurez bésoin. J'ai expédier quelques livres ensemble avec le Kāçyapaparivarta (est une liste de livres publiés par la Commercial Press, un numéro d'une journal revue musulmane chinoise etc.); si par hazard, vous désirez que je vous fasse parvenir d'autres, je serai heureux de le faire. La photographie ci-jointe représente un couvercle (?) en bronze, qui appartient à un chinois. L'autre côté (non photographié) montre deux serpents. Le "rubbing" représente une inscription sur un poignard. Je ne sais pas, d'où les objets viennent. S'ils vous intéressent, publiez les, je vous en prie. La question des droits de publication ne se pose pas.

Il y a quelques années que je vous ai envoyé le vocabulaire de Rosenberg, une autre fois je vous ai envoyé une lettre avec une dizaine de photographies archéologiques. Est ce que ces envois sont arrivés?

Je vous prie de transmettre mes salutations respectueuses a Madame Pelliot.

Cordialement à vous

AStaëlHolstein.

Bouillard a perdu sa place, mais on fait toujours encore bonne chère chez lui. Mazot se porte bien. Sir Charles Eliot n'est plus Ambassadeur, mais il va habiter le Japon comme simple citoyen jusqu'au printemps.

Paris 38 Rue de Varenne (VII)

26 avril 1931,

Mon cher ami,

M. Culty m'a remis votre mot amical et bien que la peinture qu'il annonce se trouve dans une caisse qui ne doit pas arriver avant quelques semaines, je ne veux pas attendre jusque-là pour vous dire combien je suis touché de votre pensée amicale. Voilà plus de deux ans maintenant que nous nous sommes quittés à Harvard, et depuis lors votre vie a enfin pu se fixer comme vous le souhaitiez depuis longtemps. Votre institut a une existence durable, vous même êtes marié, vous avez un bébé dont la bonne figure est venue à merveille, entre ses parents, sur la carte que vous m'envoyez; je souhaite bien vivement que tout aille longtemps pour vous au mieux de vos vœux.

Ici, après les pertes énormes qui ont atteint l'ancien orientalisme l'an passé, et dont nous avons eu notre part par la mort de Vissière, le travail se poursuit normalement. ~~Notre~~ Institut des ~~Hautes~~ Études chinoises se développe, et je

2

compilés même, si les circonstances s'y prêtent, profiter de la nécessité où il est de monter sa bibliothèque chinoise pour aller à Pékin l'hiver prochain. J'espère bien vous y voir, ainsi que Madame de Staël Holstein, à qui je vous prie de présenter mes meilleurs souvenirs et mes hommages très respectueux.

Agréez à mes sentiments bien cordialement dévoués.

Paul Pelliot.

P.S. Vous m'aviez laissé espérer fin 1928 que vous me feriez envoyer par Lambrector des matériaux sur l'Hist. secrète des Mongols. Mais rien n'est

venue. J'ai cependant l'intention de mettre [illegible]
[illegible] la dernière main à l'édition du texte, et
je serais obligé à votre confrère de tout ce
qu'il pourrait me communiquer.

P. P.

July 33

Mon cher ami,

Vous avez probablement vu le numéro du J.A.O.S. (décembre 1932) ~~qui~~ qui contient mon ~~Je vous envoie avec cette lettre tout un dossier [illegible] qui~~ article.

~~prouve que la publication de mon article~~

C'est pendant votre séjour à Pékin, que je l'ai reçu, ~~j'ai reçu le numéro du J.A.O.S., qui contient mon article,~~ Je ne vous en ai pas parlé, alors, ~~de l'article, que le J.A.O.S.~~ parce que ~~je trouvait~~ il y avait tant d'autres problèmes à discuter, ~~qui offraient un~~

Two years ago ~~(July)~~ Langdon Warner visited Peking and asked me to write an article for "Eastern Art", which I did. The article was sent to America in August 1931, ~~but it did not appear in~~ but my hope that it would be printed ~~appear~~ in the number of "Eastern Art" which appeared in December 1931 was not fulfilled.

Monsieur le Professeur Paul Pelliot
Membre de l'Institut
etc. etc. etc.
38 rue de Varenne 38
Paris VIIe
France

In September 1932 I enquired whether the article would appear in ~~[illegible]~~ the "Eastern Art" year book for 1932, and received ~~[illegible]~~ (on October 12th 1932) ~~[illegible]~~ a radiogram (informing me that) ~~the~~ the article was not appearing (photo No. 1). Thereupon I wrote to Mr. Jayne asking him to return my manuscript to Peking, ~~which he promised to [illegible] do~~ and he promised, (on December 10th 1933), to have this done (photo No. 2). In spite of ~~this~~ his promise ~~and in complete disregard of my~~ ~~Jayne sent me a tele~~ Mr. Jayne asked me (on December 29th 1932) to allow the J.A.O.S. to print my article. ~~I refused~~ (photo No. 3), and I refused categorically (photo No. 4). In complete disregard of my refusal the article was published x

~~and~~ in the J. A.O.S., ~~and the~~ which caused me a great deal of ~~much~~ annoyance. In order to repair the damage as far as possible I wrote a letter (photo No 5) to the editor of the J.A.O.S. ~~I~~ asking him to publish my explanation ~~a statement~~ ~~(photo No 6)~~ (photos No 6 and No 7) of the unfortunate duplication. You will learn ~~see~~ from Dean Chase's letter (photo No 8) that the editor of the J.A.O.S. has refused to comply with my ~~respo~~ request. ~~It would, of course, be extremely stupid to pursue this qu~~ I must, ~~of course not you~~ for obvious reasons, not quarrel with the scholars of America, and I ~~do not want you to shall in no way~~ shall refrain from protesting against the discourtesy of the editor ~~in pu~~ publicly. I communicate all this to you merely in order to convince ~~you~~ (not the public) of ~~my~~ complete innocence in the matter. ~~in order to prevent you from~~

~~because~~ All those who only read the explanation ~~adopte~~ suggested by the J. A. O. S. editors (photo № 8) will think that I am as much to blame for the duplication as the editors. ~~I am sending~~ (In a few days I shall send) you ~~(under separate cover)~~ a number of books and articles. ~~May~~ ~~I ask you to~~ Please keep one copy of the Kāçyapaparivarta commentary as well as one copy of Viller's index, and ~~to~~ present the rest to the ~~the~~ library of the Société Asiatique. Will you be so kind as to induce somebody to ~~write~~ publish a few encouraging ~~[illegible]~~ words about my efforts in the ~~Journal~~ T'oung Pao or in the Journal Asiatique ~~[illegible]~~, if you should be too busy to do so yourself? The Buddhist scholastic tradition is practically dead in India and I think that before translating Buddhist Sanskrit texts into European languages we ~~should~~ must ~~be able to~~ consult the Tibetan and Chinese ~~[illegible]~~ translations and commentaries, if we ~~want~~

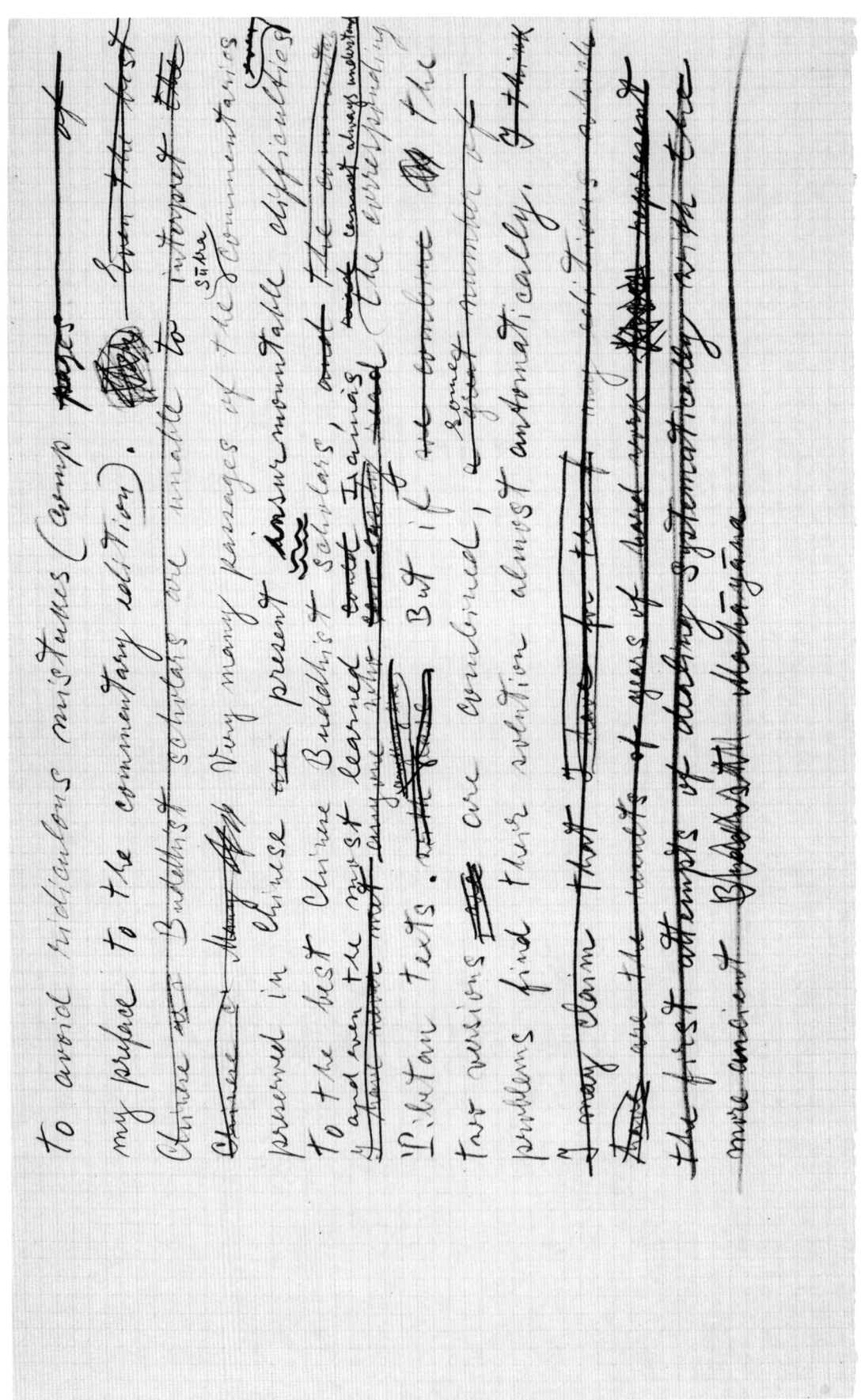

to avoid ridiculous mistakes (comp. ~~pages of~~
my preface to the commentary edition). ~~[illegible] Even the best~~
~~Chinese as Buddhist scholars are unable to interpret the~~
~~Chinese [illegible] Many [illegible]~~ Very many passages of the sūtra commentaries
preserved in Chinese ~~are~~ present insurmountable difficulties
to the best Chinese Buddhist scholars, ~~and the commentary~~
and even the most learned ~~could~~ Lamas ~~[illegible]~~ cannot always understand
~~I have never met anyone who can easily read~~ the corresponding
Tibetan texts. ~~with ease~~ But if ~~we combine~~ the
two versions ~~are~~ are combined, ~~a great number of~~ some
problems find their solution almost automatically. ~~I think~~
~~I may claim that I have for the my editions which~~
~~have are the results of years of hard work [illegible] represent~~
~~the first attempts of dealing systematically with the~~
~~more ancient Buddhist Mahāyāna~~

I think I may claim that ~~my~~ Cilinguals ~~[illegible]~~ edition of the Commentary represents a useful innovation, and I hope ~~that~~ it will ~~encourage future philologists to proceed more systematically~~ and ~~[illegible]~~ not to trans- ~~late difficult~~ prevent future translators (of texts which have commentaries) from neglecting the commentaries. The? European translations of the Saddharmapuṇḍarīka and of the Vajracchedikā which we possess are full of mistakes which could ~~have~~ been avoided if the commentaries had been con- sulted. I have studied some of those commentaries and ~~I could produce a long list of mistakes~~ I am preparing ~~an articles~~ (a series of articles dealing with them.

My edition of the Kāśyapaparivarta text has been almost completely ~~neglected~~ ignored by the philologists of Europe,

~~and I fear that the commentary will share the fate of the~~
~~Text if you~~ ~~venture to hope that they will I shall~~ and I shall be very much obliged to you indeed, if you
~~have more luck with my later efforts. I~~
will save the commentary ~~and my~~ as well as my articles from a similar fate.

It is not mere vanity which makes me ask for a printed appreciation of my work, but dire necessity.

I must be able to submit ~~some~~ at least one favorable review to the trustees. I am afraid that the review cannot ~~will not~~ be ready for the October meeting, but I venture to hope that it will reach America in time for the early Spring meeting. ~~We~~ The Japanese have after all not
~~Our friend Valyi has at last left Peking evidently Sans esprit de retour. I do not know, whether~~
~~we~~ taken Peking, and we ~~live in~~ enjoy peace once more after some very exciting weeks.

May I ask to be kindly remembered to Madame Pelliot.

Believe me yours sincerely

A. Staël Holstein.

Légation de la
République Française
en Chine.

Jeudi

Mon cher ami,

Voulez-vous me faire le plaisir de venir dîner chez moi jeudi prochain à 8 h. ½ ? Vous rencontrerez Sir Charles Eliot et deux ou trois autres amis. Smoking.

Cordialement [illegible]

THE NORTH CHINA UNION LANGUAGE SCHOOL

PEKING

DIRECTING BODIES

American Board Mission
American Methodist Mission
American Presbyterian Mission
Church of England Mission
London Missionary Society
Young Men's Christian Association

Young Women's Christian Association
American Legation
American Association of North China
British Chamber of Commerce
British Legation
Peking Union Medical College

Telephone 1633 East
Telegraphic Address "Language Peking"
Codes Used "Mission" and "C.I.M."

Principal
W. B. Pettus

May 22, 1925

Baron Staël-Holstein
7 Pi Kuan Hutung
Peking

Dear Baron Staël-Holstein:

Yenching University and the North China Union Language School are cooperating in plans for the development of a School of Chinese Studies. The plans include the strengthening of the courses now conducted at the Language School and also an expansion of the Department of Chinese in Yenching. Committees have been discussing these plans for the last few weeks. It is proposed to arrange courses in varous aspects of Chinese culture adapted to the needs of three or four groups of students, including both such students as are able to use Chinese course material and are interested in preparing for further advanced studies in the special fields of Chinese culture and also those who limit their work to sources in European languages. In every phase of the work of research and discovery which is being thought of, a strong emphasis will be paid to an interpretation of the great treasures of China's heritage to Westerners. The underlying conviction of those responsible for the undertaking is that Westerners should not only appreciate and understand the culture of China, but that Western culture itself distinctly needs to be supplemented by definite contributions from China's heritage of thought and art.

It is felt that similar aims are held by many others, both foreigners and Chinese, now living and working in Peking. Before going further with these plans, the Committees concerned are very desirous of securing the benefit of criticisms and suggestions from as many different points of view as possible. The Committee wishes to invite you to a luncheon at which those primarily interested in the study or interpretation of Chinese culture may meet together, discuss and criticize these plans, and add whatever suggestions may develop, so as to help in coordinating the new venture with existing agencies, and making the whole undertaking useful to all who are or should be interested in China. The luncheon is to be on Thursday, May 28th, at 12:30 in the new plant of the Language School at No 5 T'ou T'iao Hutung, Tung Ssu Pai Lou.

Very sincerely yours

R S V P.

W. B. Pettus

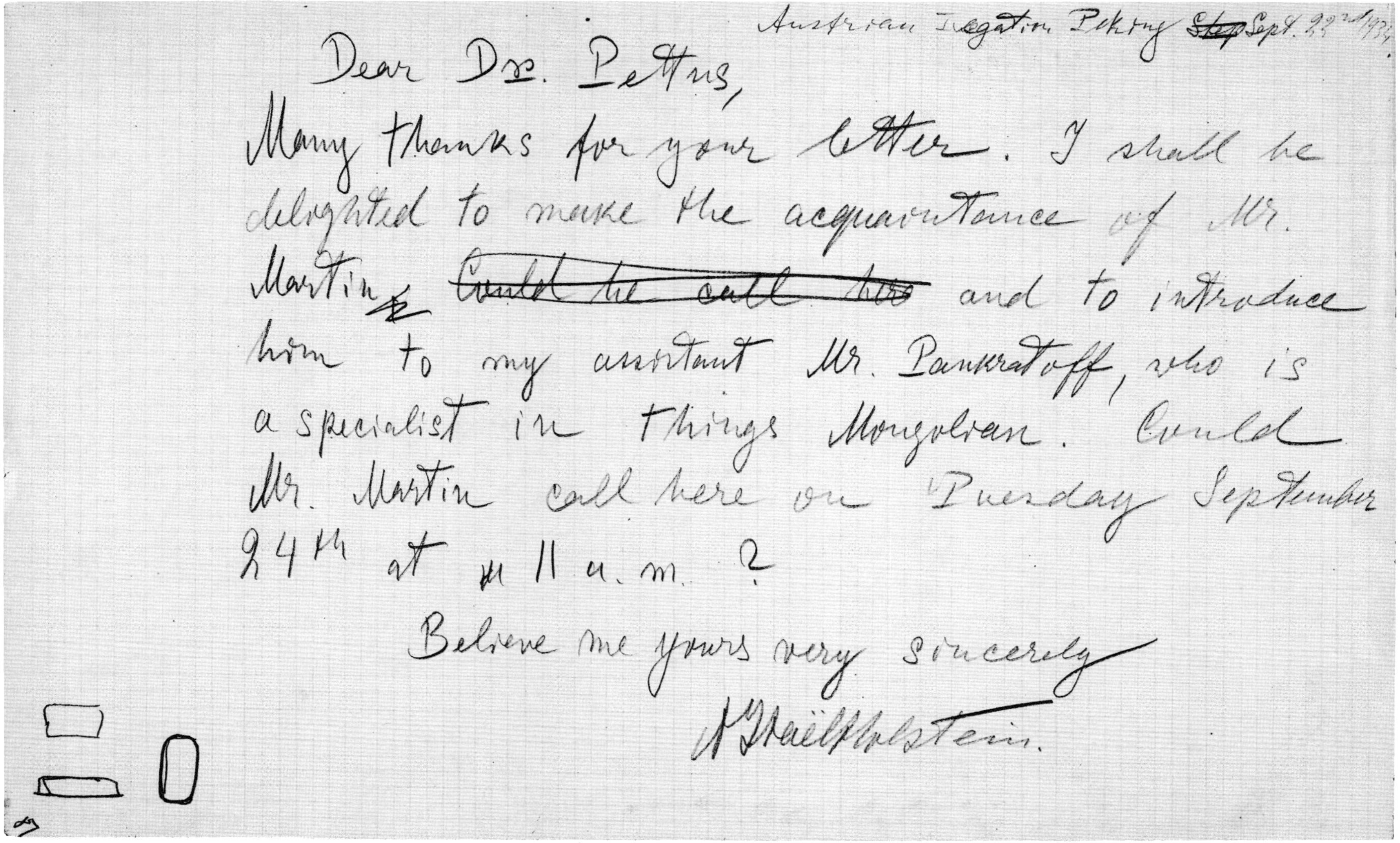

Austrian Legation Peking ~~Sep~~ Sept. 22nd 1934.

Dear Dr. Pettus,

Many thanks for your letter. I shall be delighted to make the acquaintance of Mr. Martin ~~Could he call here~~ and to introduce him to my assistant Mr. Pankratoff, who is a specialist in things Mongolian. Could Mr. Martin call here on Tuesday September 24th at 11 a.m.?

Believe me yours very sincerely

A Staël Holstein.

Dear Dr. Pettus,

Herewith I return to you with many thanks Professor Forke's "World Conception of the Chinese", ~~Chinese Cosmology~~ which you so kindly lent me some weeks ago.

Yours gratefully

A. Staël Holstein

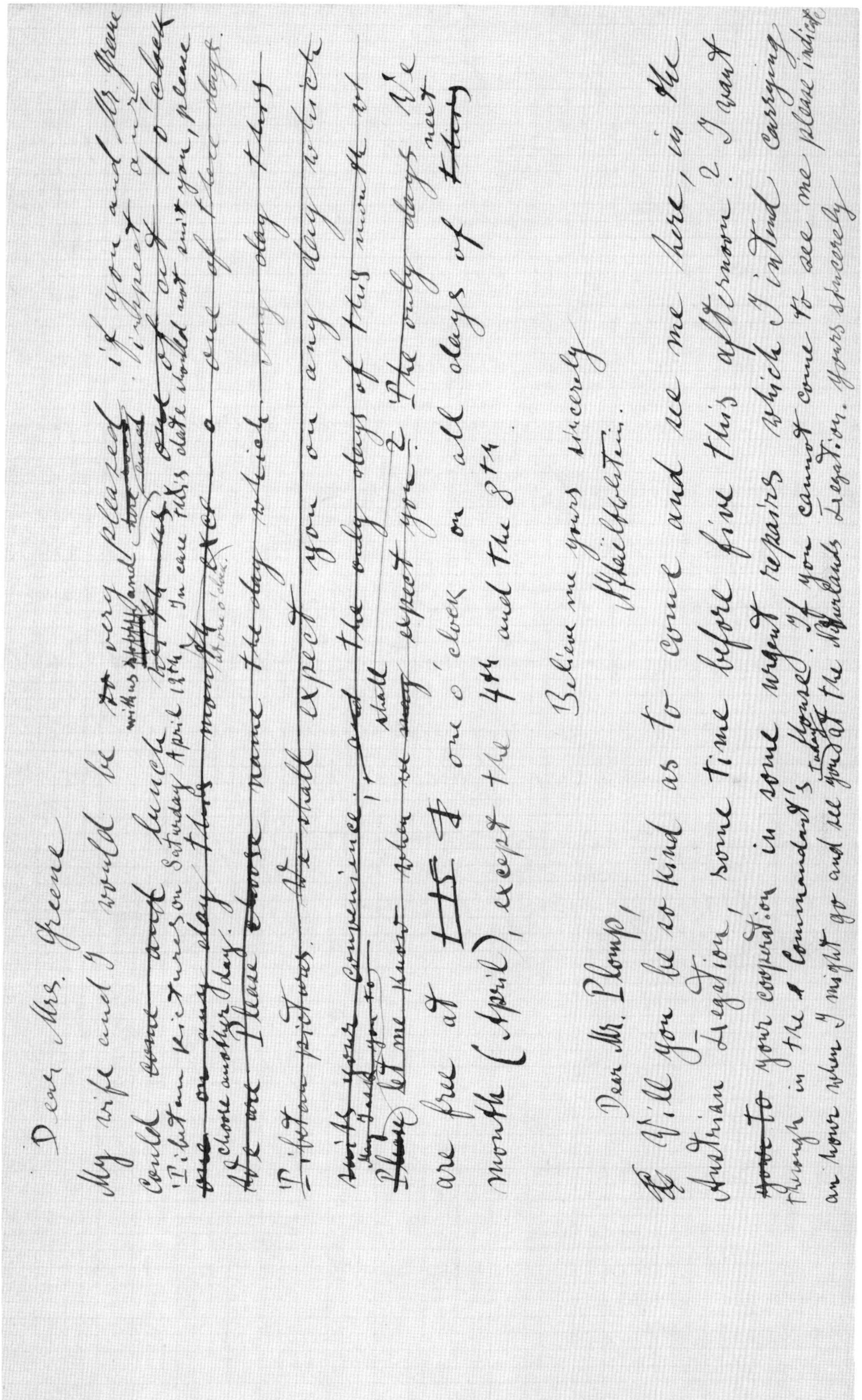

Dear Mrs. Greene

My wife and I would be ~~so~~ very pleased if you and Mr. Greene could ~~come and~~ lunch with us ~~and~~ ~~with us~~ ~~one of~~ ~~at~~ ~~1 o'clock~~ and inspect our Tibetan pictures on Saturday April 12th at one o'clock. In case this date should not suit you, please ~~one on any day this month exc~~ ~~a~~ ~~one of these days.~~ choose another day. ~~We are Please choose name the day which. Any day this Tibetan pictures. We shall~~ expect you on any day which ~~suits your convenience.~~ ~~and the only days of this month at~~ May I ask you to ~~Please~~ let me know ~~when we~~ ~~may~~ shall expect you? ~~The only days~~ We are free at ~~1.15~~ ~~&~~ one o'clock on all days of ~~this~~ next month (April), except the 4th and the 8th.

Believe me yours sincerely

AStaëlHolstein.

Dear Mr. Plomp,

~~W~~ Will you be so kind as to come and see me here, in the Austrian Legation, some time before five this afternoon? I want ~~you to~~ your cooperation in some urgent repairs which I intend carrying through in the ~~s~~ Commandant's House. If you cannot come to see me please indicate an hour when I might go and see you today at the Netherlands Legation. Yours sincerely

Dear Dr. Porter,

I send you ~~the~~ proof sheets (only partly corrected) of the Buddhist sūtra which I am publishing in Shanghai.

~~Will you be so kind as to look~~ glance o

I hope you will find time ~~to~~ to read ~~some~~ that ~~a~~ part of the ~~intro~~ preface (pages V, ~~VI~~ and XIII) in which the two ~~new~~ further volumes which I am preparing ~~and~~ ~~One of which~~ are mentioned. ~~One of those two volumes is practically~~ Mr. Yü ~~does assist~~ ~~assists me~~ ~~now~~ / assists me in comparing the ~~..~~ various Sanskrit, Tibetan and Chinese texts. ~~and that as well. He does so without being paid for it, but~~ ~~I shall~~ In case you have no further use for the proof sheets I shall send my coolie to fetch them tomorrow (Saturday) morning.

Pages 1—105 are bound separately, but they will, of course be bound together with the rest of the volume, ~~when they~~ ~~are~~ in the final edition.

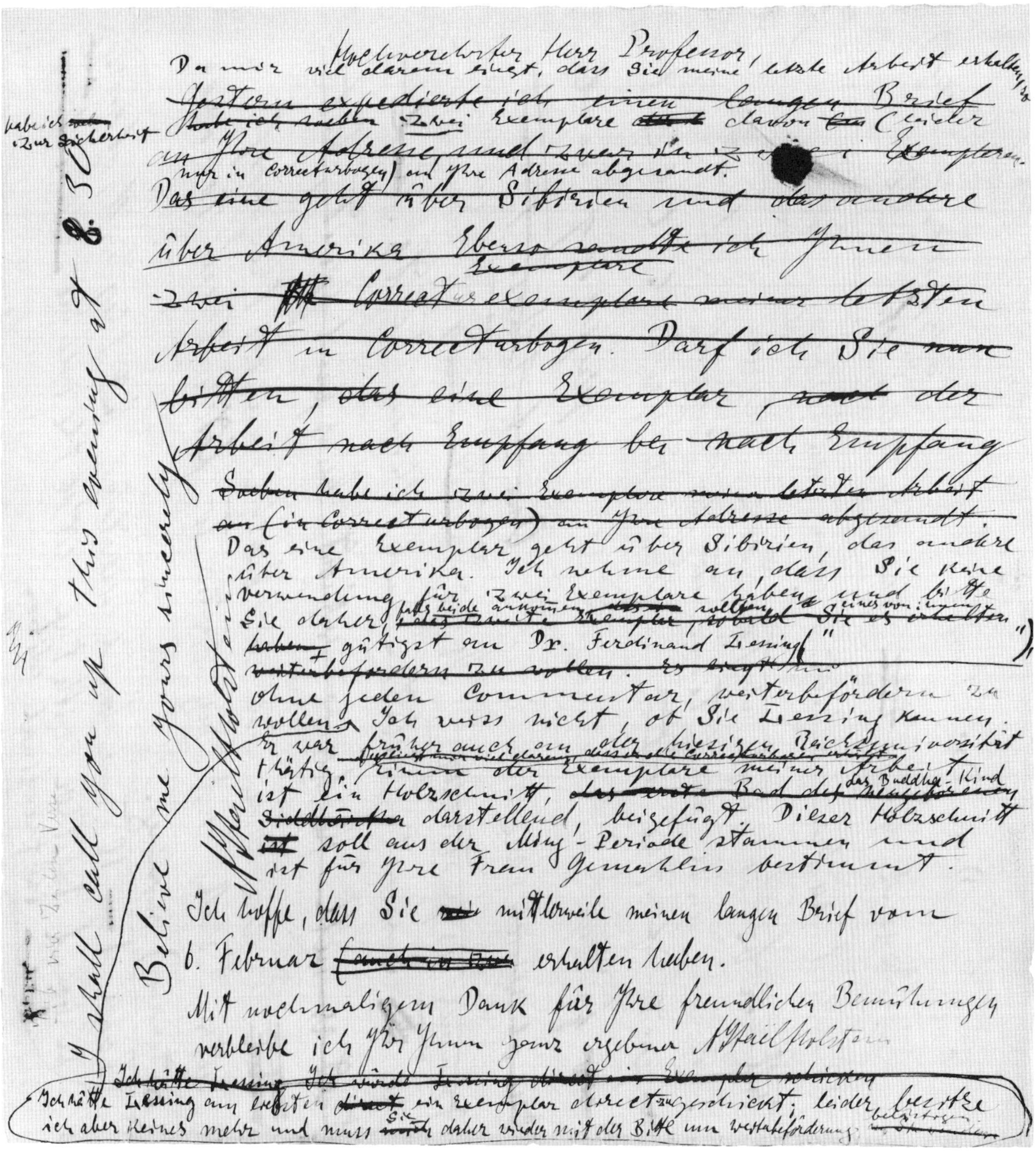

Hochverehrter Herr Professor

Da mir viel daran liegt, dass Sie meine letzte Arbeit erhalten, so habe ich zur Sicherheit zwei Exemplare davon (das letzte nur in Correcturbogen) an Ihre Adresse abgesandt.

~~Gestern expedierte ich einen langen Brief an Ihre Adresse, und zwar die zwei Exemplare. Das eine geht über Sibirien und das andere über Amerika. Ebenso sandte ich Ihnen zwei Correcturexemplare meiner letzten Arbeit in Correcturbogen. Darf ich Sie nun bitten, das eine Exemplar der Arbeit nach Empfang~~

~~Soeben habe ich zwei Exemplare meiner letzten Arbeit (in Correcturbogen) an Ihre Adresse abgesandt.~~

Das eine Exemplar geht über Sibirien, das andere über Amerika. Ich nehme an, dass Sie keine Verwendung für zwei Exemplare haben, und bitte Sie daher, falls beide ankommen, eines von ihnen gütigst an Dr. Ferdinand Lessing ohne jeden Commentar weiterbefördern zu wollen. Ich weiss nicht, ob Sie Lessing kennen. Er war früher auch an der hiesigen Reichsuniversität tätig. Einem der Exemplare meiner Arbeit ist ein Holzschnitt, das Buddha-Kind darstellend, beigefügt. Dieser Holzschnitt soll aus der Ming-Periode stammen und ist für Ihre Frau Gemahlin bestimmt.

Ich hoffe, dass Sie mittlerweile meinen langen Brief vom 6. Februar erhalten haben.

Mit nochmaligem Dank für Ihre freundlichen Bemühungen verbleibe ich Ihr Ihnen ganz ergebener A Staël Holstein

Ich hätte Lessing am liebsten ein Exemplar direct zugeschickt, leider besitze ich aber keines mehr und muss Sie daher wieder mit der Bitte um Weiterbeförderung belästigen.

I shall call you up this evening at 8.30

Believe me yours sincerely A Staël Holstein

[illegible] 2-6

YENCHING SCHOOL OF CHINESE STUDIES

(LANGUAGE SCHOOL)

DIRECTING BODIES

American Board Mission
American Methodist Mission
American Presbyterian Mission
Church of England Mission
London Missionary Society
Young Men's Chirstian Association
Young Women's Christian Association
American Legation
American Chamber of Chamber
British Chamber of Commerce
British Legation
Peking Union Medical College
Yenching University

Telephones 1633, 1629, 2959 East
Telegraphic Address "Language Peking"
Codes Used: "Missions" and "C.I.M."

PEKING, CHINA.

Monday

Dear Baron:

Herewith your package of proof. Mr Hummel & I have been glad to read the preface and to see what you are planning. I very much hope we can be of help in arranging & have Mr Yü continue to assist you. We here agree that such help should be given by this School. I hope Mr. Pettus will also agree.

Sincerely yours

Lucius C Porter

YENCHING SCHOOL OF CHINESE STUDIES

(LANGUAGE SCHOOL)

DIRECTING BODIES

American Board Mission
American Methodist Mission
American Presbyterian Mission
Church of England Mission
London Missionary Society
Young Men's Chirstian Association
Young Women's Christian Association
American Legation
American Chamber of Chamber
British Chamber of Commerce
British Legation
Peking Union Medical College
Yenching University

Telephones 1633, 1629, 2959 East
Telegraphic Address "Language Peking"
Codes Used: "Missions" and "C.I.M."

PEKING, CHINA.

Mar 6th 1926

My dear Baron Stael-Holstein:—

Upon Mr. Pettus' return I spoke to him of the opportunity to help Mr. Yü. He told me there were no funds under his control for doing this service. But I have arranged with President Stuart and can send you assurance of $40— per month for six months. This will come from funds available to help Chinese scholars and is in line with what our school hopes to do in the future. You can tell Mr. Yü that the help is assured and goes to him through you.

I am enclosing a check for the whole amount of $240=. I am very glad this will enable Mr. Yü to continue in his specialized field of study.

Sincerely yours

Lucius C Porter

YENCHING SCHOOL OF CHINESE STUDIES
PEKING CHINA

June 10th 1926

My dear Baron:-

I have talked with President Stuart about the institute for Mahayana Buddhism. He is interested in the matter. He asks to know what definite amounts would be needed to maintain you, yourself, at work in Peking, and what expenditure would be involved in carrying on your work and the plans of such an Institute, as you see them, for the next 5 years. Will you be good enough to draw up a tentative budget for one year and another for five years? we will see what can be done further.

Sincerely yours
Lucius C Porter

to Baron Stael Holstein

Peking, Tuesday June 15th 1926.

My dear Dr. Porter,

I am very glad to hear that President ~~Insti~~ Stuart is interested in ~~the pro~~ [my investigations] ~~study of the Mahāyāna~~ and I ~~will~~ feel greatly obliged to you for furthering my plans.

What I am personally most interested in at present is the development of the Mahāyāna from comparatively sober beginnings to ~~the magical app~~ the over-ornamented structure represented by the Saddharmapuṇḍarīka sūtra (妙法蓮華經) and similar texts. That development can ~~only~~ be traced [by] ~~if one compares~~ [comparing with one another] the various ~~Chinese~~ versions ~~all~~ of certain books current at different periods in the Mahāyāna world. ~~The Chinese~~ 三藏 is the only Buddhist canon ~~which contains~~ [illegible] dated versions of the same texts compiled at various epochs ranging from the II century A.D. to the X and XI. The Tibetan versions ~~still~~ can also be dated, but there are hardly any texts ~~extant in two Tibetan versions~~ I am now engaged in comparing the Sanskrit text of the Kāçyapaparivarta with four different

Chinese translations (dating from the II – X centuries A.D.) and with the Tibetan translation made during the IX century. All these texts have been already edited by me and printed at Shanghai where they must appear before the end of this month as the first volume of a series; I signed and returned the last proof sheets, containing a preface in English, some time ago.

The commentary of the Kāçyapaparivarta which exists only in Chinese and in Tibetan has been ready for print since January when I finished revising and collating the various codices. I wanted to print the commentary at once, but certain Chinese friends who were to arrange the publication have not so far found time for doing so. The two versions of the commentaries are to fill the second volume, and the third volume will contain an English translation of the text with a detailed introduction and notes discussing the various additions which have crept into the text during the centuries.

Mr. Yü to whom ~~you~~ President Stuart so kindly granted a scholarship for six months assists me very ably in comparing the various texts and in ~~studying~~ reading the commentary of the Kāçyapaparivarta.

I have also studied certain ~~[illegible]~~ hitherto unknown Tibetan commentaries, ~~the Sanscrit originals of which are lost~~, which discuss ~~[illegible]~~ the differences ~~I have~~ between the Hīnayāna and the Mahāyāna, and a treatise on those differences is practically ready for print.

I possess myself an iconographical collection ~~containing~~ (about 200 pictures and 300 statuettes) which contains much material unknown in the west and which I think worth publishing. I have already prepared a manuscript catalogue of the collection. I have further written the enclosed article on the development of certain divine personalities of ~~[illegible]~~ Aryan origin, who have undergone great changes in the course of their wanderings and who still survive in ~~North~~ China, more especially ~~[illegible]~~ at the Hsi-yü-ssŭ (comp. my article). I should like to go more deeply into those matters and to ~~publish photographs of those gods, some of which~~ photograph some of ~~those~~ the gods as ~~[illegible]~~ they are represented in China for publication together with ~~[illegible]~~ detailed historical notes.

I have, been prevented from ~~that~~ taking those photographs and even from ~~going to~~ visiting the Hsi-yü-ssŭ by the fact ~~the the National University always refused to provide me with the funds necessary for such undertakings that all~~ that practically all the funds which ought to be at my disposal have been either nationalized confiscated or withheld.

Lack of funds has also interfered with my philological studies in Peking. I was, during the last few years unable ~~to get~~ to borrow certain books ~~from the Lamas~~ from the Lamas, who must be ~~bribed~~ paid for every service, and from obtaining their advice. This is ~~especially~~ very ~~regrettable~~ the more regrettable, as the Pan-chen Lama has brought a number of quite remarkable Buddhist scholars with him to Peking. ~~In case I shall be able~~

If I get four hundred ~~Chinese~~ dollars Mex. a month for myself and about ~~two~~ one hundred and fifty dollars a month for expenses, I shall be able to realize most of my plans for the immediate future (July 1st 1926 to ~~July 1st~~ June 30th 1927). The expenses do not include books printed in European languages, ~~which are~~ (so generously ~~provided~~ provided by the Yenching School of Chinese Studies), ~~but~~ and are composed of the following items:

1) two permanent Chinese assistants — $80 a month

2) one permanent Lama assistant — $40 a month

3) miscellaneous expenses (expedition to Hei-yü-ssŭ, presents to various not permanently engaged Lamas, copying Tibetan books which cannot be bought, taking photographs etc.) ~~buying~~ Tibetan $30

~~From the sum of 6600 dollars (550 dollars a month) the salary of Mr. Yü which which has~~ (which has already been paid up to September 30th 1926) ~~for three month (120 dollars) would have to be deducted.~~

~~The sum suggested might appear as too~~

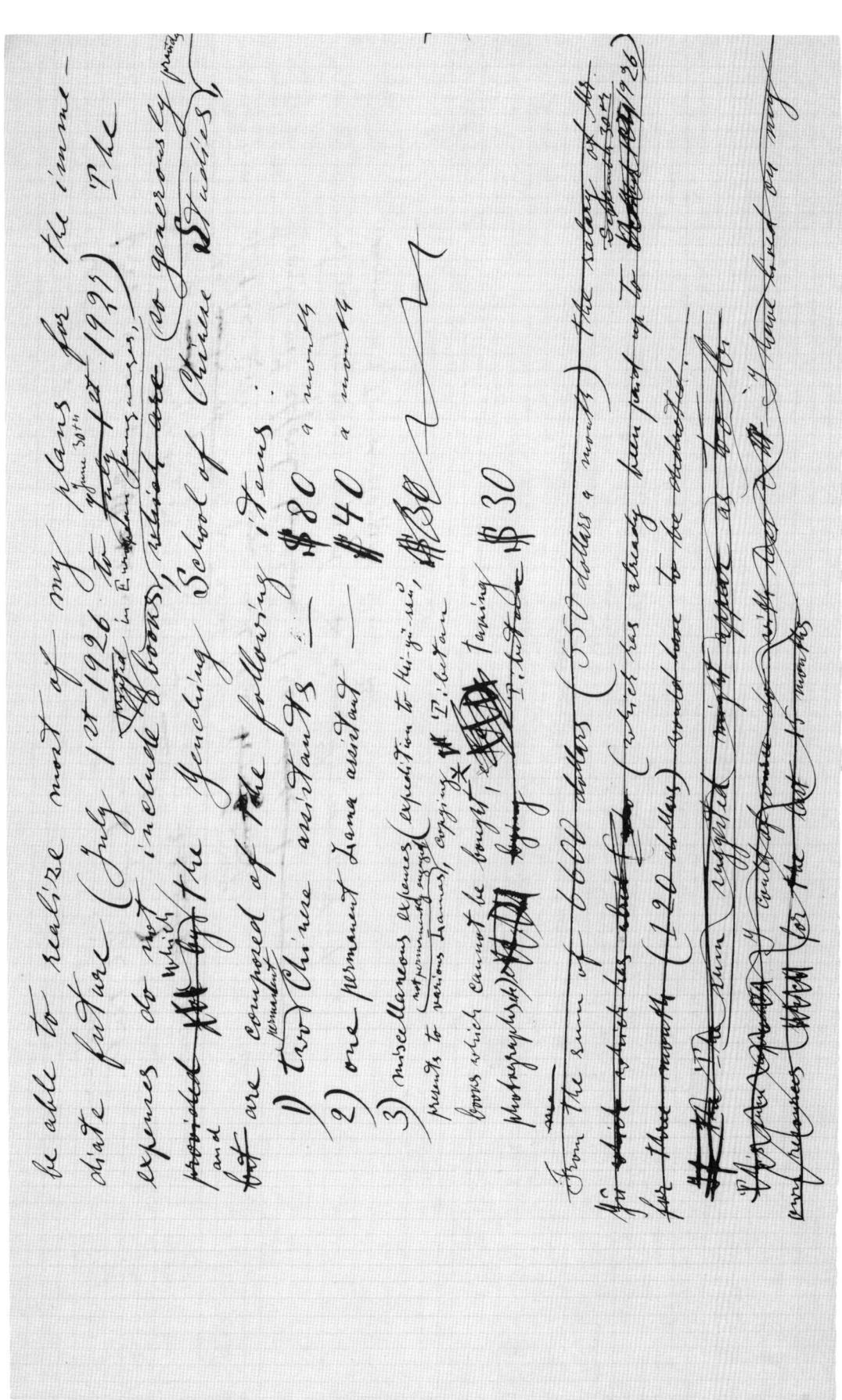

~~This sum I could of course do with less. I have lived on my own resources for the last 15 months~~

The Tibetan dictionaries which have been published so far, are very ~~[illegible]~~ inadequate and parallel texts (the Sanskrit original and the Tibetan translation) have to be ~~[illegible]~~ largely used as dictionaries by those who study religious and philosophical ~~[illegible]~~ books. ~~[illegible]~~ I possess only ~~parts of two~~ parts of the Tibetan translations of the Çikṣāsamuccaya and of the ~~[illegible]~~ Trimśikā ṭīkā, because I could not afford ~~to have~~ having the ~~whole [illegible] entire texts~~ entire translations copied. ~~As a matter of fact the copying had to be stopped when the~~

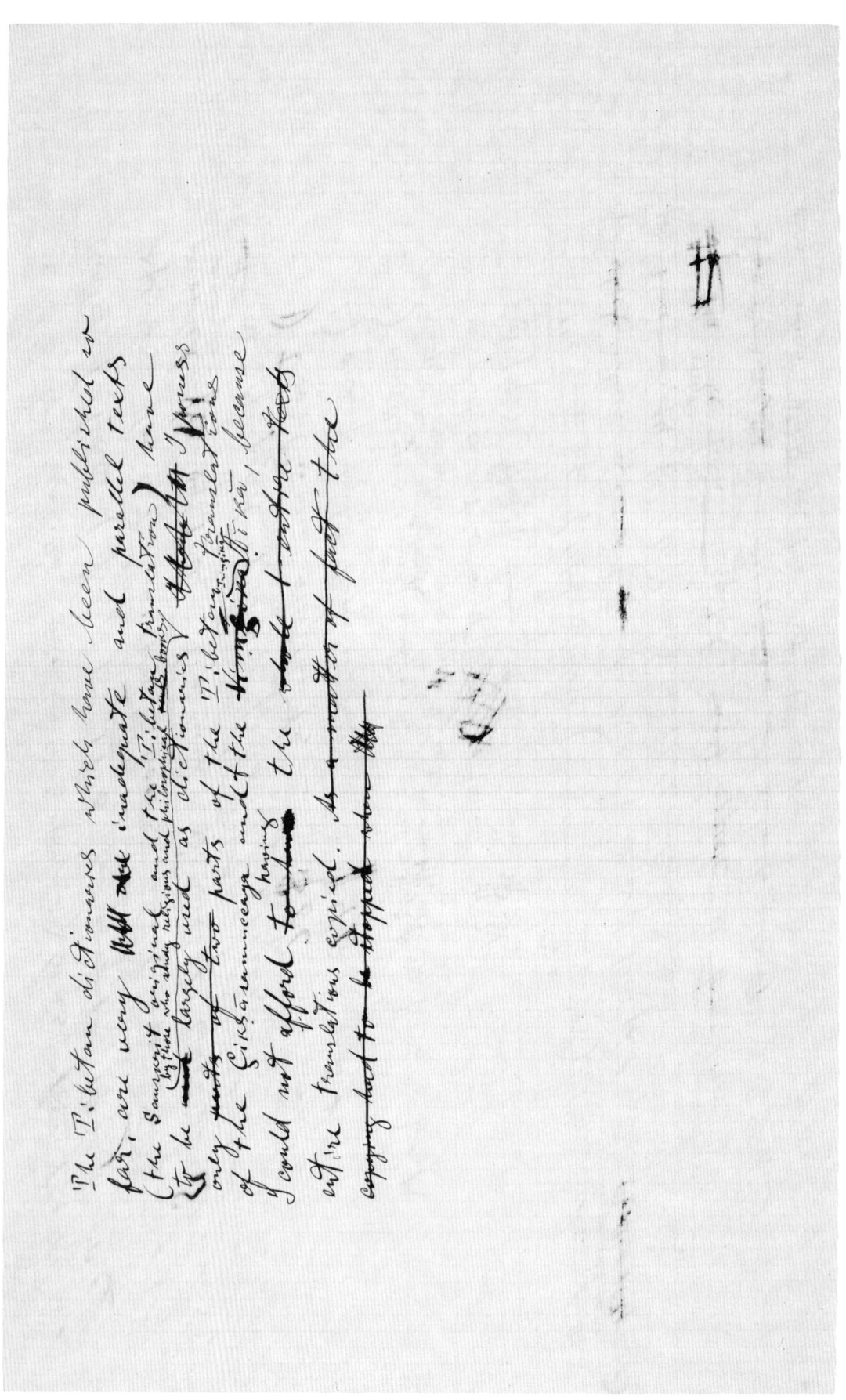

~~In case~~ this sum should be ~~too high, please let me know~~
what ~~is~~ I can get for the year ending on June 30th 1927.
~~I shall then consider what expe~~
This sum represents the minimum on which my establishment
and my work can be carried on for a year without any great discomfort,
but ~~I~~ I shall of course consider a smaller offer, ~~sum if this one should~~ if it should
~~appear as too big.~~ be impossible to let me have the whole amount.
Some ~~[illegible]~~ items could be cut down.

~~The National University (which is supposed to pay me 400 dollars a month and which [illegible] my salary to 500 dollars) has not paid me for 15 months and [illegible]~~ ~~I have practically no income of my own. If I go on using [illegible] what is left and my financial position is far from being satisfactory. I shall therefore have to be satisfied with less than ~~500~~ 400 dollars a month, in case there should be no sufficient funds available. The expenses also might perhaps be curtailed.~~ The second Chinese assistant, for instance, ~~as a second assistant~~ is not absolutely necessary. I thought of engaging ~~H~~ Mr. Chou, a graduate of the philosophical department of the National University, as a second assistant. Mr. Chou has studied Sanskrit for ~~a year~~ some time and is a very bright young man. He intended continuing his Tibet Sanskrit studies, but lately he told me, that he would have to return home and become a middle school teacher ~~for~~ on account of lack of funds. ~~[illegible]~~ I suggest keeping ~~So much for the~~ two Chinese assistants not merely for my own convenience but in the interests of ~~Indian~~ Indo-Tibetan and Indo-Chinese studies in China which ought to be represented by more than one serious indigenous scholar. I had a splendid assistant, who studied with Lessing first and then with me (altogether six or seven years) and who died three years ago. The other advanced students I ~~had~~ taught nearly all had to give up their studies for financial reasons.

Mr. Pankratoff gets his salary from the Wai-chiao-pu and his position is not as bad as mine at present. ~~If a permanent Institute~~ He has helped me a good deal in translating the Tibetan documents for ~~the~~ Mr. Rockhill's biography (not yet out) and in preparing various other papers; ~~he also~~ he comes to see me frequently and we ~~the~~ have spent many hours in comparing the Mongolian ~~version~~ translation of the Kāçyapaparivarta with the other versions. He never got anything from me for all his trouble, except some advice for his Sanskrit, Tibetan and other studies. I told him that, if an Institute should be founded here, he would get all the recommendations that I could give. ~~His salary would have to be added to the sum of 550 dollars a month.~~ It would be ~~a good thing~~ an excellent thing, if the Institute could enable Mr. Pankratoff to give up his ~~job~~ position as a teacher of ~~Russian~~ the Russian language (at the Russian University") and to devote himself entirely to ~~the study of the Mahāyāna~~ scientific work.

~~I think we could do many things~~ better ~~there in Peking which there in than anywhere else, because~~

I think we could do more for the history of the Mahāyāna at Peking than anywhere else. Peking is the only ~~place in the world where~~ great city where three out of the four "Mahāyāna languages" (Sanskrit, Tibetan, Chinese and Mongolian) are represented by permanent residents. We are already in touch with a number of competent Tibetans, Chinese and Mongolians, ~~but we have been prevented from availing ourselves of their services by lack of funds. As soon as we shall be able to pay them, they will, as we know from experience, become much more communicative than they~~ and have availed ourselves of their expert advice from time to time. As soon as ~~we shall~~ a permanent Institute gives us ~~time, security~~ encouragement and financial support we shall be able to do so regularly. ~~That will enable us to compete with those who are engaged in similar work~~

燕京大學
YENCHING UNIVERSITY
(INCORPORATED IN 1889 AS PEKING UNIVERSITY)
PEKING, CHINA.

DEPARTMENT OF PHILOSOPHY

June 18th 1928

Dear Baron Stael Holstein:

I had a good talk with President Stuart. He is much interested in the report I gave of your work and of your plan. He is in sympathy with my plan for securing support to enable you to carry out the plan and will write to America. But he wishes to wait until his return from a week's rest at Peitaiho before giving his final decision, which will be made after consulting with Mr. Pettus and with me once more. We can give the answer before July 2nd. I hope you can wait so much longer. The problem is now simply an adjustment of the proportion of your estimated budget to be carried by the University and this School of Chinese Studies.

I am very glad for my good visits yesterday. Meanwhile I am preparing a statement to the Gugenheim Foundation. President Stuart thinks we should apply there as well as to the other fund.

Very cordially yours,

Lucius C Porter

Juni · Juli 26

My dear Baron,

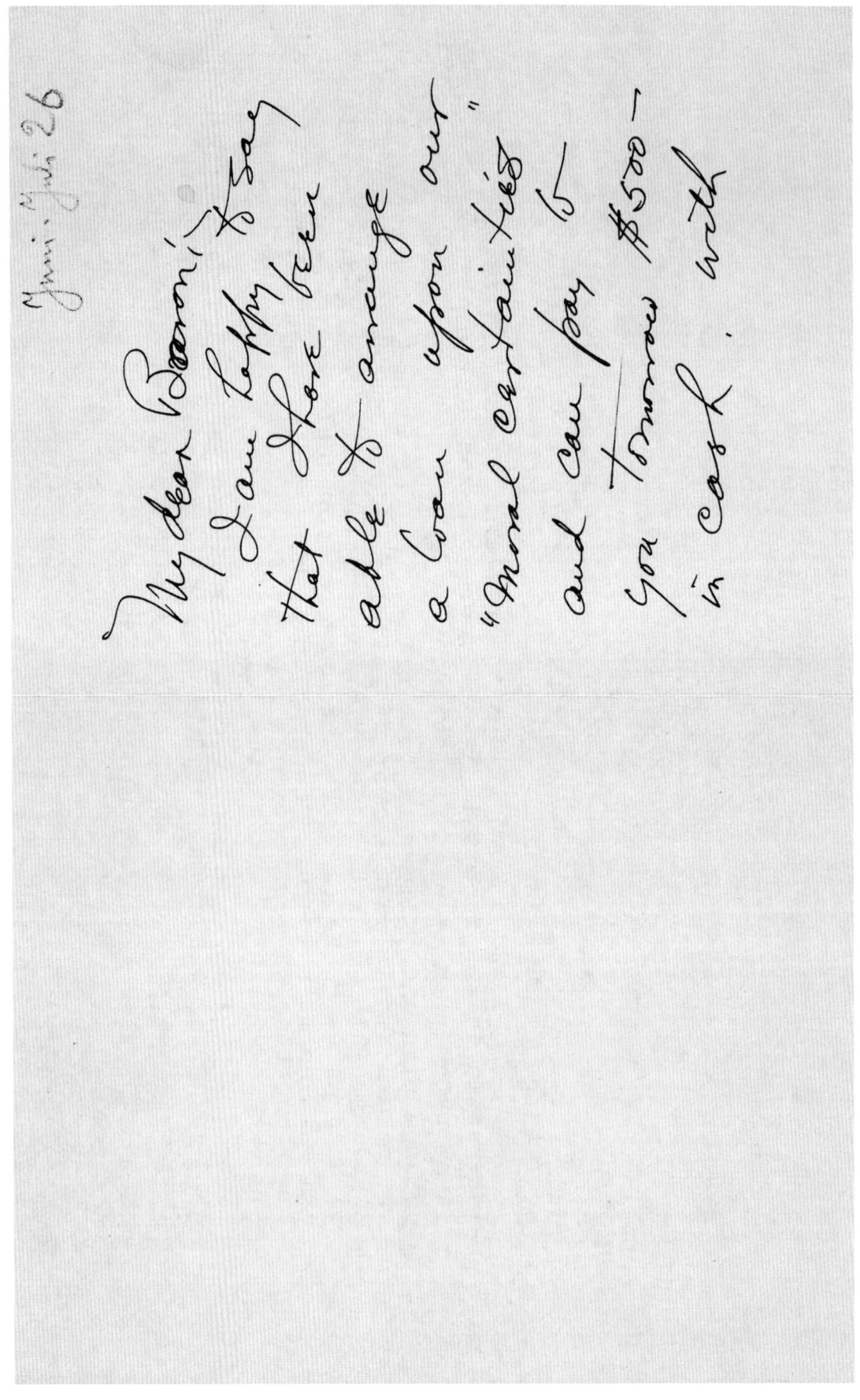

I am happy to say that I have been able to arrange a loan upon our "moral certainties" and can pay to you ~~tomorrow~~ $500— in cash. With

the guarantee of
a similar amount
next month, and
so on for a half-
year - within the
which time the
American funds
should be adjusted
and everything
smooth sailing.

I am very glad
this has been
arranged and
want to share
my pleasure with
you.
I'll see you tomorrow
about 5⁰⁰ pm or
a little after
Sincerely yours
Lucius C Porter

Summer 26

燕京大學

YENCHING UNIVERSITY

(INCORPORATED IN 1889 AS PEKING UNIVERSITY)

PEKING, CHINA.

DEPARTMENT OF PHILOSOPHY

My dear Bonni:

My interview with the Manager of the Kin Hua Press was very satisfactory. He suggested himself that he write asking the Commercial Press to send up the necessary font. I have written Dr Tiong Sec of the Commercial Press. You can read my letter and see what the situation is, and can press the matter by personal persuasion. Best luck to you. The prospects seem favorable.

Heartily yours Lucius Porter

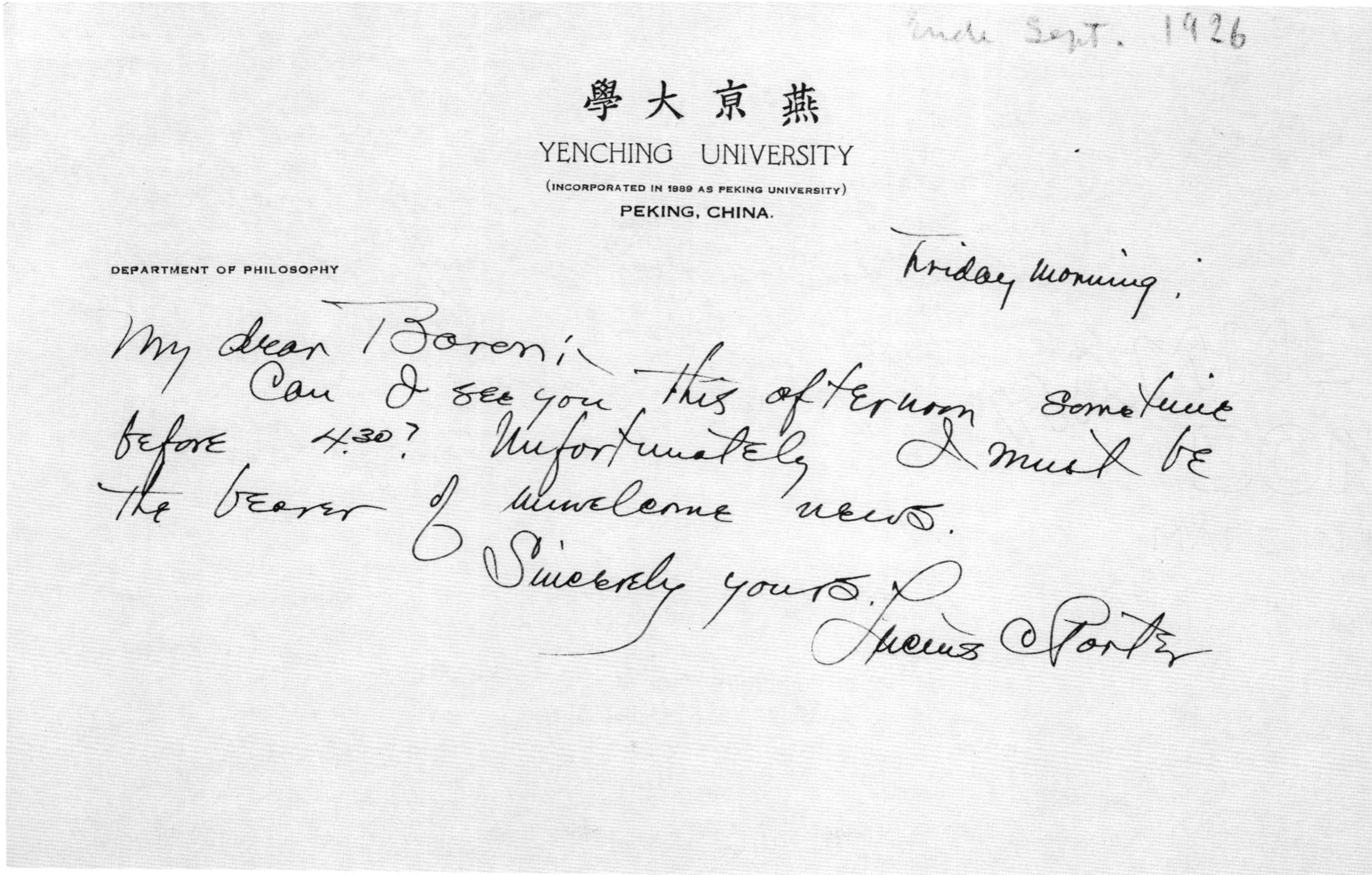

Ende Sept. 1926

燕京大學

YENCHING UNIVERSITY

(INCORPORATED IN 1889 AS PEKING UNIVERSITY)

PEKING, CHINA.

DEPARTMENT OF PHILOSOPHY

Friday morning.

My dear Baron:

Can I see you this afternoon sometime before 4.30? Unfortunately I must be the bearer of unwelcome news.

Sincerely yours,

Lucius C. Porter

燕京大學
YENCHING UNIVERSITY
PEKING, CHINA.

DEPARTMENT OF PHILOSOPHY

September 30th 1926

My dear Baron:—

Herewith a check for One Thousand Dollars local currency ($1000.00) representing payment for August + September on our half-year's plan.

Sincerely yours
Lucius C Porter

YENCHING SCHOOL OF CHINESE STUDIES
PEKING CHINA

October 27, 1926

My dear Baron:

I find that Dr. Houghton is not sufficiently interested in objects of Chinese religious art to make it worthwhile to arrange the trip to your recently discovered temple. I am sorry that it is so. We shall have to look elsewhere for help on the immediate problem.

As to the larger scheme he showed more interest and may help us by writing to America. But any such help is conditioned upon complete silence on our part as to the suggestions which I made on Monday at Madame Lauru's. This is extremely important. Any spread of those suggestions among Peking folk would injure our cause and would wreck our hopes. Anything we do further must be done without any reference to ~~any~~ the possiblity of help from Mr. Rockefeller.

Mr. Bishop and Mr. Langdon Warner seem to be the men to approach first.

I am sorry that I did not make any real progress in furthering the cause of saving those Lama images for science and art.

Very sincerely yours,

Lucius C. Porter

Oct. 29, 26

YENCHING SCHOOL OF CHINESE STUDIES
(LANGUAGE SCHOOL)

DIRECTING BODIES

American Board Mission
American Methodist Mission
American Presbyterian Mission
Church of England Mission
London Missionary Society
Young Men's Christian Association
Young Women's Christian Association
American Legation
American Chamber of Commerce
British Chamber of Commerce
British Legation
Peking Union Medical College
Yenching University

Telephones 1633, 1629, 2959 East
Telegraphic Address "Language Peking"
Codes Used: "Missions" and "C.I.M."

PEKING, CHINA.

October 29th 1926

My dear Baron:—

Herewith the check for October. No prospects as yet for anything after January 1st. I wish I knew where to turn.

Are you busy Saturday afternoon? I have a friend who would like to ask some questions about a few Lama images he has, & who would like to see your collection. If you are not free tomorrow could you name an hour some afternoon next week.

Sincerely yours
L C Porter

Oct 29th 26

燕京大學
YENCHING UNIVERSITY
PEKING, CHINA.

DEPARTMENT OF PHILOSOPHY

My dear Baron:

Since writing this morning something has come up so that I can't bring my friend to your house tomorrow. Can you let me know a convenient hour next week? Preferably some afternoon?

Sincerely yours

Lucius C. Porter

燕京大學

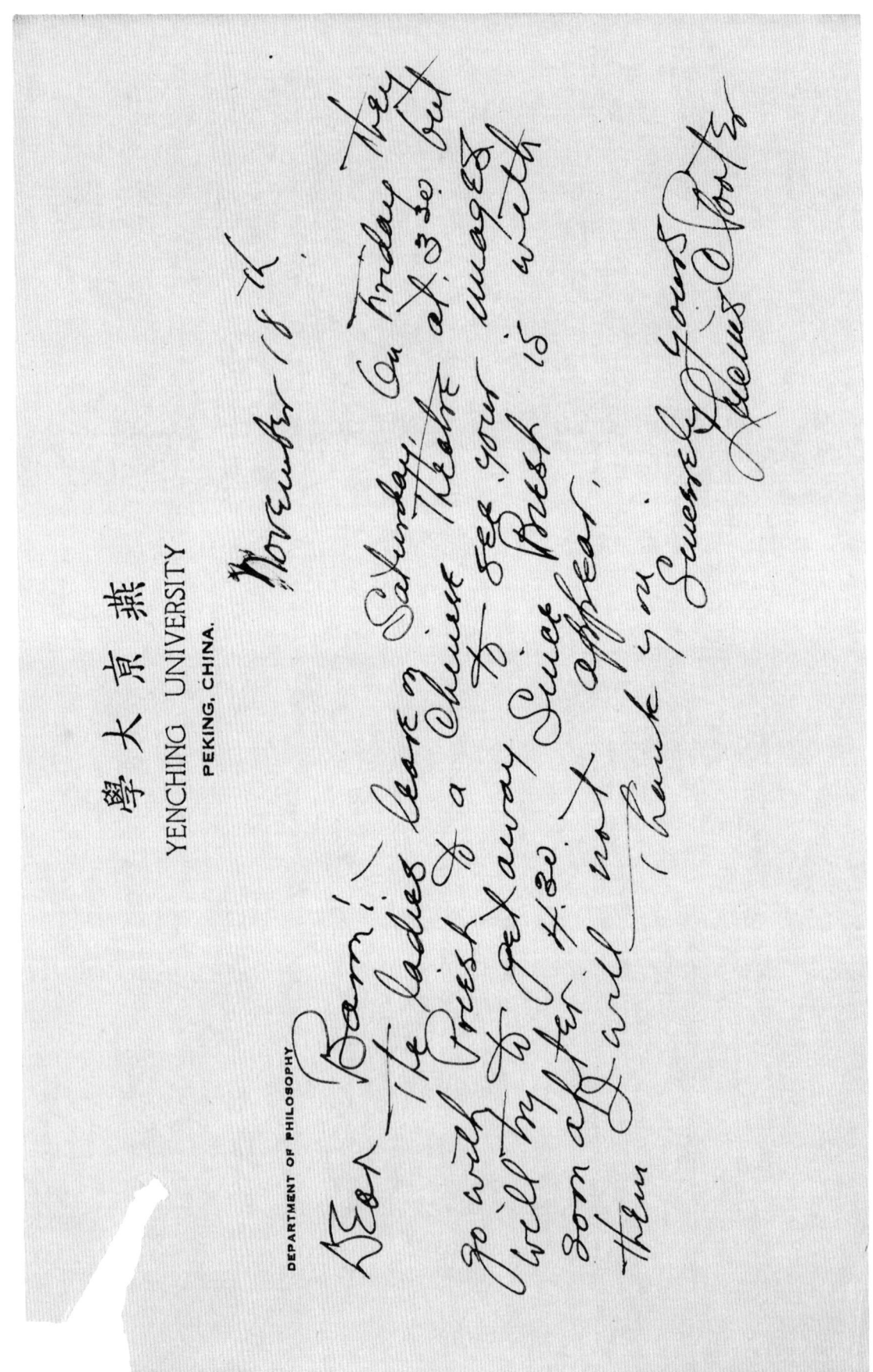

YENCHING UNIVERSITY

PEKING, CHINA.

DEPARTMENT OF PHILOSOPHY

November 18th.

Dear Baron:—

The ladies leave on Saturday. On Friday they go with Priest to a Chinese Theatre at 3:30 but will try to get away to see your images soon after 4:30. Since Priest is with them I will not appear.

Thank you

Sincerely yours

Lucius C Porter

Anf. Nov. 26

YENCHING SCHOOL OF CHINESE STUDIES
PEKING CHINA

Dear Baron:-

Herewith a check for $300= for November.

Our School is giving a tea on Monday (Dec. 6th) at 4.00 to the Charges d'affaires of the Swedish Legation and some other guests. We want you to be present as belonging to our "institute" and I hope you can surely come. I am so glad that Mr. Pettus has agreed to support our appeal to America on your behalf.

Sincerely yours
Lucius C. Porter

Tuesday noon

My dear Dr. Porter,

I have ~~much~~ great pleasure in accepting your kind invitation to tea on Monday December 6th and I thank you ~~from all my heart~~ very much ~~for the financial support which I~~ ~~of limited assistance~~ ~~(the cheque for November and the promise of~~ ~~good~~ ~~even after January 1st) which I owe to your kind offices. All The~~ ~~future~~ ~~outlook of the Sino-Indian Research Institute. It is a great relief to hear that~~ for the favourable news regarding the future of The Sino-Indian Research Institute. I am sure that the unanimity of the ~~decision~~ recommendation ~~it to~~ is due to your good offices and great energy. Even if the recommendation be not acted upon in America, the definite promise of $200 a month after ~~of~~ December 31st will enable me to carry on for some time.

I am also very much obliged to you for the November cheque.

November 26th 1926

Dear Baron:-

I believe Mr. Pettus has told you of his approval of the recommendation of our plan for your budget. That is good so far as it goes. We still have to hear from America.

There is also this good news. that Mr. Pettus and Dr Stuart can accept responsibility in any case for two-hundred dollars per month on your budget

even after January 1st. so
as to keep your work
going until funds come.
We will now try to get
assurances for the balance.
At any rate hopes are
brighter than they were.
I am glad.

Sincerely yours
Lucius C. Porter

Januar 1927

Dear Baron:—

Thank you so much for your card and greeting. I hope that 1927 will see further progress in making possible an enduring foundation for the work we are interested in.

May I use your messenger to send the check for December which I was about to mail?

Sincerely yours

Lucius C Porter

YENCHING SCHOOL OF CHINESE STUDIES
PEKING, CHINA

February 25, 1927

My dear Baron:

Thank you very heartily for the copy of your book. The outward appearance is certainly attractive. Someday I shall look more carefully into the contents. I am very glad that the book has been published.

I enclose your preface sheets with but a few suggestions.

I must see you someday about further publications. Perhaps we can arrange to have your next book appear in the Yenching series, for which the university already has an arrangement with the Commercial Press. I know that President Stuart would be glad to have your work associated with the university and to have the university share in your work. Of course, in the case of this book the prinitng had been begun sometime before we had tried to help you in any way.

Very sincerely yours,

Lucius C. Porter

YENCHING SCHOOL OF CHINESE STUDIES
PEKING, CHINA

April 11, 1927

My dear Baron:

Here is a check for $300.00 from Dr. Stuart. I will do what I can to secure more, but I am not very hopeful. The funds from America have not yet appeared, and New York is anxious about conditions in China. I am sorry that we have not accomplished anything permament for you. But the taking of the pictures preserves somethings of value.

Heartily yours,
Lucius C Porter

My dear Dr. Porter,

~~[illegible]~~ I have written to Messrs. Lévi, Thomas and Konow ~~[illegible]~~ announcing letters from you in which they will be asked for their opinions as to the ~~to recommend~~ ~~the Sino-Indi~~ S. I. Research Institute. ~~[illegible]~~ I enclose letters ~~from all the three~~ from those three scholars ~~[illegible]~~ which show that desirable statements may be expected from them. Please do return the letters to me ~~when you have done wit~~ after perusal. ~~[illegible]~~ I also enclose photographs of the following documents:

1) A letter from the Shih.

2) A ~~letter~~ letter from Ts'ai Yuan P'ei conferring the title of a 導師 upon me.

3) A letter from the President of the Palace ~~[illegible]~~ Committee appointing me a ~~[illegible]~~ 顧問 (at the time, I think, the only foreign one).

4) A letter from the ~~[illegible]~~ appointing me a 會董 (Hui Dung) ~~(I am not quite sure as to~~ the ...

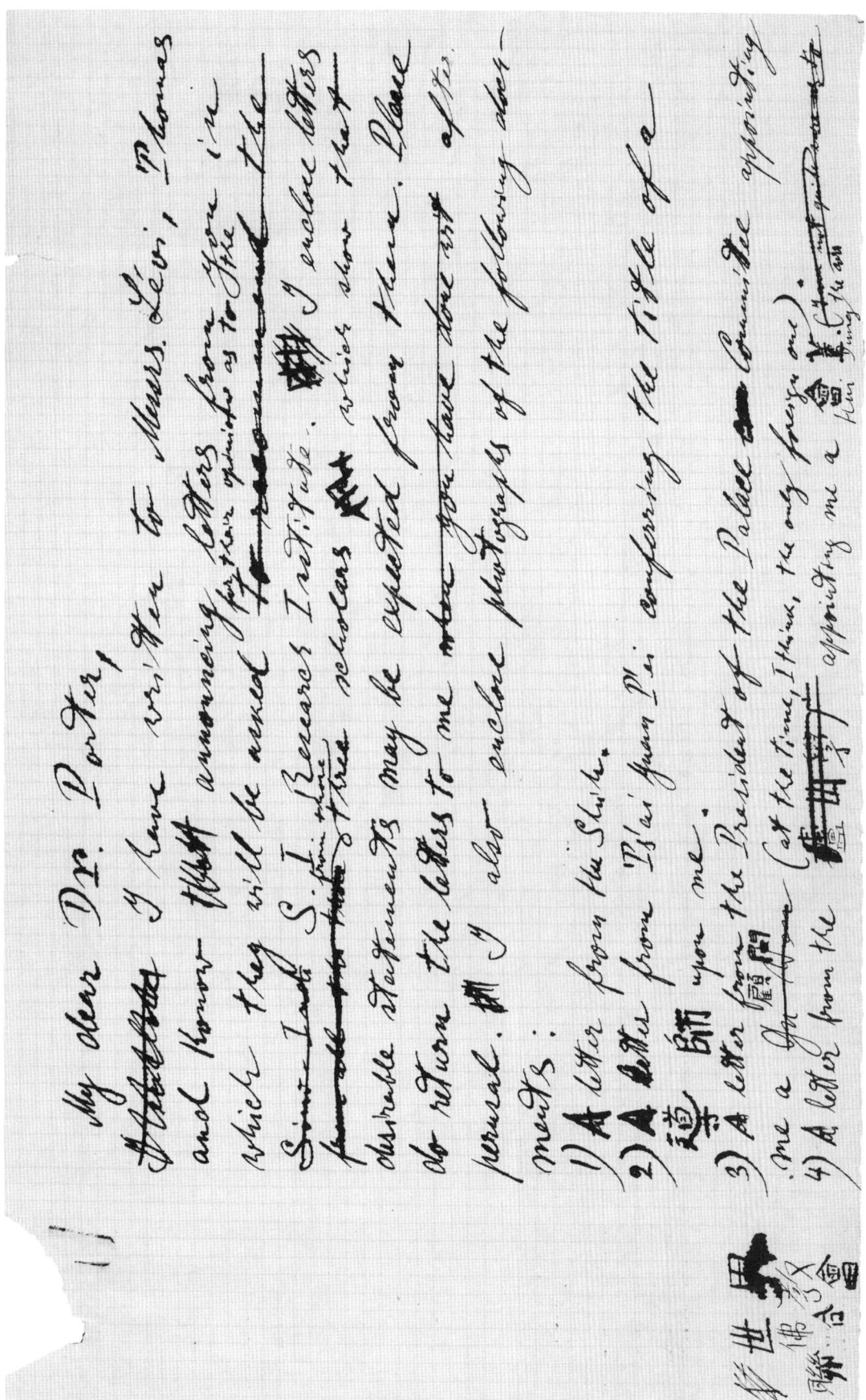

世界佛教聯合會

5) a letter from the 佛化教育社 appointing me a 社董

Monsieur le professeur Sylvain Lévi (c/o the French Embassy Tokyo) is professor of Sanskrit in the Collège de France (Paris) and has been sent to Tokyo temporarily as director of the "Maison Franco-Japonaise". I have ~~still~~ neither accepted nor declined the offer contained in his letter, so far, but ~~if~~ I do, of course, prefer staying here, if I possibly can.

Dr. F. W. Thomas ~~is without doubt certainly the~~ (the Library, India Office, London, England) is the acknowledged leader of all Britisch Sanskritists. He has declined several professorships because he prefers his present ~~post~~ position as chief librarian of the India Office, which pays him more than the Universities are able to offer.

~~Professor~~ Professor Dr. Sten Konow (Etnografisk Museum, Oslo, Norway)
has been Professor of Sanskrit in Hamburg and ~~is~~ now
occupies the same position in the University of Oslo.
He has also been teaching Indian history etc.
in Rabindranath Tagore's University and in
the Government University at Calcutta.

I have been very friendly with the Croziers through a number of years and I believe that they have much influence in Washington. I think they will do everything they can in order to further the aims of the Institute if asked to do so.

Mr. Peck is really the man who first suggested the idea of getting American support for our (Mr. Pamarotoff's and my) endeavours to me. Mme Laura promised to write to him on my behalf last year, but as she did so rather reluctantly I asked her to give it up. I think Mr. Peck is connected with the N. Y. University, who (through Mr. Schurmann) asked me to translate the Tibetan Rockhill documents (which I did).

The only American specialist in my line of studies is Dr. Laufer (a German Jew), no particular friend of mine. He has however written the following phrase (in a letter addressed to Professor Zucker and dated Chicago, August 5, 1925): "I know Baron de Staël-Holstein personally, and have a high regard for him and his work." Nevertheless I do not think that Laufer, who is very jealous, will do anything for an Institute which he might regard as a rival enterprise.

燕京大學

YENCHING UNIVERSITY

(INCORPORATED IN 1889 AS PEKING UNIVERSITY)

PEKING, CHINA

COMMISSION ON STUDIES

April 13, 1928

My dear Baron :

I have spoken to Mr. Hung and others here regarding the points you spoke of the other morning.

As to the funds, our treasurer has been authorized to pay to you the amounts due up to Oct. 1st 1928. That will be the equivalent of gold $ 4,500.00 les the Silver $2,000.00 already paid. We will report to New York that this sum has been paid. There will be Gold $ 1,500.00 for the period Oct. 1 to Dec. 31, 1928. I presume a travel allowance for the journey via the most direct route will be granted , in addition. You might keep an expense account in a general way.

As to the Tibetan volumes Mr. Hung is just now negotiating for a large purchase of Chinese documents. It is probable that he will have a sufficient balance after making this purchase to secure the Tibetan volumes, but he cannot, at the moment, guarantee to reserve the necessary $1500.00. He will know within a few days and will let you know promptly whether or not to purchase.

As to the suggestion that Mr. Ch'en Yin-k'e should go to America Mr. Hung and I feel that it might be a good thing after the general scheme of the Harvard Yenching Institute has been arranged ,but that the present is not the time to add to the group at Harvard. There is no qustion about Mr. Ch'en's superiority as a scholar. He should be associated with our institute. But for the present we need the people who see the plan as a whole and can contribute to the general scheme. Mr. Hung feels that we can make a stronger plea for including Mr. Ch'en ~~Mr. Chin~~ on the staff in China, if we do not have him with us in America this autumn.

You should hear soon from our treasurer. I hope you will let me know as soon as you decide on the time of your departure.

Very sincerely yours,

Lucius C. Porter

My dear Dr. Porter,

Many thanks for your letter and the kind way in which you have solved the financial question.

My plans have been ~~rather~~ entirely upset by a letter just received from Sir Charles Eliot in which he tells me that he has given up his ~~vis~~ planned visit to Peking and that he is leaving for England ~~at almost imme-diately~~ directly. Consequently I am not at all certain about the date of my departure.

~~I am afraid~~ I fear that somebody else might buy the Tibetan volumes and that we might miss the opportunity of ~~of buying the~~ getting a complete Kanjur, which is very rare in these parts. I trust that I will soon hear from you as to the funds available.

~~With many thanks for having dug me~~ Thanking you once more for all your kindness I remain yours sincerely

8 Sherman Hall, April 7th 1929.

40 My dear Dr. Porter, It is you who made something like a golden lily of me, and it is you who brought me to Harvard.

~~I think~~ Therefore I ought to tell you something about what passed at the trustees' meeting between your departure and mine. The Chairman ~~Hyen~~ first asked me to give him a short exposé of my aims. ~~and which I did~~ Then he questioned me about my assistants, about the ownership of the materials ~~collected~~ elaborated by our organization and about some minor matters. Finally he ~~passed to opened~~ inquired as to why I had objected to the committee which included Mmes Frame and Chu. I replied that, as far as I knew, ~~that~~ most members of that committee were not in sympathy with my endeavours and that they altogether cared ~~much more~~ for undergraduate work rather than for research. I pointed out that these matters should be kept apart, and suggested that a committee consisting of your~~self~~, President Stuart, Mr Green, Hu Shih, V. K. Ting and myself should control ~~our~~ the Sino-Indian activities ~~on the spot~~ in Peking.

I hope that I shall have an opportunity of seeing you soon after my return from Washington and that we will reach a complete agreement on all these questions.

Believe me yours sincerely and gratefully

AStaëlHolstein.

燕京大學
YENCHING UNIVERSITY
Peping China

OFFICE OF THE PRESIDENT

TELEGRAPH ADDRESS:
"YENTA"

October 14, 1929.

To Members of the Administrative Committee in Peping
of the Harvard Yenching Institute:

Dear Baron:

Enclosed please find a copy of the minutes of the meeting of the Committee held on October 1st in President Stuart's Office. Also a copy of the Regulations of the Yenching Research School in the amended form as adopted.

Very truly yours,

Lucius C. Porter

Secretary

燕京大學
YENCHING UNIVERSITY
PEIPING WEST, CHINA

Monday Morning

My dear Baron:-
An unexpected opportunity has come to me to make a trip with Prof. George Barbour to P'an Shan, a famous mountain East of Tung Chou. Almost the only time for this trip is on Saturday, Sunday + Monday of this week, namely Nov. 16. 17. 18.
But Mrs Porter + I

have already accepted
the very kind invitation
of the Baroness & yourself
for lunch on Sunday
the 17th I am writing
to ask if you could,
without undue inconvenience
to your own plans,
postpone our coming to
lunch to the following
Sunday or to some
other Sunday. Perhaps
you can telephone to me
so that we can settle the
matter. I know you will
tell me quite frankly
if you cannot easily change
your plans.

Sincerely yours
Lucius Porter

HARVARD-YENCHING INSTITUTE

Yenching University,
Jan. 9th 1930.

My dear Baron:

I have been expecting a note from you on you staff-expenses for the past quarter. The check for Mr. Pakratoff goes direct , and the quarterly payment for " representation" goes to yourself. But we have had no statement regarding the remainder of the office staff. I presume you will do as you did before, send a statement of the accounts for me to analyze, and report to our office for recording, while the office sends you a check for the total amount to be refunded to you. I have arranged a classification of the accounts of the previous quarter so that it will be a simple matter to classify the items for the last quarter.

I trust that all goes well in the New Year with the Baroness and yourself.

Sincerely yours,

My dear Professor, Porter,

I ~~am writing~~ have been asked to write an article for the "Album" which is to be presented to Professor Rapson (Cambridge, England) on the occasion of his jubilee. That article ~~has is keeping~~ (must be ready very soon,
~~me very busy and I hope you will excuse my~~
~~and ... I have been devoting all my free~~
and has kept me ~~very~~ pretty busy these days.

Please excuse me for not thanking you ~~before~~ sooner for ~~the sym-~~
~~pathy which you expressed in the~~ your kind letter ~~which~~ of sympathy.
~~you sent me after my brother-in-law's death. It mo~~
The death of my brother-in-law has made us very sad and we are greatful to all ~~those~~ our friends who mourn with us.

My statement of account is not quite ready yet, but will be sent to you as soon as possible.

The representation cheque has been received here with many thanks.

With very kind regards from us both to you and to Mrs. Porter I remain
yours sincerely A. Staël-Holstein.

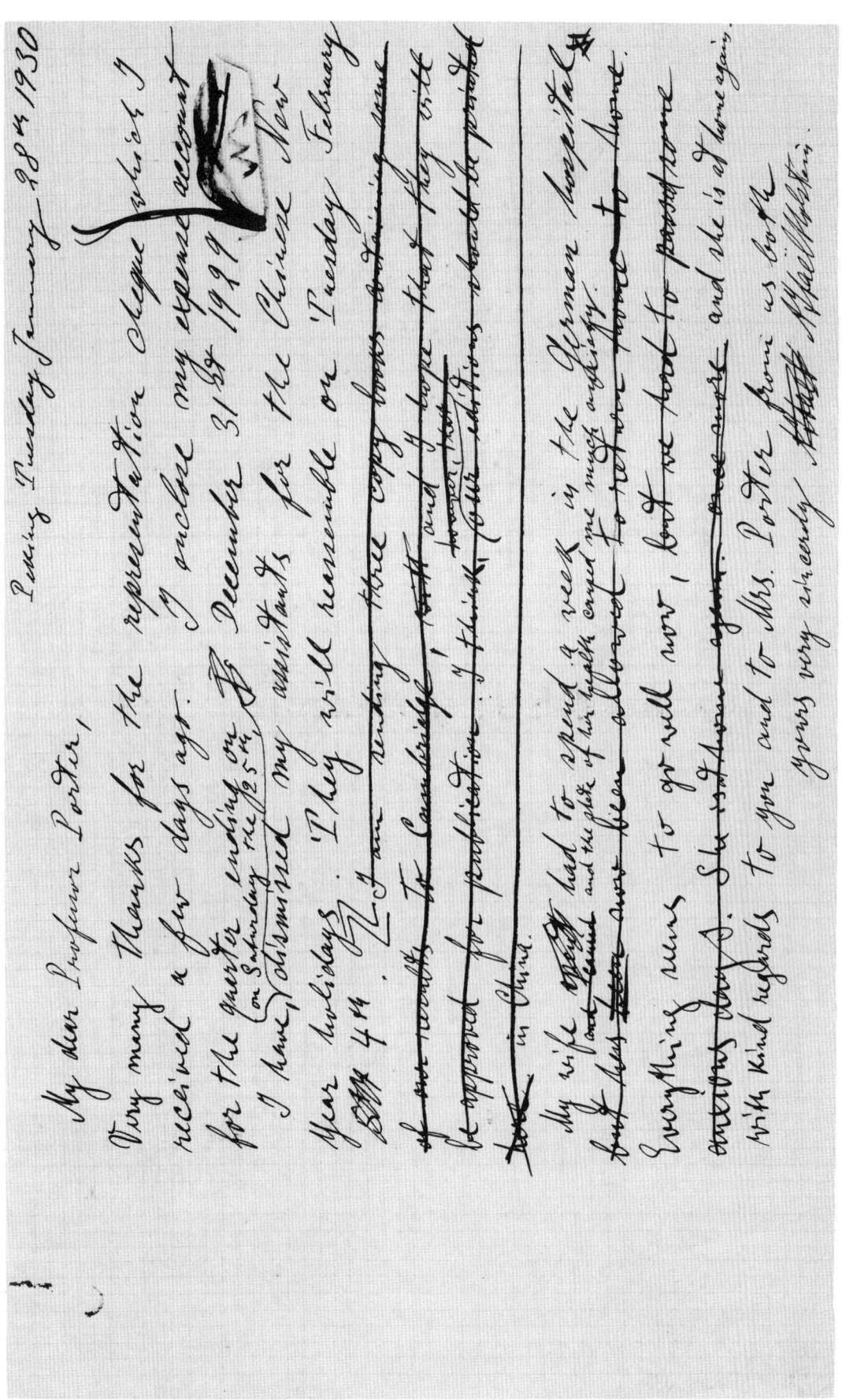

Peking Tuesday January 28th 1930

My dear Professor Porter,

Very many thanks for the representation cheque which I received a few days ago. I enclose my expense account for the quarter ending on December 31st 1929.

I have, on Saturday the 25th, dismissed my assistants for the Chinese New Year holidays. They will reassemble on Tuesday February 4th. ~~I am sending three copy books containing some of our results to Cambridge, and I hope that they will be approved for publication. I think, however, that our editions should be printed here~~ in China.

My wife had to spend a week in the German hospital and the state of her health caused me much anxiety. ~~but has now been allowed to return to home.~~ Everything seems to go well now, ~~but we had to pass some anxious days. She is at home again. once more~~ and she is at home again.

With kind regards to you and to Mrs. Porter from us both

Yours very sincerely ~~A Staël~~ A Staël Holstein.

~~The only Two names occur in the~~
~~Of the names mentioned~~ All the names which occur
in my account for the D quarter ~~are know~~ also occur in
~~the~~ [my] account for the C quarter, except two: Lama Blo
Bzan-sbyin-pa, and Mr. 于 Yü [illegible]. The latter is already known
to you, and his full ~~Chinese~~ name is: 于道泉. He
is an old pupil of mine who ~~owes his~~ [owes much gratitude] ~~is very much obliged~~
to you and to Yenching University for a subsidy which you granted
him years ago. If it had not been for your kind assistance he
would have had to abandon his career as an ~~Indo-Tibetan~~ [Orientalist]
scholar. His main occupation now is: looking after the
Tibetan, Mongolian and Manchurian books in the Metropolitan
Library. If it had not been for Yü* and your assistance no Tibetan
etc. books would form part of that library. Blo-bzan-sbyin-pa
has helped me much in studying the Tibetan texts of the
Vajracchedikā.

Peking April 25th 1930

My dear Professor Porter,

~~Kindly~~ Will you kindly ~~excuse my~~ forgive me for delaying the expense account for such a long time? ~~I did not send you~~ Preparing these accounts is not quite as easy as one might think, because I am buying books in different countries. ~~it to you earlier because I could not get certain receipts from the book sellers.~~ I have had to pay for some books out of my own pocket, because the Japanese book sellers failed to send me any receipts at all for books which they ~~sent me~~ forwarded C. O. D. ~~One~~ The two receipts which I did get from Japan (30A20 and 30A21) during the quarter ending on March 31st 1930 reached me in January 1930 though ~~has no date and one is not dated and another one~~ (30A19) ~~has been~~ issued in December 1929. Please excuse these shortcomings, and believe

~~With kind regards to you and to M~~

~~Believe~~ me yours sincerely

Staël Holstein.

14
5
70

HARVARD-YENCHING INSTITUTE
Yenching University, Peiping

Research School of Chinese Studies

June 6, 1930.

Baron A. von Stael-Holstein,
Austrian Legation,
Peiping.

My dear Baron:-

I am not sure that I told you of my plan to make a quick trip to America this summer. I expect to be back in September, but will leave on the 21st of June. I want to make arrangements for the payments that will be needed for your work at the end of this quarter. Would it be possible for you to make an estimate of your account, so that I can authorize a payment sufficient to cover it before I leave?

I have received word from Dean Chase that an appropriation has been made by the Harvard-Yenching trustees for your work on the same basis as that which was made for the current year, with the understanding that the payments will be made as they have been this year, by arrangements between you and me. I hope this will be satisfactory to you.

There is another matter in relation to which we would like to have your help. You probably know of the Yenching Journal of Chinese Studies, which our Research School here publishes. Our director, Mr. Ch'en Yuan, is very anxious to introduce this journal more fully to various sinological circles in Europe and abroad. He feels that you could be of very great value to us in assisting in this matter. We should want the journal criticized as frankly as any such journal should be, for what are regarded as its errors and mistakes, and are eager to have it become more of a medium for the exchange of opinion between Western and Chinese students in the field of Chinese culture. Mr. Ch'en feels that it would be a great help if you could furnish an article to be published in our journal, and could assume the same relationship to this journal which you once held in relation to the journal published by the National Peking University, and known as the Kuo Hsueh Che Kan. I believe you were an honorary editor of that journal, and we would be glad to have your name appear as such an editor in our journal, if you are willing to allow us the privilege. We shall be very glad to have your suggestions as to the best ways in which to introduce our journal to European students of sinology. Could you prepare a list of persons and institutions to which you think it should be sent?

Baron A. von Stael-Holstein,
Page 2.

June 6, 1930.

I shall try to see you before I get away, so as to talk over this matter with some others.

With very best wishes to you and the Baroness,

Sincerely yours,

LCP:B

Peking June 6th 1930.

My dear Professor Porter,

I am very proud to hear that you will make me an honorary editor of the Yenching Journal. I do, ~~ace~~ of course, accept the position with many thanks. I ~~will~~ also hope to be able to write an article for the Journall and will suggest the names of a number of European scholars ~~who would be grateful~~ to whom ~~the~~ copies should be sent.

Will you and Mrs. Porter come and dine with ~~us~~ us quietly (lounge suit) on Friday or on Saturday. ~~20 or on Sunday~~ We could then discuss the estimates.

Believe me yours sincerely A. Staël-Holstein.

I went to see you with Dr. Diez, ~~[illegible]~~ a professor of the history of fine arts who is travelling round the world on a H. Y. scholarship, on Sunday. I also tried to 'phone you this morning.

HARVARD-YENCHING INSTITUTE
Yenching University, Peiping

October 22, 1930.

Baron A. von Stael Holstein,
%Austrian Legation,
Legation Quarters,
Peiping.

My dear Baron:-

Mrs. Porter and I are looking forward to lunching with you and the Baroness on Sunday, the 2nd of November, as we arranged. Before I see you then, there is a little matter I wish to inquire about. I heard from Mr. Schuster that you have not received your salary checks regularly from the purser at Harvard University. Mr. Biggerstaff and Mr. Schuster likewise have failed to receive their regular July payments. I am preparing a cable to Dean Chase regarding this matter and wish to have exact information about yourself for I can include your name in the cable if it is true that the purser has neglected you. Will you send me a line regarding this matter?

I presume you are preparing the report I mentioned the last time I saw you regarding your expenditures for the current quarter, for I wish to make sure that the proper check is sent you at the end of this month.

One other problem needs to be considered. Dr. G. Ecke, as you know, has done much workin the study of pagodas near Amoy. The Publication Committee of the Harvard-Yenching trustees have agreed to publish his work and have made a considerable grant for that purpose. We have not, however, received any definite word from Cambridge regarding plans for the publication so Dr. Ecke and I are making some preliminary studies ourselves. In the meantime, Dr. Ecke is very desirous of being reimbursed for a part of the expenses he has himself met in connection with his research. Since the proper authorization has been given, already, I am sure that these funds will be available on short notice. But Dr. Ecke is in real need at the present moment. I am wondering if it would be possible for you to draw on the funds at your disposal for either a sum of $2000 silver or for the equivalent in silver of $1000 Gold, which I could pay to Dr. Ecke at once. I could give you a note for this amount and re-pay your funds as soon as money is sent out specifically for Dr. Ecke from Cambridge. This arrangement, if you are willing to make it, would be a great accommodation to Dr. Ecke and would involve no loss to yourself. Will you consider it and if possible, send a

Baron A. von Stael Holstein
Page 2.

October 22, 1930.

favorable reply. I know you are much interested in Dr.Ecke's work, and Dr. D. E. Mie's.

Anticipating the pleasure of seeing you and the Baroness soon, I am

Very sincerely yours,

Lucius C Porter

LCP:B

Tuesday Oct. 28th 1930.

My dear Professor Porter,

~~A year ago Dr. Ecke suggested ~~to me~~ that the H. Y. Institute should be asked~~ to pay for the ~~besides paying for the~~ printing of his book, ~~and also should also be asked to pay his preliminary I introduced him to Professor Woods when I introduced him to Professor Woods I never mentioned~~

About a year ago I introduced Dr. Ecke to Professor Woods, and told the latter that the H. Y. Institute would be asked to pay for the printing of the ~~book on~~ pagoda book.

~~I never mentioned When Dr. Ecke met mentioned the fact that he had spent a considerable sum for had a great deal of out-of-pocket~~ At the same time Dr. Ecke ~~mentioned~~ told me that he wished to ask the Institute to repay his preliminary expenses in addition to the ~~printing~~ cost of printing, ~~and I strongly as which I considered highly inadvisable. I~~ upon which I strongly advised him not to do so. When Dr. Ecke came to see me last Saturday I reminded him of last year's conversation, and ~~told him that I could~~ ~~he seemed to understand that I could not do anything for him in that matter. I advised him to apply to Cambridge directly in that~~ ~~told him that I would observe a benevolent~~ neutrality ~~in the~~ ~~told him that he~~ he seemed to understand that I could not do anything for him in that matter ~~not~~ at the present moment. ~~except preserving a~~

I hope that my accounts will be ready on Sunday Nov. 2nd.

~~My wife~~ We both look forward very much to seeing you and Mrs. Porter on that day at 1 o'clock.

Believe me yours sincerely

AStaëlHolstein.

~~P. S. I promised Dr. Ecke to observe a benevolent neutrality, in case anyone should ask for my~~

Peking October 30th 1930.

My dear Professor Porter,

At the time of ~~Before~~ your departure for ~~to~~ America in June 1930 I received nine thousand six hundred Mexican dollars ($Mex. 9600.00) from the Yenching treasurer. ~~One thousand~~ $Mex. 1000.00 were due to me on account of ~~for~~ representation (30B quarter), and the remaining $Mex. 8600.00 are accounted for ~~on~~ in ~~the~~ the book ~~the sheet~~ marked B which I enclose.

The ~~sheet marked~~ book marked C gives an account of the sums ($Mex. 3144.28) advanced by myself during the quarter ending on Sept. 30th 1930. ~~In addition to~~ In addition to those $Mex. 3144.28 I hope to get ~~receive~~ $Mex. 1000.00 (repr. 30C quarter) from the Yenching treasurer —— altogether $Mex. 4144.28.

Believe me yours sincerely

AStaëlHolstein.

Auf Wiedersehen Sonntag um 1 Uhr!

HARVARD-YENCHING INSTITUTE

ADMINISTRATIVE COMMITTEE IN PEIPING
OFFICE OF THE EXECUTIVE SECRETARY

YENCHING UNIVERSITY
PEIPING, WEST

January 19, 1931.

Baron A. von Stael Holstein,
% Austrian Legation,
Peiping.

My dear Baron:-

I very much hope that your little boy is much improved and has recovered from his illness.

I should be glad to send you a check for your expenses for the last quarter whenever you have time to send in a memorandum of the amount necessary. I meant to speak of this the last time I saw you. Probably your anxiety of thelast few weeks has prevented you from preparing the usual statement. There is no hurry from my point of view, but I do not wish you to feel that we have been negligent in any way.

Please present my compliments to the Baroness.

Very sincerely yours,
Lucius C. Porter

LCP:B

Peking Jan. 22nd 1931

My dear Professor Porter,

Many thanks for your kind note. ~~I send you herewith my quarterly account~~ Our little boy has returned from the hospital, and everybody seems to be well at last.

~~Please excuse the delay. I enclose my statement of account~~

With my apologies for the delay I now enclose my account. ~~May I ask Dean Chase writes in~~ In Dean Chase's letter dated Dec 12th 1930 the following passage occurs:

He [Mr. Garside] had, as you wrote, listed your balance of $ 901.53 as one which was not to be carried over. The Trustees changed the report, adding this sum to the balance to be transferred to this year's accounts."

I wonder whether the sum mentioned has actually been transferred to this (1930/31) year's account. May I ask you to let me know ~~about~~ that?

Believe me yours sincerely

AStaëlHolstein.

HARVARD-YENCHING INSTITUTE

ADMINISTRATIVE COMMITTEE IN PEIPING
OFFICE OF THE EXECUTIVE SECRETARY

YENCHING UNIVERSITY
PEIPING, WEST

January 26, 1931.

Baron A. von Stael-Holstein,
Austrian Legation,
Peiping.

My dear Baron:-

Thanks for your note together with the statement of accounts for the last quarter. I am asking our Treasurer to send you a check for the amount indicated, namely, Mex $5952.22.

I also have heard from Dean Chase reporting that at the last meeting of the Harvard-Yenching Institute trustees, the balance on your last year's account was ordered transferred to this year's account. My understanding is that this transfer has been made and has been reported to our Treasurer.

Are you planning to order a photo-stat machine? I remember you have talked about it in the past. Our group here is also considering the matter and I still have a feeling there would be an advantage if we could cooperate and avoid the expense of getting two machines.

Recently we have had a letter from the Chinese
× National Academy of Research, asking about the work conducted by your Sino-Indian Institute. I have in mind to prepare a brief memorandum indicating in outline numbers of the staff you employ and the nature of the work you are doing. I should like very much to have a draft of such report from you if you would like to send one. I remember you have been rather reluctant about giving information regarding your work less there might be interference from Chinese authorities. Now that they have sent a formal request to us, I feel that something will have to be said. Could you let me have a line by early mail?

Sincerely yours,
Lucius C. Porter

LCP:B

× P.S. Perhaps it would be better to refer this letter of inquiry directly to you for reply. We at Yenching do not wish to assume any formal relation to or connection with your work. LCPorter

HARVARD-YENCHING INSTITUTE

ADMINISTRATIVE COMMITTEE IN PEIPING
OFFICE OF THE EXECUTIVE SECRETARY

YENCHING UNIVERSITY
PEIPING, WEST

January 30, 1931.

Baron A. von Stael-Holstein,
Austrian Legation,
Peiping.

My dear Baron:-

Herewith the letter from the Central Research Institute with the questions regarding the work of your Sino-Indian Institute. I should be glad to have you answer directly to the members of the Central Institute whom you know, the questions which they ask. You will please tell them that the letter they sent was handed to you for reply. I am sure that you will be able to adjust matters with them to their satisfaction as well as your own.

Very sincerely yours,

Lucius C. Porter

LCP:B

My dear Professor Porter,

~~Our meeti~~ Many thanks for ~~your note and for the original~~ sending me ~~[illegible]~~ Mr. Fu Ssŭ Nien's letter. I ~~could~~ not dis-cuss it ~~last Saturday~~ last Saturday with Mr. Tschen Yin Koh, because ~~his wife~~ he did not appear at our meeting. His wife had fallen ~~Mr. Tschen's wife~~ ill and he had to take her to the P.U.M.C. I hope to see Mr. Tschen next Saturday and after ~~having~~ shown him the letter I shall ~~immediately~~ return it to you. ~~I shall ask~~ We shall prepare a detailed statement of ~~[illegible]~~ our work, but we shall have very little to say as to our nameless organization ~~which, [illegible] fortunately, does not even possess an officially recognized name~~. Some of our friends call it the "Sino-Indian Institute", others the ~~"Associati "Buddhist History Ass~~ "Association for the study of Buddhist History" etc., but ~~all the letters I receive from~~ none of those names has been officially recognized in America or in China. ~~I [illegible] I [illegible] [illegible]~~ You will have noticed that ~~[illegible]~~ I mention Sino-Indian expenses but never any ~~the~~ Sino-Indian Institute in my statements of account. ~~[illegible] I [illegible] You will have noticed that I never I use the expression~~

~~In case we mentioned a high sounding title like "Sino-Indian I think~~ I think our namelessness is ~~an~~ a great asset, which should be maintained.
~~Sino-Indian expenses. I have never used that the expense~~ ~~As soon~~
~~During the last two years,~~
~~I have carefully abstained from using any such expression in my correspondence~~
~~during the last two years in order to discourage avoid~~ ~~publicity~~ As soon as we assume
~~official interference.~~ ~~I am very glad that this should be so, because if we had~~ a high sounding name we ~~should~~ might be constantly bothered by official inquiries.

~~I shall~~ I shall of course inform the Ac. Sin. that we work on behalf, and at the expense, of the Harvard-Yenching Institute.

~~B B~~ With many thanks for ~~having sent me~~ the cheque and for the letter I remain yours sincerely

A Staël Holstein.

HARVARD-YENCHING INSTITUTE

April 15, 1931.

Baron A. von Stael-Holstein,
Ex-Austrian Legation,
Peiping.

My dear Baron:-

Thanks for your statement of account with vouchers for your expenditures for the quarter ending March 31st. I have asked the Yenching Treasurer to send you the check for the amount, which I hope you will receive in due time.

Please give my compliments to the Baroness, and believe me

Very cordially yours,

Lucius C Porter

LCP:MB

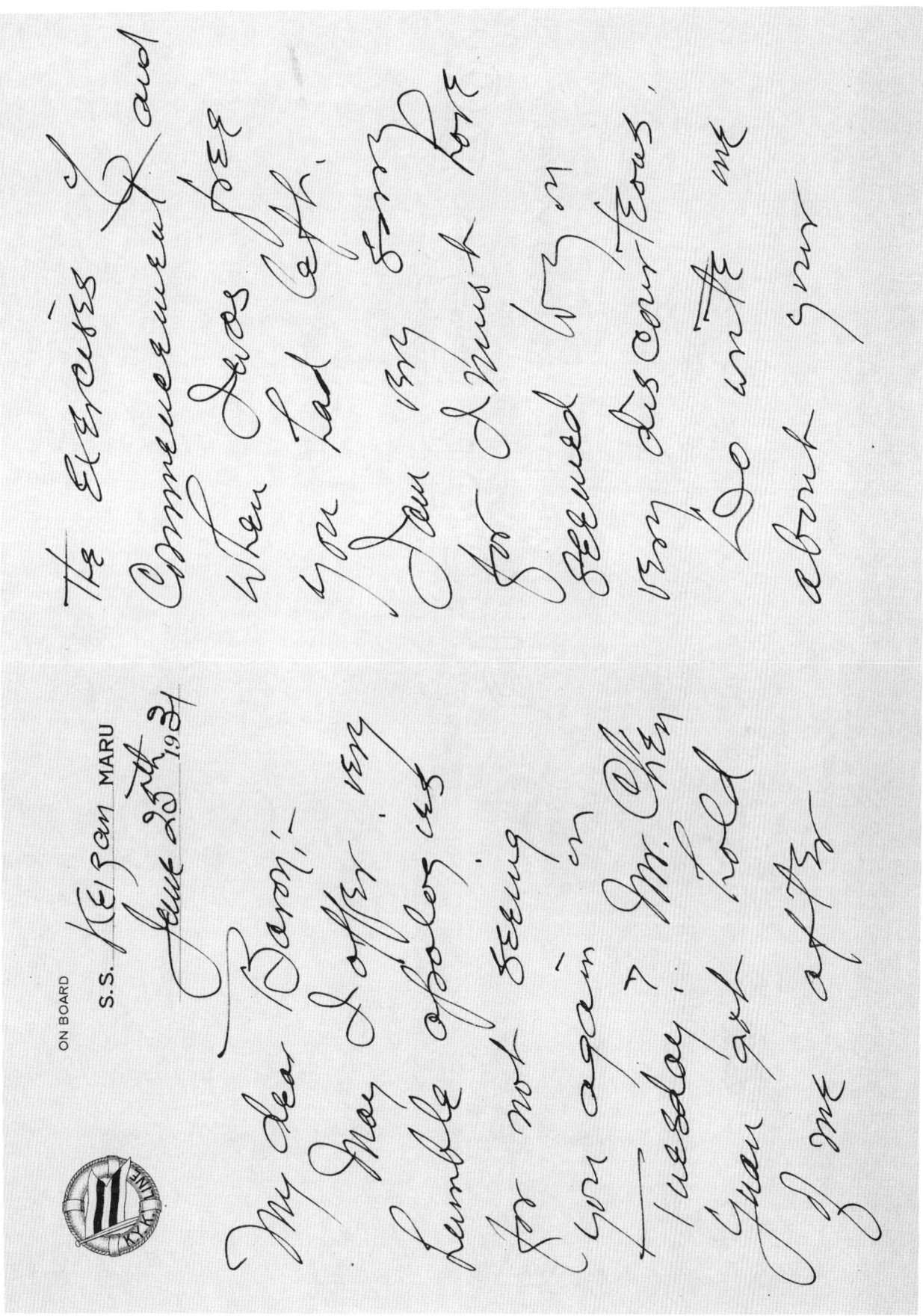

ON BOARD
S.S. Keizan MARU
June 25th 1931

My dear Baron:-
May I offer very humble apologies for not seeing you again on Tuesday? Mr. Chen Yuan got hold of me after the exercises of Commencement and when I was free you had left. I am very sorry for I must have seemed to you very discourteous.
Do write me about your

Manuscripts.

I hope all we be well with you through the year.

My compliments to the Baroness

Auf Wiedersehen

Lucius C. Porter

HARVARD-YENCHING INSTITUTE
哈 佛 燕 京 學 社

OFFICE OF THE EXECUTIVE SECRETARY
幹 事 辦 公 處

PEIPING OFFICE
北 平 辦 公 處
YENCHING UNIVERSITY
燕 京 大 學
PEIPING, WEST
北 平 西 郊

January 7, 1932.

Baron A. von Stael-Holstein,
Austrian Legation.

My dear Baron:

I write to inform you that the trustees of the Harvard-Yenching Institute at their meeting of November 14, 1932 voted the amount of L.C.$2,200 to reimburse you for the purchase of the Thibetan Kanjur. This amount has been credited to your fund by our treasurer and you may draw upon it when you desire.

I hope you received duly the check for $8094.12 sent you on December 29. I believe our treasurer has not yet received the voucher for the same.

With warm regards,

Very sincerely yours,

Lucius C. Porter

Lucius C. Porter

HARVARD-YENCHING INSTITUTE

哈 佛 燕 京 學 社

OFFICE OF THE EXECUTIVE SECRETARY
幹 事 辦 公 處

PEIPING OFFICE
北 平 辦 公 處
YENCHING UNIVERSITY
燕 京 大 學
PEIPING, WEST
北 平 西 郊

December 19, 1932.

Baron A. von Stael-Holstein,
Austrian Legation,
Peiping.

My dear Baron:

I have had a talk with Professor Ku the editor of our Yenching Journal and he bids me tell you that he will be very happy to have an article from you for some future number of the journal. He accedes to your suggestion that you get the article printed under your care at the Pei T'ang press. We will meet the expenses of the printing and will allow you 200 copies of reprints. As you have our journal you know the size of page and of print to be followed. We shall need 1,000 copies for our edition.

I will send you later a copy of the mailing list used for our journal for European correspondence which you indicated you would be good enough to check over and supplement for us.

With best wishes,

Very sincerely yours,

Lucius C. Porter

Lucius C. Porter

P.S. Prof. Ku will be glad to have you write in German if you so prefer. L.C.P.

HARVARD-YENCHING INSTITUTE
哈 佛 燕 京 學 社

OFFICE OF THE EXECUTIVE SECRETARY
幹 事 辦 公 處

PEIPING OFFICE
北 平 辦 公 處
YENCHING UNIVERSITY
燕 京 大 學
PEIPING, WEST
北 平 西 郊

Friday, December 30, 1932.

Baron von Stael-Holstein,
Austrian Legation.

My dear Baron:

In response to your note of the 26th, I am forwarding a check for your half year payment which I hope will reach you duly. You may return the receipt directly to our treasurer.

Thank you very much for your Christmas greetings and the article on the ancestry of the Thibetan Lama. I am very glad to have at hand the history of the very interesting figures in your picture which I have long admired. Mrs. Porter joins me in very warm good wishes for a happy New Year to the Baroness, your children and to you.

Very sincerely yours,

Lucius C. Porter

Lucius C. Porter

My dear Mr.

Let me wish you a ~~[illegible]~~ merry Christmas now! ~~and a happy new year. I shall be able to~~ I look forward very much to wishing you a happy new year personally at your dinner party on the 29th.

My dear Dr. Porter,

Let me wish you and your family a very merry Christmas!

I shall be so pleased if you and Mrs. Porter will come and have lunch at my house on Thursday December 29th at one o'clock. ~~If you could~~ Could you not bring ~~Mr~~ Mr. Hsü, the Sanscritist, with you? I want very much to get into touch with him.

Believe me yours sincerely

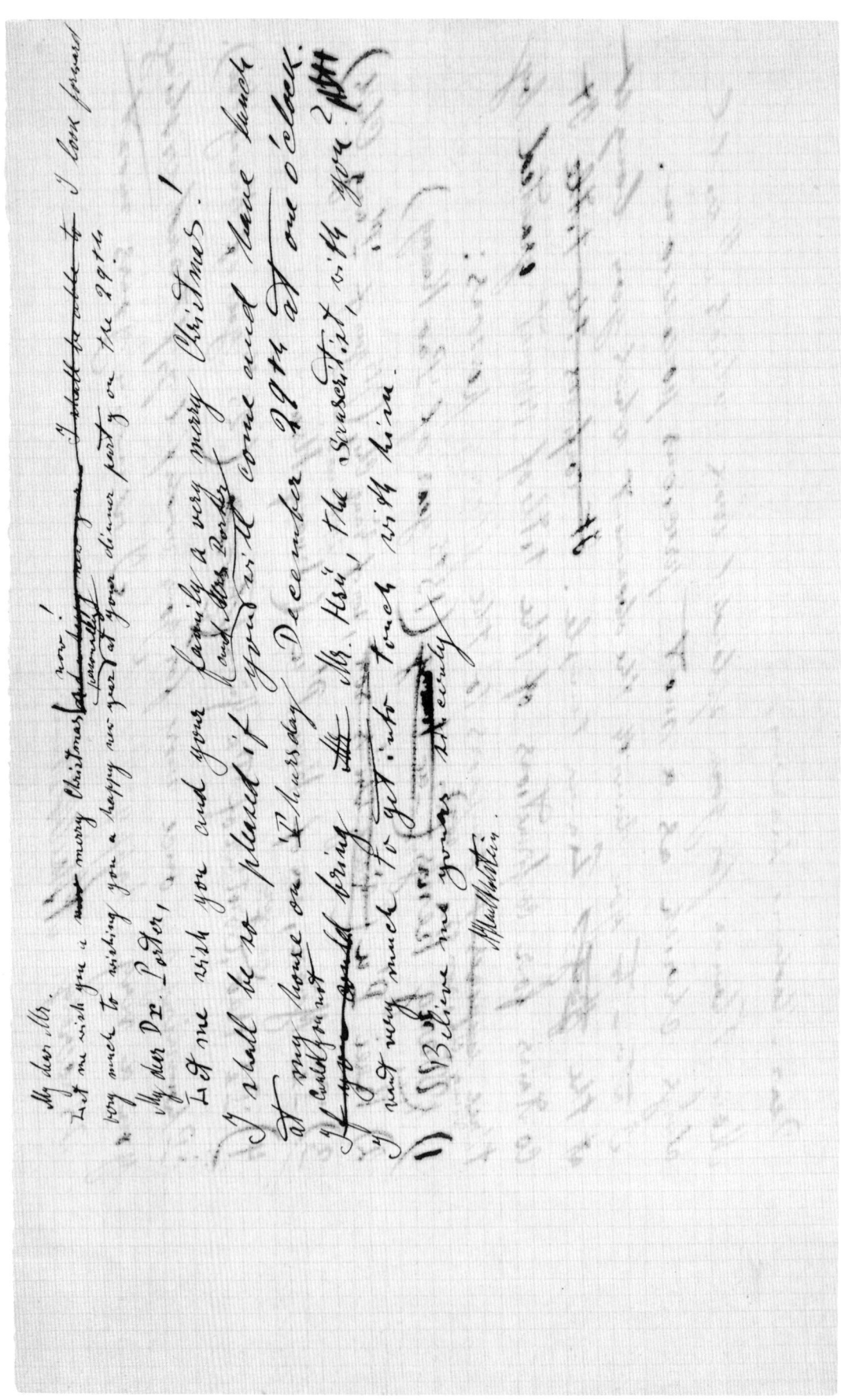

A Staël Holstein.

博

Yenching,
May 2d. 1933

My dear Baron:-

Mrs. Porter tells me ~~that~~ you have telephoned inviting us to lunch on Friday, May 12th. I am happy to say that I am free at that time and that Mrs. Porter & I are glad to accept the invitation.

I am sorry I was out on the campus when you called on Saturday.

With warm regards to the Baroness,

Very sincerely yours,

Lucius C. Porter

Sino-Indian Expense ~~Account~~ for the quarter ending on March 31st 1933

I Assistants

January 1st ~~paid to~~ Professor Weller
Mr. Pankratoff

Peking, June 5th 1933.

My dear Professor Porter

~~My wife is going~~ I am just bargaining for a house in the western hills, where my ~~wife~~ family will spend the hot season. Therefore I venture to send you my expense accounts ~~for the year ending on June 30th~~ somewhat earlier than I expected to, hoping that you will find it possible to send me a cheque before the end of this week.

I think the (original) appropriation for the 32/33 ~~Sino-Indian Institute~~ was 14000.00 Mex. dollars, to which 2200.00 Mex. dollars were ~~[illegible]~~ added later on. Of the entire sum (16000.200 Mex. dollars) I have already received 8094.12 Mex. dollars. ~~The sum total of my expense accounts for~~ If you send me a cheque for 8090.71 Mex. dollars now, a small balance (15.17 Mex. dollars) will be left with the ~~Yenching~~ treasurer of Yenching University.

Believe me yours sincerely

A. Staël-Holstein.

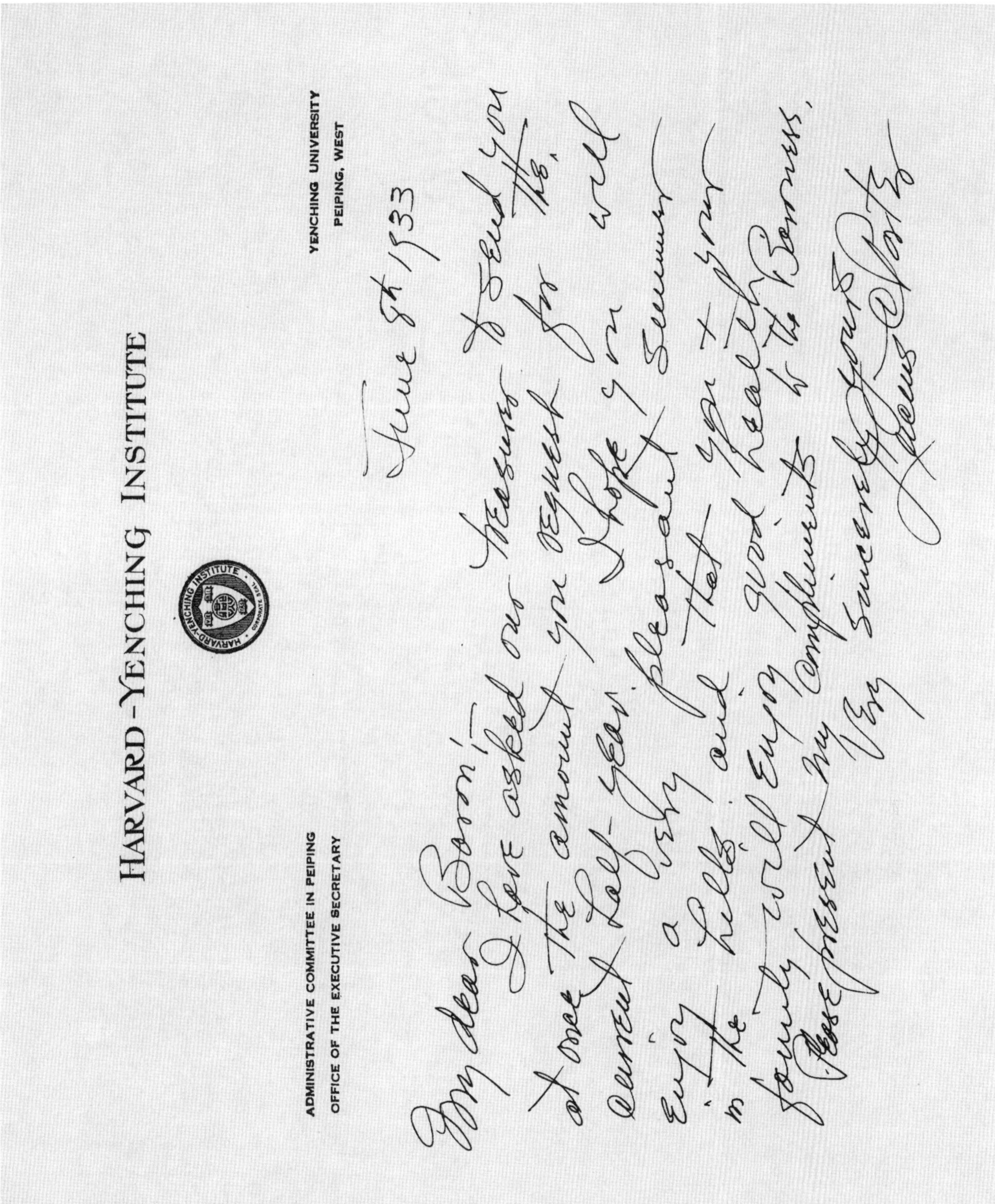

HARVARD-YENCHING INSTITUTE

ADMINISTRATIVE COMMITTEE IN PEIPING
OFFICE OF THE EXECUTIVE SECRETARY

YENCHING UNIVERSITY
PEIPING, WEST

June 8th 1933

My dear Baron:—

I have asked our treasurer to send you at once the amount you request for the current half-year. I hope you will enjoy a very pleasant summer in the hills and that you + your family will enjoy good health. Please present my compliments to the Baroness.

Very sincerely yours
Lucius C. Porter

My dear Professor Porter,

~~I [illegible] Many thanks for your note in which~~

I am very much obliged to you for having dealt so promptly with my expense account. The Treasurer's cheque ~~[illegible]~~ too has arrived, and everything seems to be in order. ~~When Professor Eliseeff arrives I~~ ~~[illegible]~~ Dean Chase writes that Professor Eliseeff hopes to be here towards the end of this ~~week~~ month. Please present my ~~My~~ compliments to Mrs. Porter.

With many thanks for your note I remain

yours sincerely

A. Staël-Holstein.

HARVARD-YENCHING INSTITUTE
哈佛燕京學社

OFFICE OF THE EXECUTIVE SECRETARY
幹事辦公處

PEIPING OFFICE
北平辦公處
YENCHING UNIVERSITY
燕京大學
PEIPING, WEST
北平西郊

June 13th., 1933.

My dear Baron:-

I have just yeard from Cambridge that Professor Serge Elisseeff is to visit China on his way from Cambridge, Mass., back to Paris. Our trustees are anxious to have him meet some of the Chinese scholars and to visit some of the institutions which receive grants from the Harvard-Yenching Institute. Professor Elisseeff is due to arrive in Shanghai on June 19th. on the S/S "PRESIDENT HARRISON". I imagine he will want to visit the work of Chinese institutions carried on at the University of Nanking and at Cheloo University in Tsinanfu. In both places, our people there can help him meet other Chinese scholars. It may be he will wish to stop at Chefoo and T'ai Shan on his way north. I do not believe he will be in Peiping before July 1st. I hope very much that you will be able to help him in his visits in Peiping about that time. I believe Professor Elisseeff was a colleague of yours once in the University of Petrograd. I will let you know as to when I hear definitely as to when Professor Elisseeff will be in Peiping, and will be glad to plan with you regarding the persons whom he should meet outside of our special Harvard-Yenching group.

With very hearty greetings to the Baroness, as well as to yourself, I am,

Very sincerely yours,

Lucius C. Porter

Baron von Stahl-Holstein,
Ex-Austrian Legation,
Peiping, China.

博

July 17, 1933.

My Dear Baron,—

How very good of you to remember Wolcott's interest in stamps! You did indeed provide him with some very unique ones of which he had no specimens. He & I both are most grateful to you for them.

What a sizzling week we have had! We are off for Peitaiho to-morrow morning and hope to find it cool enough there to pay us for the disagreeable journey we shall have getting there.

My greetings to the Baroness. I do hope the little boy has quite recovered.

Very Cordially Yours,

Lillian D. Foster

·a·hasty·little·note·

My Dear Baron -
you certainly
were a very good
friend of our
Stamp-Collector
to have remembered
him so generously.
You should have
seen his Eyes
when he saw
your big Envelope.

and the speed
with which he
turned from
skating to soaking
and pasting stamps
instead. Both he
and I send you
our grateful thanks.
Wishing you & the
Baroness and the
children the best
of years for 1934
I am
Very Cordially yours
Dec. 28,'33 Lillian D. Porter

My Dear Baron,—
Thank you so
much for your
remembrance of
Wolcott's Stamp Col-
lection. Nothing could
please him more.
A Merry Christmas to
you & your family.
Cordially Yours
Lillian D. Poster

My dear Professor Porter,

I wonder whether I am right in believing that you generally visit Peking on Sundays. ~~If you~~ ~~In case you~~ ~~I shall be so glad~~ ~~if you will call~~ on me to day ~~(at any time)~~. I have written an article for the Yenching Journal, and I want to consult you about it. If you happen to be in Town, please call on me today or on any day of this week which suits you. If you ~~cannot~~ will not call on me, I shall go to Yenching to see you, but I ~~cannot~~ can hardly take all the books etc. with me which I wanted to show you.

Believe me yours sincerely

AStaël Holstein.

Спасибо дорогая Лиля
и Баронъ за милое вни-
мание. Мы экспромтомъ
устраиваемъ маленькую
встречу Новаго Года и
просимъ очень Васъ обоихъ
придти къ намъ после 10½
вечера когда хотите.
Доставите намъ большую
радость.

Преданная Вамъ
Камилла Локкартъ

Суббота

HARVARD-YENCHING INSTITUTE

Yenching, Feb. 3, 1934

My dear Baron:

I am back from my trip to Shanghai, which I found very pleasant and interesting. Did you get my note about the printing of your article ? I got the information from our editor-in-chief, Mr. Ku Chieh-kang, to the effect

1. That he would be most happy to have your article.
2. That he would be glad to have you handle the printing of the same; 1000 copies for the regular edition of the Yenching Journal, and 200copies for yourself.
3. That the article will be publîshed as the first article in the Dec. 1934 issue of the Journal so that the paging should begin with (1), as each number is paged by itself, and not in series as was originally done.

I meant to sent this information to you before I left, and seem to remember doing so. But , as I have a fear that I did not, I repeat it now. If you did not receive it , pray pardon me for my neglect of attention.

I am reading Radakrishnan's "Indian Philosophy " with a great deal of interest. Could you give me a few of the best titles of other books in Indian and Buddhist Philosophy. I have Rosenberg's " Die Probleme der Buddhistischen Philosophie". If my interest grows I may join your Sanskirt class to learn the alphabet thereof.

Kindly give my warmest greetings to the Baroness,

Very sincerely yours,

Lucius C Porter

Dear Baron:-

Here is the set of books you want. They have not yet been catalogued. So I will ask you to be especially careful of them. You are free to keep them as long as you need them. You might send a chit acknowledging receipt so that the library records will be correct.

Do you not wish a semi-annual payment from the fund we hold for you? Let me know.

With regards to the Baroness

Very sincerely yours

Lucius C. Porter

Feb 15th 1934

My dear Professor Porter

I regret very much that I was out when you so kindly ~~I am very much obliged to you for bringing~~ brought me the books and I enclose a receipt for ~~your~~ the Yenching Library. I also highly appreciate your suggestion that a semi-annual payment from the fund you hold for me should be made now. ~~Please send me the cheque and I shall expect your cheque~~ Please send me the cheque for 7000 Mex. dollars at your convenience. May I ask to be kindly remembered to Mrs. Porter?

Believe me yours sincerely AStaëlHolstein.

Peking, February 15th 1934.

Received from the Yenching University Library: the Han Man Mêng Tsang Ssŭ T'i Ho Pi 'Ta 'Tsang Ch'üan Chou, with appendices (Mu Lu etc.) altogether eighty eight (88) fasciculi.

HARVARD-YENCHING INSTITUTE
哈佛燕京學社

OFFICE OF THE EXECUTIVE SECRETARY
幹事辦公處

PEIPING OFFICE
北平辦公處
YENCHING UNIVERSITY
燕京大學
PEIPING, WEST
北平西郊

En route
to Shanghai
June 17th 1934

My dear Baron:—

I am off for a summer trip to the U.S.A. to visit my family & to keep a little in a seminar on Far Eastern Civilization to be held at the University of California.

Before leaving I sent our treasurer a requisition for your $7000— the current half-year's appropriation for the Sino-Indian Institute.

I hope you will have a good summer. Will you send your article for our Journal to Prof. Ku Chieh-kang together with the bills for the printing of the same?

Please present my compliments to the Baroness.

Very cordially yours

Lucius C. Porter

P.S. I was sorry not to see you before leaving, but found myself too pressed by examinations. L.C.P.

HARVARD-YENCHING INSTITUTE
哈 佛 燕 京 學 社

OFFICE OF THE EXECUTIVE SECRETARY
幹 事 辦 公 處

PEIPING OFFICE
北 平 辦 公 處
YENCHING UNIVERSITY
燕 京 大 學
PEIPING, WEST
北 平 西 郊

October 15, 1934.

Baron A. von Stael-Holstein,
Austrian Legation,
Peiping.

Dear Baron:

I am sorry to have waited so long before giving you information regarding the printing of the article you have been good enough to promise for the Yenching Journal. The editorial staff has only just decided to make your article the first article in No. 17 of our journal which will appear in June 1935. You will please note the size of page for the regular numbers of the journal which I believe you have at hand beginning on the first page with the title of your article and your name, the following pages going in order from page 1. Our journal is printed on eighty pound paper which you will please use in arranging for the printing of your article. As the Chinese articles are printed in horizantal lines and in the usual western order beginning at the left, it will be very easy to follow your article with the others in Chinese. We will be glad to know as soon as it is convenient how many pages your article will occupy, so that the remainder of our No. 17 can be paged to follow your article.

You will notice that we print Yenching Hsüeh Pao 燕京學報 on the even numbered pages and the title on the odd numbered pages.

I hope you duly received from our treasury the check for your half year's appropriation. I do not find that your financial report for the half year January through June 1934 was sent to my office this summer. As we have had your report in the past it will be convenient to keep the record complete for future reference.

Please give my warm regards to the Baroness.

Very sincerely yours,

Lucius C. Porter

Executive Secretary

Peking October 23rd 1934.

My dear Professor Porter,

Many thanks for the cheque! I have already sent my receipt to ~~the your~~ the Yenching Treasurer. ~~My article~~ The first part of my article for the Yenching Journal is ready, and I intend sending it to the printers (Pei P'ang) today or tomorrow. ~~I shall not~~ ~~They will receive a~~ A number of the Yenching Journal, which I ~~ii~~ shall send along with my manuscript, will enable the printers to conform to the size required. I am afraid that I cannot tell you how many pages my article will fill before signing the last proof-sheets. ~~which will~~ Experience has taught me that revising and printing such an article takes about a month.

Four thousand dollars out of the fourteen thousand dollars, which I received from the ~~Treasur~~ Yenching 'Treasurer' (for 33/34), have been spent on representation, and I enclose photographic reproductions of the receipts ~~for~~ the remaining ten thousand dollars. ~~The receipts No. No. and No. are connected~~

I have sent photographic reproductions of the same receipts (33/34 1 — 33/34 97) to Dean Chase about six weeks ago.

I have hired a strong-room at the Deutsch-Asiatische Bank (comp. receipts 64, 77, and 89) in which I keep ~~the most~~ some very ~~valuable~~ rare books, ~~which I have bought for~~ entrusted to me by the Harvard-Yenching Institute. ~~has entrusted to me~~

May I ask to be kindly remembered to Mrs. Porter?

Believe me yours ~~si~~ very sincerely A. Staël-Holstein.

HARVARD-YENCHING INSTITUTE
哈佛燕京學社

OFFICE OF THE EXECUTIVE SECRETARY
幹事辦公處

PEIPING OFFICE
北平辦公處
YENCHING UNIVERSITY
燕京大學
PEIPING, WEST
北平西郊

November 5, 1934.

Baron A. von Stael-Holstein,
Austrian Legation,
Peiping.

My dear Baron:

I am glad that you received the check for the last current half year's payment of your appropriation. I am pleased to receive the photographic reproductions of receipts for $10,000 representingthe payments for the half year January 1 to June 30, 1934.

With regard to your article, I think there is no immediate hurry though we will be glad to know as early as possible the numbering of the pages required for your article so that Professor Jung can continue the numbering for the articles printed in Chinese.

The other day I had some little conversation with Dr. Lieventhal and discovered that he was a little concerned regarding his future plans since he had not heard definitely from you regarding your plans for his work after the conclusion of his present contract with you. Probably you have already given Dr. Lieventhal some definite statement as to whether or not you expect him to continue working with you. I hesitate to trouble you with this matter, but found Dr. Lieventhal rather anxious since he needs to make other plans in case you do not plan to continue his work for you. I am sure you will be glad to relieve his anxiety by some definite decision one way or the other.

Please present my compliments to the Baroness,

Very sincerely yours,

Lucius C. Porter

Peking November 9th 1934

My dear Professor Porter,

Many thanks for your letter, which arrived here ~~today at 7 p.m.~~ last night ~~(November 8th)~~. I have now given Dr. Liebenthal a definite answer. He tells me in a letter dated November 5th that he has been offered a job ~~[illegible]~~ in the South ("Ich habe ein Angebot nach dem Süden"), and explains his hesitation in accepting it by his consideration for our work here. In reply to his letter I wrote to him on November 8th that ~~I do not want to~~ I shall not object to his ~~leaving here after November 30th or at the expiration of our contract (January 31st).~~ ~~here even before the expiration of our contract (January 31st 1934).~~ starting the work in the South even before the expiration of our contract on January 31st 1935.

May I ask to be kindly remembered to Mrs. Porter?

Believe me yours very sincerely

A. Staël Holstein

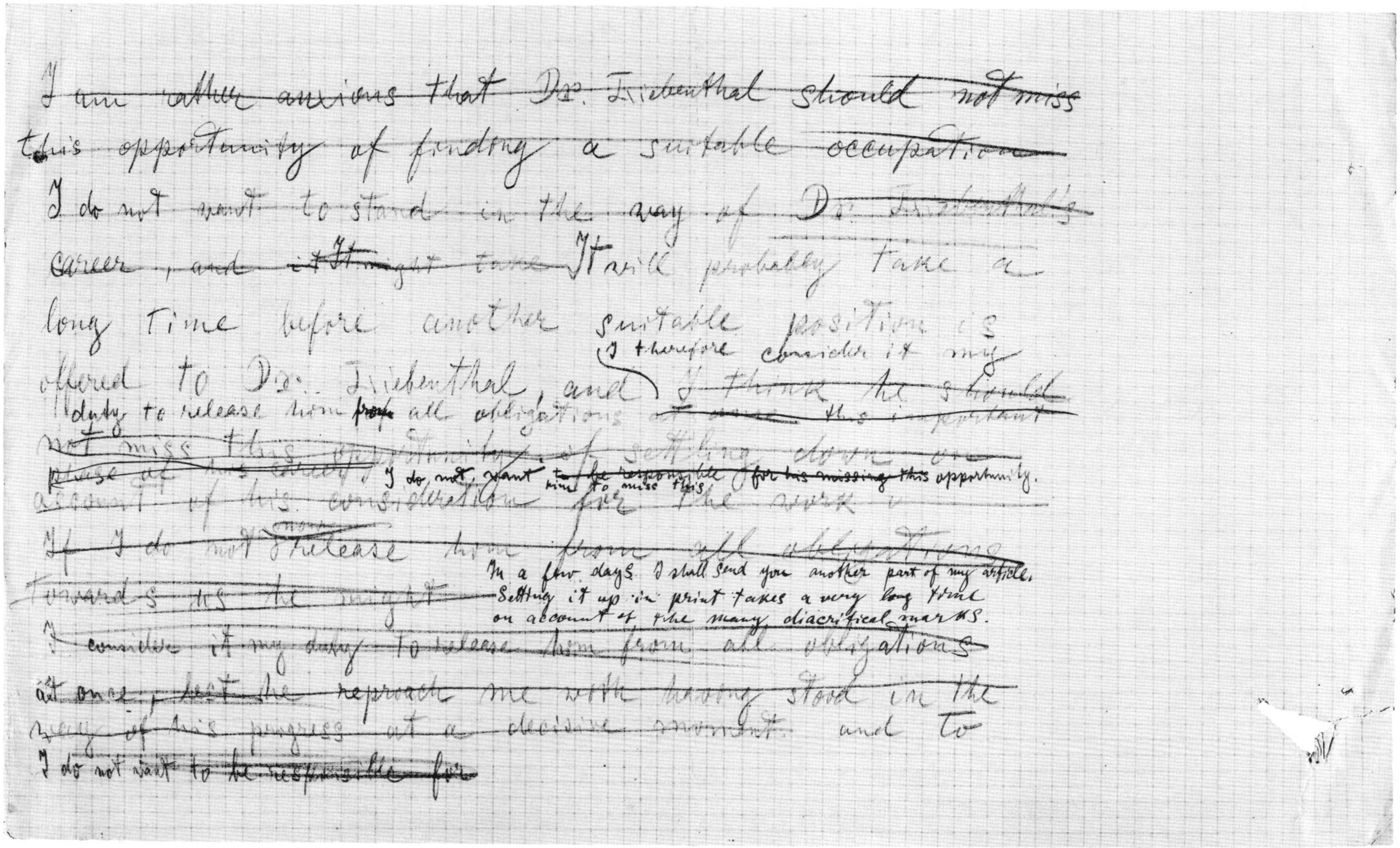

I am rather anxious that Dr. Liebenthal should not miss
this opportunity of finding a suitable occupation
I do not want to stand in the way of Dr. Liebenthal's
career, and it It might take It will probably take a
long time before another suitable position is
offered to Dr. Liebenthal, and I therefore consider it my I think he should
duty to release him from all obligations at once this important
not miss this opportunity of settling down or
phase of his career I do not want to be responsible him to miss this for his missing this opportunity.
account of his consideration for the work
If I do not release him now from all obligations
towards us he might
In a few days I shall send you another part of my article. Setting it up in print takes a very long time on account of the many diacritical marks.
I consider it my duty to release him from all obligations
at once, lest he reproach me with having stood in the
way of his progress at a decisive moment. and to
I do not want to be responsible for

HARVARD-YENCHING INSTITUTE
哈佛燕京學社

OFFICE OF THE EXECUTIVE SECRETARY
幹事辦公處

PEIPING OFFICE
北平辦公處
YENCHING UNIVERSITY
燕京大學
PEIPING, WEST
北平西郊

December 14, 1934.

Baron A. von Stael-Holstein,
Peiping.

My dear Baron:

Please find enclosed a check endorsed in your favor for $5,831.31, my repayment for the amount you were so kind as to loan to us in the emergency which I presented to you last spring. Let me express to you on behalf of President Stuart and Yenching University our very great appreciation of your friendliness in helping us to meet an emergency. We are very grateful for the loan you made to us without interest.

With warm regards,

Very sincerely yours,

Lucius C. Porter

Peking, December 24th 1934.

Dear Mrs. Porter,

I ~~am not sure whether any~~ hope ~~that~~ some of the enclosed stamps will interest your son. ~~but I h~~ He is already acquainted with the postage of all the countries represented in this small collection, but one or the other denomination may be new to him.

~~Nothing~~ My son is still in the hospital, ~~but he has not had any~~ but his temperature has been normal for almost three weeks.

~~And~~ With many good wishes for Christmas and the New Year I remain yours sincerely

AStaëlHolstein.

HARVARD-YENCHING INSTITUTE
哈 佛 燕 京 學 社

OFFICE OF THE EXECUTIVE SECRETARY
幹 事 辦 公 處

PEIPING OFFICE
北 平 辦 公 處
YENCHING UNIVERSITY
燕 京 大 學
PEIPING, WEST
北 平 西 郊

January 25, 1935.

Baron von Stael-Holstein,
Austrian Legation,
Peiping.

My dear Baron:

I am asking our Treasury Department to send you l.c.$7,000. for the current half year, so that the payment to you may be concluded before I leave for Szechwan. During my absence Miss Hilda Hague will be in charge of the office here and any enquiries or business you have should be referred to her. She will consult with President Stuart regarding any matters that may require special attention. So far as I can see, unless there is some unusual occurrence, there will be little need for consultation.

Arrangements have been made for the publication of your article in the next number of our Journal, and the payment for the printing of it has already been made. I think this clears up our business.

I hope that your family is quite recovered and that all will go well with you during the next few months. Please give my compliments to the Baroness.

Very sincerely yours,

Lucius C Porter

Executive Secretary

HARVARD-YENCHING INSTITUTE

ADMINISTRATIVE COMMITTEE IN PEIPING
OFFICE OF THE EXECUTIVE SECRETARY

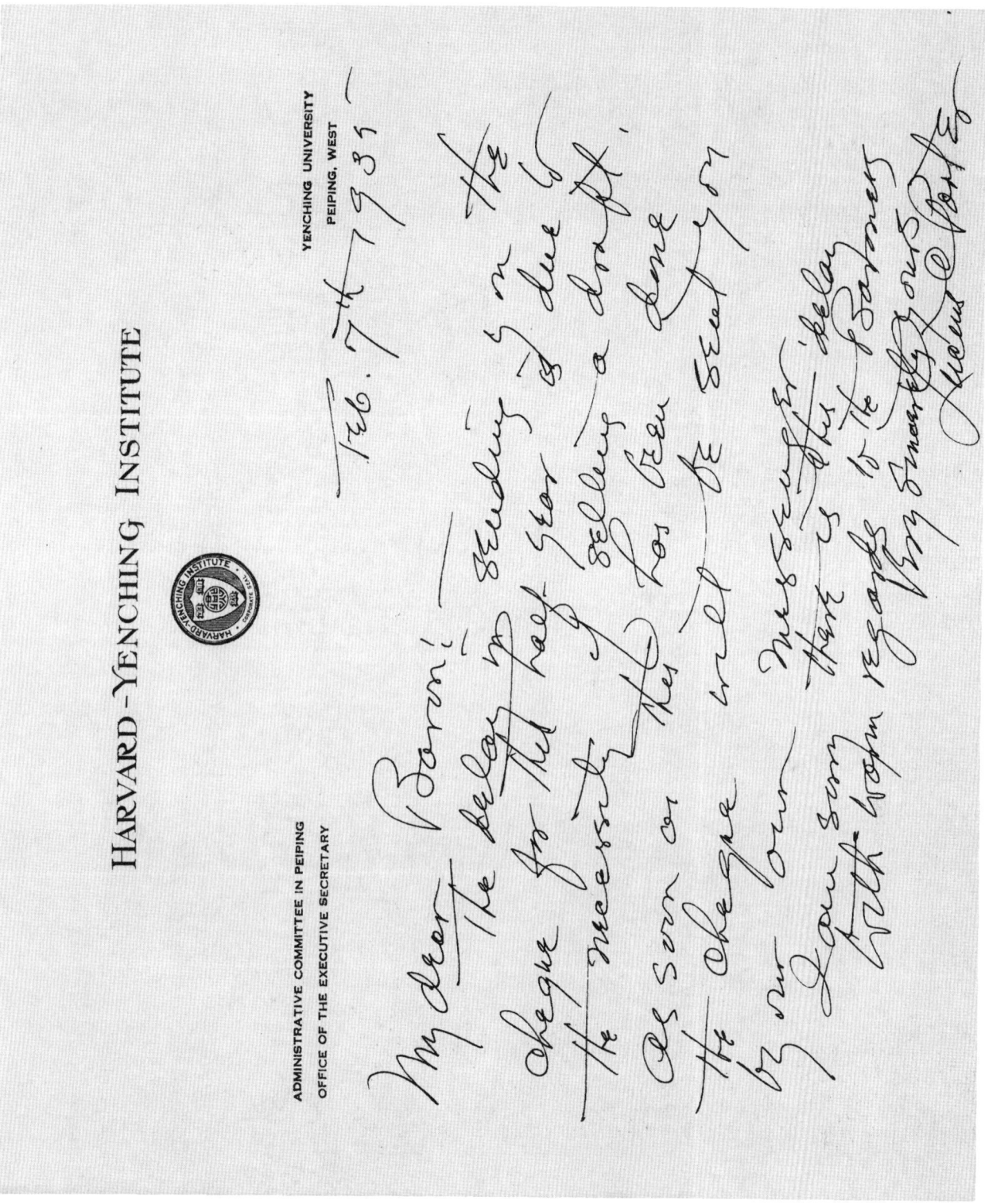

YENCHING UNIVERSITY
PEIPING, WEST

Feb. 7th 1935

My dear Baron! —

The delay in sending you the cheque for this half-year is due to the necessity of selling a draft. As soon as this has been done the cheque will be sent you by our own messenger.

I am sorry there is this delay.

With warm regards to the Baroness

Very sincerely yours,

Lucius C. Porter

Peking February 7th 1935.

My dear Professor Porter,

About a fortnight ago you very kindly wrote to me that you were asking the Treasury Department to send me l.c. $7,000. I suppose that the cheque in question is now ready. Could you ask the Treasurer to give it to the bearer of this letter? ~~The~~ In view of the impending Chinese financial crisis ~~is~~ ~~thus~~ I am very anxious to get the cheque as soon as possible.

~~My~~ ~~My wife sends you an~~

Believe me yours very sincerely

A. Staël-Holstein.

To Baron Staël-Holstein

West China Union University
Ch'engtu, Mar 25, 1935

My dear Baron:-

I am well established here & am greatly enjoying my work & the opportunity to get acquainted with this region. It is full of natural & historical interest, including many fine Buddhist temples which I am visiting. I hope to visit Mt. Omei before my return in May.

I want to write you about a plan for Sanskrit Chinese studies presented to Pres. Stuart by Prof. T. S. Hsü & Dr Liebenthal. It concerns chiefly the compilation of a Sanskrit-Chinese dictionary.

Dr Liebenthal consulted me about some such plan before I left & made a tentative outline of a program. I told him that any work in Sanskrit & Chinese studies should be related to the Sino-Indian Institute & have your hearty approval before it could be presented to the Harvard Yenching Institute. I urged him to consult with you about the possibilities & to secure your approval of the plan & of consulting with Prof. Hsü with a view to his possible cooperation.

I am very sorry that, in my absence, my advice was not followed & the plan has been presented by these two scholars directly to Pres. Stuart. I want you to know that I do not countenance any such work unless it is presented with your approval as a part of the program of your Sino-Indian Institute.

I have been disappointed that Prof. Hsü has not been more ready to work with you and prepare a plan for cooperative work that you would approve. Without your approval neither President Stuart nor I can consider any plan for Sino-Indian studies. My compliments to the Baroness.

Very sincerely yours Lucius C. Porter

West China Union University,

Ch'engtu, March 23, 1935.

My dear Baron:

I am well established here and am greatly enjoying my work and the opportunity to get acquainted with this region. It is full of natural and historical interest, including many fine Buddhist temples which I am visiting. I hope to visit Mt. Omei before my return in May.

I want to write you about a plan for Sanskrit-Chinese Studies presented to President Stuart by Professor T.S. Hsü and Dr. Liebenthal. It concerns chiefly the compilation of a Sanskrit-Chinese dictionary.

Dr. Liebenthal consulted me about some such plan before I left and made a tentative outline of a program. I told him that any work in Sanskrit and Chinese Studies should be related to the Sino-Indian Institute and have your hearty approval before it could be presented to the Harvard-Yenching Institute. I urged him to consult with you about the possibilities and to secure your approval of the plan and of consulting with Professor Hsü with a view to his possible cooperation.

I am very sorry that, in my absence, my advice was not followed and the plan has been presented by these two scholars directly to President Stuart. I want you to know that I do not countenance any such work unless it is presented with your approval as a part of the program of your Sino-Indian Institute.

I have been disappointed that Professor Hsü has not been more ready in the past to work with you and prepare a plan for cooperative work that you would approve. Without your approval neither President Stuart nor I can consider any plan for Sino-Indian Studies.

My compliments to the Baroness,

Very sincerely yours,

(signed) Lucius C. Porter

My dear Professor Porter,

Many thanks for your letter. I am very glad to hear that you enjoy your stay at Ch'êngtu and that you will return to Peking in May. ~~I highly~~ ~~apprec~~ ~~We~~ ~~When~~ As soon as you arrive I shall submit ~~con~~ ~~sult you as~~ to you my views regarding the Sino-Indian plan which ~~Professor Hsü's plan. the plan of which~~ has been presented to President Stuart. Today I only want to tell you how highly I appreciate your communication. Before the receipt of your kind note I did not ~~know that~~ ~~I never knew~~ that ~~any Sino-Indian plan had~~ ~~lately~~ the President had been approached. ~~been submitted to the President. lately.~~ Dr. Liebenthal wrote me a few days ago that he had nothing to do with the presentation of the plan ("Ich bin an diesem Schritt gänzlich unbeteiligt und bedaure ihn ....). With all good wishes from my wife and from myself I remain yours gratefully

A. Staël Holstein.

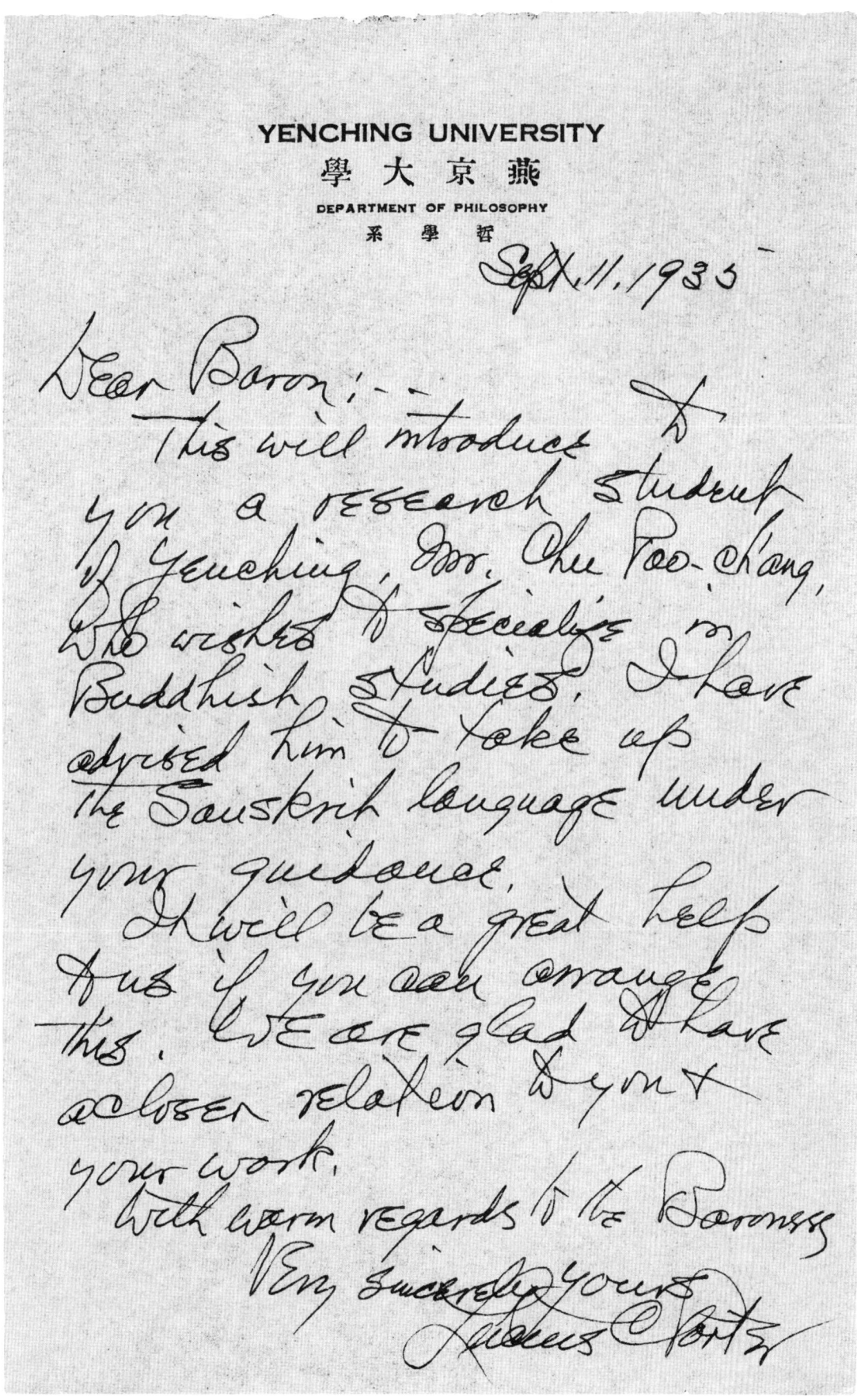

YENCHING UNIVERSITY
燕京大學
DEPARTMENT OF PHILOSOPHY
哲學系

Sept. 11, 1935

Dear Baron:--

This will introduce to you a research student of Yenching, Mr. Chu Pao-ch'ang, who wishes to specialize in Buddhist studies. I have advised him to take up the Sanskrit language under your guidance.

It will be a great help to us if you can arrange this. We are glad to have a closer relation to you & your work.

With warm regards to the Baroness

Very sincerely yours

Lucius Porter

Peking ~~September 2[illegible]~~ October 1st 1935.

My dear Professor Porter,

I enclose a copy of ~~the~~ my statement of ~~account~~ for 34/35, which I sent to Professor Elisséeff on September 24th. Will you be so kind as to send me a cheque for the first six months of $35/36? I shall be very grateful to you if you will.

Believe me yours sincerely

A. Staël Holstein.

378000
431412
1
8094.12

My dear Professor Porter,

Many thanks for ~~your~~ having arranged the matter with the authorities of the Yenching Journal so satisfactorily. ~~I shall be so~~ ~~proud~~ glad ~~to have an article of~~ I am ~~so~~ very glad to hear that they have accepted my offer, and that ~~a~~ an article of mine will appear in their periodical.

I enclose my expense accounts ~~of~~ for the 32C and 32D quarters. The funds having been drastically cut, ~~and~~ I must now ~~pay~~ buy all the books myself and pay most of ~~my own~~ the assistants out of my own funds. But there is a consolation: the accounts ~~occupy much less of my time, than they used to~~ have become much simpler. This may enable your treasurer to send ~~me~~ me the cheque before the end of the year which I would, ~~appreciate~~ for certain reasons, highly appreciate.

Wishing you and your family a happy New Year I remain yours very sincerely

A. Staël-Holstein.

HARVARD-YENCHING INSTITUTE
哈 佛 燕 京 學 社

OFFICE OF THE EXECUTIVE SECRETARY
幹 事 辦 公 處

PEIPING OFFICE
北 平 辦 公 處
YENCHING UNIVERSITY
燕 京 大 學
PEIPING, WEST
北 平 西 郊

April 16, 1936.

Baron A. von Stael-Holstein,
Austrian Legation,
Peiping.

My dear Baron:

In response to your recent request for the payment of the balance of the appropriation from the Harvard-Yenching Institute to the Sino-Indian Institute, I have asked our treasurer's office to send you the usual check for L.C.$7,000.00 which you should receive shortly.

I trust that all is going well with the development of the work of your Institute. Please present my compliments to the Baroness.

Very sincerely yours,

Lucius Porter

Executive Secretary

HARVARD-YENCHING INSTITUTE
哈佛燕京學社

OFFICE OF THE EXECUTIVE SECRETARY
幹事辦公處

PEIPING OFFICE
北平辦公處
YENCHING UNIVERSITY
燕京大學
PEIPING, WEST
北平西郊

October 20, 1936.

Baron von Stael-Holstein,
Austrian Legation,
Peiping.

My dear Baron:

Your message of greeting upon your return from holiday has been given me by Mr. Chu Pao-ch'ang. I am very glad to know that your are back, and hope you and your family have had a refreshing holiday.

Mr. Chu tells me that he is arranging with you to begin again his studies in Sanskrit, meeting you perhaps twice a week. I shall be glad to have a line from you regarding his progress in Sanskrit studies, and what you think are the possibilities for his further development in this field.

During the summer I have made acquaintance with a very interesting Buddhist monk of the Kuang Chi Szu 廣濟寺. His name is Ti Ch'en 蔽塵. He seems to be a very bright quick-minded man, and is very eager to know more of western thought and western methods of study. He is coming out to Yenching weekly as a zu hören in philosophy and psychology. I have urged him to take up the study of Sanskrit, pointing out that it is a great defect among modern-minded Buddhists that practically none of them can read the sacred language of their own religion. Ti Ch'en replies thatit is very difficult, if not impossible, for a Chinese to study Sanskrit without a knowledge of English, and that he himself lacks that knowledge. I have encouraged him by telling him that the study of English is not very difficult, and that he might easily take that up. In the meantime, I want you to consider whether or not it would be possible to help him make a beginning in the study of Sanskrit, without waiting until he has command of English. I believe that the value of your work to Chinese might be greatly increased if you could work out a method for teaching Sanskrit without first requiring a knowledge of English.

I shall hope to call on you within a few days, and discuss some of these questions with you.

Permit me to extend very hearty greetings to the Baroness.

Very sincerely yours,

Lucius C Porter

Lucius C. Porter

My dear Professor Porter,

Mr. Chu Pao Ch'ang tells me that he wants to devote ~~Experience has taught me that the~~ his whole time to the study of Sanskrit and German during the next academic year ~~§~~ (1936/1937). ~~I thoroughly I May I ask you to be so kind as to ... obtain the necessary permit to do so~~ I think that this is a most reasonable plan and I venture to hope that the Yenching authorities will allow Mr. Chu to carry it out.

~~...~~ The acquisition of Sanskrit ~~...~~ presents much greater difficulties to the Chinese than to ~~European~~ students, whose mother-tongue belongs to the Indo-European family of languages ~~who have mastered ... Latin and Greek~~. In spite of this great handicap Mr. Chu has already made very creditable progress in his studies, ~~the study of Sanskrit~~, and I shall be glad to teach him ~~...~~ Sanskrit in 1936/1937. Experience has taught me that only those Chinese Sanskrit students succeed in learning

My dear Dr. Porter,

~~I regret very much that I did not see you yesterday.~~
In case I get a good price from Langdon Warner I might sell him my collection ~~for good~~ ~~to Langdon Warner~~
as he knew it. ~~That would leave sufficient things~~
~~(acquired during the last two years)~~. The remaining things
(acquired ~~[illegible]~~ during the last two years) would still make
~~quite a good show.~~

I regret very much that ~~I~~ we did not ~~see you~~ meet yesterday.
Please do ~~not [illegible] to L. Warner~~ come and see me
before writing to L. Warner. I am practically always in
until 3.30 p.m.; but I shall have ~~to~~ to go to Tientsin
one of these days. ~~If possible~~ Please announce your arrival by "express" post card,
if possible.

With many thanks for your kind assistance I remain
yours sincerely
A. Staël-Holstein.

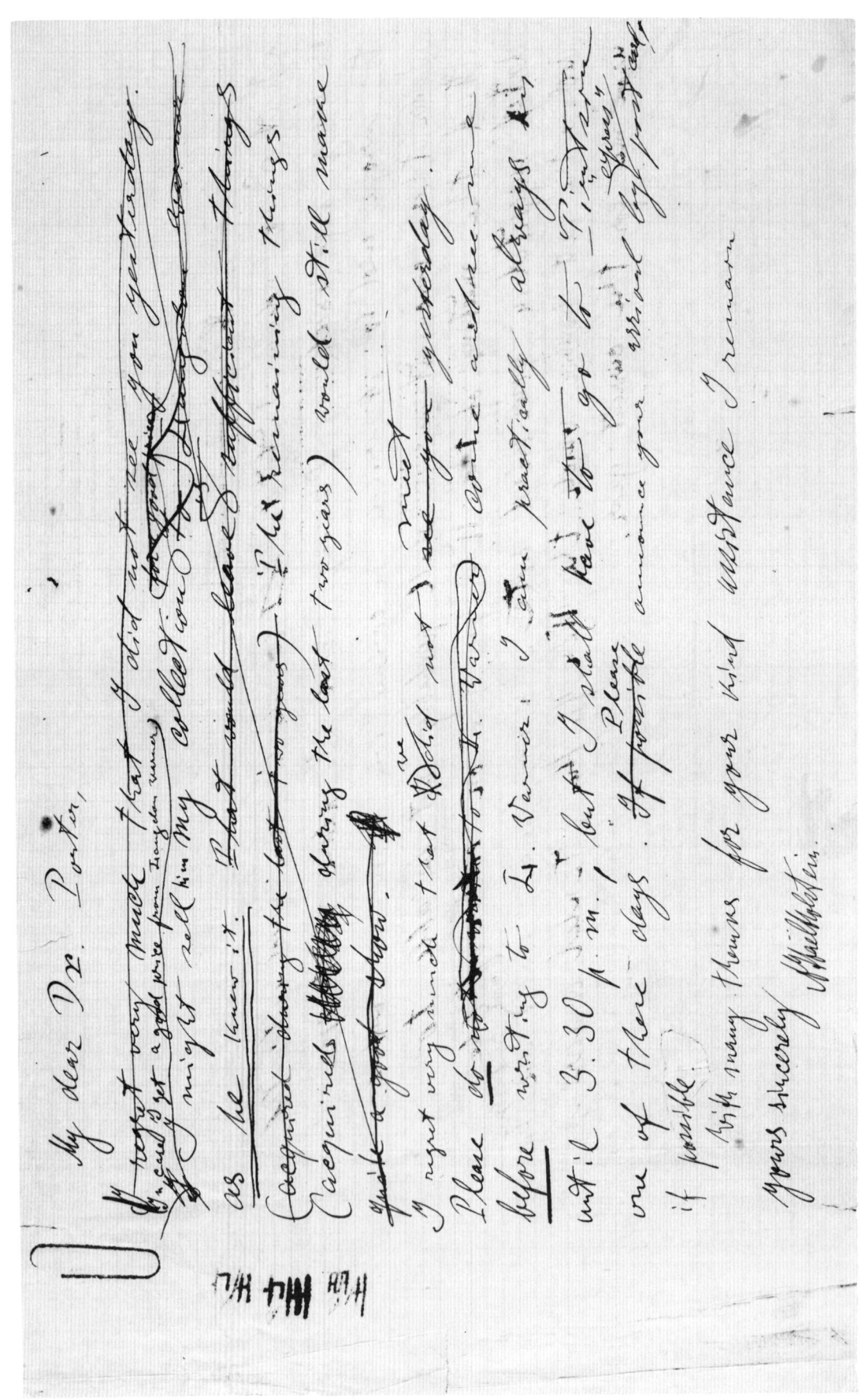

My dear Dr. Porter,

I regret very much ~~I am awfully sorry~~ that I did not see you today when ~~It was so kind of you to call~~ you called at my house. I wanted to thank you again for your kindness and to tell you how much obliged I feel to you for the support you have given me at great risk during the last 12 months. I also wanted to show you ~~the pla~~ my photographs and ask you to indicate those which you think I might send to Mrs. Bross. ~~Hartung will soon... those photographs... Hartung is the ... of ... of the images which I have in view for the present and images. Hartung is still busy with my work.~~ I hope that you will soon come again ~~...~~ and ~~see the result of his work~~.

~~Believe me~~ I remain yours gratefully

~~#~~ My dear Dr. Porter,

I have just received a letter from Dr Konow (Professor at Oslo) in which the following phrase occurs:

Sir E. D. Ross' letter which I enclose ~~might I think,~~ ~~with some profit~~ shows that the director of ~~[illegible]~~ the London School of Oriental Studies ~~[illegible] thinks~~ does appreciate my book; ~~that my book is of some use.~~ he thinks "of using it as a text book," ~~that~~ which fact might impress the Bostonians. ~~(or the Cantabs?)~~. Please do return the original of Sir E. D. Ross' letter ~~to me if possible~~ (which is better than ~~any possible~~ the best certificate) to me if possible. I can use any ~~Believe me yours sincerely~~ ~~sum~~ amount of money for a Sino-~~Indian~~ library which is ~~not~~ wanted by many people besides

THE NATIONAL UNIVERSITY OF PEKING
國立北京大學
PEKING CHINA

Baron A. von Staël-Holstein, Ph. D.
Director of Researches

Department of Indian and
Central Asian Philology.

myself. There ought to be a place here where all those interested in ~~Buddhist~~ ~~art~~ of Buddhism of Central Asia of Far Eastern art the ~~Central Asian~~ history (etc etc etc could find the books of reference which they want.

"There are such institutes in St. Petersburg, London, Paris, Berlin, Kyoto, Tokyo and even in Oslo, Gothenburg, Leipzig, Leiden, Bruxelles etc. but none ~~in P.~~ at all ~~in Peking~~ in the Capital of the country.

My own library is quite inadequate and the list of books which I ~~have prepared and shown to various~~ showed you the other day represents a minimum. Mr. Pettus once spoke of getting all those books but he ~~tried not~~ has not succeeded, ~~because he dealt I think somebody should go to Europe~~ because he dealt with the European book sellers indirectly through a New York firm (and did so half-heartedly). By dealing with the European book sellers directly one gets much better results for less money. Very many of the books and periodicals wanted are out of print and can only be ~~obtained~~ through second hand book-shops. In St. Petersburg there is a special library for the purposes of Oriental research which employs half a dozen learned specialists and a number of ordinary servants as keepers of the Oriental books alone. I think something similar ought to be started here.

which has produced the ~~greater~~ majority part of the books as well as of the works of art ~~treated~~ investigated by us and which still holds the greater part of Central Asia. It is really a shame!

There are very few Chinese who understand this and those few ~~have~~ do not possess the means ~~of remedying~~ necessary for improving the situation.

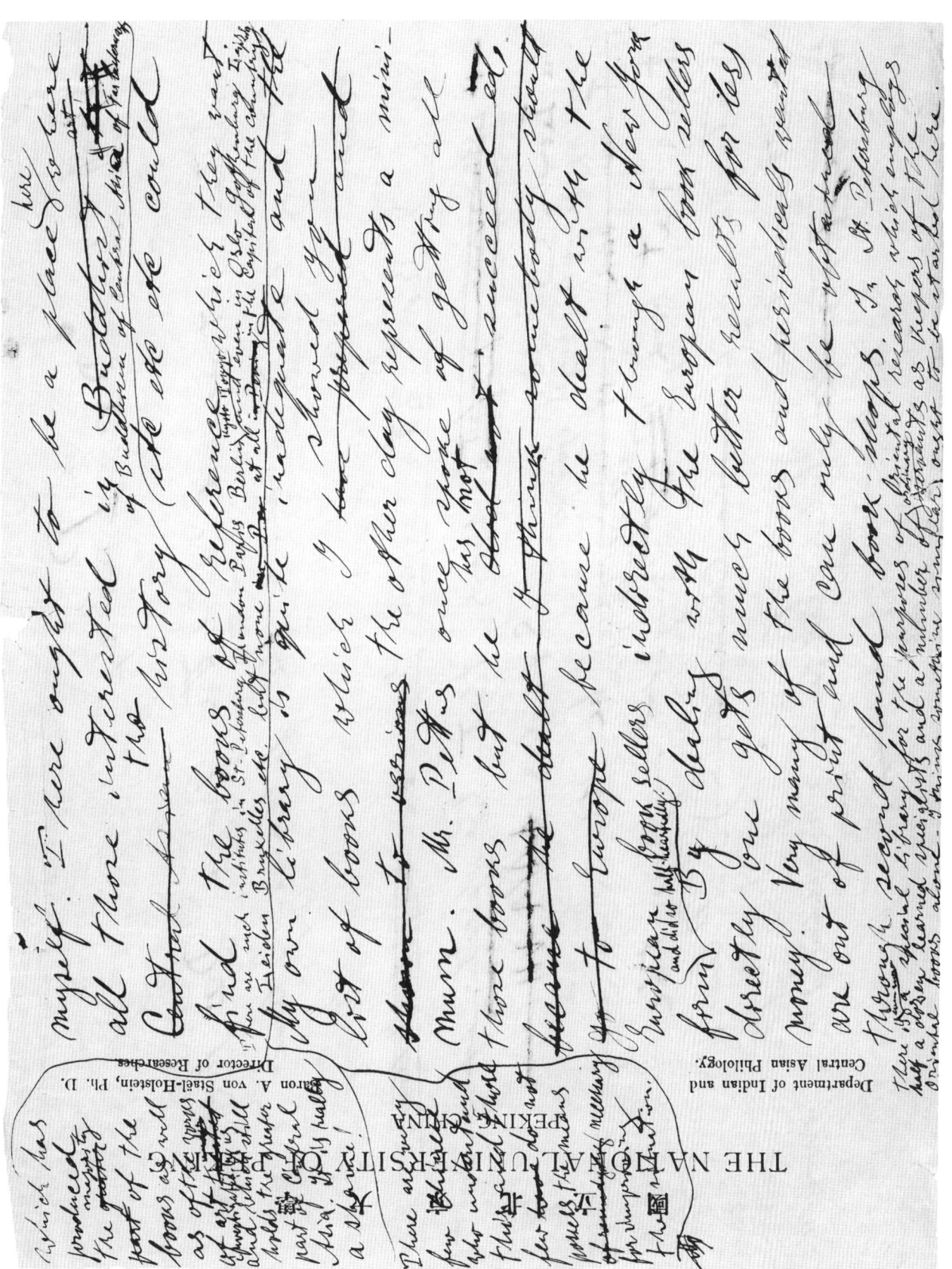

We do not of course need such a large staff because we shall only deal with Sino-Indian (including Tibetan and Central Asian) ~~lit~~ literature ~~but excluding~~ and need not buy any Egyptian Semitic or Persian books. ~~I have had infinite trouble in I have spent much time in persuading the various Peking libraries~~

~~This is~~ Providing such a library independent of the various Peking institutions which cater for ~~extensive infor~~ education rather than for research is one of the most important aims of the Sino-Indian Institute.

Another important task of the Institute will be providing competent observers of the archaeological material which is still passing through Peking and most of which is ~~lost~~

~~to science by being bought~~ sold to tourists of
various nationalities, who break up the series,
and entirely lost to science. The observers
will ~~be able~~ save single either ~~to~~ by buying the things
or taking photographs of them ~~thereby preserving~~
~~much~~ before they pass into the obscurity ~~of~~
~~suburban~~ drawing rooms.

This is how the present day Pan-chen Lama explained the
expression in an interview which
his Holiness granted me in March 1924. ~~A literal~~
is a literal translation of it.

An edi

Dear Mrs. Porter,

I enclose some envelopes (and one post card) which I received from the following countries: Sweden, Estonia, Latvia, Danzig, and Persia. I hope that your son does not possess them already. I had many other comparatively rare stamps but I have, unfortunately, thrown them away.

Believe me yours sincerely

Sehr geehrter Herr Horstmann,

Bitte schicken Sie mir die Briefe zurück. Der eine hat keine besondere Eile, und ich kann ihn ruhig ~~selbst~~ hier in Peking ~~auf dem gewöhnlichen Weg befördern~~ selbst der Post übergeben. Den Brief an Wrangell will ich aber doch durch die Bank befördern. Der Brief enthält weder politische noch sonstige Geheimnisse. Was ich vermeiden will, ist nur, dass er direct über Russland geschickt wird, denn dort gehen auch die harmlosesten Briefe sehr häufig verloren. (nach Estland adressiert) Ich ersehe aus Ihrem Schreiben, dass nur geschlossene Briefe nicht durch die Bank befördert werden sollen. Ich werde Ihnen daher den an Wrangell gerichteten Brief in einem offenen Briefumschlag wieder zugehen lassen. Ergebenste Grüsse A. Staël-Holstein

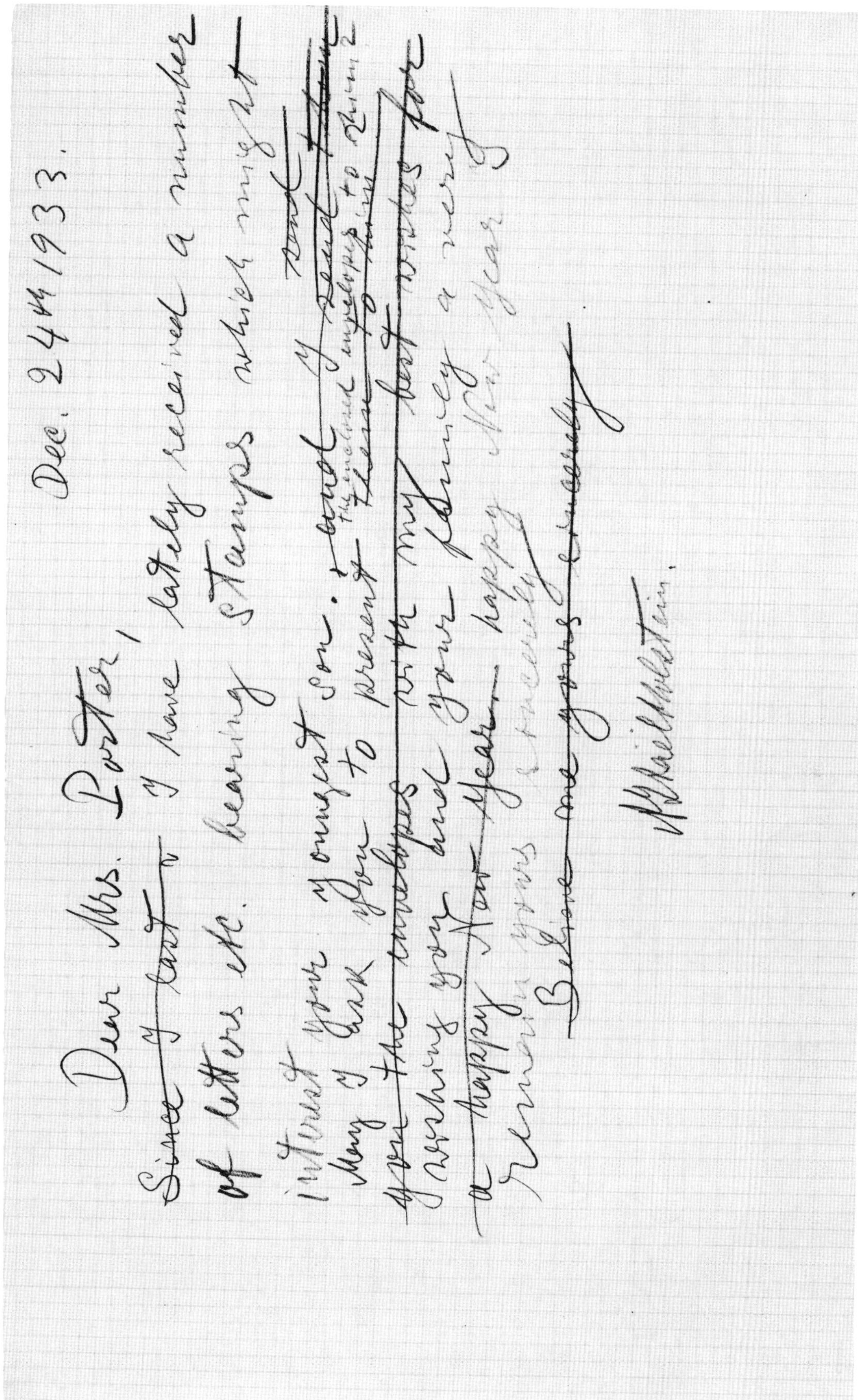

Dec. 24th 1933.

Dear Mrs. Porter,

~~Since I last~~ I have lately received a number of letters etc. bearing stamps which might interest your youngest son. ~~and I send (sent) them~~ May I ask you to present ~~them to him~~ the enclosed envelopes to them? ~~you the envelopes with my best wishes for a happy New Year.~~ wishing you and your family a very happy New Year. I remain yours sincerely

~~Believe me yours sincerely~~

A. Staël Holstein.

An die D.A.B.

Peking.

Sehr geehrte Herren,

Wollen Sie die Güte haben, sich der ~~die~~ beifolgenden Briefe recht anzunehmen? Ich bitte, die beiden Briefe in Berlin eingeschrieben nach Estland aufgeben zu lassen. Die Erfahrung hat gezeigt, dass Briefe, die ~~aus dem~~ im Fernen Osten direkt nach Estland aufgegeben werden, sehr häufig spurlos in Russland verschwinden.

Oct.-Nov. 26

My dear Madame Laurie:

Yesterday I talked
with Dr. Houghton. He
is not particularly interested
in the immediate proposal
to secure a fund to save
the Lama temple of Ch'ien Lung.
On the larger scheme he
finds more to attract him.
and is willing to send
the suggestion to America

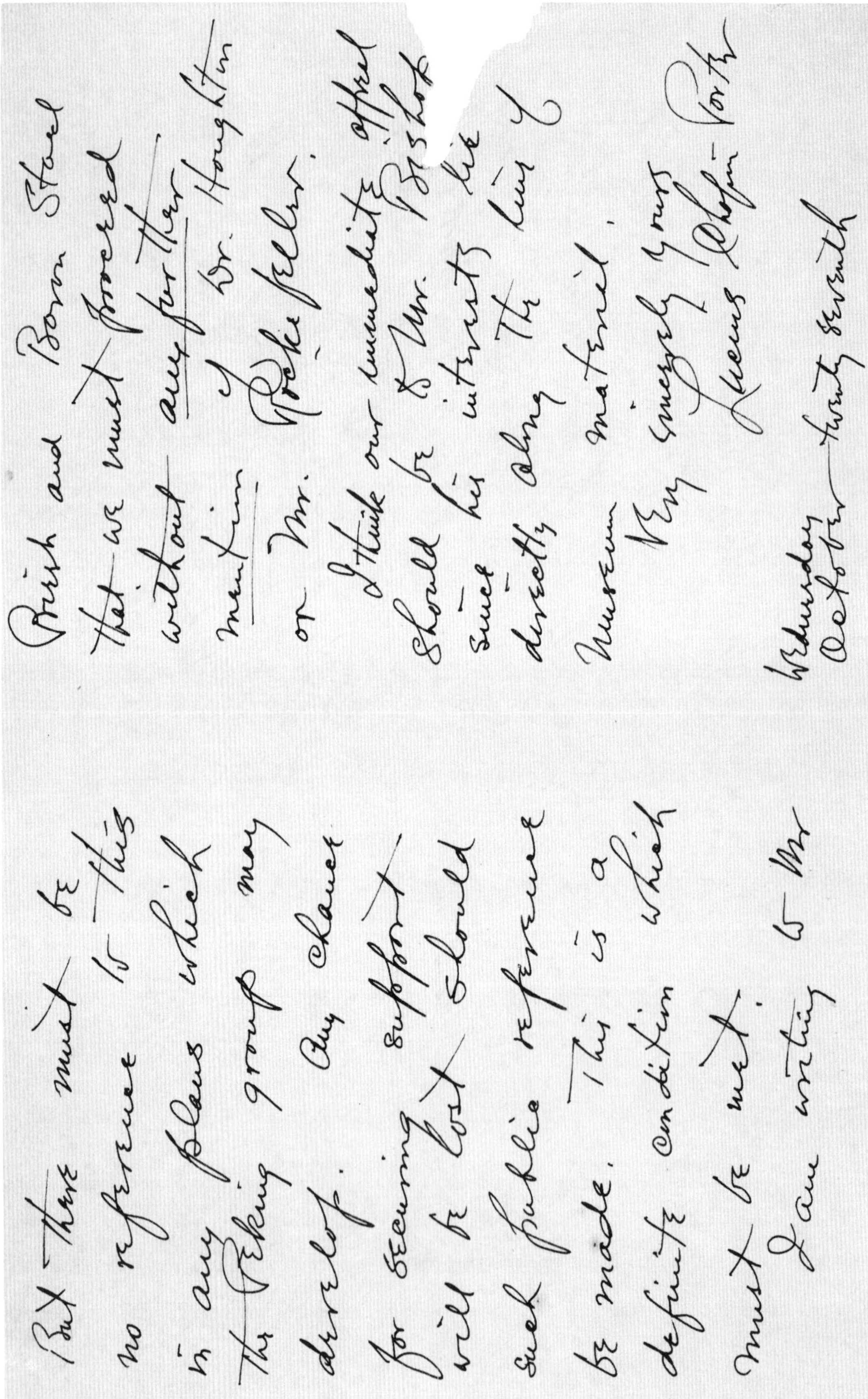

But there must be no reference to this in any plans which the Peking group may develop. Any chance for securing support will be lost should such public reference be made. This is a definite condition which must be met.

I am writing to Mr Brish and Boron Stael that we must proceed without any further mention of Dr. Houghton or Mr. Rockefeller.

I think our immediate appeal should be to Mr. Bishop since his interests lie directly along the line of museum material.

Very sincerely yours
Lucius Chapin Porter

Wednesday
October twenty seventh

July 15, 1927.

Professor Paul Pelliot,
38 Rue de Varennes,
Paris, 7 Ar.

Dear Professor Pelliot:

Let me thank you most heartily for the kind greeting which you sent through Mr. Carrington Goodrich. I am glad that he has seen you, and gladder to know that he is planning to study with you sometime during the next few years. He is a promising young man and should do a good deal in the way of Chinese studies and for the cause of supplementing interest in such studies.

The Yenching School of Chinese Studies, with which I have been connected for the last two years, has had to be reorganized owing to some maladjustment in personnel. My own university, Yenching, will probably go on with the effort to create opportunities for Westerners desiring to visit China and make use of museums, libraries and scholars here in furthering their own work. There is a Foundation in America which is considerably interested in this field, and we hope eventually to receive some financial help. Meanwhile we shall peg away on a small scale as best we can.

If anything comes of the scheme for an Institute of Chinese Studies, either in this University or under its general guidance in cooperation with the other institutions in Peking, the work of Baron Stael-Holstein should be most closely associated with it. I believe he has written you regarding ideas which he and I have discussed together for the forming of a Sino-Indian Institute. I was able to secure funds to cover his budget for this last year. He has made some astonishing discoveries of Buddhist images in the Forbidden City, and we hope to make photographs of these as well as some extraordinarily valuable Thibetan and Chinese books, which he was able to get hold of. He has material which when prepared will be of great value in the field of Buddhist iconography.

I am very happy to have been of some small use in securing money that has made possible the continuance of his work. I intend to go on and secure if possible an endowment that will provide permanently for the budget required for his studies. In presenting this matter in America it would be a very great help if you could send me a statement expressing your own opinion of the Baron's scholarship and your views of the value of his work to Oriental scholars, particularly to Indologists and Sinologists. You know the American public fairly well and the way in which we have to "work" it in order to secure the funds to maintain proper research. A statement from you which I could use in America would, I am sure, be a very great help in this endeavor to establish the Baron on a permanent basis for his work in Peking.

Some day, if the funds I have spoken of come through, I hope to be able to give you an invitation to come to Peking again and give the inspiration of your profound knowledge and methods of study to Chinese and Westerners here. We do not expect China to remain forever in a state of confusion. The next few months will, of course, be uncertain and adventurous for everybody who remains here, but a day will come when the corner will have been turned and the newer China will be ordering its own affairs more quietly and constructively than at present. May we hope for a visit from you then?

With very happy recollections of the months when I had some association with you during your American trip of 1924, and again thanking you for your greeting, I am

Very sincerely yours,

LCP:B

J U L Y
Fifteenth
1 9 2 7

Doctor Ferninand Lessing,
c/o Museum fur Volkerkunde,
120, Konigstrasse,
Berlin.

Dear Doctor Lessing:

It was very thoughtful of you to send a greeting through Mr. Carrington Goodrich and to present also a copy of your very interesting paper on Chinese grammar. It is certainly a very great addition to the studies in that field. I have talked with Baron Stael-Holstein and he has told me of the very complimentary references to your paper made by Von Sach. We will look forward with a great deal of interest to your further work in this field.

The plans for the Yenching School of Chinese Studies, of which I spoke to you when I saw you last at Peitaiho, have unfortunately not been carried out as was expected. The affiliation between Yenching University and the North China Union Language School did not turn out to be very satisfactory. This was largely due to personnel maladjustments. I have not given up hope, however, of carrying on some sort of Institute of Chinese Studies in connection with Yenching University. There is a Foundation in America with considerable resources that is really interested in our work, and it may be possible to develop something of real value to the cause of Chinese studies. We have begun in a small way with a Chinese Journal, a copy of which I am having sent to you. During the next academic year we hope to publish a journal in English.

I shall do all I can to be helpful to any foreign students who may come to Peking for study. I can be of some use in introducing them to the various scholars around the city, while we can make provision for them at Yenching University through the research staff in Chinese subjects which we are slowly developing. I will let you know how these plans progress.

One of my special interests in connection with these plans is the work of Baron Stael-Holstein. He is just the sort of scholar who should be associated with any proper

-2-

institute for Chinese Studies established in Peking. I am trying to persuade the people who are interested in our University and in the Foundation to which I have referred to set aside a sum that can be used for the development of a Sino-Indian Institute, of which the Baron would, of course, be the head; but his field of special interest is so remote from the interests of most people, even among scholars, that I find some difficulty in persuading the authorities in control to see the value of his work for Sinology and for scholarship generally. I, myself, regard it as of peculiar significance, lying as it does on the border line of Indian and Chinese studies and forming a link between the two great fields of research. He has shown me confidentially your letter to him in response to the sending of his latest book to you. I hope you will give me permission to quote from what you say in my endeavor to further the interests of this Sino-Indian effort.

If you feel inclined, I should be very glad to have a statement from you regarding the work of Stael-Holstein which I could use in presenting this cause to American scholars and the American men of business who are in charge of the Fund. You will appreciate some of the points that should be stressed to interest them. I should be very glad if you could make a statement regarding the view which scholars in Indological and Sinological studies hold toward the Baron.

Will you be good enough to convey my greetings to Doctor Schuler, Doctor Alfred von le Coq and Professor F. W. K. Muehller when you see them.

Very sincerely yours,

LCP:B

Chère Madame,

Je suis enchanté d'apprendre que je vous reverrai mardi prochain (le 24) et que Monsieur Cosme et le Comte Ostrorog, également, viendront déjeuner ici à 14 h. 15 m.

veuillez croire, chère Madame, à l'expression des mes sentiments respectueusement dévoués.

Chère Baronne,

Permettez moi de vous remercier bien vivement de m'avoir envoyé les photographies. Elles sont vraiment remarquables.

Voulez vous me faire l'honneur de venir déjeuner ici avec le Baron mardi le 24 courant à 14 h. 15 m.? Les Cosme et le Comte Ostrorog ont promis de venir.

En attendant une reponse favorable je vous prie, chère Baronne, de croire à mes sentiments respectueusement dévoués.

Mon cher Comte,

Voulez vous me faire le plaisir de venir déjeuner chez moi mardi le 24 avril à 14.15 m.? Les Cosme et le Comte Ostrorog ont promis de venir.

En attendant une reponse favorable je vous prie, mon cher Comte, de croire à mes sentiments sincèrement dévoués.

THE METROPOLITAN MUSEUM OF ART
NEW YORK
DEPARTMENT OF FAR EASTERN ART

CABLE ADDRESS
METMUSART

I will forward the photographs as soon as the slides are ready. I will keep the slides here ---then you will get some more photographs from March to keep. Its scandalous that they did not make a set for you--and it is madness for Ben to rush into such a publication with Juliet if he ever meant to have any kind of reputation in this field.

Enjoyed your visit so much--we still talk ~~fx~~ of the Sachs party with joy and glee.

[illegible]

Alan Priest

Dec 7.

D1aa

Dear Baron Stael —

I am getting a little bit cross and I assure you that if Madame Laure and I both get cross in conjunction it will be a bad day —

I keep getting frantic demands from Mr. March for a report of the Tzu Ning Kung Flower Garden — Now that really is your job and I can not do it completely without your help and I am getting frankly cross at all this mysterious rushing around — Now as to this report Mr. March tells me it is for Mr. Lodge and I assure you that Mr. Lodges wants no man's pretty phrases — he wants to know exactly what is what — Now I have done what I can — I have set down the halls — the numbers of such clusters as I saw — the names of each building and the dates from the Ritz Hsia Chin Wen K'ao the standard authority on the Forbidden City — But I have not seen the interior of the West or North towers ~~east~~ nor the small palace to the east and some statement must be made of the contents important or not — I can do it if you will take me there and help me for about an hour and a half but the description of the Mahayana Pantheon as it exists there ought to be more complete than I am able to do —

My typewriter is broken so Mr. March will get the school stenographer to do it — Please ask him for ten copies of this garden information and for five copies of the report I have already sent you — They have stenographer people and might as well do it — I can't at the moment — as I said my typewriter has gone smash — Sorry —

Sincerely

Alan Priest

Tuesday December 8 —

Dear [illegible]on Stael,

This is all excellent but I xxxxxx must have more ! I have made certain notes on a copy I am sending you and beg you to give me that information. But I want also to know more exactly about the Tzu Ning Kung Hua Yuan temple. It is Ch'ien Lung --do you know the year ? That I can find but please tell me just what Pantheon of Lama deities is there, apporximately how many, a little about these thousands of mud images with four languages and their importance.

Also I want to know a little more exactly about what Europea scholars are writing what books on this particular phase of Buddhism or Lamaism with very limited sources. Also just what connection you have with the palace board and just what encouragement you will have to catalogue photograph and publish.

When I have this I will do you another statement and I want to do it before the visit to the palace. I am keeping the statement all in the third person and will take responsibility for it so please give me all the swank you can muster for me to make a gilded lily of you.

I have just come from Mrs. Cal's. and find them all (or both) very much pleased with your many graces and already enthusiastic about the temple.

Sincerely ,

Alan Priest

P.S. – and shortly I want a half dozen prints of Fonder's letter – ARP –

My dear Mr. Priest,

I ~~regretted~~ regret very much that you ~~were~~ are out. ~~when I went to call upon you this afternoon.~~ I wanted to tell you that your non-photographic ~~for a~~ visit ~~to the palace can easily be arranged. I visit~~ to the palace can take place ~~on any day you choose~~ very soon on a day to be ~~arranged~~ fixed by yourself ~~and~~ in consultation with Professor Yüan T'ung Li ([illegible] 同), who is an influential member of the Palace Committee.

Professor Yüan, a friend of mine and a very obliging young man asks you to come and see him on Thursday October 13th at 9.30 a.m. at the Metropolitan Library in the Pei Hai enclosure (on the top of the mountain which bears the Tibetan pagoda). Please do go there at the appointed time and give Professor Yüan a list of the places which you want to visit.

Yours very sincerely A Staël Holstein

Dear Baron Stael,

I have opened up a new avanue of possible help and beg you to take a hand. It is a bother I know but I want Mrs Cal and her two gxxxx guests to see the Llama temple in the plxxxx palace, to have a glimpse of the main throne courts and one courtyard of the Ning Shou palace. They are going to America, Washington and Chicago within the fortnight all three of them and will at least talk for us. Also Miss Staunton at once suggested Lodge and Bishop, and said she could help with them. Lucius Porter is a relative of Mrs Bross and could with advantage be included especially as he has not seen the temple and should to talk it up. I can go or not to drum up this that or the other as you think advisable. Mrs Cal leaves on Saturday a week from tomorrow so that Tuesday Wednesday Thursday I should think would be best.

This may come to nothing or to a great deal and while I feel like a dog to urge you into all this bother I think it must be done if you can.

Sincerely,

Alan Priest

Dear Mr. Priest,

Mr. Bishop has gone to Ta-t'ung-fu and will not return to Peking before the middle of November. I saw Dr. Porter again yesterday and he told me that he intended ~~th~~ to be present at our meeting ~~on Monday (L~~ at Madame Liang's house on Monday at 4.30. ~~I told him that~~ the object of the meeting would be the preservation of the ~~temples~~ unique Lamaist collections discovered by us ~~temples~~ in the P'u-ning-kung-hua-yüan. ~~If you see~~ ~~In case you see Dr. Porter before the meeting please try to avoid any discussion of my personal future with him.~~ I suppose you will not see Dr. Porter before the meeting. But ~~supposing~~ in case you happen to meet him ~~do~~, please ~~avoid~~ do not discuss my personal future with him, if you possibly can avoid that subject.

~~the hasties (Hotikai) and the Tib. translation of mantra~~ again ~~[illegible]~~ "secret words".

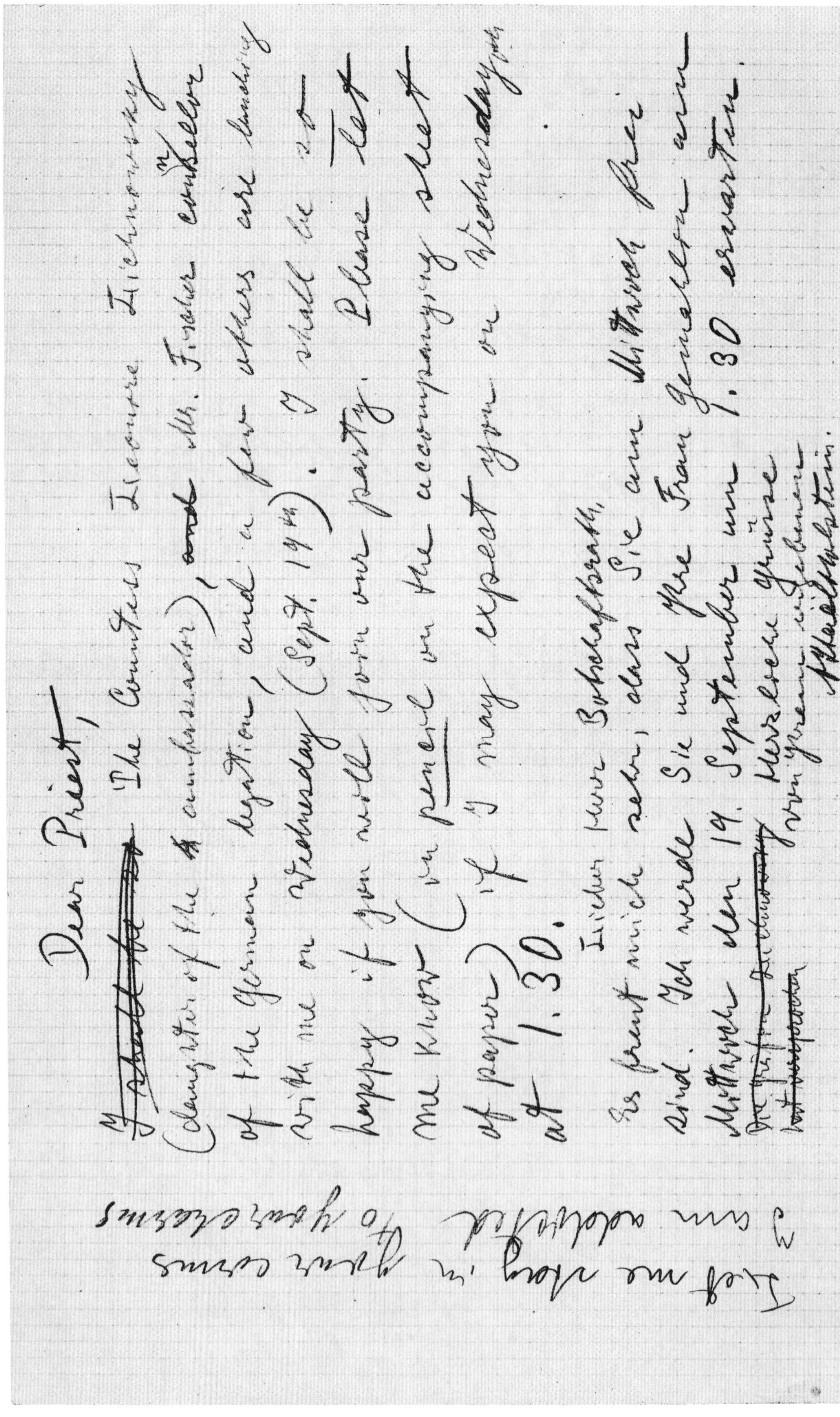

Dear Priest,

~~I shall be so~~ The Countess Leonore Lichnowsky (daughter of the ambassador), ~~and~~ Mr. Fischer counsellor of the German legation, and a few others are lunching with me on Wednesday (Sept. 19th). I shall be so happy if you will join our party. Please let me know (in pencil on the accompanying sheet of paper) if I may expect you on Wednesday at 1.30.

Lieber Herr Botschaftsrath,

Es freut mich sehr, dass Sie am Mittwoch frei sind. Ich werde Sie und Ihre Frau Gemahlin am Mittwoch den 19. September um 1.30 erwarten.

~~Die Gräfin Lichnowsky hat versprochen~~

Herzliche Grüsse von Ihrem ergebenen

A Haidtstein.

Let me stay in your arms
I am addicted to your charms

Oct. 10, 1934

Dear Preast,

Many thanks for your letter. I fear that Mr. 陳's ~~is just as~~ diet is just as strict ~~and mi~~ as mine and that it is of no use asking him to the feast. He practically never accepts any invitations to Chinese meals. ~~I suppose that~~ I am, however, sure that Pankratoff will come if you invite him. I enclose his address. We gave it to your coolie last night when he came here with a letter addressed to Pankratoff but he has evidently not delivered the letter yet. ~~I~~ My boy has just telephoned to Pankratoff (who enjoys a holiday today on account of the double tenth) and learnt from him that no letter from you has arrived at his house.

Believe me yours sincerely A Staël Holstein.

Dear Mr. Priest,

I am awfully sorry that I must not see you off. Herewith the ~~[illegible]~~ lecture sheets and some ~~other~~ more printed matter. If you think it ~~takes too much room~~ too heavy to carry all the way to Boston, please present it to the Peking Society for the prevention of cruelty to ~~[illegible]~~ In China ~~and [illegible] scoundrels~~ or to some other deserving institution.

My compliments to Mr. Warner. I shall be ~~very happy~~ to deliver a dozen or so ~~some~~ lectures in Cambridge, ~~if they want me to,~~ if desired, provided that I shall be able to stay at a comfortable hotel during the time.

Wishing you ~~a happy~~ bon voyage (and with many thanks) I remain yours sincerely

My cable address is:
Holstein
Peking Club
Peking.

Dear Baron Staël —

You should have had these yesterday but I have had another *palace revolution and was helpless — sorry — Please tell me where you secure this checked paper? I must have quantities of it for maps —

Sincerely

Alan Priest

Tuesday —

* Which largely accounts for the bad temper in which yesterday's mission was written — A.P.P.

Dear Priest,

~~I shall be so~~ The Countess Leonore Lichnowsky (daughter of the ambassador), ~~and~~ Mr. Fischer counsellor of the German legation, and a few others are lunching with me on Wednesday (Sept. 19th). I shall be so happy if you will join our party. Please let me know (in pencil on the accompanying sheet of paper) if I may expect you on Wednesday at 1.30.

Lieber Herr Botschaftsrath,

Es freut mich sehr, dass Sie am Mittwoch frei sind. Ich werde Sie und Ihre Frau Gemahlin am Mittwoch den 19. September um 1.30 erwarten.

~~Die Gräfin Lichnowsky hat versprochen~~

Herzliche Grüsse
von Ihrem ergebenen
A. Staël-Holstein.

Let me stay in your arms
I am addicted to your charms

July 33

Dear Professor Przyluski

I am sorry to say that ~~my knowledge of Chinese is~~ my ~~[illegible]~~ knowledge of Chinese is extremely limited and that I cannot ~~write~~ myself ~~review~~ report on the latest Chinese contributions to ~~[illegible]~~ ~~Buddhist~~ the ~~scientific~~ study of ~~literature on~~ Buddhism. ~~[illegible]~~ I asked Professor Y. K. Tschen of Tsinghua University ~~whether he could~~ the best Buddhist scholar in Peking, whether he could not do it, but he refused on account of his health, and said that Professor T'ang of the National University of Peking would be able to ~~do it.~~ take his place. ~~I sent~~ Thereupon I sent two volumes of your "Bibliographie" to Professor T'ang and asked him to undertake the task, but he has left Peking for the long vacation without giving me a definite answer. In case Professor T'ang should refuse~~s~~, I ~~[illegible]~~ shall ask Mr. L. K. Lin, one of my collaborators at the Sino-Indian Institute, to write the reports ~~for you~~ the year ending in May 1933, and I think

(~~May~~ ~~June~~ 1934.)

you ~~can~~ may count upon receiving them ~~report~~ before ~~[illegible]~~
I am very glad to hear that you ~~[illegible]~~ as well
as some of your pupils were interested in my articles,
~~and I am sending you under separate cover~~ and I shall, in a few days, send you a copy of my
edition of the commentary to the Kāçyapaparivarta. ~~, which has just appeared.~~

With many thanks for your letter I remain yours
Sincerely

Registered A.R.

A Monsieur le Professeur J. Przyluski
9 rue de Luynes 9
Paris VIIe
France

Dear Mr. Reid,

Many thanks for your note. I am very glad to hear that you are free tomorrow morning and that you would like to see me. Will you give me the pleasure of your company at lunch tomorrow (Thursday) at 1 o'clock at my house. I shall be delighted to see you. Hoping for ~~the~~ a favourable answer (or on the accompanying sheet) I am yours respectfully

A Staël Holstein.

Lieber Herr Doctor,

~~Erlauben Sie mir, bitte,~~ Nur eine Zeile, um Sie daran zu erinnern, dass ich Sie morgen ~~zum~~ um 12 hier zum Lunch ~~zum~~ erwarte. Ich freue mich sehr darauf Sie zu sehen.

Ihr Ihnen ganz ergebener

A Staël Holstein.

Monsieur Le ~~de~~ Docteur R. Wilhelm
Attaché Scientifique

Baron A. de Staël-Holstein has much pleasure in accepting Mr. & Mrs. Boyd-Carpenter's kind invitation to dinner on Friday the 29th.

Peking Sept. 27th 1922

Dear Dr. Reid,

Many thanks for your kind letter in which you ask me ~~for~~ to ~~contribute~~ write an article ~~for~~ for your ~~own~~ paper. I ~~am~~ feel ~~very much~~ greatly honoured by your request and I hope to be able to comply with it in the near future. I ~~hope~~ look forward very much to seeing you on December 1st and to ~~be able~~ discussing the subject of my paper with you on that auspicious day.

Please excuse my late answer; the delay was chiefly due to unusual pressure of work.

Believe me yours sincerely

A. Staël-Holstein.

labour for hire was considered as a degradation by the husbandmen who were Vaiçyas and was done as a rule only by Çûdras, ~~to the~~ which included artisans mechanics and so forth.

~~Of~~ Professor Rhys Davids thinks that the claim of the Brahmins to social superiority was not accepted by Çâkyamuni's contemporaries as a whole. The Professor arrives at this conclusion

Dear Mr. Reid,

Many thanks for your note. I am very glad to hear that you are free tomorrow morning and that you would like to see me. Will you give me the pleasure of your company at lunch tomorrow (Thursday) at 1 o'clock at my house. I shall be delighted to see you. Hoping for ~~the~~ a favourable answer (on the accompanying sheet) I am yours respectfully

A Staël Holstein.

Lieber Herr Doctor,

~~Erlauben Sie mir, bitte,~~ Nur eine Zeile, um Sie daran zu erinnern, dass ich Sie morgen ~~zum~~ um 12 hier zum Lunch ~~zu~~ erwarte. Ich freue mich sehr darauf Sie zu sehen.

Ihr Ihnen ganz ergebener

A Staël Holstein. Monsieur Le ~~Dr~~ Docteur R. Wilhelm Attaché Scientifique

Baron A. de Staël-Holstein has much pleasure in accepting Mr. & Mrs. Boyd-Carpenter's kind invitation to dinner on Friday the 29th.

Peking Sept. 27th 1922

PALACE MUSEUM
PEIPING, CHINA.

A copy of Mr. John D. Rockefeller' s letter

26 Broadway
New York

January 23, 1930.

My dear Sir:

I beg to acknowledge the receipt of your letter of December 12th, advising me that the repairs to the Lama temples in the Palace Museum grounds have been completed. The two books of photographs which you were good enough to send me make it evident how much the temple was in need of repairs and also show in a most gratifying way the results of your labors. Please accept my thanks for these photographs that my congratulations upon the fine piece of work which you have now completed.

One of the things that gave me greatest sorrow when I visited China was the condition of disrepair in which I found so many of the temples. If the people of China appreciated the wonderful beauty of their architecture as foreigners do, I am sure they would long since have sought to stay the hand of destruction, which will I fear ultimately bring to complete ruin many of these architectural treasures.

May I say in closing that it has been a pleasure and satisfaction to me to participate in the preservation of the Lama temple, and may I also express the hope that the Museum may seek to extend its afforts to preserve the num-monuments of China.

Very sincerely,

signed.

Mr. Yeh Pei Chi,
Director General of the Palace Museum,
Peiping, China.

Lieber Rolf,

~~Dein Hase ist mit einer gewissen Verspätung eingetroffen, und hat Willy Olga und mich~~ Dein Hase, der mit einer grossen Verspätung hier eingetroffen ist, ~~Er~~ hat Olga und mich sehr erfreut. Er ist ein in hohem Grade würdiger Vertreter der porcelaine craquelée und nimmt in unserem Haushalt einen wichtigen Platz ein. Tausend Dank! Das Lexicon ist ~~auch~~ (danke Euren gütigen freundlichen Bemühungen) ebenfalls eingetroffen und wird von meinem neuen japanischen Assistenten ~~Herrn~~ Narita San eifrig benutzt. (Ich habe Balfour vor einigen Tagen einen Dankesbrief nebst Chèque abgeschickt.) Ein Absolvent der Domschule, ~~Herr~~ Dr. Behrsing, ~~aus~~ ~~Er~~ der zuletzt Assistent am Indologischen Institut in Leipzig war, gehört jetzt auch zu meinen Mitarbeitern; er ist nicht nur estnischer Staatsangehöriger, sondern kann auch vorzüglich Estnisch "lassen", was mitunter sehr bequem ist. Ausser uns versteht, glaube ich, kein ~~Mensch~~ Bewohner Pekings ~~Estnisch~~ die Sprache Kreutzwalds und Tõnissons.

Wie schade, dass Ihr nicht hergekommen seid! Hoffentlich kommt Ihr im nächsten Jahr. Herzliche Grüsse von Deinem treuen Vetter Alec.

B.O. 2 r. 15.

18/viii 16

Cher baron,

Je viens de recevoir votre carte portant le timbre Tokyo 7/8/16, & suis très heureux de savoir que vous y allez à toute vapeur. Sûr que l'hiver passé a été abnorme sous tous les aspects; de là aussi ce que vous appelez the last winters stupor. Les 9 hres a.m m'imposent énormément & je ne doute pas que votre séjour là bas portera de bons fruits. Cette carte est le n°4

les deux premières étaient sans texte,
je n'ai reçu aucune de Sibérie et je
que du Japon aussi d'après ce que vous
dites, ne me sont pas toutes parvenues.
Très fâcheux. Quant à mes lettres, la
présente est le n° 5 – elles n'ont pas été
recommandées et traînent peut-être
quelque part dans la boue du conti-
nent. J'ai eu de vos nouvelles par
mon homonyme, mais seulement
par téléphone, puisque le temps de
chien, les tracas de la douane etc.
l'ont empêché de réaliser sa visite
annoncée, ce que je regrette profondément. Et que peut on se causer par

Notre doyen va très bien. Je ne l'ai pas
vu depuis. Ce séjour à Raivola dont
je vous parlais dans la dernière
lettre aura été pour moi le grand
événement de l'été 1916. Sans la fièvre
typhoïde de Lilian j'aurais répété
l'expérience. — Dans les nouvelles conditions de travail et de vie vous
n'aurez guère songé à la Festschrift
qu'on prépare pour le 80ème anni-
versaire de Radloff. Cependant il
serait tellement à souhaiter que vous
y contribuiez aussi. Le cadre est bien
large, et puisqu'il s'agit surtout d'un
hommage, le ~~[illegible]~~ sujet n'a pas
besoin d'être strictement turcologique

ni ethnographique. Si vous pouvez,
cher baron, tâchez de donner une
copie. Par les temps qui courent ça
a vraiment de l'importance. Comme
terminus ad quem on donne le 1 Octobre
mais c'est je crois en vue de ce qu'on est
habitué à marchander. Moi je fais
une grande machine sur le rôle du
vin dans le Shahnâme. Voilà
comment des vieux vicieux, doués d'une
certaine force de fantaisie se consolent
de l'affreuse actualité. Du reste „les coupes
de rubis" de l'épopée persane se maté-
rialisent parfois...

Adieu, cher baron, puisse la science
vous être douce, aussi douce que ces

sa part ce ne serait que la restitution d'une dette.
Vous n'avez aucune idée à quel point notre bourbier
est dégoutant cet été. Été? par un thermomètre qui
ne dépassai jamais 10°, sans un rayon de soleil. Ces
quinze jours du juillet où il y avait moyen de se
réchauffer le nez sont depuis longtemps oubliés & on grelotte
comme d'habitude. Le climat du marais asiatique n'a
jamais été plus insupportable & même notre jeunesse
& le Kagabon endurci au borée de Terioki éternuent,
toussent, pestent comme en plein hiver. Que dirai-je de
moi-même! — L'année académique a commencé, rentre
qui peut. Ne peuvent pas tous. Les journaux vous
ont appris la mort de Backlund. Deux jours avant
il a été en ville, enjoué, tout en sève. Mauvais augure.

téléphone! Du reste il a confirmé que vous alliez
bien lorsqu'il est parti & qu'après un labeur
intense vous alliez prendre du repos. Il m'a
appris aussi qu'il était porteur de quelque chose
de votre part à mon intention, hormis votre bon
souvenir. Je ne sais pas ce que c'est, mais trouve
ça tellement inutile. [redacted]. R. devait
aller voir Stcherbatskoi à Novgorod ces jours-ci &
ce ne sera qu'après son retour que j'aurai l'occasion
de lui causer plus intimément. Excellente idée
de prolonger votre séjour. Je ne doute pas qu'il y
aura moyen de l'arranger du moment que ça
dépend principalement du principal. D'ailleurs de

bewildering creatures & le bon whisky par une suave nuit fleurie de chrysanthèmes

Je vous serre la main & suis

Yours most truly

F. Rosenbg

Mon oncle va clopin-clopant, en général pas trop mal. Oldenburg a quantité de projets bouddhistes, toujours affairé, toujours festinans lentissime ou bien plutôt à rebours.

Il vaudrait mieux adresser (3. O. 2 n. 15 pour éviter les retards & les poches restantes 15/IX 16

Cher Baron,

Je suis vraiment tout confus devant votre superbe kakémono. Ça diffère du tout au tout de ces petites aquarelles brossées à la hâte pour l'exportation dans de barbares pays, auxquelles je songeais en vous priant de penser à moi, quand vous en rencontrerez sur votre route. Déjà avant de savoir qu'il était signé j'avais résolu de le faire passer pour un Okyō. Vous m'en avez fait une grande joie pour laquelle je vous remercie de coeur.

Reçu aussi votre carte sur laquelle vous constatez qu'une partie seulement de mes lettres vous est arrivée. Il n'y avait pas grande chose dedans, mais je suis quand-même fâché d'avoir eu trop confiance en le service international des postes. Dorénavant je fais enregistrer.

Maintenant causons affaires! Le fait est que le Comité est un peu froissé de votre silence & vous demande une espèce de compte-rendu sur vos travaux actuels et à venir, pour figurer dans l'opuscule de la fin de l'année. Ça n'a pas besoin d'être officiel, une lettre particulière à Radloff, Stcherbatskoi ou Oldenburg suffirait; on en donnerait lecture à une des séances. Il ne serait pas superflu d'y ajouter une demande de prolongement, question purement académique à ce qu'il paraît. ~~non pas seulement~~ Mon illustre chef, qui (d'ailleurs ne va que clopin-clopant) en fait une affaire d'état au point que les oreilles vous ont dû tinter plus d'une fois, les autres sont plus calmes, mais même notre brave doyen V.V. ne laisse pas d'être quelque peu grippé à vous voir faire tellement le mort. Tâchez d'arranger ça au plus tôt; d'autant plus que parmi les membres du Comité il y en a, paraît-il, qui ne regardent pas votre mission d'un oeil favorable.

Nous végétons tant bien que mal, beaucoup plus préoccupés de sucre & de bois que de questions scientifiques. Je bûche avec une énergie inouïe sur l'article pour le Recueil dont le ms. doit être présenté au plus tard le 1 octobre. N'avez-vous pas, & où dans ce cas, écrit sur gramarana = shamsana? Je ne puis trouver l'endroit. Ou bien était-ce en causant de nava vihāra, pur-buddha etc.? J'en aurais besoin pour une note & vous serai reconnaissant pour un tirat. Avez-vous vu le compte-rendu de Sir Aurel dans le Geographical Journal fr August & Sept. s.t. A third journey of exploration in Centr. Asia 1913-16

Ces derniers temps nous recevons quelques journaux.

Adieu, cher baron, tâchez de vous porter bien, évitez les salaisons merci & croyez-moi Yours sincerely F Rosenberg

V.O. 2 l. 15

8/21 X 16

Il y a longtemps que je n'ai de vos nouvelles.

Cher Baron,

Navré de vous avoir pu causer des
ennuis par ma lettre d'il y a une
quinzaine de jours. Depuis vous avez
reçu, j'espère, ma carte postale et
la dépêche du 9/22 X: Faculty has
accorded prolongation April. A cette
dernière m'autorise l'entretien télé-
phonique que je viens d'avoir avec
Stcherbatskoi. Les craintes exagéra-
tions du doyen étaient nées, paraît-
il, dans son cerveau japhétique

par parthenogenèse. Vous considérez, n'est-ce pas, que je ne pouvais pas admettre pareil miracle, autant plus qu'à ma question, s'il fallait vous écrire il répondit très affirmativement. La faculté, hier, n'a pas seulement accordé votre demande, mais a résolu, à l'unanimité, pour pouvoir vous conserver vos émolu-ments, de changer le congé en omission-komandirovka jusqu'au 1 avril. Stch. a lu un compte rendu de vos travaux qui a pleinement satisfait et contenté le saint collegium et le ministère au lieu de se rebiffer a, au contraire, déclaré que votre cas lui serait de preuve bienvenue du rapprochement scientifique des puissances amies & alliées. Voilà. En voulez vous encore des z homards?

J'espère que vous allez beaucoup mieux que nous qui billons par l'absence de bienêtre, mais .... dulce et decorum est & le reste.

Mon pauvre Nif file un mauvais coton. L'asthme augmente & le nez se fait d'un bleu intense, ce qui est très mauvais signe. Serge n'est pas très fort non plus & fourre de la politique jusque dans des nécrologies (Auguste Barth). Grande perturbation dans mon home. Ma brave Elsa est condamnée. Il y a huit jours Dr. Lufinger s'est mis à l'opérer, mais s'étant convaincu que le cancer avait ~~[illegible]~~

progressé au point de rendre toute opération impossible
on a recousu l'entaille, lui laissant l'illusion d'une ~~conva~~ -
lescence. Je ne sais pas ce que j'en ferai quand elle aura quitté
l'hôpital. C'est pas seulement du point de vue égoïste que je
plains cette brave personne.

Vass. Vass. est d'une jeunesse admirable, la bella signora parfois
souffrettante mais toujours charmante, notre jeunesse insou-
ciante et en général gentille. Vient de paraître la terrible „tuile"
d'Alexeieff – près de 800 pages in 8 lex, dont 500 ne servent qu'à
rendre indigeste la portion nutritive (je ne demanderais pas mieux
que d'être démenti par des sinologues poète-philosophes).

Adieu, cher Baron, pardonnez à mon zèle ~~lequel~~ vous aura
peu causer quelques fâcheux moments, mais avouez que, connaissant
l'aversion de mes contemporains au sujet des lettres à écrire, je n'ai
pas pu ne pas saisir le calame. Jouissez au mieux des biens de
la civilisation

Votre très dévoué

J. Rosenberg

B.O. 2.I.15

Postscriptum Cette nuit 30/13/XI est ~~parti~~ décédé Salemann, évidemment d'un anevrisme; le matin on l'a trouvé 29/XI/16 mort près de son lit.

Cher Baron,

Many, many thanks pour vos cartes dont la dernière du 5 XI m'est parvenue hier 11/XII. La précédente avec les geishas-passablement dégoûtantes d'ailleurs, n'est pas encore déchiffrée parceque, les lumières d'Alexéeff & de Polivanoff n'étant pas suffisantes, je n'ai pas pu depuis attrapper un vrai japonisant ne voulant pas soumettre la dite inscription à l'examen du prof. Yebouki dont dans peu de temps vous allez faire la connaissance. Il parait

depuis lu en entier

qu'il est terriblement savant; ici on le croit bonze.

Je vous félicite d'avoir pu ressusciter l'âge d'or, noyé dans des flots de champagne dont émergeaient d'énormes bouquets de vives chrysanthèmes, ce qui je suppose a dû vous réconcilier quelque peu avec le retour à l'Imperial Hôtel & ~~le manque~~ l'absence des moines de Nikko. J'ose croire que la vie dans le dit hôtel est malgré tout un peu moins malcommode que celle que mènent ici certains de vos contemporains.

Vous ne dites pas mot de mes lettres concernant la faculté etc. Avec celles-ci il n'y aurait rien de perdu, l'achat serait

Qui court – les trams qui ne courent guère je ne vois absolument pas comment je ferai…
Adieu cher baron, gorgez-vous de la sagesse & des beautés du soleil levant & soyez assuré que le moindre reflet qui m'en revienne est accueilli à cœur & à bras ouverts
Truly yours FR

seulement si s'était égarée la dépêche qui devait vous
annoncer au plus vite possible le résultat des délibérations
de la faculté.

Dénudés à peu près de tout ce petit superflu qu'un individu cultivé a
besoin pour vivre on est nourri par échange par des potins
et des chichis dont la quantité est en proportion directe à
leur imbécilité. En général on se croirait facilement entouré
de rien que d'idiots.... L'autre dimanche a eu lieu la
dispute de notre sinologue. Eh bien, oui, je m'étais attendu
à bien des choses, mais ça a tout de même dépassé
tout ce qu'on pouvait prévoir. Mauvaise farce mal et ridiculement jouée, absence complète de tact et d'éducation,
prétentieuses tendances à faire de l'esprit de mauvais goût...
J'avoue que l'attaque que j'avais soupçonné aussi bien assai-

donnée, a été correcte tout plein, bien que incolore & n'atteignant
pas son but parceque qu'elle s'est laissée désarçonner par des
contreattaques menées de manière à dérouter un meilleur stratège.
En général assez mauvaise presse. – L'examen & de même le cours
d'essai de mon „fils" (Smirnov s'est, paraît-il, encore payé – la quantième
fois? des élucubrations là dessus) sont, à l'unanimité, censés brillants
tout court, ce qui est d'autant plus rafraîchissant que tous ces Kalantar,
Martinovitch, même Malov etc. n'ont eu qu'un succès purement de
scandale, mais, pour ne pas entraver la science qui enfin ~~secoue~~ secoue le
joug qui l'écrasait, on ... passe l'éponge. Le „riche propriétaire & commerçant"
victime dernièrement des lazzis quotidiens de „politeurs", vient de s'habiliter
à la faculté philologique où, à un auditoire relativement bien garni et
avide de science il explique le Rigveda. Séance de ~~gala[?]~~ gala à l'Université au sujet de la découverte de la Grande Inscription cunéiforme de
Vase de Sardur II. Excessivement important, patriotique & maladroit comme
de coutume. – On vit... (cf. Heine) Mon cher principal est toujours mal, ne sortira pas
de sitôt de sa cage; en sortira-t-il? Le vieux Younoche n'est pas trop vaillant non plus
influenza traînant; la belle-charmante & rajeunie (l'aîné beaucoup). Moi-même moins
mort que l'année passée, candidat à la prochaine session de la Cour d'assise! Par le froid

B. O. 2 mn. 15
19 II / 4 III 17

Ecrivez quand-même. Adressées au Musée les lettres ont certaines chances d'arriver.

Cher Baron,

Il est à présumer, que cette fois-ci ma lettre ne manquera pas de se présenter entre vos mains, puisque M. de Hartmann s'en charge. Щербатской a l'intention d'y joindre une sienne. Il vient de (non, il y a un bon moment) recevoir la vôtre du 15/I dont il m'a donné lecture. Moi aussi j'ai reçu celle du 30/I de Kobe. Le même jour (v. st.) la poste m'a retourné ~~la~~ une seconde (recomm.) lettre adressée à l'Imperial Hôtel. Depuis je vous avais envoyé une carte à l'Ambassade. Très fâcheuses ces incorrections du service des postes. Enfin il faut s'y faire comme à bien d'autres choses. La dépêche au moins est arrivée, le reste n'a pas d'importance. Si je vous renvoie quand-même ma lettre du 30/XI, ce n'est pas que je la croie autrement digne d'un second voyage, mais ~~parce~~ parce que elle vous donnera, dans un moment de loisir, quelques impressions alors toutes fraîches de certains "événements" concernant la FACULTÉ comme vous dites si bien. Vos ~~dernières~~ lettres sont excessivement intéressantes & devraient, me semble-t-il, satisfaire aux prétentions du Comité & de la Faculté, car Uhl. y a communiqué ce qu'il fallait. Cependant ni Radloff, ni Oldenburg ne s'en contentent évidemment pas[x] & croient nécessaire d'insister sur des rapports officiels qui pourraient être rédigés

x s'en contentent plutôt seulement grâce à leurs „sentiments amicaux" pour vous

tout à fait ds le style de la lettre à Uz., mais portant
l'enseigne „[illegible] [illegible] [illegible] ..... [illegible] ....“ Uz. vous écrira
ces dessins je suppose. Vos envois sont arrivés en bonnes mains
celui à Oldenburg a déjà trouvé son chemin au Musée, celui
à Radloff ne tardera pas de le suivre. Hartmann vous donnera
des détails sur les desiderata de R. quant au [illegible].

Rentrerez-vous au terme? J'avoue que j'en doute & ne le souhaite pas pour vous, mais tâchez de prendre vos mesures à
temps & saison par rapport à la faculté, pour éviter des [illegible]
des pertes pécuniaires. Recommencer à vivre notre vie après
une année d'absence – ah non zut! Au surplus Lubet forme,
du moins déclare urbi & orbi être décidé à former boutique.
Que vous dirai-je de notre Musée? Il y aurait des volumes à
~~[illegible]~~, puisque dans toute chose il n'y a que la quantité qui compte.

Oh, God gracious, nous avons tout, nous avons l'abondance de tout, nous n'avons besoin que de cligner de l'œil pour que les écluses des « cefsefkesnous sorafofka » s'ouvrent, en nous inondant de forces telles que ce piètre Occident rien jamais vit en rêve ! A nous l'Orient, à nous l'étude de l'Orient ! C'est là notre domaine à nous ! Arrivé le jour, où ces pauvres hères, enfin, capissent, qu'ils n'y voient mèche, que c'est nous seuls qui de par le caprice souverain de notre ~~de~~ ડ્ડ ખ્ગ્ગ avons tous les droits naturels, officiel, intellectuel, spirituel, corporel, perpétuel, éternel, sans appel, sumberel, ~~cultur~~ général, individuel & pas moins constitutionnel & surtout culturel, d'accaparer tout. Enfin, du moment que le mot d'ordre ~~la devise~~ générale s'appelle impérialisme, — que d'étonnant que la Science s'y rallie, risquant sinon, sans appui, de force rentrée ne pas tenir debout. Le fait est que l'enceinte sacrée de notre Musée a dû accueillir une ruche ~~essaim~~ de collaborateurs de toutes les couleurs & dont quatre sont des idiots avérés. Jamais la ~~belle~~ devise viel obs mutzig ne m'a mieux fécondé le saint giron de Mme la science que par les temps qui courent. — Fouilles, déblaiements, excavations, réparations de fautes du passé, musiques d'avenir, finances illimitées. Du reste notre nouveau principal est charmant, parfait, mais fantaste, exubérant & hélas telle. —

2

ment surchargé de fonctions, (d'un mot tout comme vous le connaissez. Projets pyramidaux au sujet du centenaire (fin 1918) de notre „[illegible] (c'est le nom courant) catalogues imprimés, publications de luxe etc. etc. etc. Si je prenais au sérieux seulement un dixième de ces belles paroles, il ne me resterait que de claquer tout court, car je suis (pour ainsi dire actuellement le seul représentant du vieux fond, Lemm passant presque tout son temps à chercher des trésors cachés dans la bibliothèque du défunt, achetée par l'Académie à raison de 6000 roupies, Alexeieff venant de rentrer d'un sanatorium où il a achevé de soigner les suites de la dissertation, lesquelles chez lui s'étaient portées à une partie du corps extrême-ment importante pour la science, surtout quand au lieu d'une sciatique il y a du plomb dedans.

Le petit Ivanov, excessivement précieux pour le Musée à cause de son ~~[illegible]~~ satyriasis par rapport ~~à~~ à des mss. puants, nous sera à ce qu'il paraît, ravi par l'Amérique amie qui, prétend t'on, éprouve un besoin urgent de l'accueillir comme sécrétaire de notre agent militaire, si toutefois le scorbut dont il souffre actuellement ne s'y oppose; quant à la politique personne, bien entendu, ne s'en inquiète.

~~[illegible]~~ La Faculté ~~on~~ continue de prodiguer les grades académiques. La victime échéante est celui qui pendant cinq longues années a dû puiser, bien malgré lui d'ailleurs, ~~de~~ la sagesse iranienne dans les courriers de la bourse. Je suis à même de constater à mon profond regret, qu'en effet il n'a pas eu d'autre source. Mais à l'heure qu'il est osera-t-on jamais, s qui en aurait le front! d'avouer que telle (chaire ^ou telle^ demeure vacante faute de quoi la remplir, ah non par exemple! Et puis — Marr-fils, ivanisant éminent, pour obtenir à son tour les grades, ne pourrait guère se passer de quelqu'un, ne fût ce que d'un mannequin, qui occupât, en le remplaçant pendant qu'il mûrit, sa chaire à lui. Vous voyez, il n'est que logique qu'au cas donné certaines insuffisances, de prépuce par ex. entre autres, ne peuvent être prises en considération. D'abord on s'est insinué à voulait ~~faire~~ jouer cette farce à un autre qui a refusé net. Du reste Freiman y trouve, je suppose, son compte. En tout cas est-il incomparablement plus digne que tous ces Kalautay Barets, Parnackelums & Cie. En étoile sur ce fond terne brille seul le petit R. (espèce de barre hélas!) Son cours d'ouverture d'avant-hier a été un succès extraordinaire, même Tuksorau Ubanubun a dû le constater.

On ne parle politique qu'en tout petit comité, et encore..! ~~Par~~ L'irritabilité d'humeur nerveuse générale empêchent de s'entendre même ceux qui au fond sont d'avis peu différent. Ah, comme on se fait mauvais caractère! ~~[illegible]~~ Avec Bae-Bae nous nous entendons à merveille, mais parfois son esprit devient inquiétante. Mais quel tempérament! La belle est toujours charmante ~~bien~~ quoique souvent souffrante. Il n'y a que les femmes ~~qui ne sont~~ pas trop stupides, pour causer avec pas les temps qui courent. Savez-vous que depuis 70 jours nous jouissons des températures terribles, & sans un jour de relâche! Enfin, tout concourt pour rehausser l'enthousiasme pour cette belle & noble guerre. Vous ne lisez pas nos journaux, j'espère. Dans une lettre à Alexeieff Pelliot regrette de vous n'avoir pas vu pousser une pointe vers Pékin en passant au Japon; ibidem il constate avec satisfaction que Sir Aurel s'est fait si profondément anglais qu'on ne sent plus l'odeur de son pays d'extractions (ce n'est pas textuel).

Voilà des potins, des potins! Ne m'en veuillez pas & soyez indulgent. Vous lirez ça quand vous n'aurez rien d'autre à faire; peut-être y aura-t-il alors à côté (une grande bouteille de Sherry ou d'un autre bienfait des dieux, ça me donnerait une grande satisfaction. Bien des choses de tout notre monde. Je vous serre la main & suis très yours truly F. Rosenberg

B.O. 2.v.15

Depuis votre télégramme du 28 mars, le Comité vous a expédié deux envois à 600; V.V. me charge de constater ceci. 10/23 V 17

Cher Baron,

Ce matin j'eus la grande joie de voir arriver votre lettre du 4 ce qui fait en tout 19 jours de route, phénomène inouï! La précédente est datée du Oriental Hotel, Kobe 30 janvier; j'en ai donné lecture à qui de droit. Depuis, Hartmann a bien voulu se charger d'un gros paquet de lettres pour vous, mais il ne vous a plus trouvé au Japon ; à ce que je vois nos missives, - il y en avait aussi de la part de Uzegotabeskaïa

Adieu cher baron, tâchez de vous bien porter et de faire provisions de santé pour l'hiver qui s'annonce insupportable. Bien des choses et autres

Truly yours FR

ont dû vous arriver avec un retard imprévu. Actuellement vous les avez, je n'en doute pas et vous conviendrez que je ne mérite pas sans réserve que vous soyez "very angry with me" (ce qui d'ailleurs me flatte). Depuis le départ de H. je n'ai plus écrit, par ce.. que .... Ah bon rien, que tout cela est odieux, ignoble et idiot et sale! Jamais pessimiste n'osa l'être assez pour prévoir pareil épanouissement de la bêtise humaine. Les chiffons écarlates ne font que rehausser la désespérante grisaille physique, morale et mentale. Ils sont comme tout ce verbiage, à ~~force de traîner~~ dans la boue l'un et l'autre en assument les qualités. Personne n'y fait plus attention, comme on ne fait plus attention aux odeurs qu'exhalent les rues, veuves de balai & d'arrosage. Que voulez-vous, payant 200 roubles par mois les citoyens condescendant à se charger du balayage, la mairie a bien le droit de les filtrer au tamis fin. Enfin passe pour la canaille; mais ceux qui sont le sel de la terre, la fameuse intelligence! Il faut voir ça de ses propres yeux. Dans ses défauts, dans ses abominations on dépasse ce que nous apprend l'histoire, pour tout Gironde ne s'écrit pas par K-d, & s'il y a bien plus d'un Baboeuf, plus d'un Marat (en vertu pour le moment) je ne vois pas l'ombre d'un Carnot, ni d'un Dumouriez pour ne pas parler des „grands". Piètre calque aussi l'évangile de la félicité universelle, auquel on prétend de croire réellement. Mentalité de nègres tribadisant avec la psychologie d'un troupeau de bêtes, demain peut-être féroces. La machine craque dans tous ses engrenages; s'il y a encore des parties qui marchent tant bien que mal, c'est à force d'inertie. Je sais que vous qui avez une foi si profonde en la mission messianique de la sainte Russie, je sais que vous pardonnerez à un vieux désabusé dont la vue baisse sensiblement & qui ne peut voir que ce qu'il voit. L'académie est en fermentation tout plein le personnel savant se dépasse. Pour moi les meetings - toujours aux heures de

travail ça se comprend — n'existent pas. Personne n'y songe que, en se révol-
tant ils signent l'acte de ~~leur~~ esclavage d'antan. Présomption illimitée, point
d'orgueil; horreur générale de tout ~~ce qui est~~ travail comme indigne du peuple
libre et souverain. Moi-même je n'ai pas manqué un seul jour au musée;
quant à l'horreur du travail, c'est une infection (à causes variées, mais à laquelle il est très difficile de se soustraire. Un jour la promenade au M. s'est faite sous cette
fameuse „pluie de poules", moins horripilante d'ailleurs que je n'aurais cru.
— Vous savez sans doute que Щербатской va en Mongolie et qu'il vous
a chargé de ses cours? Hélas l'Europe qui vous donne le mal de pays,
vous ne la trouverez point en rentrant à P. Mais où la trouverez-vous,
la trouverons-nous? Je ne doute pas non plus que ce ne soit plus la bonne
madame un peu vieillotte et molle, pourtant gracieuse et si divinement accommo-
dante! Notre standart of life? N'en parlons pas. À propos, plus de Cubat; Contant
continue de fonctionner. Mon chef, dernièrement nommé membre de la commission
suprême d'enquête, se démène comme quatre, ne dort qu'autant d'heures; principe
politique: la douma et mobile. À la Faculté quantité de nouveaux gradés. Là comme
ailleurs on ne fait que s'organiser. Pauvres organes, que deviendrez-vous si ça continue. Notre bon vieux V.V. a été très malade (fluxion de poitrine), il l'est hélas
encore; vieilli de 10 ans, je ne plaisante pas. Pauvre vieux, il est tout seul; j'y
vais presque tous les jours. L'air de Finlande le retapera-t-il? — Quand comptez-vous
rentrer? Donc, lassitude d'Orient et des hsiensheng parfumés; profonde sympathie.

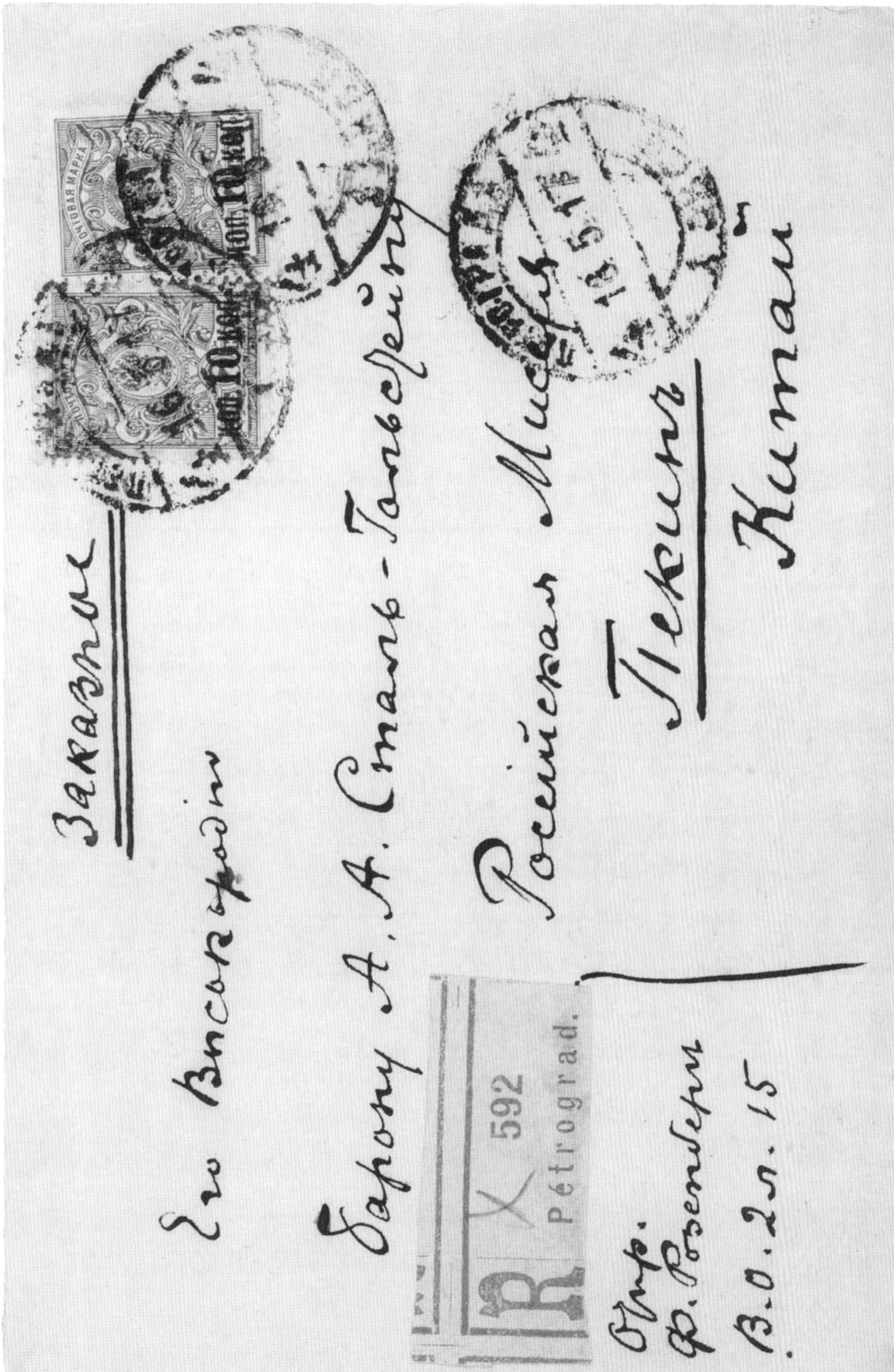
Заказное
Его Высокородію
Барону А. А. Сталь-Гольстейну
Россійская Миссія
Пекинъ
Китай
R 592
Pétrograd.
Отпр.
Ф. Розенбергъ
В.О. 2л. 15

V.O. 2 ligne 15
19/ix 17

Cher baron,

Evidemment mes lettres font comme celles de Mme de Keyserling, ou bien les vôtres ne trouvent pas le chemin jusqu'entre mes mains. Après tant de vaines tentatives je n'ai plus le courage d'écrire quelque lettre d'affaire, bien que celle-ci, présomptivement partira ~~dans~~ la valise de France. — Le fait est que Halvorsen avant de partir (neuf jours après la prise de Riga) m'a confié un chèque aux 1500, le reste, dit-il de votre dépot. A cause de certaines formalités par rapport au ministère des finances, comme vous savez, l'envoi de la dite somme a dû être remis à la fin septembre. Dès hier la bourrage a été rédigée et Radloff espère que cette fois encore il réussira à arranger l'affaire au temps d'antan. Ma dépêche a été inutile, la remesse de Londres l'ayant précédée. — Tâchez de ne rentrer pas dans notre rôtisserie du diable. On y demeure quand on ne peut pas faire autrement, mais on n'y va ni n'y rentre

de son gré. Vous ne pouvez avoir idée de ce que c'est. —
Stch. repart, dit on, pour la douce Mongolie, mais puisque l'alma mater cette année fera la nourrice sèche, ça ne vous oblige à rien, me semble-t-il. Notre musée est en train de se suicider. Partout des caisses; public pas admis. Tout cela dicté non pas autant par l'ordre de ces espèces de mouf-flés(?) que par la marotte cavette(?) du ci-devant ministre. Je suis dans tous les états, d'autant plus que, à côté de myriades d'avanies, depuis un mois près(?) je fais mon petit Robinson dans le monde tout d'une espèce de Vendredi. —

Vous souhaitant tous les biens que le Céleste Empire (la Céleste Margot, c'est-il rigolo!) est capable de fournir, je vous serre la main et suis

truly yours

F. Rosenberg

20/IX

Je viens d'apprendre de source sûre que quant à la Fac. des l. Orient. contre ordre a été reçu, et qu'elle ouvre ses portes dès le 2 Oct.

25/I 18

Cher baron,

Enfin de vos nouvelles! J'ai fini par en
avoir faim & soif presque à l'égal des nom-
breux предметов первой необходимости
dont nous sommes privés. La veille j'ai reçu
la lettre de Pelliot portant l'inscription de
votre main, le lendemain votre carte, écrite
le jour de votre naissance & de celle de l'année
(8400 voeux pour l'un & l'autre). Je ne dirai pas
qu'elle m'ait extraordinairement rassurée, pourtant on se contente de peu par les temps qui
courent & elle contient tout de même des choses
qui ne sont pas mauvaises au superlatif. ~~Entre~~
les lignes je lis que la science of personal
economy n'est pas la seule que vous cultiviez.
Ma lettre précédente vous a expliqué l'arrêt des
finances déposées entre les mains de notre
~~Altmeister~~. Quant aux rations suivantes je ne
doute pas que M. de H. vous tient au courant.
Mme Egoroff n'a plus téléphoné de sorte que je n'en
sais rien; j'espère que les nouvelles de cette source

concernant Testama a ont été effacées comme tout ce qu'on dit et fait dans le pays Ioïstia. De source sûre je tiens que, bien que extrêmement sérieuses, les affaires de chez nous ne sont pas désespérées. Ne songez pas de réintégrer vos pénates du quai Tambotkoff! Pour quiconque a quitté la brillante capitale d'un puissant empire, de se retrouver dans cet ignoble bouge d'assassins et de larrons (il y a qui applaudissent à Xan-Sypu) est chose tout bonnement impossible. Nous autres, faits à la dure, nous continuons à y végéter, repliés sur nous mêmes, ne sortant guère de nos tranchées respectives, réduits comme p. ex. votre obéissant serviteur à une seule chambre, la moins froide, et nous étonnant chaque matin de nouveau de nous réveiller sans avoir été préalablement assommés ou tout au moins dévalisés. La faculté n'a pas cessé de fonctionner; il y a des drôles qui prétendent que l'intensité du travail en rachète tout plein et plus la réduction du semestre qui se termine le 1 mars i.e. en escomptant le nouveau style décrété aujourd'hui même, à la mi-février. Donc il n'y a pas lieu de vous faire du mauvais sang à ce sujet. J'ai causé avec le doyen et d'autres gros bonnets de la boutique. Quant à votre Chinesenmüdigkeit je la comprends et j'y compatis, pourtant elle ne vaut pas, je suppose, ~~celle~~ son analogue laquelle, avec peu, finira par nous achever nous autres. – On travaille quand même, ou bien faute de mieux, autant que les doses homéopathiques d'électricité et de pétrole le permettent. Ni l'académie, ni l'université, n'ont pas saboté (idiot tous ces mots dont même les efforts se rendent compte au point de dériver celui-ci p.ex. de sabbath + adresse pour télégrammes du gouvernement „Generalpostamt" Hine!), mais on a tout le temps mandé à la cadet (prière de transcrire en russe) pour finir par aller à Canossa, ce qui vient d'avoir lieu le jour d'hier. Sont-ils idiots, ces cadets! Du reste tous ces crétins, n'importe de quelle couleur, se disputent la palme à droits égaux. Le musée travaille, moi j'en fais les honneurs, donne des audiences [et autres choses utiles], suis un peu chef d'orchestre.

Mon premier fragment sogdien-bouddhique est sous presse, le second en voie de préparation. Vous riez? Pourtant je n'exagère pas. En général on ne va pas encore trop mal, tout le monde moins plus réduit en poids & volume, surtout les cadets qui prétendent avoir lutté des luttes inouïes; moi même statu quo puisque j'ai Bertha, la suédoise. Avez-vous appris la mort de [illegible]? Il est devenu depuis un des plus grands iranistes de tous les temps. Notre bon Vass. Vass. me fait de la peine. A son âge des avaries pareilles sont terribles & tragiques.

Adieu, cher baron, je ne doute pas que vous avez recueilli des matériaux énormes; espérons que l'avenir ne refusera pas les loisirs de les mettre à profit. Je vous remercie bien vous même et également Pelliot pour le renseignement au sujet du livre de Gauthiot. Ce serait tentative vaine que de s'adresser à Meillet — plus de communications avec l'Europe, plus de — enfin on ne finirait pas avec tous ces „plus de". Stoss-seufzer perpétuel: quousque tandem! J'ai vendu Felline. Ce serait pas mal du tout si ... si ... si ... Enfin on verra, ou on ne verra pas. Je vous serre la main & fait bien des voeux pour vous. Yours truly [initials]

Peking den 7ten Juli 1924.

Lieber Herr Rosenberg,

Es freut mich sehr von Boris Alexejewitsch Wassiljeff zu hören, dass Sie von Jahr zu Jahr jünger werden und dass Sie die Sommermonate nach wie vor in Pawlowsk am Busen der Natur zubringen. Hoffentlich fühlen Sie sich dort auch in diesem Jahr so wohl wie in alten, längst entschwundenen Zeiten.

Als ich im Jahre 1916 Leningrad verliess, übergab ich einen Theil meiner ~~[illegible]~~ Kunstgegenstände dem ethnographischen Museum, wo sie auf Befehl des seligen Wassili Wassiljewitsch, wenn ich mich nicht irre, ~~[illegible] glaube ich~~ im Cabinet des Directors im verpackten Zustande aufgestellt wurden. Von diesen Sachen halte ich die ihnen bekannten sechs Arhatstatuetten (Goldbronze) und die drei indischen Silbervasen für die werthvollsten. Ausserdem befindet sich noch ~~ist~~, wie mir Alexei Iwanowitsch mittheilt, mein grosser persischer Kronleuchter im ethnographischen Museum. Vielleicht sind die beiden grossen chinesischen Bilder, die in meinem Speisezimmer hingen und die, wie ich jetzt weiss, sogar in China einen ~~[illegible]~~ sehr grossen Werth repräsentieren,

Gruss an Jäschke(?) Alexejeff Giesz[illegible], Whitney, Waddell [illegible] Ivanoff etc.

auch in's ~~ein~~ ethnographische Museum gerathen. ~~Dasselbe hoffe ich~~

~~Der~~ Wo mag der gestickte chinesische Wandschirm geblieben sein, der in meinem Salon

stand, ~~und~~ der chinesische Tisch, die indischen Miniaturen, die an den Wänden hingen, die entzückenden Stickereien, meine angefangenen Arbeiten (Notes on the Indo-Scythes) meine andern Papiere, Briefe, Photographien etc etc.?

Vielleicht wissen Sie etwas von diesen Sachen? Wenn Sie die Kunstgegenstände diese Sachen, und

~~mir~~ den geretteten Theil meiner Bücher dem ~~vereidigten Rechtsanwalt~~ Herrn Woldemar

Hartmann, vereid. Rechtsanwalt, Dorpat Altstrasse 2 ~~übergeben~~ übersenden wollten, so wäre ich Ihnen sehr

dankbar. Ich habe Herrn Rechtsanwalt Hartmann gebeten über den Modus des Transports der Sachen

mit ihnen zu correspondiren. ~~Von den Büchern~~ Alexei Iwanowitsch ist ja

~~wie sehr präcis in seinen~~ Angaben, ~~Trotzdem scheint mir aus soviel glaube ich doch mit seinen Erzählungen~~

Ich bin Ihnen sehr zu Dank verpflichtet dafür, dass Sie sich an der Rettung meiner Bücher betheiligt

haben und dass Sie sie ~~jetzt~~ jetzt im Asiatischen Museum aufbewahren. Ich sehne mich schon seit Jahren

nach meinen Büchern und habe Sergei Fjodorowitsch mehrfach brieflich gebeten, sie mir zurückzuschicken

(durch Miss Dreier, Alexei Iwanowitsch und Sylvain Lévi), ausserdem habe ich ihn noch mündlich durch

Sven Hedin an die Angelegenheit erinnern lassen — aber alles vergeblich, er hat mir überhaupt nicht

ein Mal geantwortet. Anfänglich ärgerte ich mich darüber. Jetzt weiss ich aber, dass er sich verheirathet

hat, und kann dem jungen Ehemann nicht mehr zürnen. Er hat ~~jetzt~~ natürlich als solcher alle Hände voll zu thun

und man kann von ihm nicht ~~so~~ erwarten, dass er Briefe schreibt. Bitte schreiben Sie mir ausführlich via Dorpat über Ihre Stellungnahme zu Wein Weib und Gesang und zu den Tagesereignissen. Ist es wahr, dass Sie Ihr Chinesisches [illegible] Rubel an Zarubin verkauft haben?

Herzliche Grüsse von Ihrem ergebenen

AStaëlHolstein.

Дополнение к французск. письму

Truly yours FR

28 IX / 11 X

-вич сохранил свой более спартанский но всё-таки вполне здравый разум; он и отказался от эвакуации. Будьте здоровы и старайтесь не эвакуироваться.

Дорогой барон,

Наконец пришла весточка. Страшно рад что живётся вам не дурно и что имеете вокруг себя людей, а то у нас остаются одни только отвратные за очень редкими исключениями. Поздравляю с покупкою Капищки и надеюсь что нет недостатка и соответствующих капиталов. Поздравляю также с возведением в сан доцента, состоявшимся на этих днях. В чем состоит его

его преимущества, вы со временемъ узнаете.
Но придется пожалуй вернуться въ
нашъ сумасшедшій домъ т.к. факультетъ
окончательно начинаетъ функціонировать
съ 1 октября. Если найдете какой-нибудь
способъ отвлечь возвращеніе, то не упус-
кайте его изъ рукъ; это очень серьезно,
особенно для стараго человека.
Что касается финансовъ, то все выслано
что было получено, два раза по 1200
и последній разъ 1500 = 3900. Сегодня
должна была пойти бумага о следую-
щихъ 1500; но застанутъ они васъ еще
въ Пекинѣ? Такъ-какъ вы сами

въ телеграммахъ и письмахъ указали
адресъ Légation Pekin, то конечно и деньги
были отправлены туда, а не въ Японію.
Дайте телеграмму пригодятся-ли или остаются въ Пекинѣ,
я тогда снесусь съ бар. Унгерномъ или m-me
Егоровой на к-рыхъ указалъ Тельтерессъ и вообще
какъ быть съ финансами. — Вообще вся и даже
горе тощій запасъ разума превращается въ
всеобъемлющую грусть. Указываешь мнѣ вовсе
нашу прекрасную коллекцію рукописей, во
избѣжаніе одного риска подвергаю ее тысячамъ
другихъ. Сердце болитъ, нервы окончательно
расшатались и руки съ трудомъ поднимаются
на такое мученіе и безсмысленное самоуби-
ство. Je ne décolère plus depuis. Что за мука!!

Когда нибудь расскажу разныя детали. Моя робинзонада конечно теперь не действуетъ успокаи-вающе на нервы, и нередко является мысль бросить всю эту работу и удрать въ Пб. пока еще есть возможность... При этомъ конечно мои санскрито-буддійскіе штудіи не могутъ прогрессировать, тоже съ [illegible] своими занятіями; много времени уходитъ съ функціями горючей, сухомойки, повара и прочихъ. Но всё-таки одна просьба — Вы всё узнать у Pelliot к-ый напечатанъ въ журналѣ Азіат. ~~[illegible]~~, какъ обстоитъ со второй частью Essai de grammaire sogdienne покойнаго Gauthiot. Въ заметке въ Journ. As. 1916 (последн.) онъ самъ говоритъ о ней въ дополнительномъ томе. Но нетъ-ли возможности ее раздобыть, если она существуетъ, хотя бы какъ Communication privée, въ какомъ виде у него издана и первая часть (или быв. Записками). Мои помощники въ Петербурге пока остаются безучастными. Думаю скоро воспользуюсь ими отправкою привезенныхъ Вами рукописей. Искренній привѣтъ отъ Вас. Вас. Это единственный изъ всей компаніи